D1559511

OATHS AND THE ENGLISH REFORMATION

The practice of swearing oaths was at the centre of the English Reformation. On the one hand, oaths were the medium through which the Henrician regime implemented its ideology and secured loyalty among the people. On the other, they were the tool by which the English people embraced, resisted, and manipulated royal policy. Jonathan Michael Gray argues that since the Reformation was negotiated through oaths, their precise significance and function are central to understanding it fully. *Oaths and the English Reformation* sheds new light on the motivation of Henry VIII, the enforcement of and resistance to reform, and the extent of popular participation and negotiation in the political process. Placing oaths at the heart of the narrative, this book argues that the English Reformation was determined as much by its method of implementation and response as it was by the theology or political theory it transmitted.

JONATHAN MICHAEL GRAY is Assistant Professor of Church History at Virginia Theological Seminary.

Cambridge Studies in Early Modern British History

Series editors

JOHN MORRILL
Professor of British and Irish History, University of Cambridge,
and Fellow of Selwyn College

ETHAN SHAGAN
Professor of History, University of California, Berkeley

ALEXANDRA WALSHAM
Professor of Modern History, University of Cambridge,
and Fellow of Trinity College

This is a series of monographs and studies covering many aspects of the history of the British Isles between the late fifteenth century and the early eighteenth century. It includes the work of established scholars and pioneering work by a new generation of scholars. It includes both reviews and revisions of major topics and books which open up new historical terrain or which reveal startling new perspectives on familiar subjects. All the volumes set detailed research within broader perspectives, and the books are intended for the use of students as well as of their teachers.

For a list of titles in the series go to www.cambridge.org/earlymodernbritishhistory

OATHS AND THE ENGLISH REFORMATION

JONATHAN MICHAEL GRAY

CAMBRIDGE
UNIVERSITY PRESS

CAMBRIDGE
UNIVERSITY PRESS

University Printing House, Cambridge CB2 8BS, United Kingdom

Cambridge University Press is part of the University of Cambridge.

It furthers the University's mission by disseminating knowledge in the pursuit of education, learning and research at the highest international levels of excellence.

www.cambridge.org
Information on this title: www.cambridge.org/9781316635575

© Jonathan Michael Gray 2013

First published 2013
First paperback edition 2016

A catalogue record for this publication is available from the British Library

Library of Congress Cataloguing in Publication data
Gray, Jonathan Michael, 1979–
Oaths and the English Reformation / Jonathan Michael Gray.
p.   cm. – (Cambridge studies in early modern British history)
Includes bibliographical references (p. 247) and index.
ISBN 978-1-107-01802-0 (hardback)
1. Reformation – England.   2. England – Church history – 16th century.   3. Oaths.   I. Title.
BR377.G73   2012
274.2'06 – dc23   2012016543

ISBN 978-1-107-01802-0 Hardback
ISBN 978-1-316-63557-5 Paperback

Contents

Acknowledgements

It is neither possible nor desirable to publish a scholarly book without accumulating a vast array of debts of gratitude. This book would not have been possible without the resources of numerous libraries. I am grateful to the staff of the following institutions who allowed me to consult their collections and provided assistance when necessary: the British Library, the National Archives, Lambeth Palace Library, Cambridge University Library, the Bodleian Library, Corpus Christi College Library (Cambridge), Emmanuel College Library, Corpus Christi College Library (Oxford), Christ Church Library, Guildhall Library, Inner Temple Library, the Canterbury Cathedral Archives, the Centre for Kentish Studies at Maidstone, the Lancashire Record Office, the Haus-, Hof- und Staatsarchiv, the Huntington Library, the Folger Shakespeare Library, Bishop Payne Library at Virginia Theological Seminary, and most importantly, Green Library at Stanford University. I also thank Stanford University, the Huntington Library, and Virginia Theological Seminary for supporting me financially through fellowships, grants, and employment.

I have had the great fortune of working under truly excellent advisors and mentors at every stage of my academic development. Eric Carlson kindly agreed to supervise me as an undergraduate and has continued to follow my academic career at each subsequent stage, offering valued advice and friendship. I am grateful to Jeff Watt for overseeing my Masters thesis, helping me learn sixteenth-century French, and providing a model of a balanced history professor who finds time to exercise, enjoy life, and serve his family while still doing excellent work. Jeff has also read portions of this manuscript and provided feedback. I thank as well Joe Ward for talking me out of quitting graduate school during my first few trying months in Mississippi and then convincing me to apply to Stanford's Ph.D. program when I was ready to stop with an M.A. When I first arrived at Stanford, Carolyn Lougee accepted me as an orphaned advisee. My conception of the field of early modern Europe is a result of her patient tutelage and teaching. I also thank her for reading and commenting on portions of this text. Paul Seaver taught me palaeography and guided me as I first stumbled onto the topic of oaths. I have never encountered a better listener! Barbara Pitkin welcomed a history student into religious studies and read much of my manuscript. At VTS I have been blessed with wonderful colleagues who have encouraged my scholarship. I thank Bob Prichard for taking me under his wing and sharing with me his great knowledge of church history and seminary life. My largest academic debt is to David Como. Professor Como is a paragon of a learned, nurturing advisor. He taught me the history of Tudor-Stuart England, guided this manuscript from inception to publication, strengthened my raw skills as a teacher, and mentored me in all aspects of the discipline of history. To all of these professors I offer my sincerest gratitude.

No matter how excellent the professional guidance, this project would not have come to fruition without the amazing support of friends and family. At Stanford the members of Inter-Varsity Graduate Christian Fellowship provided essential community, without which scholarship dries out. Special thanks go out to Paul Leu, Greg Koehrsen, and Pete Sommer. Throughout my entire development as a scholar, Ashley Jensen has been there for me. He has listened to countless phone diatribes in which I lamented on the travails of being a graduate student and new professor. He also introduced me to my incredible wife, who quickly became my biggest cheerleader. Even after our marriage removed ulterior motives for flattery, Karin has continued to encourage me in every way! She also has read this entire manuscript, offering valuable advice and suggestions. Yet no one can equal the positive influence of my parents on this project. Their support – financial, emotional, and spiritual – has moulded me into the scholar and person who I am today. It is to them that I gratefully dedicate this book.

Omnia ad Dei gloriam

Notes on the text

When quoting early modern texts, I have kept the original spelling but expanded all abbreviations. Some punctuation has been amended for clarity. I take the new year to start on 1 January and have changed some dates accordingly. Unless otherwise noted, all translations from Latin and French are my own. This includes Chapuys' letters to Charles V. Whenever the original letter is cited from the Haus-, Hof- und Staatsarchiv, the English quotation in the text is my translation.

Small parts of Chapters 1 and 3 were previously published in my 'Vows, Oaths, and the Propagation of a Subversive Discourse', *Sixteenth Century Journal* 41 (2010): 731–56 and my 'The Sixteenth-Century Background to the Current "Oath" of Conformity of the Episcopal Church', *Journal of Episcopal Church Canon Law* 1 (2010): 33–59, used here with permission of the journals. Appendix E, II (instructions for the visitation of Franciscan Observants) previously appeared in Henry de Vocht, ed. *Acta Thomae Mori: History of the Reports of His Trial and Death with an Unedited Contemporary Narrative.* Humanistica Lovaniensia, 7 (1947). It is reprinted with kind permission of Publications of the Institute for Economics of Leuven University and Librairie Universitaire Ch. Uystpruyst.

Abbreviations

BI	Borthwick Institute for Archives
BL	British Library
Cal SP Spain	*Calendar of Letters, Despatches, and State Papers, relating to the Negotiations between England and Spain Preserved in the Archives at Simancas and Elsewhere.* Ed. Pascual Gayangos. Vols. IV and V. London, 1879–88
Cal SP Venice	*Calendar of State Papers and Manuscripts, Relating to English Affairs, Existing in the Archives and Collections of Venice, and in Other Libraries of Northern Italy.* Ed. Rawdon Brown et al. London: Longman Green, 1864–1947
CAP	*Church Authority and Power in Medieval and Early Modern Britain: The Episcopal Registers.* Ed. Dorothy Owen and David Smith. 9 vols. Brighton: Harvester Press Microform, 1986
CCCC	Corpus Christi College, Cambridge
CIC	*Corpus Iuris Canonici.* Ed. Aemilius Friedberg. 2 vols. 1879–81. Reprint, Union, NJ: Lawbook Exchange, 2000
CUL	Cambridge University Library
Foxe, *AM* (1583)	*Acts and Monuments (1583) . . . The Variorum Edition.* [online]. Sheffield: HriOnline 3 2004. www.hrionline.shef.ac.uk/foxe/ Accessed May 2005 to June 2011
Foxe, *AM* (Townsend)	*Acts and Monuments of John Foxe; with a Life of the Martyrologist, and Vindication of the Work.* Ed. George Townsend. New York: Ams Press, 1965
GL	Guildhall Library, London
HHS	Haus-, Hof- und Staatsarchiv, Vienna

KAO	Kent County Archives Office (now Kent History and Library Centre, Maidstone)
LP	*Letters and Papers, Foreign and Domestic, of the Reign of Henry VIII, Preserved in the Public Record Office, the British Museum, and Elsewhere.* Ed. J. S. Brewer, R. H. Brodie, and James Gairdner. 2nd edn 1920. 21 vols. in 37. Reprint, Vaduz: Kraus Reprint, 1965
LPL	Lambeth Palace Library, London
NA	National Archives, Kew
PS	Parker Society

Introduction

The English Reformation was as much about oaths as it was about Henry's marriage, succession, and headship over the English Church. The London Charterhouse knew this well. On 4 May 1534, royal commissioners visited this famously austere Carthusian monastery to tender to them the oath of succession. According to a recently passed act of Parliament, all English subjects were required to swear fidelity to Henry, to Henry's new wife Anne Boleyn, and to their heirs. They also had to swear to observe and maintain the whole contents of the act, and these contents explicitly declared Henry's first marriage to Katherine of Aragon unlawful. When the commissioners arrived, the prior of the Charterhouse, John Houghton, attempted to turn them away. Houghton declared that it was not his business to meddle with the affairs of kings. The king could repudiate and marry whomever he wanted without the Charterhouse's consent. But the commissioners held firm, responding:

> We require you without disguise, evasion or sophistry to swear obedience to the King's law and laying your hands upon Christ's Holy Gospels – we shall stand by and administer the oath – to declare without qualification that the former marriage was unlawful and therefore rightly annulled; that the later marriage shall be held lawful and in accord with divine law and therefore rightly entitled to the approval of all.[1]

Houghton refused the commissioners' demand. He could not see how a marriage 'celebrated according to the rite of the church and observed for so long' could be declared void.[2] The commissioners then imprisoned Houghton and the procurator of the house, Humphrey Middlemore, in the Tower of London. After about three weeks of captivity, Houghton

---

[1] Chauncy, *Passion and Martyrdom* (1570), 61. This is printed from a manuscript edition of 1570. All English quotations from the 1570 version are the translation of A. F. Radcliffe. I will also make use of the first printed edition of the work: Chauncy, *Historia aliqvot* (1550). All English quotations cited from this version are my own translation.

[2] Chauncy, *Historia aliqvot* (1550), sig. M3ᵛ.

and Middlemore were persuaded that the oath of succession was not a matter of faith, nor worth dying for, and they agreed to submit. Yet the rest of the Charterhouse was not convinced. At the next visit of the royal commissioners, the monks all stoutly refused to swear. During a third visit, Houghton and half a dozen other brothers took the oath. Finally, after a speech by Houghton and under threat of imprisonment, the rest of the house swore the oath, 'but only under the condition "as far as it was lawful"'.[3] We do not know the exact form of their oath nor how they attached this condition. All that survive today are notarial attestations verifying that the monks took their 'oaths and fidelities'.[4]

Swearing the oath of succession did not end the troubles of the London Charterhouse. In the summer of 1534, the London Carthusians seem to have been tendered an acknowledgement of royal supremacy. At that time, Henry was administering an oath to all clerical institutions. In this oath each member of an institution had to acknowledge that Henry was the supreme head of the church in England and that the Pope had no more power in England than any other foreign bishop. The actual profession of the Charterhouse does not survive, and our main source for the events at the London Charterhouse, Maurice Chauncy (a monk of the Charterhouse in the 1530s who in the reign of Edward VI wrote an account of the trials of the London Charterhouse), was strangely silent on the events of the summer of 1534. However, a list of various clerical institutions that professed the royal supremacy at that time survives. Under the heading of London, it reads: 'nine Carthusians contumaciously refused to undertake the oath'.[5] There is no record of Henry taking any punitive action against the nine Charterhouse monks who refused the oath.

The plot thickened in November 1534 when Parliament passed the Act of Supremacy. Despite the fact that no oath was prescribed by the act, Houghton, along with Robert Laurence and Augustine Webster (the priors of the Charterhouses of Beauvale and Axholme respectively), 'anticipated' the coming of another royal commission and sought an interview with Secretary Thomas Cromwell to forestall the visit in the spring of 1535.[6] Cromwell first declined to meet with them, but eventually he demanded that they reject the authority of the Pope and abnegate 'all other external

---

[3] Chauncy, *Historia aliquot* (1550), sig. M4ʳ. Only the 1550 version of Chauncy's narrative notes that the Charterhouse swore the oath of succession *conditionally*.

[4] The original notarial attestations are NA E25/82/3 (*LP*, VII 728). They are printed correctly in Rymer (ed.), *Foedera*, XIV:491–2. The first one is from 29 May, and the second from 6 June 1534.

[5] BL Cotton MS E VI, fol. 209ᵛ (*LP*, VII 891 (ii)).

[6] Chauncy, *Historia aliquot* (1550), sigs. N4ᵛ–O1ʳ.

powers, jurisdictions, obediences to whatever person or order they had owed or promised' and affirm that Henry alone was the supreme head of the church.[7] The priors replied evasively that 'they would do all that true Christians, dutiful and loyal subjects, ought to do for their prince; in all things they would willingly obey the King as far as divine law permitted'.[8] But Cromwell would not accept such an equivocal answer. He allegedly retorted:

No reservation whatever shall be accepted by me. My will and command is that without delay before this honorable assembly you shall make the simple declaration without addition or disguise, confirming and approving all that is submitted to you. Moreover – for fear lest heart and voice be not in accord – I require you to testify by a solemn oath that you believe and firmly hold to be true the very words – my decision is irrevocable – which we propound to you for an honest confession of faith.[9]

The priors were unwilling to make this oath. After a show trial at the end of April, Houghton, Laurence, and Webster were executed on 4 May 1535. Immediately before his execution, Houghton countered the oath of supremacy with his own oath, calling 'to witness heaven and earth and God the Lord of heaven and earth' that he refused to consent to the king and his law 'not from malice or obstinacy or wish to rebel, but from fear of God', lest he offend God's 'glorious majesty' by believing something contrary to 'the pillar of truth, the Catholic Church'.[10]

After the execution of the Charterhouse's leader, Henry continued to try to bully the Carthusians into submission. On 4 June Henry executed three other leaders of the London Charterhouse (Humphrey Middlemore, William Exmew, and Sebastian Newdigate) for refusing to acknowledge his supremacy. For the next two years, the brethren of the London Charterhouse endured extreme pressure. Henry reduced their rations, subjected them to systematic sermons in favour of his supremacy, and sent some of the brothers to monasteries supportive of Henry's supremacy.[11] According to John Whalley, a commissioner Cromwell sent to try to convince the Charterhouse to submit and leave their order, the Charterhouse's resistance to Henry's will centred around a previous oath they had made to the Pope: 'they feare that in case they shulde nowe swarue and goo from theire Religion, and hereafter the pope and his adherentes shulde prevayle, that then they shulde be grevyously punnyshed (yea vnto the deathe) for

---

[7] Chauncy, *Historia aliqvot* (1550), sig. o1ʳ.   [8] Chauncy, *Passion and Martyrdom* (1570), 79.
[9] Chauncy, *Passion and Martyrdom* (1570), 79.   [10] Chauncy, *Passion and Martyrdom* (1570), 91–3.
[11] For a detailed account of these two years, see Thompson, *Carthusian Order*, 411–35.

breakyng of the othe that they have made to the pope'.[12] Finally, under the threat of dissolution, twenty-one brethren of the London Charterhouse gave in and took a new form of the oath of supremacy on 18 May 1537.[13] Yet while they swore outwardly, according to Chauncy 'in their hearts' they prayed to the Lord:

We beseech your mercy, so that you may not regard this way which we act externally in placing our hands on the book of the holy Gospels and kissing it, and neither accept it as if we are confirming or consenting to the will of the king, but rather in veneration of the sacred words described in the Gospel you may receive this our external pretence as made for the preservation of our house.[14]

Their oath did not end the matter. On 15 November 1538, the London Charterhouse was suppressed. As for the ten monks who refused to swear in May 1537, they were imprisoned at Newgate and systematically starved to death.

The story of the London Charterhouse in the 1530s illustrates the central argument of this book: oaths were crucial to the implementation of and response to the Henrician Reformation. Oaths were the means through which the Henrician regime sought to enforce the parliamentary revolution of 1534 on the Charterhouse. Oaths were also fundamental to the Charterhouse's resistance and acquiescence to this same revolution. And while the exact details of the above narration may be exceptional in that our knowledge of the Charterhouse is greater than our knowledge of other institutions, the role of oaths in the story is representative of the Henrician Reformation in general. Oaths were a primary language of the Henrician Reformation, an important medium through which the Henrician regime negotiated key aspects of its religious policy with the English populace.

The focus of this book is the role of oaths in the Henrician Reformation. Its novelty lies in its placement of the oath – as opposed to a person, movement, or set of ideas – as the protagonist in the story of the Henrician Reformation. Previous historiography has of course mentioned oaths, but the emphasis has almost solely been on the content of oaths. Oaths are depicted as important insofar as they provide insight into what the Henrician Reformation was about: divorce, succession, papal authority, royal

---

[12] NA SP1/96, fol. 61ʳ (*LP*, VIII 600), printed in Thompson, *Carthusian Order*, 415–17. The oath to which Whalley referred was probably the Carthusians' initial monastic profession, specifically their vow of obedience.
[13] The form of this oath with the monks' original subscriptions and a notarial attestation survives. It is NA E25/82/2 (*LP*, XII (i) 1232). It is printed in Rymer (ed.), *Foedera*, XIV:588–9.
[14] Chauncy, *Historia aliqvot* (1550), sig. Q2ᵛ.

supremacy, and obedience to the king. Clearly the content of oaths was important, but this book claims that the actual device was of equal significance. Post-structuralist philosophers have taught us that language is not simply a transparent reflection of reality; it constitutes reality. If oaths were a language of the Reformation, then oaths are important not only because they communicated the Reformation but also because they constituted the Reformation. The English Reformation was just as much about its method of implementation and response as it was about the theology or political theory it transmitted. This is the central insight of this book.

The first part of my argument is that oaths were the principal means through which the Henrician regime implemented its Reformation on the ground and in the parish. After all, a close reading of the story of the Charterhouse indicates that the London Carthusians were tendered at least four different professions: an oath of succession in the spring of 1534, an institutional profession of Henry's supremacy in the summer of 1534, another oath of supremacy in the spring of 1535, and yet another form of the oath of supremacy in 1537. And as Chapter 2 demonstrates, the oaths administered to the Charterhouse were simply a selection of a much larger pool of professions that Henry employed to enforce the Boleyn (and then Seymour) marriage and succession, the abrogation of papal authority, and the establishment of royal supremacy over the English Church. Furthermore, Chapter 6 shows how oaths to tell the truth and abjuration oaths were a significant part of the Henrician regime's campaign against heresy.

My claim that oaths were essential to the implementation of the Reformation needs to be set in the context of other historians' accounts of the Henrician Reformation. Current debates about the Reformation usually fall into two schools. The first is the revisionist school, whose members include J. J. Scarisbrick, Eamon Duffy, Christopher Haigh, and G. W. Bernard. Scarisbrick explored the implementation of and response to the dissolution, spoilage, and appropriation of monasteries, chantries, schools, hospitals, guilds, and churches.[15] His focus, then, was primarily institutional. By contrast, Eamon Duffy's description of the Henrician Reformation centred on traditional parish religion: the veneration of images, the cult of the saints, the enjoyment of Holy Days, the practice of pilgrimages, and the industry of purgatory. Duffy investigated how the Henrician regime reformed these practices and how this Reformation was contested

---

[15] Scarisbrick, *Reformation and the English People*, 65–135.

on the ground.[16] Christopher Haigh's narrative of the Henrician Reformation focused less on the implementation of reform and more on the
political circumstances that led to reform. Parliamentary contests, court
intrigue, and international diplomacy all featured prominently in Haigh's
story.[17] G. W. Bernard covered all three of these themes – institutions,
traditional parish religion, and politics – in his magisterial explanation of
Henry's Reformation.[18] What unified all of these revisionist accounts of the
Henrician Reformation was an emphasis on the strength of the Henrician
regime and its ability to enforce its Reformation through intimidation and
violence. Scarisbrick claimed that the Henrician regime 'was astonishingly
efficient and formidable'.[19] It accomplished its Reformation through a
combination of manipulation, trickery, and bullying – particularly imprisonment and death.[20] Duffy argued that the 'Treasons Act was a formidable
instrument, and complaint against the King's proceedings liable to back-
fire on the complainer'.[21] Haigh then narrated how the Henrician regime
carried out the Treasons Act, executing its foremost opponents.[22] Haigh
claimed that 'a combination of government coercion and individual conversion drove traditional Catholicism from the churches', but he amended his
argument by noting that most people 'experienced the reformation as obedience rather than conversion', thereby prioritizing government coercion.[23]
Finally, Bernard's account of the Henrician Reformation depicted Henry
as a bloodthirsty tyrant who used intimidation, imprisonment, and execution to overawe his subjects into submission. In Bernard's own words, 'the
power of a determined, devious and ruthless king and his councilors was
too great'. People 'had little option but to acquiesce and comply'.[24]

In opposition to the revisionist school, historians such as Ethan Shagan, Alec Ryrie, and Kevin Sharpe (often labelled as post-revisionists)
have underscored the weakness of the Henrician regime and its inabil-
ity to enforce its Reformation without the cooperation of the provincial gentry and even the populace at large. After all, noted Shagan and
Sharpe, Tudor government had no police force, no standing army, and no
provincial bureaucracy.[25] If the Henrician regime wanted to implement its

[16] Duffy, *Stripping of the Altars*, 379–447.
[17] Haigh, *English Reformations*, 88–136, 152–67. Haigh highlighted his emphasis on politics on page 21: 'Religious change was governed by law, and law was the outcome of politics. The Reformations were begun, defined, sustained, slowed, and revitalized by political events.'
[18] Bernard, *King's Reformation*.
[19] Scarisbrick, *Reformation and the English People*, 81.
[20] Scarisbrick, *Reformation and the English People*, 61–8, 77–9, 109.
[21] Duffy, *Stripping of the Altars*, 385.   [22] Haigh, *English Reformations*, 119–21, 139, 141.
[23] Haigh, *English Reformations*, 3, 21.   [24] Bernard, *King's Reformation*, 601.
[25] Shagan, *Popular Politics and the English Reformation*, 2; Sharpe, *Selling the Tudor Monarchy*, 81.

Reformation effectively, then it had to win the consent of the people, claimed post-revisionists. Ethan Shagan thus explored the reasons why the English people chose to 'collaborate' with the Henrician regime, arguing that the Henrician regime was able to implement its Reformation only because local authorities and other 'collaborators' negotiated with the regime.[26] Shagan further argued that people negotiated because they had something to gain by accepting reform, be it political patronage, royal support in a local dispute, financial gain, or social emancipation. Other historians have stressed that people cooperated with the regime in implementing reforms because of ingrained habits of loyalty to their lawful sovereign.[27] While not invalidating the 'hard', coercive power of the regime, this 'soft, ideological' power was, in the words of Alec Ryrie, the 'decisive' reason behind Henry's ability to secure his subjects' assent to his divorce.[28] Sharpe, however, asserted that another form of ideological power was pre-eminent in 'securing compliance', the power of representation.[29] Sharpe has analysed in great detail the propaganda (texts, images, and performances) of the Henrician regime, stating that 'power and authority, the legitimation of monarchy and dynasty, depended on representations'.[30] Although there is therefore great diversity among post-revisionist explanations, what sets them apart from revisionists is their claim that the operative means by which the Henrician regime implemented its Reformation was persuasion not intimidation, negotiation rather than physical coercion.

This book modifies both the revisionists' and post-revisionists' explanations of the Reformation by arguing that oaths were a central way (if not *the* central way) in which Henry both coerced his subjects into obedience and secured their consent to many of his policies. Note that I am not arguing that oaths were the *only* way in which the regime implemented its Reformation. Proclamations, injunctions, visitations, executions, representations of the monarch, and the various 'carrots' the regime offered to those who collaborated with it remain important.[31] Yet what undergirded all of these methods of implementation was the belief that Henry had the right to change his succession, reform the church, and punish

---

[26] Shagan, *Popular Politics and the English Reformation*, 22.

[27] Marsh, *Popular Religion*, 201–4, Marshall, *Reformation England*, 55–6. Revisionists like Scarisbrick and post-revisionists like Shagan also recognize the validity of this point. See Scarisbrick, *Reformation and the English People*, 81, 109; Shagan, *Popular Politics and the English Reformation*, 88.

[28] Ryrie, *Age of Reformation*, 123.   [29] Sharpe, *Selling the Tudor Monarchy*, 84.

[30] Sharpe, *Selling the Tudor Monarchy*, 15.

[31] For example, Henry did not use oaths to force his subjects to destroy images or to win their assent to a new English Bible.

those who opposed his will. Obedience was 'the essence of Henrician religion',[32] the thread on which all other Henrician reforms hanged, and oaths were paramount in coercing and convincing Henry's subjects to be obedient.

My claim that oaths were essential to the implementation of the Reformation is novel in that oaths do not play a major role in the standard accounts of either the revisionists or post-revisionists. Oaths are absent from Duffy's *Stripping of the Altars*, Shagan's *Popular Politics and the English Reformation*, and the sections on the Henrician Reformation in Ryrie's *Age of Reformation* and Sharpe's *Selling the Tudor Monarchy*. Haigh has only a paragraph on the oath of succession, a few sentences on the punishment of those who refused Henry's oaths, and a few more sentences on the role of oaths in the Pilgrimage of Grace.[33] Scarisbrick overlooked oaths in his section on the Henrician Reformation, and then when talking about the Elizabethan oath of supremacy, he questioned 'how much oaths mattered anyway'.[34] Oaths do play a notable role in Bernard's story, but even he minimized their significance. Refusing to swear the oath of succession was not, for Bernard, an 'overtly political activity'.[35] Bernard treated oaths not so much as a means of coercion but rather as 'tests of loyalty' which were 'intended rather to flush out secret and internal opposition'.[36] In the end, oaths were less important to Bernard than the penalties Henry imposed on those who refused his oaths, notably imprisonment and execution.

The primary reason why historians overlook oaths is because they misunderstand the nature and importance of oaths in the sixteenth century. We view oaths through our modern bias. Today, oaths are insignificant. They matter only insofar as they increase the likelihood of truthful testimony in courts of law by imposing the formal penalty of perjury on those who lie after swearing an oath. Oaths provide a legal incentive to tell the truth, an incentive that is absent in unsworn testimony or everyday conversation, whether confirmed with an oath (the common expletive 'God' is a derivative of oath-taking) or not. Outside of court, oaths today have no power. This modern bias is present in two generally excellent histories that do emphasize the role of oaths in the Henrician Reformation: David Martin Jones' *Conscience and Allegiance in Seventeenth Century England* and Geoffrey Elton's *Policy and Police*. Jones focused on the legal power of Henrician state oaths, noting that 'an oath widely and unreservedly accepted was superfluous, as it merely confirmed a pre-existing natural

---

[32] Rex, 'Crisis of Obedience', 894.   [33] Haigh, *English Reformations*, 119, 121, 141, 146, 149.
[34] Scarisbrick, *Reformation and the English People*, 137–8.   [35] Bernard, *King's Reformation*, 125.
[36] Bernard, *King's Reformation*, 160; Bernard, 'Tyranny of Henry VIII', 119.

obligation'.[37] Elton, whose depiction of the Henrician state oaths remains the most nuanced to date, nevertheless concluded by claiming that 'by themselves oaths could not achieve very much'. They were useful only to the extent that they 'made people solemnly aware of their new duty'.[38]

The problem with such a modern understanding of oaths is that it fails to recognize the great spiritual power of oaths in the sixteenth century. Oaths did not merely 'confirm a pre-existing natural obligation'; they also cemented this natural obligation by adding to it a spiritual bond. Oaths did more than simply make people 'aware of their new duty'; they made God the enforcer of their new duty. Indeed, the argument of Chapter 1 is that oaths were seen as powerful because the act of swearing gave the juror access to Almighty God, and God would not allow his person to be abused by false or vain swearing. Accordingly, this book contends that the principal means of coercion of the Henrician Reformation was not physical (as the revisionists claimed) or ideological (as some post-revisionists emphasized) but theological. The English Reformation was not just about theology; it was achieved through theology.

And this explains why the Henrician regime implemented its Reformation through oaths. Jones stated that the Henrician regime turned to oaths because they were flexible, because they had a 'long constitutional and common-law pedigree', and because the regime had no 'viable alternatives'.[39] While these factors were certainly important, Chapter 1 argues that the primary rationale behind the Henrician regime's employment of oaths was its desire to make the most powerful being in the universe (God) enforce the obedience of its subjects. Similarly, Elton maintained that the Henrician regime used oaths selectively because it recognized that oaths were inefficient and ineffective – they 'could not achieve very much'.[40] By contrast, Chapter 3 argues that Henry employed oaths selectively precisely because he was aware of the power of oaths. Henry administered the most detailed, strongest oaths to groups of his subjects who had sworn previous oaths, oaths potentially subversive to royal authority. Henry took oaths seriously because his subjects did. After all, Whalley observed that the London Charterhouse would not submit to Henry because of their previous oath to the Pope. The only way to invalidate such a powerful bond was to meet it with an equally powerful bond, another oath. It is possible to view the Henrician Reformation as a spiritual arms race, where both Henry and his subjects sought to best each other by swearing stronger and stronger oaths.

---

[37] Jones, *Conscience and Allegiance*, 61.   [38] Elton, *Policy and Police*, 230.
[39] Jones, *Conscience and Allegiance*, 61.
[40] Elton, *Policy and Police*, 230. See also 381–2 for another dismissal of oaths as ineffective.

Of course, my claim that oaths were the primary means through which the Henrician regime implemented its Reformation does not completely invalidate revisionist or post-revisionist explanations. The Henrician regime's use of oaths does, for example, support the post-revisionist claim that the Henrician state was weak. It relied on God to police its Reformation because it was unable to police its subjects on its own. Oaths also demonstrate that the Henrician regime sought to win its subjects' consent. This consent was not, however, always voluntary. The penalty for refusing to swear, as Bernard has clearly reminded us, was imprisonment and (eventually) execution. The regime's use of spiritual coercion was thus still backed up with raw physical coercion. Finally, propaganda remained important, for in order for the oath to be completely valid, the juror had to be convinced that the content of his oath was true. But even if propaganda persuaded the juror that his oath was right and violence persuaded him to take the oath, it was the oath itself that was the chief guarantee of the juror's continual loyalty after the act of swearing. Oaths were therefore central to the implementation of the Henrician Reformation.

The second part of my argument is that oaths were crucial to the English people's response to the Henrician Reformation. For simplicity's sake, the key themes in the English people's response to the Henrician Reformation can be divided into three parts: what the majority of the English people generally did, why they did this, and how they did this. My analysis of oaths increases our knowledge of all three of these questions, though my argument chiefly relates to the third part. Nevertheless, the first question – what did the majority of the people generally do in response to the Henrician Reformation? – is the most basic. A. G. Dickens, writing in the Whig tradition, argued that the majority of the English people *embraced* the Reformation. They were discontented with medieval piety and the church, so they welcomed reform.[41] Revisionists have destroyed Dickens' depiction of medieval English Catholicism, convincingly arguing that most English people were pleased with their church and its style of piety at the beginning of the sixteenth century.[42] As such, revisionists have emphasized the English people's *resistance* to the Reformation as their primary response.[43] Revisionists were initially split on the effectiveness of this resistance, but the general trend has been to acknowledge that in the long run, popular

[41] Dickens, *English Reformation*.
[42] Scarisbrick, *Reformation and the English People*, 1–60; Duffy, *Stripping of the Altars*, Part 1; Haigh, *English Reformations*, 25–55.
[43] Scarisbrick, *Reformation and the English People*; Duffy, *Stripping of the Altars*, 379–447; Haigh, *English Reformations*, 137–51; Bernard, *King's Reformation*, 73–224.

resistance was unable to halt the progress of reform.[44] Revisionists could maintain this because they saw the Tudor regime as powerful and ruthless, able to overcome popular resistance no matter how widespread it was. Yet since post-revisionists have called into question the strength of the Tudor state, they have likewise called into question the prominence of resistance as a response to the Reformation. Instead, post-revisionist historians like Ethan Shagan, Christopher Marsh, and Norman Jones have stressed that the most salient popular response to the Reformation was 'collaboration' (Shagan's term), 'compliance' (Marsh's term), or 'choice' (Jones' term).[45] In essence, post-revisionists argue that although the English people may have not been happy with Henrician reforms, the majority of them *acquiesced* to these reforms, even if such acquiescence was combined with low levels of resistance.[46] The real dividing line between revisionists and post-revisionists here is not so much whether the majority of the English people eventually complied with the Reformation but rather the degree to which most people's compliance involved their consent. There is a measure of popular agency present in terms like 'collaboration' and 'choice' that is absent from the accounts of a historian like Bernard.[47]

My focus on oaths allows us to test the extent to which the English people embraced, resisted, or acquiesced to the Reformation, to verify which kind of response really was the most prevalent. A decision to refuse the oaths of succession or supremacy suggests that the nonjuror opposed some part of the oath, while a decision to take these oaths indicates some kind of acceptance of the content of the oath, or at least a willingness to cooperate with the regime regardless of the juror's own personal opinions. The beginning of Chapter 4 therefore explores who took and who rejected the oaths of succession and supremacy. I find that most people did take the oaths administered to them, which sides with the post-revisionists' claim

---

[44] Haigh initially depicted the popular resistance to the Reformation as quite effective. It caused Henry to reverse his policies in the fall of 1538, and in the end, Elizabethan popular religion was not that different from pre-Reformation popular religion; Haigh, *English Reformations*, 137, 285–95. Duffy was more subtle. Although he stated that popular resistance did contribute to an official policy of 'studied moderation' after 1537, he saw reforms as continuing and in the end, he admitted most parishes eventually complied with and even accepted the Reformation; Duffy, *Stripping of the Altars*, 587–93, 402; Duffy, *Voices of Morebath*, 151, 171, 175–81. Bernard was most adamant in his avowal that despite the presence of much opposition, it was ineffective in halting the will of a ruthless king; Bernard, *King's Reformation*, ch. 2, *passim*.

[45] Shagan, *Popular Politics and the English Reformation*, 13–18, Marsh, *Popular Religion*, 197–8; Jones, *English Reformation*, 5–6.

[46] For a penetrating discussion of how low levels of resistance to one kind of reform involved implicit collaboration with another kind of reform, see Shagan, *Popular Politics and the English Reformation*, 17–18.

[47] Bernard, *King's Reformation*, 598, 601.

that acquiescence was people's primary response. Yet whether the English people consented to the policies outlined in the oaths they swore is another matter, and Chapters 4 and 5 also show that it was possible to resist the spirit of the oath even while displaying minimum levels of compliance.

The second theme in the English people's response to the Reformation is why they responded in the way that they did. This is the question that has most occupied historians in recent years. Duffy argued that people resisted the Reformation because they liked traditional Catholicism.[48] Bernard believed that people complied with the Reformation because they were afraid of the wrath of a tyrant king.[49] Marsh, Watt, Walsham, and Wabuda emphasized that people acquiesced with the Reformation because it was not a complete break with the past; the primary Christian virtues of charity, community, and peace; the themes of popular cheap print; the doctrine of Providence; and the prevalence of Christocentric devotion and preaching were consistent throughout the sixteenth century and gave people a sense of familiarity amid change.[50] Shagan averred that people collaborated with the Reformation because they stood to gain something, and that something was usually political or economic rather than spiritual.[51] Similarly, Norman Jones noted that people chose to accept distasteful religious changes because religion was just one facet of their lives – not necessarily the most important facet. Concerns for property or family solidarity, for example, sometimes trumped religion and made people more likely to accommodate to the Reformation in order to preserve or augment what was of most value to them.[52] By contrast, Diarmaid MacCulloch and Alec Ryrie re-emphasized the importance of religion as an explanation, though unlike the revisionists their focus was on Protestantism. MacCulloch and Ryrie argued that the message of evangelical Protestantism – particularly its message of spiritual, social, sexual, and chronological liberty – had inherent appeal and explains why some people embraced the Reformation.[53] Finally, many historians have reiterated that inherent loyalty to the king was another reason why people acquiesced to the Reformation.[54]

All of these explanations have some degree of truth to them. After all, the English people were not homogeneous. The reasons behind the English

[48] Duffy, *Stripping of the Altars.* [49] Bernard, *King's Reformation.*
[50] Marsh, *Popular Religion*; Watt, *Cheap Print and Popular Piety*; Walsham, *Providence in Early Modern England*; Wabuda, *Preaching during the English Reformation.*
[51] Shagan, *Popular Politics and the English Reformation.* [52] Jones, *English Reformation.*
[53] MacCulloch, *Boy King*, 121–6, 129–40; Ryrie, 'Counting Sheep, Counting Shepherds', 98–105.
[54] See for example Scarisbrick, *Reformation and the English People*, 81, 109; Marsh, *Popular Religion*, 201–4; Marshall, *Reformation England*, 55–6.

people's response to the Reformation were as varied as the people themselves. Chapter 4 supplements these reasons by examining why people chose to take or decline the oaths of succession and supremacy. Although this might initially appear to be a rather modest contribution to historical knowledge, my exploration of why people chose to take or decline oaths gains significance when one realizes that swearing oaths was the primary manner in which the English people responded to the Henrician Reformation. The theme of *how* the English people responded to the Reformation (the third theme of popular response) has of course been treated by other historians, but oaths have not been a prominent part of their explanations. This oversight is unfortunate, for oaths were not only the principal mechanism through which most people manifested their resistance or acceptance of the Henrician Reformation but also explain how they justified their opposition or acquiescence with a specific rationale. In other words, this book argues that oaths were the chief vehicle through which the English people exhibited and legitimized their response to the Reformation.

Take, for example, resistance to the Reformation. Traditionally historians have divided resistance to the Reformation into two categories: active and passive.[55] Active resistance was open rebellion like the Pilgrimage of Grace. Passive resistance was refusal or reluctance to cooperate. It generally consisted of foot-dragging and evasion – parishioners rarely refused to hand over parish goods but rather stalled for time or hid parish goods in their homes and then told royal officials that they did not possess the sought-after goods. This same pattern of passive resistance is evident in the popular response to the oaths of succession and supremacy. While few people refused to swear them outright, some people utilized equivocation, conditional protestations, and mental reservation to mitigate the full force of these oaths. The monks of the London Charterhouse took their oaths this way, and the second half of Chapter 4 explores these practices in great detail.

Oaths were also a major part of active resistance to the Reformation. One common means of active resistance was to swear an oath of one's own devising. Just as Prior Houghton swore an oath declaring his opinion on the oath of supremacy before his execution, Englishmen in the North swore their own oaths during the 1536 rebellion known as the Pilgrimage of Grace. Chapter 5 examines these rebel oaths and argues that the pilgrims swore them in part as a response to the oath of succession. By declaring the people's interpretation of the oath of succession, the pilgrims publicly commented

---

[55] This dichotomy is Ryrie's. See his *Age of Reformation*, 139–41.

on the king's recent religious policy, set the parameters of their allegiance, and attempted to manipulate the king's future course of action. And these oaths not only demonstrated the pilgrims' resistance to the Henrician Reformation, they also legitimized it, for they made the pilgrims' obedience to God and the king dependent on the pilgrims' rejection of the regime's recent religious policies. Oaths sworn before the start of the Reformation could have a similar effect. The London Charterhouse justified their refusal to swear the oath of supremacy by citing their previous oath to the Pope. Oaths were therefore both a means of and justification for resistance.

Oaths played an equally important role in how people acquiesced to the Reformation. In many ways, resistance and acquiescence were opposite sides of the same coin. For example, while swearing the Henrician state oaths with mental reservation may have been resistance from the point of view of the juror, it was acquiescence from the point of view of those who witnessed the oath. Any act short of outright refusal to swear contained at least an element of acquiescence. Since oaths were the primary point of contact between the Henrician regime and the people, and since the majority of the English people swore the oaths administered to them, oaths were the principal way the people acquiesced to the Reformation. Moreover, just as oaths sworn against the regime legitimized resistance, so did the various state oaths administered by the regime legitimize acquiescence, for they propagated the idea that it was subjects' duty to obey the crown and its policies, and then cemented that obedience with a spiritual bond. If, as I have already mentioned, inherent loyalty to one's lawful sovereign was an important reason why the English people complied with the Reformation, then oaths were the primary means through which this loyalty was inculcated and intensified.

By arguing that the English people responded to the Henrician Reformation through oaths, this study takes for granted that the English people participated in the Reformation. The Reformation was not a one-way process, be it top-down or bottom-up. It was often a process of negotiation between the Henrician regime and the people, as Houghton, Laurence, and Webster's interview with Cromwell illustrates. G. W. Bernard has contended that, when it came to the state oaths of Henrician Reformation, 'no "negotiation" was possible', for those who dared to defy the Henrician regime ended up on the execution block.[56] While this was true for Houghton, Laurence, and Webster, Chapter 6 shows that persecuted evangelicals often secured substantial concessions from the ecclesiastical

---

[56] Bernard, *King's Reformation*, 600.

authorities during their heresy trials. In particular, evangelicals successfully negotiated with the regime what they would swear in their abjuration oaths, and even whether they would swear an oath at all! And even if the negotiation failed (as was the case with the London Charterhouse), the English people were participants in the process of implementation in that they swore oaths. *Pace* Bernard, I maintain that the act of swearing or refusing to swear an oath was an act of real political significance.[57] Oaths gave the people a voice. It is true that the Henrician regime tried to limit the range of this voice by attempting to restrict the people's choice to two options – swear this state oath or suffer the consequences – but a restricted voice is still a voice, and this book clearly demonstrates that many people added their voices in ways that fell well outside the regime's score. The beauty of oaths was that anyone could swear them. This study therefore contributes to the growing literature on popular politics, arguing that oaths were the vehicle through which the English people commented on, contributed to, and even exercised agency over the national politics of the Henrician Reformation.[58]

If oaths thus gave agency to both the ruling regime and the English people, which group benefited most from oaths? The crown implemented its Reformation through oaths because oaths added spiritual muscle to a weak police force. Was that muscle effective? The English people responded to the Henrician Reformation with oaths because oaths gave them access to a power higher and greater than the king. Was this power operative? The conclusion of this book addresses these questions, exploring the ramifications of the prodigious use of oaths during the Henrician Reformation. Historians often argue that the Henrician Reformation (and the European Reformations in general) increased the power of the state.[59] I claim, however, that in the long run, the Henrician regime's employment of oaths empowered its subjects more than it empowered the English monarchy.

Finally, because oaths were highly important to the Henrician Reformation, any examination of them inevitably touches on issues other than the implementation of and response to the Reformation. In particular, the prism of oaths sheds new light on the stories of Thomas More and

---

[57] Bernard, *King's Reformation*, 125.
[58] For more on popular politics, see Shagan, *Popular Politics and the English Reformation*; Walter, 'Public Transcripts, Popular Agency and the Politics of Subsistence', 123–48; Zaret, *Origins of Democratic Culture*; Lake and Pincus (eds.), *Politics of the Public Sphere in Early Modern England*.
[59] Elton, *Tudor Revolution in Government*; Sharpe, *Selling the Tudor Monarchy*, 84, 475, 481; Jones, *Conscience and Allegiance*, 25; Reinhard, 'Reformation, Counter-Reformation, and the Early Modern State', 123–8.

John Fisher, the extent to which court faction influenced the policies of Henry VIII, the relationship between Mary and her father, the connection between Lollardy and evangelicalism, and the nature of evangelical heresy trials. Oaths, then, do much to increase our understanding of the Henrician era.

CHAPTER I

The theoretical basis of swearing oaths

In his Sermon on the Mount, perhaps the most influential sermon in Western history, Jesus proclaimed:

Agayne ye have herde howe it was sayd to them off olde tyme, thou shalt not forswere thy silfe, but shaltt performe thyne othe to God. But I say vnto you swere not at all: nether by heven for hyt ys goddes seate: nor yet by the erth, ffor it ys hys fote stole: Nether by Jerusalem, ffor hit ys the cite of the grete kynge: nether shalt thou sweare by thy heed, because thou canst not make one heer whyte, or blacke: But your communicacion shalbe, ye, ye: nay nay. For what soever is more than that, cometh off yvell.[1]

It appears that Jesus taught simply to tell the truth at all times and cease swearing oaths altogether. Indeed, many of the early Church Fathers (Origen, Cyprian, Gregory Nazianzen, and Basil) interpreted Jesus' words in this way.[2] Chrysostom even went so far as to dedicate an entire Lenten sermon series to the eradication of all swearing in Antioch.[3] Yet other fathers (notably Augustine and Jerome) did not interpret Jesus' teaching as completely forbidding the practice of swearing. They noted that Matthew 5 could not be taken literally since God commanded his people to swear in the Old Testament (Deut. 6:13, 10:20) and the apostle Paul swore in his epistles (Rom. 9:1, Gal. 1:20, Phil. 1:8). They then constructed a whole theory of oath-taking, a theory that was codified in canon law and greatly elaborated in medieval sermons and manuscripts.

This theory of oath-taking is the subject of this chapter. It is the essential backdrop to why Henry used oaths to implement his Reformation and why the English people responded to these state oaths in the way that they did. The theory of oath-taking must be examined before we can understand

---

[1] Matt. 5:33–37, Tyndale, *New Testament 1526*. For a similar statement, see James 5:12.
[2] Roberts and Donaldson (eds.), *Ante-Nicene Fathers*, IV:368, V:470; Schaff and Wace (eds.), *Nicene and Post-Nicene Fathers*, VII:429, VIII:128, 238, 239.
[3] Schaff (ed.), *Nicene and Post-Nicene Fathers*, IX:317–489.

the practice of oath-taking in Henrician England. Of course, the reign of Henry VIII was a time of great religious change. Protestant ideas filtered in from the Continent and influenced reformers like Thomas Cranmer, Thomas Becon, and John Bale. Yet the triumph of Protestant ideology was far from complete in Henry's reign, and historians continue to debate the extent to which Henrician England can justifiably be classified as Protestant. Henry's church was fluid; it contained a continuously changing body of members, members influenced by both Roman Catholic and Protestant theology in varying degrees. This means that any examination of the theory of oath-taking in Henrician England must explore both the medieval Catholic heritage and the Protestant modification of this heritage, for both theories had some currency in Henrician England. This chapter will thus extend temporally and geographically beyond the parameters of the title of this book. It may be objected that any temporal extension forward into the reigns of Henry's children is unwarranted since the future obviously cannot influence the past. Granted, but the circumstances of Henry's reign (specifically the danger of voicing any opinions contrary to those of the king) meant that it was quite possible that many people held beliefs in Henry's reign that they did not declare openly until after Henry's death. For example, it is probable that the theories contained in the Homily against Swearing and Perjury published in Cranmer's Book of Homilies were held by some English people before the publication of the homily shortly after Henry's death. By covering the whole spectrum of theological views on oaths available in the sixteenth century, we can establish a base theory from which we can safely assert that all Henrician English people (be they conservative, evangelical, or radical) drew.[4]

Such a base theory is possible because the differences between Catholics and Protestants were minor when it came to oaths. Both Catholics and Protestants, whether medieval or early modern, centred their theories of oath-taking around the idea that oaths were a vital gateway through which human society was able to experience God. An oath was a kind of ark whereby human beings gained access to God's power and could harness

[4] I am aware that it is historiographically unfashionable to write of English 'Protestants' during the reign of Henry VIII. Yet because the chronological span of this chapter extends beyond the death of Henry, I will continue to use the word Protestant to refer both to genuine Protestants who lived during the reigns of Henry's children and also to the evangelical reformers who also lived and wrote under Henry. This is appropriate when writing of oath theory, for although Henrician evangelicals like Thomas Cranmer or John Bale were not necessarily Protestant in the full sense of the word, their writings on oaths in Henry's reign were consistent with Continental Protestant oath theory. In Chapter 6, when sticking strictly within the temporal parameters of Henry's reign, I will refer to these same individuals as evangelicals. For more information, see footnote 1 of Chapter 6.

his omniscience and omnipotence as a guarantor of the truth of their statements. Yet like the ark of the Hebrews, oaths as manifestations of God's power and majesty had to be approached with reverence and awe, lest the majesty of God be insulted and he punish his people. Oaths could be sworn only in specific circumstances and in certain ways. The more one valued the majesty of God's name and, as a result, oaths, the stricter one constrained the use of oaths. Yet few people condemned swearing oaths altogether, for to do so would deprive God of a form of worship and humans of a crucial way to access God, a way that allowed them to harness the very power of God. It was this divine power emanating from oaths that made it such an attractive means of implementing the Reformation in England and also of resisting this same Reformation.

OATHS AS A FORM OF WORSHIP OF GOD

An oath, most simply and universally defined, is citing someone (or something) as witness to the truth of one's statement. Yet because the purpose of an oath is to make the person to whom it is sworn believe that the swearer's statement is true, the person or being cited as witness must possess greater authority than the swearer, otherwise the witness adds nothing to the credibility of the swearer. For example, if I attempt to convince my friend that I did indeed lock the door by citing my dog as witness, this oath does not make my statement any more believable, for my dog lacks both the ability to recognize the locking of a door and the power to communicate to my friend the truthfulness of my statement. So in the words of Hebrews 6:16, humans 'sweare by him that is greater then them selues'.[5] For medieval and early modern religious writers, the person cited as witness in an oath was – or at least should be – always God. Why? The simplest answer was that God commanded that oaths be sworn in his name.[6] But there were deeper reasons for swearing by God, reasons that explain why God would command his people to swear by him. First, the person whom one cited as witness had to have the ability to discern whether the swearer's declaration was true or false. Who but God had the capacity always to know the veracity of any statement?[7] John Hooper, a Cistercian monk who underwent a Protestant conversion under Henry and became bishop of Gloucester

---

[5] *Coverdale Bible of 1535.*

[6] 'Thou shalt feare the Lorde thy God, and him onely shalt thou serue, and sweare by his name'; Deut. 6:13; 'Thou shalt feare the Lorde thy God, him onely shalt thou serue, vnto him shalt thou cleue, & sweare by his name'; Deut. 10:20, *Coverdale Bible of 1535.*

[7] Frequently quoted passages are 1 Chron. 28:9 and Jer. 17:10.

and Worcester under Edward, wrote: 'To swear is to protest and promise the thing we swear to be true before him that knoweth the thoughts and cogitations of the heart: that knoweth only and solely God.'[8] Thus, by swearing by God, the swearer recognized God's omniscience. Second, the person by whom one swore had to have the power to punish the swearer if his or her statement was false; otherwise there would be no incentive for the swearer to be truthful. Some oaths included an explicit malediction, in the words of Thomas Aquinas, 'as when one obliges himself or someone close to him to punishment if what he alleges be not true'.[9] Even if such a curse was not vocalized in an oath, it was always implied. Hooper, for example, believed that every oath contained an 'execration', while the equally fervent English Protestant John Bale specified that when you swear, 'thou makeste him iudge of the thinge to auenge it of thee yf it be false but in the least pointe'.[10] Other writers agreed.[11] If oaths, then, always implied punishment of perjury, who but God had the power to punish all men regardless of their circumstances? In swearing by God the swearer recognized God's omnipotence. Finally, the person whom the swearer cited as a witness had himself to be always truthful; otherwise his credibility as a witness was tarnished. Yet the psalmist declared that 'all men are lyers'.[12] God, however, was always truthful, for, as the 'Bishop's Book' of 1537 put it, 'if he could be false, he were not God'.[13] By citing God as witness in an oath, one recognized his essence as truth. Thus, by calling on God in an oath, one proclaimed and acknowledged that he was indeed God.[14]

If by citing God as witness, the swearer acknowledged his omniscience, his omnipotence, and his essence as truth, then in the very act of taking

---

[8] Hooper, *Early Writings*, 477.   [9] Aquinas, *Summa Theologiae*, II-II, q. 89, a. 1.

[10] Hooper, *Early Writings*, 477; Bale, *Christen exhortacion*, sig. B5^v.

[11] For example, see Calvin, *Institutes of the Christian Religion*, book 2, ch. 8, para. 24; Tyndale and Frith, *Works of the English Reformers*, II:291; Bicknoll, *Swoord agaynst Swearyng*, fol. 12^r.

[12] Ps. 115:11 (116:11 in modern Bibles), *Coverdale Bible of 1535*.

[13] Lloyd (ed.), *Formularies of Faith*, 139.

[14] Thomas Wygenhale, a medieval priest who wrote a large manuscript on oaths, cited Jerome and wrote that perjurers denied God: 'Sed quociescumque nomen dei in vanum assumimus vel sine tribus comitibus iuramus tociens vincun^r [vincuntur?] a viciis atque peccatis. Ergo quociescumque nomen dei in vanum assumimus vel sine tribus comitibus iuramus tociens mortalier peccamus cum deum negemus'; CUL MS II. 1. 39, fol. 5^r. Alexander Carpenter implied the same idea when he asserted that false swearers deny Christ's divinity: 'patet quod omnis periuria quantum in se est deum falsum facit & mendacem & inquitum in se est tollit a deo etiam veritatem: & cum deus sit veritas quantum in se est aufert illi diuinitatem suam'; Carpenter, *Destructorium viciorum*, sig. G5^r. This same idea is repeated in the Bishop's Book of 1537: 'And so such perjured men, as much as is in them, make God no God'; Lloyd (ed.), *Formularies of Faith*, 139. Finally, the seventeenth-century Protestant Edmond Bicknoll applied this idea to Anabaptists, saying that they deny that God is God because they refuse to swear oaths; Bicknoll, *Swoord agaynst Swearyng*, 12^v. Thus, this idea was constant from the fourteenth century to the seventeenth century.

an oath the swearer actually worshipped God. The Swiss reformer Henry Bullinger and the English evangelical minister Roger Hutchinson averred that one gave honor to the person by whom one swore.[15] The ecclesiastical lawyer Richard Cosin likewise declared: 'Swearing is a kinde of religious acte, whereby wee giue worship to God, as most true, most iust, and knowing all thinges.'[16] Thomas Aquinas claimed that oaths were *latria* (supreme worship that is due to God alone), while the author of *Dives and Pauper*, as well as John Calvin (a century later) stated simply that oaths were a kind of divine worship.[17] The medieval priest Thomas Wygenhale proclaimed that one venerated, loved, and feared whatever one swore by.[18] John Bale went so far as to say that one deified whatever one swore by.[19] Indeed, the idea that swearing was a form of worship lay behind the extremely common denunciation of oaths by creatures. To swear by a creature was to give that creature the honour, worship, and glory that belonged only to God. It was a kind of idolatry. Virtually every medieval and early modern treatise that discussed oaths condemned swearing by creatures.[20] Indeed, many writers followed Jerome and construed Jesus' command in Matthew 5 to mean that one should not swear by creatures since Jesus qualified his statement to 'swear not at all' by disallowing oaths by heaven, earth, Jerusalem, or an individual's head.[21] Oaths by creatures were a serious sin. According to medieval canon law, clerics who continued to use them should be excommunicated.[22] Hooper declared: 'Before all things beware of an oath by any creature, except ye will be glad to have God's displeasure.'[23] Oaths were a form of worship, and worship should be given to God alone. The seventeenth-century Puritan writer John Downame summarized: 'whatsoever we sweare by, that we deifie, in communicating vnto it Gods incommunicable attributes, as his omnipresence, omniscience, omnipotence, whereby he can powerfully

---

[15] Hutchinson, *Works*, 21; Bullinger, *Decades*, PS, VII:248.   [16] Cosin, *An Apologie*, part 3, 33.

[17] Aquinas, *Summa Theologiae*, II-II, q. 89, a. 4; Barnum (ed.), *Dives and Pauper*, 232–3; Calvin, *Institutes*, bk. 2, ch. 8, para. 23.

[18] CUL MS II. I. 39, fol. 86[r]. Wygenhale (also known as Wignhal or Wygnale) was a canon of the Monastery of the Blessed Mary of West-Durham (Norwich) and perpetual vicar of the Church of the Holy Trinity in Cambridge. Wygenhale's treatise is the only full-length medieval work dedicated to swearing, as far as I am aware. It survives only in manuscript.

[19] Bale, *Christian exhortacion*, sig. C3[r].

[20] Brandeis (ed.), *Jacob's Well*, 153; Diekstra (ed.), *Book for a Simple and Devout Woman*, 1, 62; Barnum (ed.), *Dives and Pauper*, 226, 232–3; Carpenter, *Destructorium viciorum*, sig. G4[v]; Wycliffe, *Johannis Wyclif tractatus de mandatis divinis*, 201–2; Swinburn (ed.), *Laterne of Liȝt*, 89; White, *Of oathes*, 5–8; Bond (ed.), *Certain Sermons or Homilies*, 130; Bullinger, *Decades*, PS, VII:248; Bale, *Christian exhortacion*, sigs. B3[v], C2[v]–3[r]; Downame, *Foure treatises*, 12. This list is not exhaustive, but the idea should be clear.

[21] Jerome, *S. Hieronymi Presbyteri Opera, Pars I, 7: Commentariorvm in Mathevm*, 32–3.

[22] *CIC*, C. 22 q. 1 c. 9, Friedberg, 1:863.   [23] Hooper, *Early Writings*, 479.

protect his truth, and punish al falsehood; al which are so peculiar to God as that they cannot be communicated with any creature'.[24]

WHAT TO SWEAR BY: OATHS AND THE WORSHIP OF GOD IN MEDIEVAL CATHOLICISM

Catholics and Protestants alike asserted that oaths were a form of worship and, as such, humans should not swear oaths by creatures. Yet medieval Catholics worshipped God in a different manner from sixteenth-century Protestants. Medieval Catholics believed that the power of God was diffused throughout the material world in certain sacred persons, objects, and ceremonies. Saints, relics, books of the Gospels, and the consecrated host, for example, reflected or channelled God's power. As a result, medieval Catholics swore oaths by them, believing that such oaths were more effective because the objects by which they swore gave them greater access to God.

First, oaths were often sworn before or by relics. For example, in 1538, Thomas Hore, prior of Cardigan, narrated the story of the finding of an image of the Virgin Mary. No matter how many times the image was brought to the church of Cardigan, it returned to the spot of its discovery. When the Church of Our Lady was built on the spot of its discovery to house the image, a taper was lit before the image that burned for nine years continuously without using wax until someone swore falsely on the taper. Thenceforth, the taper was 'enclosed and taken for a greate relyque, and so worshipped and kyssed of pylgremes, and used of men to sweare by in difficill and harde matters'.[25] Crosses and altars were other examples of sacred objects upon which oaths were often made. The vicar of Halywell recounted the story of a man who swore falsely on a 'holy rood', after which he was unable to remove his hands. When he applied more force in the effort, he lost his footing and hung suspended on the cross for three days until he repented his perjury.[26] Similarly, included in the *Alphabet of Tales* (a medieval collection of didactic legends) was a story emphasizing the gravity of swearing on the grave of a saint. When a justice of the peace could not determine which party was truthful in a local dispute, he made both parties swear an oath before the altar. The guilty party 'bagan to wax all seke & ill at ease'. The justice, not totally satisfied, then took both parties to St. Pancras' grave and made them swear again. This time, the perjurer

---

[24] Downame, *Foure treatises*, 12.   [25] Wright (ed.), *Three Chapters of Letters*, 186 (*LP*, XIII (i) 634).
[26] Whitford, *Werke for householders*, 27–8.

was not able to remove his hand from the grave, and his hand began to swell up. As a result of this episode, residents of this unnamed county continued the practice of swearing on St. Pancras' grave in disputed matters.[27] In the absence of saints' relics, oaths were sometimes sworn simply by saints themselves. 'By Saint Mary', (often shortened to 'Mary') was so common an oath that even the zealous reformer Hugh Latimer confessed to using it.[28] Hence, even though oaths were theoretically restricted to the worship of God alone, medieval people often connected them to the more accessible, tangible manifestations of God's power in the world: relics and saints.

The most tangible manifestation of God's presence in the world was of course the corporal body and blood of Christ transubstantiated from bread and wine during the Mass. As such, medieval people naturally associated oaths with the Mass. Indeed the Latin word *sacramentum*, from which we derive the English word 'sacrament', originally meant 'oath'. Just as soldiers professed their loyalty to and bound themselves under their captains in the Roman Empire with an oath of allegiance, so Christians professed their loyalty and allegiance to Christ through the sacraments.[29] Yet the connection between oaths and the sacrament of the altar was not merely etymological, it was also practical. Treaty oaths between sovereigns, for example, were usually sworn immediately following the Mass.[30] William Tyndale, the great Henrician reformer who translated the New Testament into English, lamented how oaths sworn on the holy sacrament were so lightly broken.[31] After the Gospels, the most common book used to solemnize an oath was the Mass book. The Mass also had relevance to sinful oaths. Some medieval writers believed that God would forgive light or forgotten oaths when the offender heard Mass.[32] Conversely, the author of *Dives and Pauper* averred that a perjuror was 'vnable for to reseyuyn þe sacrament of þe auter þat is Crist hymself, souereyn trewþe, vndyr forme of bred'.[33] It makes sense that people would associate the calling forth of God as their witness with the 'making' of God since in both activities, God was made accessible to the common person. Indeed, since Christ was corporally present in the consecrated host, swearing by the Mass was

[27] Banks (ed.), *An Alphabet of Tales*, 286–7. This story is also recounted by Wygenhale: CUL MS II. 1. 39, fol. 38ᵛ.
[28] Latimer, *Sermons and Remains*, 79.
[29] Bullinger, *Decades*, PS, VII:235; Zwingli, *Zwingli and Bullinger*, 264–5. Medieval writers sometimes used *sacramentum* to refer to an oath, but usually they employed *iusiurandum* or, even more commonly, *iuramentum*.
[30] *Cal SP Venice*, VII 76.   [31] Tyndale and Frith, *Works of the English Reformers*, 1:446–7.
[32] Simmons (ed.), *Lay Folks Mass Book*, 367; Hill, *Songs, Carols, and Other Miscellaneous Poems*, 70; Brigden, *London and the Reformation*, 13.
[33] Barnum (ed.), *Dives and Pauper*, 235.

equivalent to swearing by God to some medieval Christians. For instance, a commonplace book written at the start of Henry VIII's reign contained a song against swearing by the Mass. It commenced:

> The Mass is of so high dignytee,
> þat no thyng to it comprehendid may be;
> For ther is present in the trynyte,
> On God in persones thre.
> (Refrain) I consaill you both more & lesse,
> [Beware of sweryng by þe masse.][34]

It is clear that the writer discouraged swearing by the Mass not because it was a creature, but because it was so holy that it should be approached only with reverence and solemnity. The writer's concern was that the Mass (like the name of God) should not be taken in vain! By contrast, sacramentarian Protestants were believed to reject oaths by the Mass based on their denial of the real presence. In 1536, Robert Wymond was accused of saying 'that eny man may swere by the masse for the masse was not of godes makyng'.[35] Ten years later, Richard More allegedly proclaimed, 'If he swere by the masse, he swereth by none othe, for godd was not in the Sacrament of the Aultare.'[36] These examples demonstrate that the connection between oaths and the Mass was based on the presence of God in the Mass.

Although the holiness of relics, saints, and the Mass led to their association with oaths, no sacred object was more connected to oaths than the Gospels. The majority of solemn oaths in medieval and early modern England were sworn on the Gospels. Charles V swore his treaty oath to Henry VIII 'by God our creator in the word of the king on our faith and honor and the holy Gospels of God corporally touched'.[37] Fifteenth-century jurors in criminal and civil cases placed their hands on the Gospels when they swore, afterwards kissing the book.[38] Oaths of canonical obedience usually ended with the phrase 'God help me and the holy Gospels of God'.[39] Recantation oaths like that of Christopher Grebill in 1512 included the expression 'I swere by thies holy euangelies by me bodely here touched'.[40] Oaths of

---

[34] Hill, *Songs, Carols, and Other Miscellaneous Poems*, 42.

[35] Wymond, however, denied the accusations made against him; NA sp1/113, fol. 90ʳ (*LP*, XI 1424).

[36] Richard More admitted this, but repented of his heresy. Bishop Bonner concluded that he was a 'symple' man and had learned the opinion from others; NA sp1/218, fol.140ʳ (*LP*, XXI (i) 836).

[37] BL Cotton MS Vespasian C VII, fol. 23ʳ.

[38] Reynes, *Commonplace Book of Robert Reynes*, 143–4.

[39] LPL Warham's Register, fol. 2ᵛ. This is Archbishop Warham's oath of canonical obedience to the Pope, but virtually every oath by a bishop, prior, abbot, or simple parish priest ends in a similar – if not identical – form, as can be seen in any medieval episcopal register.

[40] LPL Warham's Register, fol. 159ʳ.

office almost always concluded with similar phrases such as 'so god helpe you and the holie euangelies', or 'by the holy contents of this book'.[41] Examples of swearing on or by the Gospels could be continued endlessly, but it should be clear that a book of the Gospels was the most common accoutrement to a solemn oath.

But why were oaths sworn so often on or by the Gospels? Put simply, the Gospels were the word of God. Since the word of God incarnate was Jesus Christ, the Gospels were, in a sense, God.[42] Archbishop Thomas Arundel, in his attempt to make the Lollard William Thorpe swear on the Gospels, declared: 'it is all one to swear by the word of God, and by God himself'.[43] The Gospels were also tangible witnesses of the Incarnation, death, and Resurrection of Jesus and his promise that those who believe in him will have eternal life. By swearing on the Gospels, then, the swearer called the second person of the Trinity (Christ) as his or her witness since it was in the Gospels that Jesus Christ's divinity was revealed. The Gospels were the means through which people came to know Christ. As a consequence, when a man forswore himself on the Gospels, he denied their contents and forsook their benefits.[44] The sermon on perjury in Cranmer's Book of Homilies expanded:

So that whosoever wilfully forsweareth hymself upon Christes holy evangely, thei utterly forsake Gods mercy, goodnes and truth, the merites of our savior Christes nativitie, lyfe, passion, death, resurrection and ascencion. They refuse the forgevenesse of synnes promised to all penitent sinners, the joyes of heaven, the company with angels and sainctes for ever, all whiche benefites and comfortes are promised unto true Christian persones in the Gospel.[45]

The same held true for swearing by the missal, by the saints, or by relics. When one swore falsely by them, one forsook their benefits.[46] Medieval writers also believed that the act of laying one's hand on a

---

[41] For some examples of common oaths of office, see BL Cotton MS Vespasian C XIV, fols. 425^r–444^r; BL Royal MS 9 A XIV, fols. 15^v–20^v; BL Lansdowne MS 155, fols. 50^v–51^r, 286^r–290^v; BL Lansdowne MS 621, fols. 105^r–112^v; BL Lansdowne MS 762, fols. 40^r–45^v; BL Harleian MS 160, fols. 185^r–199^r; BL Harleian MS 433, fols. 301^r–305^v; BL Harleian MS 785, fols. 90^v–93^v; BL Harleian MS 6873, fols. 2^r–15^v. Although this list is not comprehensive, it certainly will provide the reader with a sense of the standard forms of oaths of office.
[42] 'In the begynnynge was that worde, and that worde was with god: and god was thatt worde'; John 1:1; Tyndale, *New Testament 1526*.
[43] Bale, *Select Works*, 113.   [44] Carpenter, *Destructorium viciorum*, sig. G5^r.
[45] Bond (ed.), *Certain Sermons*, 133. For a similar quote from a fifteenth-century source, see Barnum (ed.), *Dives and Pauper*, 235.
[46] See for example Diekstra (ed.), *Book for a Simple and Devout Woman*, 279; Carpenter, *Destructorium viciorum*, sig. G5^r.

book (or relic) re-enforced this idea in a tangible, corporal way. The *Fasciculus Morum*, a guidebook for preachers from the fourteenth century, taught:

> And one should notice here that a person who knowingly lies with perjury first of all commits himself to the devil; and when he touches the Book or some sacred object with his hand, by this hand the devil holds him until he returns to penance, to the extent that when he takes food, he takes it from the devil's hand; likewise, if he crosses himself or does something of this sort, it all is done from the devil's hand.[47]

The swearer's physical contact with the Gospels while taking his oath was the means through which the devil took hold of him. Hence, medieval Catholics swore on or by the Gospels (as on or by relics or saints) because they were a kind of window to God, a way in which God's divinity and power could be understood and accessed in the everyday human world.

Although relics, the Mass, and the Gospels all reflected and mediated God's power, they did not all do so equally. It followed that not all oaths were equally solemn or potent. The more a particular object on or by which one swore had access to God, the more convincing and binding was one's oath. When Richard Duke of York was forced to swear loyalty to Henry VI after Richard's capitulation at Dartford in 1452, Richard emphasized the power of his oath by covering all the bases. He swore 'by the holy Evangelies conteyned in this Boke that I lay my hande upon, and by the holy Crosse that I here touche, and by the blessed Sacrament of oure Lordes body that I shall nowe with his mercy receyve'.[48] Andrew Chertsey, the early sixteenth-century translator of French devotional treatises, would have approved, for he maintained that an oath by God and the evangelists is more binding than an oath just by God, which in turn was more binding than an oath by the evangelists alone.[49] Most people, however, considered oaths upon the Gospels ('book oaths') to be of greater weight than simple oaths. For example, when John Danyell in 1556 asked Edward Horsey to divulge information which Horsey had sworn to secrecy 'on a testement', Horsey replied, 'I wyll not breake my noth [oath] on a boke for all the good [gold?] yn yngland, how wolde you or any man trust me whan I swear a symple othe yf I break my boke othe?'[50] The profusion of oaths by the Gospels and relics in medieval England was a result of the belief that these kinds of oaths were more powerful since the book or relic gave one more direct

---

[47] Wenzel (ed. and trans.), *Fasciculus Morum*, 165–7.   [48] *Rotuli Parliamentorum*, v:346–7.
[49] Chertsey, *Floure of the commaundementes*, fol. 25ᵛ.   [50] NA sp11/8, fol. 61ʳ.

access to God, and that access to God (specifically his knowledge of truth and his ability to punish falsehood) was the primary end of an oath.[51]

Relics and books of the Gospels thus were created things that were treated as conduits of the divine. Through their connection to God, they ceased to function as creatures when cited in an oath. The opposite phenomenon happened when humans treated God himself as if he were a creature. According to medieval Catholics, this happened when one swore an oath by God's blood, bones, feet, or any other corporal feature. This kind of swearing was blasphemous because, in the words of Edwin Craun, 'to swear oaths *per membra* is to treat God as a created thing, to speak of God as if he were another human being or a physical object, not the transcendent God of Christian tradition'.[52] Of course, God did in one sense have corporal members in the Incarnation of Jesus Christ, the second person of the Trinity. And because oaths gave the swearer access to God, medieval Catholics taught that blasphemous oaths by God's members gave the swearer access to Christ's corporal body. Yet because these oaths were sinful, the access such oaths granted was harmful, equivalent to crucifying Christ's body anew.

The genesis behind the connection of blasphemous oaths by God's body to the crucifixion is not clear, but it may be that the original idea was to tap into the powerful devotional impulse in medieval Europe that empha-sized Christ's passion, and then use it for a didactic purpose.[53] Meditation upon Christ's passion might logically lead to an abhorrence of the sins for which Christ suffered – and still suffers according to some of the more vivid medieval writers. And blasphemous oaths were especially keen candidates for such an application because the exact nature of the sin (speaking of Christ's members in an irreverent way) called to mind the suffering that these same members underwent on the cross. This association is obvious in a fifteenth-century homily on swearing preserved at the Bodleian Library. The preacher first claimed that blasphemous oaths hurt God '*asmeche as* is in hem þe dou god[e]s sone cst [cast?] vp on þe cros'. He then elaborated:

and ne hadde he [Christ] wepte salt water with his eyne for our gilt & nouȝt for his own shulde we neuer ell asworny be godes eyȝin. And ne hadde he be stougyn to

[51] By way of contrast, Thomas Wygenhale wrote that perjury in common speech was just as serious and solemn as perjury upon a book, for in both cases the perjurer cited God as witness and was thus doomed; CUL MS II. I. 39, fols. 22ᵛ–23ʳ.

[52] Craun, '"Inordinata Locutio": Blasphemy in Pastoral Literature', 151.

[53] For the importance of the devotional impulse on Christ's passion in late medieval Europe, see Duffy, *Stripping of the Altars*, 234–8; Febvre, 'Origins of the French Reformation', 61. For a hypothesis of the possible biblical roots of the idea that blasphemous oaths mutilated Christ's body, see Gray, 'So Help Me God', 33–4.

the herte & schad his precious blod to washe vs from our synys shulde we neuer ell aswern be godes herte ne be godes blod. And ne hade he suffrid the depe wondes & bitter peynys yn his bodi & in his bonys to sauyn vs from helle pyne shuld we neuer ells sworn be his wondes bodi blod ne bonys.[54]

The idea was to call a person's mind to the suffering of Christ's body on the cross and then suggest that blasphemous oaths were just as painful to Christ as his passion. Of course, the implication of this is that the mutilation of Christ's body by blasphemous oaths was more figurative than literal. The more theologically astute medieval writers such as Vincent of Beauvais and Thomas Wygenhale shared this figurative interpretation of blasphemous oaths.[55]

Yet representations of popular piety from the fifteenth century suggest that blasphemous oaths literally dismembered Christ. First, some of the didactic books aimed at the laity did not simply compare blasphemous oaths to Christ's past passion; they depicted blasphemous oaths as causing his passion afresh whenever they were sworn. For example, the author of *Jacob's Well* asserted that when you swear by God's (or his saints') soul, body, heart, flesh, bones, pain, death, feet, nails, or other limbs, 'þanne þei rende god iche lyme fro oþer, and arn werse þan iewys, for þei rentyn hym but onys, and swiche swereys rendyn him *iche day newe*'.[56] Second, the visual juxtaposition of blasphemous oaths with Christ's dismemberment also suggested a more literal association. For example, in Corby Church, Lincolnshire, the remnants of a wall painting show the Virgin holding the crucified Christ. Surrounding this pietà scene are seven fashionably dressed men (gentlemen are often cited in medieval writings as blasphemous swearers) and their demons with little caption boxes above the men's heads. Although most of the text has faded, the bit that is still legible reads 'ones', and it is likely that the full box contained the phrase 'by God's bones'. Furthermore, demons are piercing the hand, foot, and side of three of the men respectively.[57] Finally, the most common and forceful examples of the belief that blasphemous oaths actually dismembered Christ are contained

[54] Bodleian Library, Ashmole MS 750, fol. 47[r–v].
[55] Vincent of Beauvais, Thomas Wygenhale, and the author of the *Myrour to Lewde Men and Wymmen* emphasized the figurative nature of the mutilation of Christ's body through blasphemous oaths by using such words as *quasi, quantum in ipsis est, as if,* and *seemeth.* See Vincent of Beauvais, *Speculum quadruplex,* III:1181–2; CUL MS II. I. 39, fol. 89[r]; Nelson (ed.), *Myrour to Lewde Men and Wymmen,* 216–17.
[56] Brandeis (ed), *Jacob's Well,* 153. My italics. For another example, see Laurent, *Book of Vices and Virtues,* 62.
[57] Also notable is the example of Broughton church, Buckinghamshire. For details on both of these churches, see Woolf, *English Religious Lyric,* 397; Rouse, 'Wall Paintings', 157–63; Woodforde, *Norwich School of Glass-Painting,* 185–6.

in the poetry and illustrative stories of the fourteenth and fifteenth centuries. Robert Mannyng's influential poem *Handlyng Synne* has a poignant stanza on Christ's members being mutilated by blasphemous oaths.[58] The entire premise of Stephen Hawes' poem *The conuercyon of swerers* was Jesus writing a letter to the princes of the world, explaining how 'cruell swerers whiche do god assayle / On euery syde his swete body to tere / With terryble othes as often as they swere'.[59] Among popular exempla, the most common story described a man of upright character (usually labelled as a justice of the peace) devoted to the Virgin Mary. This man's only vice was swearing blasphemously. One day, this man had a vision of the Virgin. In the Virgin's arms was a mutilated, bloody infant. Mary asked the man what judgement he would give on the malefactor who had so harmed her child. Indignant, the protagonist cried that the offender should be hanged. He then inquired who did this brutal crime. Mary replied: 'Thysilff . . . hast thus hym yshent / And al to-drawe my deere, blessed childe, / And with grete othes his lyemes al to-rent / And all his noble bodye thus hast þou defoiled.'[60] Another story recounted Christ himself appearing on the day of judgement, displaying his wounds, and accusing vain swearers of tearing his body.[61] These didactic books, wall paintings, poems and stories suggest that many medieval people believed that oaths by Christ's members really did tear into his corporeal body.

The representations of blasphemous oaths in popular piety thus moved beyond comparing blasphemous oaths to Christ's passion and suggested that blasphemous oaths caused Christ's passion anew. In doing so, they highlighted the special, sacred power of oaths. Medieval theologians taught that when one swore by the Mass, by saints, by relics, or by the Gospels, the swearer gained access to the particular quality of God manifested in the process, person, or thing by which he or she swore. That is why oaths by items that more directly mediated God's holiness (such as the Gospels) were more powerful than oaths by items that less directly reflected God's holiness (such as minor relics). The popular belief that oaths by Christ's members allowed the swearer to access and mutilate Christ's body is simply an extension of this logic. Christ's body was certainly a direct manifestation of God's holiness, but to call it as witness in common conversation (oaths by Christ's members were never required in formal or legal situations)

---

[58] Mannyng, *Handlyng Synne*, 25.   [59] Hawes, *Conuercyon of swerers*, sig. A2[r].

[60] Quote from Idley, *Peter Idley's Instructions*, 119. For other sources that contain this story, see Bodleian Library Ashmole MS 750, fols. 47[v]–48[r]; Barnum (ed.), *Dives and Pauper*, 240–1; Mannyng, *Handlyng Synne*, 25–9; Mirk, *Mirk's Festial*, 113–14.

[61] Smith (ed.), *Common-Place Book*, 79; Reynes, *Commonplace Book of Robert Reynes*, 281–3.

in an irreverent way, as if it were a creature, was to scorn it. Just as perjurous oaths by the Mass, saints, relics, or the Gospels abused the aspect of divinity mediated through it, so did blasphemous oaths by Christ's members abuse his body. Oaths gave the swearer the ability to contact God, either gloriously through the proper worldly embodiments of God's divinity or blasphemously through the worldly embodiments of Christ's humanity.[62]

WHAT TO SWEAR BY: OATHS AND THE WORSHIP OF GOD IN
PROTESTANT ENGLAND

The Reformation changed the way people worshipped God. Protestants favoured a more direct approach to God through the word; the mediation of the saints was unnecessary and derogated the power of Christ. Moreover, the adoration of the host was idolatry and the veneration of relics was superstition. And since oaths were a form of worship, the Reformation affected oaths as well. More specifically, Protestants restricted the acceptable nouns by which one could swear, rejecting oaths by relics, saints, the Mass, and the Mass book. Although John Bale had been clamouring against oaths by these objects throughout the 1540s, the issue rose to national prominence when John Hooper was elected bishop of Gloucester in 1550. Like Bale, Hooper considered oaths by saints and the Mass to violate God's commandment on swearing. He was particularly angered by the ordinal of the first Edwardian prayer book of 1549, since in it all clergymen at their ordination were required to swear the oath of supremacy, which ended with the phrase 'so help me God, all saints and the holy Evangelist'. As a result of this offending clause (and his distaste for ecclesiastical vestments), Hooper initially refused to be ordained as bishop. In July 1550, Hooper explained his reasoning before Edward VI and the Privy Council, whereupon the king conceded to Hooper's wisdom and struck out the concluding clause of the oath that had displeased Hooper. In the second Edwardian prayer book, the oath of supremacy closed with the phrase 'so help me God through Jesus Christ'.[63] After 1550, English Protestant condemnations of oaths by the Mass and saints were common. Hutchinson, for example, specified that swearing by the Mass or by saints was idolatry.[64] Likewise, Downame

---

[62] For more on the claim that blasphemous oaths gave the swearer the power to mutilate Christ's body, see Mohr, 'Strong Language', 19–26.

[63] Russell, 'Lollard Opposition to Oaths', 680–3. Also see Calvin's letter to Edward VI, where Calvin wrote: 'Now there are manifest abuses which are not to be endured; as, for instance, prayer for the dead, placing before God in our prayers the intercession of the saints, and adding their names to his in taking an oath'; Robinson (ed. and trans), *Original Letters*, 709.

[64] Hutchinson, *Works*, 21.

condemned all 'Papisticall oathes, by the Angels, Saints, and their reliques; by their Idols, the Masse, Roode, and such like'.[65] Indeed, the revised code of ecclesiastical law (the *Reformatio legum ecclesiasticarum*) drafted in the later years of Edward's reign summed up this change in oath-swearing when it declared: 'It is our will that a lawful oath shall be taken in these words and no others: "May God so help me through our Lord Jesus Christ."'[66]

The Protestant condemnation of oaths by saints, relics, and the Mass, however, was not as discontinuous with medieval tradition as it may seem. The dividing point was not whether people could lawfully swear oaths by creatures, but what exactly counted as a creature. Everyone condemned oaths by creatures, but some medieval writers, as we saw above, maintained that when oaths were sworn by relics, saints, and the Mass, they did not operate as creatures but rather reflected or channelled God's power. Other medieval writers, such as Peraldus, condemned oaths by creatures without adding a qualification allowing oaths by relics, saints, or the Mass. St Jerome had gone even further by explicitly condemning oaths by saints.[67] Furthermore, Protestants who rejected oaths by saints, relics, and the Mass did so for the same reasons as medieval Catholics had forbidden oaths by creatures in general: such oaths deified creatures and robbed God of his glory.[68] As such, Protestants inherited and repeated the medieval Catholic view that oaths were a form of worship to be given to God alone. What Protestants disputed was *how* God should be worshipped. Medieval Catholics worshipped God (in oaths and otherwise) through saints, relics, and the Mass. For Protestants these practices were idolatry and superstition. In oaths, as in all forms of worship, humans should approach God directly.

Although English Protestants rejected oaths by the Mass and saints, they did not generally end the practice of swearing on and by the Gospels. Yet there was not unanimity on this issue. Some sects of medieval Lollards had taken a firm stance against book oaths. The Lollard tract the *Laterne of Liȝt* clearly stated: 'But neiþir on bookis schullen we swere ꞏ neithir bi Goddis creaturis . . . But we mai in no case swere bi bookis ꞏ as we han seide aforne, neiþir bi lyueli [lively] creaturis ꞏ as bi seyntis or ony such oþir.'[69] Similarly, the Lollard preacher William Thorpe refused to swear upon a book before Archbishop Arundel, saying, 'Sir, a book is nothing else but a thing coupled together of divers creatures; and to swear by any creature, both God's law and man's law is against.'[70] When Arundel argued that the Gospels, as the

[65] Downame, *Foure treatises*, 14.
[66] Bray, (ed. and trans.), *Tudor Church Reform*, 550–1.   [67] Ross (ed.), *Middle English Sermons*, 23.
[68] See for example Downame, *Foure treatises*, 12.   [69] Swinburn (ed.), *Laterne of Liȝt*, 89.
[70] Bale, *Select Works*, 74. See a similar quote on 111.

word of God, were God, Thorpe responded 'that the holy gospel of God may not be touched with man's hand'.[71] John Bale, the sixteenth-century editor of Thorpe's examination, took an identical stance: 'A dampnable vse haue ye brought into the worlde amonge manye other, to sweare vpon a boke whych ys but a creature, where as mennys othes ought to be vpon God onlye.'[72] Yet despite this opinion, the Homily against Swearing and Perjury of 1547 allowed book oaths, even emphasizing their gravity.[73] The Elizabethan oath of supremacy ended with the phrase, 'So helpe me God and by the Contentes of this Booke', as did many of the official oaths of office during Elizabeth's reign.[74] Witnesses and jurors continued to swear oaths on the Gospels in court as well, evidently with no objection. It was not until the rise of Separatism that we see this practice being called into question again. The Separatist leaders Henry Barrow and John Greenwood, for example, refused to swear an oath upon a Bible because they considered it an oath by a creature.[75] Likewise, when Francis Johnson's Brownist congregation was examined by a special commission in 1593, many of his congregates refused to take an oath to answer all questions truthfully (the *ex officio* oath), specifying that they 'denieth to sweare vpon any booke'.[76] These objections did little good, for oaths upon the Gospels continued to be the predominant manner of swearing in seventeenth-century England.[77]

Why did English Protestants continue to swear upon the Gospels? Perhaps swearing 'on' something did not necessarily mean one swore 'by' the thing, even if the phrase '*by* the contents of this book' was common. After all, two seventeenth-century Protestants, John Downame and Christopher White, pointed out that swearing 'by my faith' or 'by my soul' should not be interpreted as calling one's faith or soul as witness to the truth. Rather, it pledged the object to God as a surety and bound it to undergo punishment if the oath was false.[78] While the swearer could not pledge the

[71] Bale, *Select Works*, 114.

[72] Bale, *Yet a course at the Romyshe foxe*, fol. 90ᵛ. See also Bale, *Christen exhortacion*, sig. c3ᵛ.

[73] See the above quote on page 25.   [74] *Statutes of the Realm*, 1 Eliz. 1, c. 1, IV:352; NA C254/179.

[75] Barrow, for example, boldly proclaimed to Archbishop Whitgift 'that that book was not the eternal word of God, that eternal God himselfe, by whom onely I must sweare, and not by any bookes or Bibles'; Barrow, *Writings*, 194. For similar statements, see pages 93–4, 656; Greenwood, *Writings*, 22, 170–1.

[76] BL Harleian MS 6848, fols. 32ʳ–36ʳ, quote from fol. 33ᵛ. See also BL Harleian MS 6849, fols. 181ʳ–182ʳ; BL Harleian MS 7042, fols. 36ᵛ–38ᵛ; Greenwood and Barrow, *Writings*, 377, 380.

[77] Spurr, 'Profane History of Early Modern Oaths', 46. By way of comparison, it is worth mentioning that Gerard ter Borch's portrait *The Swearing of the Oath of Ratification of the Treaty of Münster* (1648) shows that in contrast to the Catholics, who had their hands on a book, the Protestants swore with one of their hands raised when swearing the Treaty of Westphalia. This suggests that some Continental Protestants did not like to swear upon a book.

[78] Downame, *Foure treatises*, 2; White, *Of oathes*, 5.

Gospels in the same way, he or she did implicitly admit to forfeiting the promises within the Gospels if the oath was false, a practice somewhat similar to Downame and White's position. The fact that people traditionally saw book oaths as more binding probably contributed to their persistence as well, for English Protestants had no desire to weaken the power of an oath or provide an excuse for oath-breaking. This was Richard Cosin's explanation for the continuation of book oaths in Elizabethan England: 'The vse of this [a book of the Gospels] in particular; is to strike a more aduised feare & reuerence into vs: when wee consider the reuerence due to an oathe, as it is described in that booke; & the curses there threatened against those, that forsweare themselues, or shall take the name of God vainely.'[79] Yet Cosin also went on to cite Aquinas, Bonaventure, and other scholastics' assertion that oaths by the Gospels were not oaths by creatures since the Gospels were a transparent window of God's majesty.[80] Keeping oaths on the Gospels, after all, does seem to fit with the heightened significance among Protestants of the word of God as the primary means through which God accomplishes his salvation. Yet no matter why Protestants approved of book oaths, it is clear that by doing so they continued to emphasize the connection between oaths and God, thereby stressing that oaths must be treated with reverence and awe.

The Protestant condemnation of blasphemous oaths by Christ's members as mutilating his body also proved continuous with medieval rhetoric. In some sense, this was counter-intuitive. After all, Reformed Protestants denied the 'making' of Christ's body in transubstantiation. They averred that Christ's corporeal body remained at the right hand of the Father in heaven. As such, should they not also have denied the tearing of his body by blasphemous oaths? Melissa Mohr thought so, arguing that 'post-Reformation swearing has lost its ability to access and control God's physical body', undergoing a spiritualization like that of the Lord's Supper.[81] It is true that English Protestants placed less emphasis on the dismemberment of Christ through blasphemous oaths. For example, this belief was not mentioned at all in the Homily against Swearing and Perjury. Yet many English Protestants continued to depict blasphemous oaths as mutilating Christ's body. For example, a draft of an Elizabethan Parliamentary bill proposed that at every quarter session, 'there shall be inquirie made the Iustices chardging the grand inquest for commen blasphemers of the most reverent name of god that is which teare god as it were in peaces swearing by

---

[79] Cosin, *An Apologie*, part 3, 29.   [80] Cosin, *An Apologie*, part 3, 34–5.
[81] Mohr, "Strong Language," 30.

the heart, nayles, feet, or any other true or imagined part of god, or by his death, life, or any like thing'.[82] Bale claimed that if thou swore by Christ's body, thou 'doest as moche as in the lyeth (lyke as the holye doctours confesse) to plucke him oute of heauen with violence, & to crucifie him agayne a fresh'.[83] Like Vincent of Beauvais, the author of the parliamentary bill and Bale connected oaths by Christ's members to his Passion figuratively with the phrases 'as it were', and 'in as much as'.[84] Yet the language of Thomas Becon, the most popular evangelical propagandist of Henry VIII's reign, was more direct. Becon simply declared: 'these wicked caytiffes crucify him dayly with theyr vnlawefull oothes'.[85] John Downame also used vivid, unqualified language implying the actual dismemberment of Christ by vain oaths. He wrote: 'but most of all [they] blaspheme our Sauiour Christ himselfe, pulling his soule from his bodie, and tearing peecemeale his precious members one from another, diuersifying their oathes according to the diuers parts of his sacred bodie'.[86] There was nothing spiritualized in this mutilation of Christ's body.

   In general, Protestants continued to suggest that blasphemous oaths had the power to mutilate Christ's body not because they wanted to make a theological statement on the exact accessibility of Christ's corporeal body after the Resurrection, but because such stories emphasized the gravity of these oaths and warned the laity against employing them. For both medieval Catholics and sixteenth-century Protestants, the depiction of Christ being wounded by blasphemous oaths served a useful didactic purpose. It stressed the serious nature of misusing oaths and provided the laity with a vivid image which religious writers hoped would prevent them from uttering blasphemous oaths in the future. Protestants shared with medieval Catholics the belief that oaths, as a form of worship, must never be uttered in an irreverent manner. Indeed, the changes Protestants made concerning how an oath could be sworn only served to increase the sanctity of oaths. Whereas medieval Catholics allowed the swearing of oaths by the Mass, by relics, and by saints as manifestations of God's divinity, Protestants rejected this practice and claimed that such oaths scorned God by bestowing upon a creature the glory owed only to him. It follows that Protestants would be just as zealous – if not more – in using any strategy open to them to decry the use of blasphemous oaths that scorned God by treating the

---

[82] BL Lansdowne MS 105, fol. 200ᵛ.   [83] Bale, *Christen exhortacion*, sig. B6ᵛ.

[84] For another clearly figurative equation of oaths by Christ's body with the tearing of his members, see Foxe, *AM* (1583), 2103.

[85] Becon, *An Inuectyue*, sig. C2ᵛ. My italics.

[86] Downame, *Foure treatises*, 24. See a similar quote on 28.

second person of the Trinity as a creature. The key for both Protestants and Catholics was to stress how an oath gave the swearer access to God, and to emphasize that such power should not be abused.

THE CONDITIONS OF A LAWFUL OATH

Because an oath invoked the name of the one holy, omniscient, and omnipotent God, it was not something to be taken lightly. Religious writers of the fifteenth and sixteenth centuries, both Catholics and Protestants, thus developed a fairly standard exposition on the conditions under which one could swear a lawful oath: that is, an oath that would not provoke the wrath of God. Inevitably, religious writers based their account on Jeremiah 4:2: 'et iurabis vivit Dominus in veritate et in iudicio et in iustitia'.[87] They usually glossed swearing 'the Lord liveth' as meaning that one should swear by the name of God alone, a point already discussed. But they also specified that for an oath to be lawful, one had to swear in truth (without deception or guile), in judgement (not vainly, ignorantly, or unwillingly), and in justice (not for an evil purpose or ungodly end). They often called these three conditions the 'companions' of a lawful oath.

The first condition of a lawful oath was that the oath must be sworn in truth. At its most basic level, religious writers used this companion to attack perjury. Although perjury could mean the abuse of oaths in a general sense, it also had the specific meaning of confirming a lie with an oath.[88] Taken in this sense, religious writers decried perjury as a mortal sin. Andrew Chertsey asserted that only a bishop could absolve perjury done in court, while canon law maintained that unconfessed perjurers should be expelled from the community of the faithful.[89] Thomas Wygenhale declared that

---

[87] Vulgate. *Biblia sacra iuxta Vulgatam versionem.* Coverdale translated this verse as follows: 'And shalt swear: The Lorde lyueth: in treuth, in equite and rightuousnesse'; *Coverdale Bible of 1535.*

[88] The ambiguity in the definition of perjury is best illustrated by Thomas Wygenhale, who first gave a specific definition of perjury and a few sentences later gave a more general definition: 'periurium est mendacium iuramento firmatum. vnde quibusdam placet non esse periurium vbi non est mendacium & sicut dicitur falsum sine mendacio ita iurari falsum sine perurio nec esse periuium nisi mens ab ore diffenceat . . . iuramentum tres habere comites veritatem & iudicium & iusticiam vbi ista defunt. non est iuramentum sed periurium'; CUL MS II. I. 39, fol. 39ʳ. Alexander Carpenter defined perjury as 'veritatis abnegatio fraudulenta cum diuine attestationis acceptione'; Carpenter, *Destructorium viciorum,* sig. G3ᵛ. Downame defined perjury as 'nothing else but false swearing. Or more fullie, It is a knowne or imagined vntruth, confirmed by oath, ioyned with deceit, which was either purposed and intended before the oath was made, or resolued on afterwards'; Downame, *Foure treatises,* 47. Bale, however, used the more general definition of perjury, saying it was simply 'to abuse the name of God'; Bale, *Christen exhortacion,* sig. B2ʳ. The standard gloss to Jeremiah 4:2 in the Vulgate defined perjury as any oath missing the standard three companions; *Biblia Latina cum glossa ordinaria.*

[89] Chertsey, *Crafte to lyue well,* fol. 31ᵛ; *CIC,* C. 22, q. 1 c.17, Friedberg, I:866.

perjurors should be excluded from the order of the priesthood. Wygenhale went so far as to say that one should choose the hardest death rather than offend God by perjury.[90] According to canon law, perjury was worse than homicide, for homicide killed only the body while perjury murdered the soul.[91] The author of *Dives and Pauper* agreed, noting that perjury was worse because while homicide was committed against man, perjury was a sin against God.[92] Reformers (whether partly or fully Protestant) could be equally vehement in their condemnations of perjury. Thomas Becon, for example, wrote: 'O wyckednesse, more than can be expressed. O shameful synne worthy [of] all kynd of punyshment. O incomparable vice worthy to be reuenged not with papers wearyng only, but wyth the moost bytter & intollerable paynes that are prepared in hell for Satan and hys ministers.'[93] The sermon on perjury in Cranmer's Book of Homilies similarly taught that perjurors give themselves to the Devil, provoke God's wrath, and will be condemned to everlasting shame and death.[94] Clearly, lying under oath was not to be taken lightly.

Yet to medieval Catholics, swearing in truth meant not only never confirming an objective falsehood with an oath but also avoiding using an oath to deceive someone, even if the content of the oath was objectively true.[95] This idea sprang from the Augustinian theory of lying. Augustine defined a lie as 'a false statement made with the desire to deceive'.[96] Although all lying was wrong, the actual false nature of the statement mattered less than the intention of the mind. The main fault in a lie was 'the desire to deceive'.[97] Since late medieval religious rhetoric was 'overwhelmingly Augustinian', and since perjury was simply a lie confirmed with an oath, religious writers decried any deception through oaths.[98] Gratian, the twelfth-century editor of canon law, believed that the person who thought 'to go around' [*circumuenire*] his oath by using 'cunning of words' [*verborum calliditate*] was guilty of perjury.[99] The *Book of Vices and Virtues* condemned swearing 'bi art, or bi sophymme [sophistry]', while an anonymous fifteenth-century

---

[90] CUL MS II. I. 39, fol. 86ᵛ.   [91] *CIC*, c. 22 q. 5 c. 5, Friedberg, 1:883–4.
[92] Barnum (ed.), *Dives and Pauper*, 252.   [93] Becon, *An Inuectyue*, sig. F2ʳ.
[94] Bond (ed.), *Certain Sermons*, 133.
[95] 'Potest igitur dici periurium iuramentum quod sit de falso vel cum dolo vel sine dolo. & de vero cum dolo'; CUL MS II. I. 39, fol. 39ʳ.
[96] Augustine, *Lying (De mendacio)*, trans. Sarah Muldowney, in *St Augustine: Treatises on Various Subjects*, 60.
[97] Augustine, *Lying (De mendacio)*, trans. Sarah Muldowney, in *St Augustine: Treatises on Various Subjects*, 55–6. For a general discussion of Augustine's theory on lying put in the context of dissimulation, see Zagorin, *Ways of Lying*, 19–25.
[98] For the Augustinian nature of late medieval thought on lying, see Craun, *Lies, Slander, and Obscenity*, 40–7.
[99] *CIC*, c. 22 q. 5 c. 8–9, Friedberg, 1:885.

sermon decried swearing 'for defect and gile'.[100] Such an oath was a double sin, for the shifty swearer both took God's name in vain and deceived his fellow Christian.[101] The author of *Dives and Pauper* brought this point home with a story. Once a Christian borrowed some gold from a Jew and refused to pay him back, claiming he had already repaid the gold. The Jew took him to court, and the judge made the Christian swear an oath on a book that he had repaid the Jew. In order to place his hand on the book, the Christian swindler handed his staff to the Jew. Unbeknown to the Jew, the staff was hollow and contained all his gold. The Christian swore: 'Be God, and be Sent Nicolas, and so helpe me God at þe holy doom, Ye tok þe al þat monye þat þu chalangist & more þerto', which was technically true since he had handed the Jew his gold-filled staff. But God would not allow such an oath to stand. On his way home from court, the Christian grew weary and took a nap by the side of the road. While he slept, a cart ran over the Christian, killing him, breaking open his staff, and scattering the gold.[102]

Sixteenth-century English people (be they Catholic or Protestant) also accepted the medieval claim that oaths sworn in truth precluded deception or equivocation. The Henrician canons held true to medieval canon law and stated that oaths must be understood according to the hearer.[103] The Protestant-informed Edwardian *Reformatio legum ecclesiasticarum* was more overt in its denunciation of deceptive swearing:

A perjurer is defined as someone who knowingly and cleverly cheats someone with an oath designed to deceive, or who willingly violates a lawful oath, or who twists his words when swearing in such a complicated way that the meaning of the oath is not clear. Against this deceit we want this rule to be always maintained, that what the person to whom the oath is sworn understands by it according to the normal custom of speech, is what will be believed as having been sworn.[104]

Radicals like John Bale and John Hooper also decried the use of guile when swearing.[105] By Elizabeth's reign, both Puritans like James Morice and their conformist opponents like Richard Cosin could agree that no

[100] Laurent, *Book of Vices and Virtues*, 62; Bodleian Library Ashmole MS 750, fol. 46ᵛ. For a similar quote, see Barnum (ed.), *Dives and Pauper*, 235.
[101] Both the claim that God understands oaths in the same way as the person to whom the oath is sworn and the argument that using equivocation (ambiguity of words) in an oath for deception is a double sin are repeated often throughout late medieval writings. See for example: Laurent, *Book of Vices and Virtues*, 63; Aquinas, *Summa Theologiae*, II-II, q. 89, a. 7; Mannyng, *Handlyng Synne*, 98; Chertsey, *Floure of the commaundementes*, fol. 24ᵛ; *CIC*, c. 22 q. 5 c. 9, Friedberg, 1:885; Brandeis (ed.), *Jacob's Well*, 153.
[102] Barnum (ed.), *Dives and Pauper*, 235–7. [103] Bray (ed. and trans.), *Tudor Church Reform*, 24–5.
[104] Bray (ed. and trans.), *Tudor Church Reform*, 550–1.
[105] Bale, *Christen exhortacion*, sig. A8ᵛ; Hooper, *Early Writings*, 477.

one should use equivocation or deception when swearing.[106] Thus, for both Catholics and Protestants, to swear in truth meant to swear truly without equivocation, dissimulation, or guile.

The second condition of a lawful oath was that the oath must be sworn in judgement. Oaths could be sworn outside judgement in multiple ways, but the most common way was to swear an oath in a trivial situation when it was not necessary. Clerical writers referred to these oaths as vain oaths and further described them as customable, idle, frivolous, light, trifling, rash, of sport, for nought, or without necessity. It is clear that vain oaths were common oaths sworn in everyday conversation and not in a solemn liturgical, legal, political, or otherwise serious setting. Fifteenth and sixteenth-century religious writings are full of denunciations of vain oaths.[107] Some medieval writers considered vain oaths to be only a venial sin, while perjury was a mortal sin.[108] But the general trend was to emphasize the gravity of vain oaths, to impress upon the listener or reader the severity of the sin of vain swearing.[109] This was because vain oaths, like oaths by Christ's members, were a form of blasphemy. They were a way to despise or scorn the name of God by not treating it with majesty. To swear vainly was to rob the name of God of its reverence.[110]

The other reason vain oaths were denounced so fervently was because they were thought to lead to perjury. Augustine famously preached: 'Swearing is a narrow ledge, perjury a precipice. If you swear, you're near the edge; if you don't swear, you're far away from it.'[111] Henceforth it became common to the point of banality to write that the more you swear, the greater your chances of perjury.[112] To swear vainly and habitually was sooner or

---

[106] Morice, *A briefe treatise of Oathes*, 5; Cosin, *An Apologie*, part 3, 12–13.

[107] Virtually every religious treatise that mentioned oaths condemned vain swearing to some extent. For a sampling, see CUL MS II. 1. 39, fol. 19ᵛ; Brandeis (ed.), *Jacob's Well*, 153; Carpenter, *Destructorium viciorum*, sig. G4ʳ; Wycliffe, *Johannis Wyclif tractatus de mandatis divinis*, 186–92, 194–5; Wycliffe, *Select English Works*, III:84–5; Swinburn (ed.), *Laterne of Liȝt*, 89; Bullinger, *Decades*, PS, VII:240–1; Lloyd (ed.), *Formularies of Faith*, 139; Becon, *An Inuectyue*, sigs. CIᵛ–FIʳ; Bale, *Christen exhortacion*, *passim*; Bicknoll, *Swoord agaynst Swearyng*, fol. 20ᵛ; Downame, *Foure treatises*, 19–23.

[108] Laurent, *Book of Vices and Virtues*, 1–2.

[109] Wygenhale went to great lengths to show that every oath – no matter how slight – uttered without all of the three companions was a mortal sin that killed the swearer's soul and would send him or her to hell unless repented; CUL MS II. 1. 39, fols. 6ʳ, 20ʳ, 36ʳ, etc. Protestants, of course, rejected the distinction between venial and mortal sins.

[110] Diekstra (ed.), *Book for a Simple and Devout Woman*, 266–8; Bradford, *Writings*, 10–11; Tyndale and Frith, *Works of the English Reformers*, II:292; Bicknoll, *Swoord against Swearyng*, fol. 20ᵛ.

[111] Augustine, 'Sermon 180', 316.

[112] Examples of this statement are too common to cite fully. For a sampling, see Diekstra (ed.), *Book for a Simple and Devout Woman*, 278; Carpenter, *Destructorium viciorum*, sig. G5ᵛ; Vulgate Gloss on Matt. 5, *Biblia Latina cum glossa ordinaria*; Barnum (ed), *Dives and Pauper*, 227; Bale, *Christen exhortacion*, sig. B8ᵛ.

later (usually sooner) to fall into the pit of perjury. This raises the greatest paradox of late medieval and early modern rhetoric on swearing: the more a writer esteemed swearing, the more he discouraged it. For example, John Bale, arguably the hottest, most aggressive, and least compromising Henrician reformer, a man greatly concerned about the sanctity of oaths, forbade all manner of private oaths. Unlike other English writers who allowed private oaths in weighty matters, Bale declared that only oaths sworn before a magistrate or for a public function beneficial to the commonwealth were licit.[113] Oaths were a sacred gateway whereby humans could call on the omniscience and omnipotence of God, but the very sanctity, holiness, and majesty of God restricted the use of oaths to special circumstances. Because medieval and early modern religious writers took oaths seriously, they proclaimed that oaths must be sworn with discreet judgement, not vainly.

Of course, vain oaths were not the only oaths lacking judgement. Clerical writers sometimes included two other kinds of oaths in this category. The first was an oath sworn in ignorance, for in order for the oath to be in accordance with judgement, the swearer had to have knowledge of the matter promised. This is why some medieval didactic books condemned oaths sworn concerning matters of doubt.[114] This is also why the suspected Lollard Robert Best refused to swear an oath to answer truthfully all the questions asked of him by Bishop Cuthbert Tunstall in 1527. Best was ignorant of the content of the questions. Yet once Tunstall read to Best a bill of articles explaining the content of the questions, Best could swear in judgement and thus took his oath.[115] The claim that a promise was licit only if the promisor had full knowledge of the situation was much more common in clerical discussions on vows, but the principle was based on Jeremiah 4:2 and thus applied just as easily to an oath as to a vow.[116] Another oath that could be construed as lacking judgement was an oath obtained through force, compulsion, or intimidation. Such an oath lacked judgement because the swearer did not have a choice in the matter. The degree to which these oaths were binding was a matter of controversy. On

---

[113] Bale, *Christen exhortacion*, sigs. A6^r–A7^r, B5^r–B6^r. For a comparison to other English Protestants see Becon, *An Inuectiue*, sigs. 14^r–15^v; Downame, *Foure treatises*, 10. Tyndale seems to have approached a similar level as Bale: Tyndale and Frith, *Works of the English Reformers*, II:292–3. The extent to which private swearing was allowed also varied among Continental Protestants. Zwingli, for example, condemned all private oaths, as did Calvin in the 1536 edition of the *Institutes*. By 1559, however, Calvin had changed his mind and allowed private swearing in grave matters; Calvin, *Institutes*, pg. 393, n. 34.

[114] Brandeis (ed.), *Jacob's Well*, 153; Diekstra (ed.), *Book for a Simple and Devout Woman*, 278; Laurent, *Book of Vices and Virtues*, 62.

[115] BL Harleian MS 421, fol. 20^r.   [116] Gray, 'So Help Me God', 95–7.

one hand, canon law stated that an oath extorted through fear must still be kept unless keeping it would endanger the swearer's salvation. On the other hand, canon law also decreed that the church was accustomed to absolve people from oaths exhorted through fear, and if someone broke an oath obtained by force, the transgressor (even if he or she had not been formally absolved from his oath) was not to be punished as a mortal sinner.[117] English Protestants were also ambivalent on this issue. Sixteenth-century Protestants who attacked the binding nature of vows often claimed that a forced promise (whether a vow or oath) was not binding, though seventeenth-century Protestants such as John Downame and Christopher White argued that unless it was unambiguously evil, a forced oath still bound the conscience of the swearer, even if it might not be binding in all courts. This was because the oath was never completely forced; the swearer always consented to some degree in every oath.[118] As we shall see, the question of whether a forced oath was binding or not became a key issue in the campaign to enforce the Henrician Reformation. Yet whether or not a forced oath was binding, the key point here is that oaths should be taken in judgement, and judgement required both knowledge and at least a degree of autonomy.

The final condition of a permissible oath was justice. Catholics and Protestants uniformly condemned oaths that were unjust, illicit, or against the law. Indeed, to Thomas More, if the oath was not lawful, breaking it was not perjury.[119] An oath administered improperly was sometimes considered to be unlawful. For example, the Court of Star Chamber ruled that when a person lied under oath after the oath had been tendered to him by someone without authority, such a lie was not technically perjury.[120] But when religious writers spoke of an unlawful oath, they usually referred to an oath to commit an evil or unjust act. For example, Hugh Latimer, the zealous reformer and bishop of Worcester in the later 1530s, preached that if a group of thieves make an evil oath not to reveal each other and then one of them gets caught, it is better for him to break his oath and betray his fellows than keep his oath and thus facilitate future robberies.[121]

[117] *CIC*, x.2.24.8, Friedberg, II:361; *CIC*, x.2.24.15, Friedberg, II:364.
[118] Downame, *Foure treatises*, 60; White, *Of oathes*, 30–4; For a discussion of the Protestant attack on forced vows, see Gray, 'So Help Me God', 97–8.
[119] More, *Dialogue concerning Heresies*, 765.
[120] This conclusion comes from a case that took place in Michaelmas, Anno 23 and 24 of Elizabeth. The plaintiff Robert Ruckell accused Robert Bridges and William Lockett of lying under oath. Lockett was able to demonstrate that a clerk of London had tendered him his oath, a man who 'had noo Aucthoritie to give an oath'. So Lockett was not found guilty of perjury but rather a misdemeanour, while Bridges was found guilty of perjury; BL Harleian MS 2143, fol. 11ᵛ.
[121] Latimer, *Sermons by Hugh Latimer*, 519–20.

The most common examples of evil oaths were biblical: David's oath to kill Nabal and his sons, Jephthah's vow to slay the first thing that he saw upon returning home, Herod's oath to grant any request of Herodias, and Joshua's oath to spare the Gibeonites.[122] Such oaths, religious writers uniformly declared, should be broken rather than kept.[123] Most people would have agreed with William Tyndale's statement: 'to swear to do evil is damnable, and to perform that is double damnation'.[124] The sin of swearing an illicit oath should not be compounded with the further sin of fulfilling it.

Nevertheless, the breaking of an evil oath was not always as straightforward as it might seem. The story of Joshua's oath to the Gibeonites was particularly thorny for religious writers. On the one hand, the oath clearly was illicit. God had commanded the Israelites to destroy all the pagan tribes of Canaan. In spite of the Gibeonites' deception of claiming not to live in Canaan, Joshua's sworn peace treaty with them clearly violated this divine command. On the other hand, Israel kept this oath and God approved of it, for later, when Saul executed the Gibeonites, God punished Israel for breaking its oath.[125] This led to the distinction in canon law between an oath made illicit because of what was sworn and an oath made illicit because of the manner of swearing.[126] The former, such as homicide or adultery, was illicit in its nature (*in sui natura*) and should always be broken. The latter, such as swearing to marry after having vowed chastity, was not inherently illicit but made so because of the particular circumstances of the swearer. This kind of evil oath could still be kept, though penance had to be done for making it. The other example Gratian mentioned was that of swearing not to do something expedient to one's salvation. As long as the person could still be saved without impediment, he or she was not prohibited from fulfilling this oath even though it should not have been sworn in the first place.[127] Thus, while everyone agreed with the simple statement that an oath sworn without justice should be broken, there was an underlying haziness concerning what actually made an oath unjust and when an unjust oath could still be fulfilled.

---

[122] 1 Sam. 25; Judg. 11; Matt. 14; Mark 6; Josh. 9. Joshua's oath to the Gibeonites was the only ambiguous example.

[123] This axiom held true for all religious writers, Catholic or Protestant, fifteenth or sixteenth century. For a representative example, see Carpenter, *Destructorium viciorum*, sig. G3ᵛ; Idley, *Peter Idley's Instructions*, 153–4; Chertsey, *Floure of the commaundementes*, fol. 24ᵛ; Bond (ed.), *Certain Sermons*, 132; Bale, *Christen exhortacion*, sigs. A7ᵛ–A8ᵛ; Becon, *An Inuectiue*, sigs. G4ʳ–H3ʳ; Gardiner, *Obedience in Church & State*, 163.

[124] Tyndale and Frith, *Works of the English Reformers*, II:293.   [125] Josh. 9; 2 Sam. 21.

[126] *CIC*, c. 22 q. 4 c. 23, Friedberg, I:882.   [127] *CIC*, c. 22 q. 4 c. 23, Friedberg, I:882.

For an oath to glorify God, then, the oath had to be sworn in the name of God (or one of the corporeal manifestations of his divinity for Catholics) and it had to be sworn truthfully without an intention to deceive, gravely before a magistrate or in some other equally solemn circumstance, willingly and with knowledge of the matter, and justly so that what one swore to do was not wrong. Medieval Catholics and sixteenth-century Protestants agreed on these basic guidelines. Oaths that lacked any of these conditions were sinful and a serious offence to the majesty of God.

GOD'S WRATH AGAINST ILLICIT SWEARING

And in medieval and early modern England, God did not take insults to his majesty lightly. In order to protect his honour and reputation, God kept careful watch over the use and abuse of oaths. Any person who swore falsely, vainly, blasphemously, or unjustly implied that God either could not or would not punish his transgression, for otherwise the person would not have sworn the illicit oath in the first place. Thus, by not swearing correctly, the individual was denying either God's power or his nature as truth. In essence, the swearer was denying that God was God, a claim that God would simply not tolerate. The Lord himself proclaimed that a curse (manifested to Zechariah as a large flying book) 'shal come to the house of the thefe, & to the house of him, that falsely sweareth by my name: & shal remayne in his house, & consume it, with the tymbre & stones therof'.[128] Medieval religious writers were keen to authenticate this claim. For example, the Bridgettine monk and author of devotional best-sellers Richard Whitford declared: 'For his othe [God] may slee or infecte your chylde in the cradle, or stryke your beestes in the feeldes, destroy your corne and grayness, and cause pryuely many myscheues.'[129] To prove this was indeed true, medieval authors often peppered their writings about oaths with stories of providential punishment on false and vain swearers. The fourteenth-century poet and historian Robert Mannyng told a tale of a rich man who, in his attempt to defraud a poor one, swore a false oath. The rich man bent down to kiss the book to confirm his oath and was struck down by God, never to rise again.[130] Another common story was that of a blasphemous boy who, accustomed to vain oaths, was carried away by demons before the eyes of his father.[131] Sometimes God tailored

---

[128] Zech. 5:1–3; *Coverdale Bible of 1535.*   [129] Whitford, *Werke for Housholders*, 23–4.
[130] Mannyng, *Handlyng Synne*, 96–8. For a similar story see Idley, *Peter Idley's Instructions*, 152.
[131] Carpenter, *Destructorium viciorum*, sig. G5ᵛ; Idley, *Peter Idley's Instructions*, 180–1. This story seems to have its origin in St Gregory.

the punishment to suit the specific way in which the swearer abused his name. Gulielmus Peraldus, the thirteenth-century writer of the highly influential summa of virtues and vices, told the story of a knight playing a game who swore 'by God's eyes'. Immediately, his eyes burst forth from his head and fell onto the board.[132] Whitford narrated a tale about one 'mayster Baryngton' who was a great swearer by God's blood. One day in a tavern, Baryngton swore 'By goddes blode this day is vnhappy'. He soon started to bleed through his nose. This aggravated him to the point that he swore in anger by the different parts of Christ's body. Each time he named a new body part of Christ, that part of his own body began to bleed until Baryngton finally expired.[133] Many more examples could be given. Melissa Mohr made an astute observation when she wrote: 'The God of anti-swearing tracts is a great fan of poetic justice.'[134]

Did the emphasis on God's punishment for vain or false oaths wane with the coming of the Reformation? Did Protestants dismiss all these stories as superstition just as they swept aside stories of miracles done by saints and relics? Keith Thomas believed so, arguing that Protestants 'diminished the role of supernatural sanctions in daily life'. Thomas continued: 'The Protestant emphasis upon the individual conscience inevitably shifted the ultimate sanction for truthfulness from the external fear of divine punishment to the godly man's internal sense of responsibility.'[135] Concerning oaths, this statement is not true. Protestant tracts against illicit swearing are just as full of stories of providential punishment as the tracts of medieval Catholics. Perhaps the most famous and influential example of this is the last section of *Acts and Monuments*, which John Foxe devoted to narrating stories of providential punishment. Many of the victims of divine wrath mentioned by Foxe were Roman Catholic persecutors of Protestants (thereby showing God's approval of Protestantism), but a good number of them were perjurers and vain swearers of unspecified doctrinal leaning.[136] Similarly, Edmond Bicknoll dedicated a full fourth of his treatise against vain and false swearing to telling stories of providential punishment.[137] Not content to stop there, both Edmond Bicknoll and Christopher White included stories from the Continent of providential punishment on vain and false swearers. White concluded: 'It is a large common place, and all

---

[132] Peraldus, *Summarium summe virtutum et vitiorum*, fol. 168ʳ; Diekstra (ed.), *Book for a Simple and Devout Woman*, 267.

[133] Whitford, *Werke for Householders*, 25–6.   [134] Mohr, 'Strong Language', 12.

[135] Thomas, *Religion and the Decline of Magic*, 76–7.

[136] See for example the story of M. Burton on 2100–1, John Apowel and Denis Benfielde on 2102–3, or the Cornish gentleman under Edward VI on 2104–5; Foxe, *AM* (1583), 2100–5.

[137] Bicknoll, *Swoord agaynst Swearyng*, fols. 30ᵛ–47ʳ.

parts of the world can administer examples of Gods publike and priuate reuenging hand on periur'd persons.'[138] John Downame went so far as to assert that God does not limit his punishment to individual swearers but will visit the entire community with his wrath. Like sixteenth-century Parisian Catholics who believed that they had to purify their communities of all heretics to avoid God's anger, Downame averred that God would punish the entire realm unless vain swearers were stopped.[139] The compilers of these stories took pains to specify that these stories were not mere hyperbole. Whitford, Foxe, and Bicknoll all provided the locations of these events and names of witnesses so the reader could verify for himself that these stories were indeed true.[140] Clearly, stories of providential punishment were an essential part of both medieval and early modern oath theory. These stories were important because they illustrated in graphic terms the theological significance of oaths. Foxe hit the nail on the head when he wrote:

Fourthly and lastly, heere may also be a spectacle for all them which be blasphemous and abhominable swearers, or rather tearers of God, abusing his glorious name in suche contemptuous and despitefull sort as they vse to do. Whome if neither the woorde and commaundemente of God, nor the calling of the preachers, nor remorse of conscience, nor rule of reason, nor theyr wytheringe age, nor hory haires will admonish: yet let these terrible examples of Gods districte Iudgement, somewhat mooue them to take heede to them selues.[141]

Stories of providential punishment reminded the reader or listener that no matter how grave or light the social and legal ramifications of one's oath might appear, an oath was an invocation of the power and majesty of God, and God would not allow his name to be abused.[142]

RAMIFICATIONS OF THE THEORY OF OATH-TAKING FOR THE HENRICIAN REFORMATION

How does all this oath theory apply to the Henrician regime's campaign to implement and enforce its Reformation through oaths? The fundamental

---

[138] White, *Of oathes*, 18.
[139] Downame, *Foure treatises*, 34. Wygenhale espoused a similar doctrine; CUL MS ii. i. 39, fol. 84^r. For an account of the sixteenth-century Parisian fear of the consequences of heretical pollution, see Diefendorf, *Beneath the Cross*, 37–8, 178.
[140] Whitford, *Werke for Householders*, 26–8; Foxe, *AM* (1583), 2105; Bicknoll, *Swoord agaynst Swearyng*, fol. 36^v.
[141] Foxe, *AM* (1583), 2103.
[142] This paragraph confirms the more general conclusions of Alexandra Walsham on Protestant providentialism in her *Providence in Early Modern England*.

point of oath theory was that oaths gave swearers access to God. God had the ability to know whether an oath was true, the power to punish perjurors, and the will to do so, for he desired to protect the majesty of his holy name. It was commonly assumed that God would punish swearers who lied or broke their promises, even to the point of eternal damnation. This theory made oaths an ideal means of testing the beliefs of subjects and of binding them to behave in a certain way in the future. For example, asking the question, 'do you believe that the Bishop of Rome is the supreme head of the church?' was a weak way to implement the abrogation of papal authority. The questionee could simply respond 'No', and the only way for the questioner to enforce this belief would be to respond by saying: 'If I find out in the future that you are lying, I will punish you.' Conversely, the oath, 'swear that you do not believe that the Bishop of Rome is the supreme head of the church', was a more powerful device. Here God was the enforcer of truth. He knew whether the juror was lying or not, and he would not let a false oath stand unpunished. Likewise, the command, 'be loyal to me', was much weaker than the oath, 'swear allegiance to me'. The former could be enforced only by threats of temporal punishment if the subject were caught committing a disloyal act. The latter, however, would be enforced with temporal and eternal punishment if the swearer committed a disloyal act, whether or not he or she was actually caught by the state. This great power of oaths is why Henry turned to them to implement his Reformation.

This also meant that there was a strong difference between an oath and an oathless promise, declaration, or subscription. God was the power behind oaths, and God was not cited as a witness in these weaker professions. Oaths were thus placed on a higher plane than oathless promises or declarations. John Downame, for example, claimed that while the person to whom you made a promise could release you from your obligation, he could not release you from a promissory oath since an oath invoked the unchanging name of God.[143] The standard medieval gloss on Hebrews 6 read, 'just as men [are bound] profusely by promises, [they are bound] more profusely by oaths'.[144] Augustine recognized that while some people allowed simple lies in certain circumstances, no one condoned confirming a lie with an oath:

---

[143] Downame, *Foure treatises*, 65–6. It is worth pointing out that not all writers agreed with Downame that promissory oaths could *never* be dissolved by the party to whom the promise was sworn. See for example Barnum (ed.), *Dives and Pauper*, 245–6; White, *Of oathes*, 52.

[144] *Biblia Latina cum glossa ordinaria*.

Only in the worship of God may they grant that we must not lie; only from
perjuries and blasphemies may they restrain themselves; only where God's name,
God's testimony, God's oath is introduced, only where talk of divine religion is
brought forth, may no one lie, or praise or teach or enjoin lying or say that lying
is just.[145]

Augustine was admitting that everyone knew that professions where God
was not cited as witness were less solemn and less binding than oaths. The
ramification of this was that if Henry or one of his commissioners opted
for an oathless subscription or promise in lieu of an oath, they did so for a
reason. Likewise, whether a particular profession contained an oath or not
certainly factored into the decisions of many early modern people when
they decided to accept or resist this profession. Historians who overlook
the distinction between an oath and an oathless profession risk losing sight
of a significant variable in the English Reformation.

The theory of how to swear (that is, the conditions of a lawful oath) also
benefited the Henrician regime's campaign to implement its Reformation
through oaths. As we have seen, when theorists taught that an oath must
be sworn in truth, they meant not only that one should not swear an oath
to confirm a false statement but also that one should not swear an oath to
confirm a true statement in a way that deceived the person administering
the oath. In essence, this precluded any kind of dissimulation in swearing.
Equivocation (the deliberate manipulation of ambiguity in words) and
mental reservation (the adding of a qualifying statement to one's oath
inside one's own mind) were anathema in oath-taking, according to oath
theory. This meant that oaths allowed people less wiggle room. When
Henry presented his subjects with an oath, his subjects were (theoretically)
supposed to respond in an honest and straightforward manner. The same
applied to oaths administered in heresy trials.

The claim that an oath must be in accordance with judgement also
strengthened the state oaths of the English Reformation. The most common interpretation of this theory was the condemnation of blasphemous,
vain, or rash oaths. These oaths had the potential to harm the Henrician
regime because they led to the devaluation of oaths in general. The person
who did not blink at abusing God's name by swearing in common, everyday situations or swearing by God's body would probably not bat an eye
at abusing God's name by committing perjury when swearing the oath of

---

[145] Augustine, *Against Lying (Contra mendacium)*, trans. Harold B. Jaffee, in *St Augustine: Treatises on Various Subjects*, 173. See also 175. A similar though truncated statement is found in Andrew Chertsey's *Crafte to lyue well and to dye well*: 'and yet it shole be worse yf a man affermed y* lesynge by othe for than a ma[n] sholde forswere hym'; fol. 31ᵛ.

supremacy, or so the logic went. The condemnation of vain and blasphemous oaths, however, emphasized the sanctity of God's name. It endowed oaths with a gravity and weight that made them well suited for the designs of the Henrician regime. It is probably not a coincidence that the sixteenth century witnessed both the increased use of oaths by the English state and the first attempts by the English state to legislate against the swearing of vain oaths.[146]

Yet not every aspect of oath theory dovetailed so nicely with the goals of the Henrician regime. The claim that an oath exhorted by force or through fear was an illicit oath against judgement had the potential to invalidate the state oaths of the English Reformation, for Henry and his bishops (when judging over heresy trials) threatened those who refused to swear their oaths with substantial penalties such as imprisonment and execution. Did this not make their oaths forced? If so, were their oaths still binding? Even more destabilizing to the Henrician regime was the theory that oaths had to be sworn in justice, that is, the content of the oath had to be lawful. The problem here was that not everyone agreed on what was just and lawful. The ultimate authority in these matters was of course the word of God, but in the age of the Reformation, Christians did not agree on the proper interpretation of the word of God. Catholics believed that vows of celibacy were in accordance with Scripture. Protestants disagreed. Roman Catholics believed that papal superiority was consistent with Scripture. Protestants (and some Henrician Conservatives like Stephen Gardiner) believed that such superiority conflicted with the scriptural precept of obedience to one's secular magistrate. As such, Protestants and Roman Catholics could both use the word of God as the basis for evaluating the legality of the content of a particular oath of obedience (to the Pope or to Henry VIII) but still arrive at contradictory conclusions. Thomas Cranmer's debate with the Marian Catholic Thomas Martin during Cranmer's heresy trial of January 1556 clearly demonstrated this phenomenon. Using the scriptural examples of Herod's oath and Jephthah's vow, both Martin and Cranmer agreed that one 'oughte not to haue conscience of euery othe, but if it be iust, lawful and aduisedly taken'. But they then applied this logic to different oaths: Cranmer claimed that this logic allowed him to break his oath of canonical obedience to the Pope and Martin claimed that this logic allowed him to

---

[146] The main goal was to impose a twelve pence fine for every vain oath sworn. Attempts were made to impose this rule in 1551, 1553, 1559, 1571, and 1601, but all these attempts failed. It was not until 1624 that Parliament passed a temporary act against profane swearing. For details on this campaign, see Bray (ed. and trans.), *Tudor Church Reform*, lxxxviii–xcix, 548–9; Jones, *English Reformation*, 163, 168; *Statutes of the Realm*, 21. Jac., c. 20, IV:1229–30.

break his oath of supremacy to Henry VIII.[147] For an oath to be lawful, its content had to be in accordance with truth and justice, but since truth and justice were in dispute in the sixteenth century, what was lawful for one religious group was not lawful for another.

Of course, the chief point of clerical arguments against unjust oaths was not to provide a pre-packaged excuse for breaking an offensive oath but rather to prevent people from swearing illicit oaths in the first place. Yet the natural corollary to this argument, as we have seen, was that it was better to break an illicit oath than to keep it, for to keep it would be a double sin. This argument was not necessarily subversive to the Henrician regime. For example, in his treatise *De vera obedientia* Stephen Gardiner (the Henrician Bishop of Winchester) used this argument to justify the breaking of his oath of canonical obedience to the Pope and the swearing of the oath of supremacy to Henry VIII:

> ffor in othes or promises, the forme ought not so muche to be respected, as the mater. But let a man, saye, sweare, or promise as faithfully as he can, that thing that he ought not to doo nor performe, the promise shall not be aboue the nature of the mater selfe . . . for the othe ought to be a seruaunt of truthe, & can not, nor ought to be preiudiciall vnto the truthe . . . he that maketh an vnlauful othe, and gothe on stil to put it in execucion, thrusteth downe him selfe deper and deper, from whence he can neuer escape, except he com out arsewarde.[148]

Yet while Gardiner deployed this argument against an oath that Henry VIII did not want his subjects to keep, this same logic could be applied against the oaths Henry himself imposed. Edward Fox, the Henrician Bishop of Hereford, recognized this. When Fox first read Gardiner's manuscript of *De vera obedientia* in 1535, Fox wrote to Thomas Cromwell:

> Oon thing i thinke necessarie to be observed in the booke whiche I beseche youe to kepe to yourself or ells secretly as of yourself to aduertise the kinges highnes therof whiche is the excuse my lorde makethe for his oothe whiche if it might be lawfull for euery man to make the like and to draw the same in to exemple youe know and considre how the malice of men might elude soche oothes as we have now lately made. And therfor although this excuse be sufficient and valleable ynough against my lorde for his own deade yet paraduenture som hurte might com therof yn tyme comyng in case it shuld be invulged or spredd abrode.[149]

The 'oothes as we have now lately made' were obviously the oaths of succession and supremacy, which Henry had been tendering throughout the realm in 1534 and 1535. Fox thus feared that the publication of Gardiner's

---

[147] Foxe, *AM* (1583), 1876.   [148] Gardiner, *De vera obedientia*, sigs. G7^r, H1^v–H2^r.
[149] BL Cotton MS Cleopatra E VI, fol. 201^r (*LP*, IX 403).

excuse for breaking his oath of canonical obedience would provide Englishmen hostile to Henry's religious settlement a ready-made justification for the breaking of their recent oaths to the king.

Fox's advice to Cromwell was to keep this particular aspect of oath theory (that one should break an illicit oath) under wraps, and this certainly would have been more conducive to the Henrician regime. Yet the problem was that at precisely the same time as English reformers were echoing medieval Catholic rhetoric on the sanctity of oaths, they were also flooding the printing presses with attacks on monastic vows. These works stressed that monastic vows were forced, taken in ignorance, contrary to the word of God, or in some other way against truth, judgement, and justice. As such, monastic vows were illicit and should be broken. Although English reformers never explicitly applied this logic to the state oaths of the Henrician Reformation, the great similarity between vows and oaths (both are forms of divine promises) and the fact that much of this logic originated in oath theory itself meant that many people could and did apply these arguments to the oaths of the Henrician Reformation.[150] Hence, English attacks against monastic vows emphasized the very aspect of oath theory that Fox had hoped would not be 'invulged or spredd abrode'.

To conclude, then, the theory behind oath-taking was a double-edged sword to the Henrician regime. On one hand, it lent power to the oaths of the English Reformation by stressing the sanctity of oaths and proclaiming the vengeance of God against those who swore falsely, deceptively, or flippantly. On the other hand, by stressing that oaths against truth, judgement, and justice were illicit and should be broken, it provided those who had a different definition of truth and justice a convenient means of resistance to these oaths. Finally, we should also remember that the practice of swearing oaths did not necessarily line up with the theory behind it. Jacques de Vitry (a thirteenth-century monk who collected sermon models for preachers) told the story of a priest who exhorted a penitent woman in confession to cease swearing customably:

She replied: 'Sir, God help me, I'll not swear again.' The priest said: 'You have just sworn.' 'By God, I'll refrain from it again.' The priest told her her speech should be 'yea, yea', and 'nay, nay', as the Lord had commanded, for more than this was wrong. She replied: 'Sir, you are right, and I tell you by the blessed Virgin, and all the saints, that I will do as you command me, and you shall never hear me swear.'[151]

---

[150] Gray, 'Vows, Oaths, and the Propagation of a Subversive Discourse'.
[151] Vitry, *Exempla or Illustrative Stories*, 91–2, 222.

Although a simple laywoman's persistent use of oaths in everyday conversation may not have been much of a threat to the Henrician regime,
the story does illustrate that oath theory was often more prescription than
description. What if a bishop or an earl decided to ignore another aspect of
oath theory and swear the oath of supremacy falsely or deceptively? Clearly
it is important to examine how the English populace actually took the
oaths of the Reformation. Yet before we examine how the English people
responded to the oaths of the Reformation, we must explore how Henry
used oaths to implement his Reformation. It is to that we now turn.

CHAPTER 2

Oaths, subscriptions, and the implementation of the parliamentary reforms of 1534

How did Henry VIII implement his Reformation of 1534? What were the steps the Crown took between 1533 and 1537 to propagate, coerce, and enforce its Reformation on the ground? The textbook answer that Henry administered two oaths – an oath of succession in the spring and summer of 1534 to all males over the age of twelve, and an oath of supremacy sometime in 1534 or 1535 to all clergy and political office holders – is clearly wrong.[1] Ann M. C. Forster, in her article documenting the various oaths tendered against Roman Catholicism, likewise oversimplified what happened, mentioning only an oath of succession, an oath bishops swore against the papacy, and a new oath against papal supremacy from 1545.[2] Historians such as John Guy, Geoffrey Elton, and Philip Hughes have done well in presenting more nuanced accounts. Guy noted that the subscription signed by the parish clergy differed from the oath of the diocesan clergy, while the oath sworn by ecclesiastical and lay office holders differed from either of the purely clerical professions.[3] Elton went further, observing that the secular clergy simply subscribed to a rejection of papal authority, that the institutional clergy and the bishops swore a comprehensive oath concerning Henry's supremacy over the English Church, that the Parliament of 1536 devised new forms of both the oath of succession and the oath of supremacy, and that these two new forms were rarely administered.[4] But the most detailed account came from Philip Hughes. Hughes noted the oath of succession and the clerical declaration against the bishop of Rome, but he also referenced professions sworn by the universities, friars, monks, and bishops.[5] Yet even the descriptions of Elton and Hughes failed to do justice to the plethora of different professions Henry employed to gain adherence to his divorce, new succession, and royal supremacy. Hughes, for example,

---

[1] For examples of such textbook accounts of these two oaths, see Ridley, *Tudor Age*, 287; Brigden, *New Worlds, Lost Worlds*, 121.
[2] Forster, 'Oath Tendered', 86–7.   [3] Guy, *Tudor England*, 136.
[4] Elton, *Policy and Police*, 227–30.   [5] Hughes, *Reformation in England*, 1:270–6.

sometimes conflated the various professions, and his account is far from systematic. Indeed, the attempt to summarize such a complex situation in one paragraph (Guy) or in a handful of pages (Elton and Hughes) leads more to confusion than to clarity. No historian has yet mapped out the exact number and order of the different professions of Henrician England and compared the professions to each other in a detailed manner. This chapter seeks to correct this historiographical oversight by reconstructing the step-by-step process whereby Henry administered to his subjects professions in support of his Reformation of 1534. This reconstruction reveals that Henry employed a number of distinct professions of different strengths that varied in form, content, and extent of administration depending on Henry's target subject group.

THE RELATIONSHIP BETWEEN OATHS AND SUBSCRIPTIONS

Before delving into our narrative, we need to examine the relationship between oaths and subscriptions. Since an oath was simply a declaration or promise in which God was cited as witness to the truth of a statement, it did not need to be accompanied by a written subscription. Undoubtedly, most common oaths employed in quotidian conversation did not include a written subscription. Yet the majority of public oaths in the fifteenth and sixteenth centuries were indeed endorsed by some kind of subscription. Coronation oaths, treaty oaths, and other formal political oaths were usually confirmed by subscriptions.[6] If the swearer was not able to sign his or her own name, he or she could make a mark as a substitute. This was common in oaths of abjuration since heresy sometimes infiltrated the ranks of the illiterate.[7] The purpose of a subscription was to serve as evidence for anyone not actually present at the oath-taking that the person did indeed swear the oath. For the same reason, notaries were often present to witness these oaths.[8] The practice of subscribing one's name after swearing a public oath was thus well established in the sixteenth century. Brian Cummings' interpretation of the dual nature of the succession acknowledgement – both an oath and a subscription – as an 'official ambiguity' that meant that

[6] For an example of a coronation oath accompanied by a subscription, see Doleman, *Conference abovt the next svccession*, 104. For a treaty oath, see LPL, Warham's Register, fols. 14^r–15^r. For an oath of fealty, see *Rotuli Parliamentorum*, v:346–7.
[7] See for example BL Harleian MS 421, fols. 175^r–176^v, 181^r.
[8] See for example BL Cotton MS Vespasian C XIV, fol. 443^r, where Lord Burghley served as a notary for an oath.

the 'oath itself was insufficient as a guarantee' fails to recognize the general context of public oath-taking in early modern England.[9]

But if public oaths were often accompanied by subscriptions, subscriptions themselves did not necessarily signify that an oath had been sworn. Subscriptions by the Elizabethan clergy to Archbishop Parker's Advertisements in 1566 or to Archbishop Whitgift's Three Articles of 1584 did not include an oath. It was possible to indicate one's assent to a doctrine or belief without actually swearing an oath by simply signing one's name after a written profession or acknowledgement. These oathless subscriptions, while still formal documents, lacked the spiritual muscle that made oaths so binding. The essential point, then, is to determine whether a signed profession was accompanied by an oath or not. If the content of the profession contained the words 'so help me God' or some variant, we can assume an oath was sworn, since God had been called as witness. The issue is trickier when a list of subscriptions exists without the actual profession accompanying the signatures. In such cases, we cannot assume an oath was sworn unless corroborating evidence exists for an oath, evidence such as a notarial instrument mentioning the 'oath' or 'juramentum' or an explicit commission that demanded the tendering of an oath to the people whose signatures survive.

THE USE OF OATHS AND SUBSCRIPTIONS TO ENFORCE THE SUCCESSION AND SUPREMACY

The drive to gather documented acknowledgements of the positions codified by the acts of Parliament in 1534 had begun well before 1534. The main issue was of course Henry's marriage to Katherine of Aragon. Katherine had been married to Henry's elder brother Arthur, but Arthur died less than five months after the marriage. Young prince Henry had stepped in to marry Katherine to cement the relationship between England and Spain, but in order to marry his brother's widow, Henry needed a dispensation from the Pope, for according to canon law Henry was now technically a sibling of Katherine. Pope Julius II duly granted the dispensation, and Henry and Katherine were married in 1506. But in 1526 or 1527, after years without the birth and survival of a male heir, Henry began to wonder if his marriage to Katherine displeased God, notwithstanding the papal dispensation. Did not Leviticus 20:21 state that it was illicit to marry your brother's wife and

---

[9] Cummings, 'Swearing in Public: More and Shakespeare', 212.

that such a marriage would produce no sons?[10] At the same time as Henry's conscience became stricken with doubts on the validity of his marriage to Katherine, his heart became infatuated with a young courtier named Anne Boleyn. Accordingly, Henry asked Pope Clement VII for an annulment of his marriage to Katherine. Katherine, however, resisted Henry's scheme, claiming that her original marriage to Arthur had never been consummated. Clement's hands were also tied since Katherine's nephew Charles V was now master of Italy. Clement dispatched Cardinal Lorenzo Campeggi to England to decide the matter between Henry and Katherine, but he secretly informed Campeggi not to grant the annulment. By the summer of 1529, Campeggi had suspended the official trial without granting Henry his annulment.[11]

At this time Henry altered his strategy in an effort to put pressure on the Pope. Upon the suggestion of a Cambridge don named Thomas Cranmer, Henry began obtaining declarations from the universities of Europe which stated that the prohibition of marriage to the widow of a deceased brother was a divine law with which the Pope could not dispense. Henry's own universities proved embarrassingly obstinate. The junior members of both universities (the lower house of the Convocation of the universities) initially persisted in stating that such a marriage as Henry's was indeed licit by divine law and natural law. After the exertion of royal pressure, Cambridge delegated the decision to a group of sixty, who gave Henry the opinion for which he was looking. The juniors of Oxford refused to do this and remained intransigent in the face of numerous delegations from the king. It was only after the chancellor of Oxford decreed that the juniors of the university were unworthy to make this decision, appointing a select group in their place, that the king received the judgement he wanted.[12] In 1531, Henry began to exert pressure on the clergy of England as a whole, accusing them of exercising illegal spiritual jurisdiction. In exchange for a pardon, Henry demanded a subsidy of £100,000 and that the Convocation of Canterbury subscribe to a statement that he was 'the sole protector and supreme head of the church and clergy of England'. Convocation, however, refused to acknowledge Henry's new title unless the following phrase was added after it: 'as far as it is allowed by the law of Christ'.[13]

---

[10] Whether Lev. 20:21 referred specifically to sons or more generally to children was a point of debate at the time. See Bernard, *King's Reformation*, 17.

[11] For details on the events described in this paragraph, see Henry Ansgar Kelly, *The Matrimonial Trials of Henry VIII.*

[12] Wood, *History and Antiquities*, II:40–4.

[13] Bray (ed.), *Records of Convocation*, VII:133–4; Ortroy (ed.), 'Vie du bienheureux martyr Jean Fisher Cardinal, évêque de Rochester', 10 (1891): 359–65; 12 (1893): 251–2; Lehmberg, *Reformation Parliament*, 109–116.

Seventeen members of the lower house of Convocation then signed two protestations declaring that they did not understand this title to detract in any way from papal primacy, while some clergy from the province of York issued a protestation rejecting Henry's new title altogether.[14] Henry may have gained a new title, but it was apparent that many of his clergy interpreted the conditional clause as essentially nullifying Henry's headship. A year later, Henry pressured the clergy of England again, this time demanding that Convocation subscribe to a document that abrogated the independent jurisdictional power of the church in England, the so-called Submission of the Clergy. Again, Convocation tried to add qualifying conditions to their subscription, but this time Henry refused to accept them.[15] In the end some members of Convocation did subscribe to this document, but Michael Kelly, the primary historian of this Convocation, estimated that 'at least one-third and probably as much as a majority of the clergy then present refused to ratify the Submission'.[16] Notably, only six bishops subscribed, and three of these added qualifying reservations.[17] Clearly Henry's attempts to intimidate the church by gathering communal subscriptions from his English clergy were not working.

By the start of 1533, Henry decided to take matters into his own hands. He secretly married Anne Boleyn in January, and then he began to seek recognition of his annulment from individual bishops. On 23 February Ambassador Eustace Chapuys wrote to Charles V that Henry had asked the archbishops of York and Canterbury, the bishops of London, Winchester, and Lincoln, and some English and Italian doctors 'to subscribe a little document he has had set down in writing at his fancy, one which is very strange'.[18] Chapuys reported that while Edward Lee (York) and Stephen Gardiner (Winchester) had not yet agreed to do this, Cranmer (elect of Canterbury) had gleefully subscribed. The actual document to which Cranmer subscribed does not survive, and no other evidence exists of this strange subscription. Yet considering the context in which Chapuys

---

[14] The two protestations from the lower house of Convocation are printed in Bray (ed.), *Records of Convocation*, VII:134–6. For information on the protestation of the clergy of York, see *Cal SP Spain*, IV (2) 721 (*LP*, V 251). Part of the protestation itself survives in Tunstall's Register, and the rest of it can be reconstructed from Henry's letter in response to it. See Wilkins (ed.), *Concilia*, III:745, 762–5.

[15] For relevant documents on the Convocation of 1532 and the Submission of the Clergy, see Bray (ed.), *Records of Convocation*, VII:181–9; Wilkins (ed.), *Concilia*, III:748–55; Gee and Hardy (eds.), *Documents Illustrative*, 154–78. I have reconstructed the exact chronology of this Convocation in Gray, 'So Help Me God', 171–5.

[16] Kelly, 'Submission of the Clergy', 116.

[17] For the conditional subscriptions of the bishops of St Asaph (Standish), Lincoln (Longland), and London (Stokesley), see Wilkins (ed.), *Concilia*, III:749.

[18] HHS, Staatenabteilungen, England, Berichte, Karton 5, 1533, 23 February (*LP*, VI 180).

mentioned the subscription, the document was obviously about Henry's annulment.[19] Whatever the content of the document, it was soon made irrelevant, for Henry's new Archbishop of Canterbury Thomas Cranmer officially granted Henry his annulment from his marriage with Katherine of Aragon in the spring of 1533, and Anne Boleyn was crowned queen in June 1533.

By the end of the year, Henry may have circulated among select bishops his first device seeking an explicit rejection of papal authority in England. In a letter dated 9 December 1533, Chapuys told Charles V that he had heard that in the last few days 'the king has been soliciting certain bishops to consent to the derogation of papal authority'. With the exception of Cranmer, all of them refused to consent to it.[20] No other evidence for this device exists. Yet even if Chapuys was mistaken about what actually happened, his letter surely indicates that at the very least, a rumour of a device requiring the abrogation of papal authority was in the air at the end of 1533.

At the start of 1534, the Crown again targeted a select group of subjects and sought their documented adherence to the Boleyn marriage. This time, however, it was Bishop John Stokesley of London and the nuns of Syon Abbey who were tendered a subscription. Syon was an influential Bridgettine abbey at Isleworth on the Thames that was famous for its learning and austerity. On 4 January, Stokesley wrote to Thomas Bedyll, one of Thomas Cromwell's men. (Cromwell was by now Henry's principal minister and chief councillor.) Stokesley wrote that he had received from Bedyll's servant letters 'subscribed vpon condition with thands [the hands] of thabbesse and systers of Syon'.[21] Stokesley added that he would not subscribe to this letter because the clergy had never expressly given any kind of judgement about Henry's second marriage. They had only declared Henry's first marriage invalid. Although it is not absolutely clear what was going on here, it appears that Cromwell had sent a profession to the sisters and abbess of Syon containing a statement that the clergy of the realm (presumably in Convocation) had declared the king's first marriage invalid and his second legitimate. The sisters subscribed with a condition, but Stokesley refused to subscribe because he recognized that the English clergy had not yet made an official statement concerning Henry's marriage to Anne. Stokesley then wrote that if he subscribed to the letter as it was worded now, he would seem to do so out of affection rather than truth.

---

[19] For two different theories on the exact content of this document, see Chibi, *Henry VIII's Conservative Scholar*, 82–3; Chibi, *Henry VIII's Bishops*, 115.

[20] *Cal SP Spain*, IV (2) 1158 (*LP*, VI 1510).   [21] NA SP1/82, fol. 11[r] (*LP*, VII 15).

Before the letter was published with subscriptions, Stokesley observed that this oversight should be reformed. He said he would subscribe to a clean copy of the letter once the indicated changes had been made.[22] A day later, Stokesley signed a new letter, probably an altered but related profession that had taken into account his suggested changes. Stokesley then wrote to Syon to encourage their subscription to this new letter. The sisters of Syon, however, probably never signed this new letter because their confessors had told them that they had done wrong subscribing to the first letter.[23]

The subscriptions offered to Cranmer, Lee, and Gardiner, and the letters presented to Stokesley and Syon Abbey, foreshadowed the policy that the regime would pursue after the Act of Succession. The Crown was putting out feelers, giving its policy a test run before the real campaign was launched with the Act of Succession. The Crown targeted a select yet influential group of subjects – the most important bishops of the realm (Canterbury, York, London, and Winchester) and a well-esteemed abbey close to London – and tendered them some kind of acknowledgement of Henry's divorce and remarriage. That the Crown was tentative in this initiative is supported by the fact that it took no punitive steps against those (everyone but Cranmer) who refused to subscribe. On the other hand, that this was more than a simple test run is evident by the apparent plan of the regime to publish the subscription of Stokesley and Syon, a document that the Crown probably hoped would influence others to follow in Stokesley's and Syon's lead and accept the Boleyn marriage.

The real campaign to enforce Henry's Reformation came at the end of March 1534 when Parliament passed the Act of Succession. It declared that Prince Arthur had carnally known Katherine and thus that Henry's marriage to Katherine was against God's law, a law with which no one could dispense. It then proclaimed Henry's marriage to Anne valid and rejected the power of the Pope to interfere with the succession of any realm. The act set the succession through the male heirs of Henry and Anne or, failing them, a subsequent wife. If Henry had no male heirs, the throne was to pass to Elizabeth, the new daughter of Henry and Anne. The act also established penal measures against those who violated it. Anyone who wrote or published anything against the act was guilty of treason, for which the penalty was death. Anyone who spoke against the act was guilty of misprision of treason, for which the penalty was imprisonment and loss

---

[22] NA sp1/82, fols. 11^r–12^r (*LP*, VII 15).

[23] We can infer this from a letter from James Mores, a servant of Bedyll, to Bedyll on 6 January. See NA sp1/82, fol. 37^r (*LP*, VII 22).

of goods. 'And for the more sure establishement of the succession', the act further decreed:

that as well all the nobles of your Realme spirituall and temporall, as all other your subjectes now lyvyng and being or that hereafter shal be at theire full ages, by the commaundement of your Majestie or of your heires at all tymes hereafter frome tyme to tyme when it shall please your Highnes or your heires to appoynt, shall make a corporall othe in the presence of your Highness or your heires, or before suche other as your Majestie or your heires wyll depute for the same, that they shall truly firmely and constantly without fraud or gyle observe fulfyll maynteyne defende and kepe to theyre cunnyng wytte and uttermoste of theire powers the hole effectes and contentes of this present acte.[24]

Accordingly, on 30 March Henry commissioned Archbishop Cranmer, Lord Chancellor Thomas Audley, and the Dukes of Norfolk and Suffolk to administer the oath. That same day, at the close of the session, these four tendered the oath of succession to all the members of Parliament then present.[25]

After Parliament, the first group of subjects to take the oath of succession was the clergy of London, who were tendered the oath by the aforesaid commissioners on 13 April at Lambeth Palace.[26] The actual content of the oath of succession tendered on this day is unknown. The commission that was granted to Cranmer, Audley, Norfolk, and Suffolk and read in the House of Lords at the end of March authorized them to take an 'oath and faithfulness' of all the king's subjects 'according to the power, form, and effect of this statute, made and put forth in the current Parliament concerning our security, position, and succession, and according to the tenor of the oath annexed to the present' documents.[27] As such, it is likely that the form of the oath tendered on 13 April was the same as the form sworn by Parliament at the end of March. On 20 April the majority of the city of London took the oath of succession.[28] That same day, a commission went out to Lord Thomas West, Sir William Fitzwilliam, and others to tender the oath in Sussex. The form of the oath of succession included in this commission is similar to the one sworn in Parliament, which further suggests that the form of the oath sworn throughout the realm in the spring

[24] *Statutes of the Realm*, 25 Hen. 8, c. 22, III:471–4 (474).
[25] *Journal of the House of Lords*, I:82; Hall, *Hall's Chronicle*, 814. Hall claims that Parliament took the oath on 30 March. For the text of the oath, see Appendix D, I.
[26] Strype, *Cranmer*, I:36–7.   [27] *Journal of the House of Lords*, I:82.
[28] Byrne (ed.), *Lisle Letters*, II: 129–30 (*LP*, VII 522).

of 1534 was analogous to the one sworn in the House of Lords.[29] Other commissions for the rest of the realm must also have gone out at this time.

The administrative effort in tendering the oath of succession throughout the realm was Herculean, and many letters survive describing the process. On 5 May Bishop Stephen Gardiner wrote to Cromwell explaining the process in Winchester. Gardiner had received his commission on 29 April. Five days later, he assembled at the castle of Lord Audley the commissioners, a great number of local gentlemen, and all the abbots, priors, wardens of friars, and curates of the shire. After everyone present took the oath, the abbots and priors presented Gardiner with a list of names of all those in their houses, while the curates provided the names of all male parishioners over the age of fourteen in their parishes. Gardiner then divided up the county and assigned specific areas of coverage to each commissioner. Gardiner warned Cromwell that the whole process would not be accomplished quickly: 'Wherein ye shall perceive [it is] a long work and will require a long tracte of ty[me], and it be not divided among many commissioner[s], considering specially that every man's name mus[t] be written as our commission purporteth and cert[ified].'[30] Lord Thomas Audley wrote to Lord Lisle in Calais on 9 June with similar instructions. After taking the oath himself, Lisle was to divide the commissioners into groups of two or three, give each group a copy of the oath, three or four 'of the books of the acts', and a roll of parchment on which every person who took the oath was to subscribe his name. Audley excused the actual town of Calais from this tedious task, asserting that if the mayor made a 'little schedule mentioning that the whole inhabitants of the town be sworn, and the day, year, and place, and afore whom they were sworn, and put their common seal to that schedule, this were a good sufficient declaration for the Town without any particular name to be written'.[31] The requirement that all those taking the oath subscribe their names certainly contributed to the administrative headache. Cranmer was unsure of what to do with those who could not sign their names. He decided provisionally to have them make their mark and then have his secretaries subscribe the swearer's name next to the mark, but he wondered if he should not take their seals instead

---

[29] BL Harleian MS 7571, fol. 25^{r-v}. This document is a copy and thus must be taken with a grain of salt. It is possible that the original commission did not contain a copy of the oath of succession and the copyist added it from another source. See also Appendix D, II.

[30] Gardiner also informed Cromwell that they planned to take the oaths only of males, yet he was unsure enough to suggest that if the king desired females to swear as well, they would alter their course; BL Cotton MS. Otho C X, fol. 171^{v}; printed in Pocock (ed.), *Records of the Reformation*, II:536–7 and in Gardiner, *Letters*, 56–7.

[31] Byrne (ed.), *Lisle Letters*, II:178–9 (*LP*, Add., 941).

of their subscriptions.[32] The sheer scope of the task of administering the oath to every adult male in the realm also stretched the royal bureaucracy to its limit. More than one area of the realm was overlooked when the initial commissions went out.[33] Nevertheless, the great number of surviving letters about the tendering of the oath of succession from the spring and summer of 1534 attest to the fact that in the end, the regime managed to accomplish it.

Yet the oath of succession was not the only controversial device tendered in the spring of 1534. On 31 March Radulphus Pexsall, a royal clerk, read in Convocation a document concerning the response of the 'lower house' (*domus inferioris*[34]) to the question, 'Whether the Roman high priest has any greater jurisdiction conferred to him in Holy Scripture in this realm of England than any other foreign bishop?' Thirty-two denied that the Pope had greater jurisdiction than any other foreign bishop, four affirmed that he did, and one was doubtful.[35] No other details from the Convocation of 1534 have survived, so nothing else is known about the origin or development of this statement in Convocation.[36] Yet regardless of its origin, the question read in Convocation on 31 March became the basis of a statement rejecting papal authority tendered in one form or another to every member of the English clergy by the end of 1534. For example, a document preserved in the British Library commences with the phrase 'Romanus episcopus non habet maiorem aliquam iurisdictionem collatam sibi a deo in sacra scriptura in hoc regno Angliae quam alius quiuis externus episcopus [The Roman bishop has no greater jurisdiction conferred

---

[32] Cranmer, *Miscellaneous Writings and Letters*, 291. A roll of these subscriptions to the oath succession has survived from Lancashire. The roll is headed 'These be the names and syrnames of all the persens aswell spirituall as temperall that Mr Thomas Halsall knight and I[]mies Ecares[] of Bicurseath esquier Commissioners and Iustices of peax in the Countie of lanc have swone afore vs according to the o[the] forme & effect of the statuts made by Acte of parlyament for the Kinges Succession as souerigne lord dwellin in all these . . . [cownties?] to vs alloted in the wapentate of derbiss.[r] [Derbyshire] vs and ou[r]felowes commissioners in the said Countie of lancastre.' After this heading, a long list of names follows, well over one thousand. The names are organized by location, usually by parish. Each new parish commences with original signatures, usually by gentlemen, priests, or other clergymen. Following these original signatures, the rest of the names from that parish (by far the majority) are all written in the same hand; NA DL41/1182.

[33] NA sp1/84, fol. 19[r] (*LP*, vii 656); NA sp1/88, fols.141[r]-143[r] (*LP*, vii App. 23 and 24); Elton, *Policy and Police*, 225.

[34] In this case, the 'lower house' probably refers to the lower house of Convocation. The same phrase, however, is used in the records of Convocation to refer to the House of Commons of Parliament, which makes the reference in this case rather ambiguous.

[35] Bray (ed.), *Records of Convocation*, vii:199–200.

[36] For a theory that this statement was related to the act of Parliament abolishing Peter's Pence, see Gray, 'So Help Me God', 126–7.

to him by God in holy Scripture in this kingdom of England than any other foreign bishop]'. The original signatures of many of the top clergy of the realm follow this statement, including signatures by both archbishops, the bishops of Carlisle, Chichester, Coventry and Lichfield, Durham, Ely, Exeter, Lincoln, London, and Winchester, five archdeacons, the provincials of the orders of Carmelites and Franciscans, twenty-two abbots, eleven priors, one warden and fifty-two others.[37] The document is undated, but it must have originated between 19 April (the date of the consecration of Thomas Goodrich and Roland Lee as bishops of Ely and of Coventry and Lichfield respectively) and 27 May (the date of the death of Richard Sydnor) 1534.[38] On 2 May the University of Cambridge issued a similar declaration. This document, however, contained no signatures but simply the seal of the university.[39] Three days later, the Convocation of the Clergy of York arrived at the same conclusion.[40] Finally, the University of Oxford as a corporate body rejected papal jurisdiction in England with the same statement on 27 June 1534.[41]

But it was not just the convocations, the universities, and the top prelates of the realm who signed such documents. Two books of signatures of parish priests and other members of the secular clergy from various dioceses in the province of Canterbury exist in the National Archives. At the head of each page is the familiar statement that the Pope has no greater power in England than any other foreign bishop. Below each statement are the name of a location (usually a deanery) and the subscriptions of the clergy associated with that location. Most of the pages have no dates, but the few that do are from July 1534.[42] Some of these subscriptions may have been collected as early as April 1534, perhaps even at the same time as the tendering of the oath of succession. On 28 April, for example, Cranmer wrote to Cromwell:

Mr Roodd hath also been with me at Croydon, and there hath subscribed the book of the king's grace's succession, and also the conclusion '*quod Romanus Episcopus non habet majorem auctoritatem a Deo sibi collatam in hoc regno Angliae quam quivis*

---

[37] BL Additional MS 38656, fols. 3ʳ–4ʳ.   [38] Gilson (ed.), *Catalogue of Additions*, 186.

[39] NA E25/24 (*LP*, VII 602), also printed (with additional preamble) in Wilkins (ed.), *Concilia*, III:771–2.

[40] The fullest report of the Convocation of York's decision that the Pope has no greater jurisdiction in England than any other foreign bishop is BL Cotton MS Cleopatra E VI, fol. 207ʳ (*LP*, VII 769). This document also contains many signatures, but the document is a copy and the signatures are not original. An abbreviated report of York's decision without any signatures is NA E25/45. Also see Rymer (ed.), *Foedera*, XIV:492–3 and Wilkins (ed.), *Concilia*, III:782–3.

[41] BL Cotton MS Cleopatra E VI, fol. 209ʳ (*LP*, VII 891). This is a copy without any signatures. It is printed in Wilkins (ed.), *Concilia*, III:775–6.

[42] NA E36/63, E36/64 (*LP*, VII 1025).

alius externus episcopus;' and hath promised me, that he will at all times hereafter so conforme himself.[43]

Thus, it is possible that at least some of the secular clergy simultaneously rejected both papal authority and swore to the new succession. Even if some of the secular clergy rejected papal authority on a different day from when they swore the oath of succession, the fact that both professions were in circulation at the same time suggests that they were closely related. Yet there is one important distinction between these two professions. Unlike the oath and subscription to the succession, there is no evidence that the secular clergy's rejection of papal authority was ever accompanied by an oath. Secular clergymen merely signed their names after a simple profession.[44]

This was not the case, however, for the mendicant orders in England. They were tendered a long, detailed, and explicit profession of royal supremacy and acknowledgement of the Boleyn succession accompanied by an oath. On 13 April – the same day when the London clergy took the oath of succession – Henry issued a grant to George Browne, Provincial Prior of the Friars Hermits, and to John Hilsey, Provincial Prior of the Friars Preachers, to visit all the houses of friars of whatever order, to make inquiry into their morals and fealty to the king, to instruct them how to conduct themselves with safety, and to reduce them to uniformity.[45] Two undated sets of instructions that relate to this visitation also survive: one for the friars in general and another specifically for the Observant Franciscans. The instructions ordered the friars to 'exhibit' (*exhibere*) fidelity to the king, to swear an oath to discharge faith and obedience to the king, Anne, and their children, to confess Henry's marriage to Anne was lawful and legitimate, to confirm that Henry was the supreme head of the church in England, and 'to confess that the Roman bishop who uses the name pope in his bulls and who claims for himself the first position of supreme high priest has no more dignity or authority than other bishops' in England or elsewhere.[46] Thus, the profession of the friars went further than both the oath of succession and the clerical subscription against papal authority (though both of these were incorporated into the friars' profession) in that it explicitly acknowledged Henry's supremacy over the church in England.

---

[43] Cranmer, *Miscellaneous Writings and Letters*, 287.

[44] Elton recognized this fact; Elton, *Policy and Police*, 229.

[45] NA c66/663, m. 6d (*LP*, VII 587 (18)).

[46] The instructions also explained how the friars should refer to the king and Pope in their preaching and prayer, as well as other general business of the visitation. The document of instructions to the friars in general is BL Cotton MS Cleopatra E IV, fol. 11[r–v] (*LP*, VII 590). The document of instructions to the Observant Franciscans is printed in Vocht (ed.), *Acta Thomae Mori*, 208–9. Both of these professions are printed in Appendix E.

Although the only explicit oath mentioned in the body of the instructions was the oath of fidelity to the king, queen, and their offspring, the instructions to the friars in general ended with the command that all the priors, convents, and their successors 'bind themselves with an oath . . . to observe faithfully each and every of the aforesaid [articles]'.[47] Furthermore the actual professions of the friars closely parallel the instructions for visitation and conclude with the prescribed oath to observe all the aforesaid articles.

The first of these professions was made on 17 April by the Franciscans, Augustinians, Carmelites, and Crutched Friars of London.[48] The Friars Preachers of Langley Regis, the Minors of Alisbury, the Preachers of Dunstable, the Minors of Bedford, the Carmelites of Hechynge and the Minors of Ware made an identical profession on 5 May.[49] These professions were signed only by the various heads of houses, who a few days later acknowledged their professions in the Chancery, Henry's court of records. Yet it is likely that each friar took his oath individually, for the instructions command that 'all and singular of the brothers . . . personally present be gathered' and 'examined apart and separately'.[50] Moreover their professions specifically state that 'we the priors and convents of brothers . . . with one mouth and voice and with unanimous consent and assent of all and singular . . . do profess, witness, and faithfully promise'.[51] Hence Henry forced each of the friars to acknowledge his new marriage, his succession, his supremacy and to confirm these acknowledgements with an oath.

Henry soon extended the friars' profession to all clerical institutions of the realm. On 14 May 1534, the prioress and convent of the Priory of Dartford in Kent made a profession identical to that of the friars, except that it omitted the articles on how to interpret Scripture and how to exhort people to pray when preaching.[52] The profession of the Priory of Dartford, however, is exceptional in its form and in its early date. The next institutional profession dates from 13 June, and the form is again slightly altered. This new form is essentially the same as the friars' original profession – each person promises fealty and obedience to Henry, Anne, and their offspring, recognizes Henry as the supreme head of the Church of England, rejects papal authority, and confirms all the articles of profession with an oath – but the new profession omits the section about Parliament,

---

[47] BL Cotton MS Cleopatra E IV, fol. 11[v].

[48] NA c54/402, m 33d, printed in Rymer (ed.), *Foedera*, XIV:487–9 (*LP*, VII 665(1)).

[49] NA c54/403, m 18d, printed in Rymer (ed.), *Foedera*, XIV:489–90 (*LP*, VII 665(2)).

[50] BL Cotton MS Cleopatra E IV, fol. 11[r].

[51] NA c54/402, m 33d, printed in Rymer (ed.), *Foedera*, XIV:487–9 (*LP*, VII 665(1)).

[52] NA E25/39/2; Rymer (ed.), *Foedera*, XIV:490–1 (*LP*, VII 665 (3)). The articles on preaching were probably omitted because nuns did not preach in public.

Convocation, and Cranmer having declared Henry's marriage to Anne as legitimate, abbreviates the clause about renouncing the Pope's laws and canons, and adds a clause about calling the Pope the Bishop of Rome rather than pope or high priest.[53] This form of the institutional profession effectively remained constant for the duration of 1534 into the first months of 1535; variations were negligible.

Unlike the friars' profession, no sets of instructions survive for this general institutional profession. There are, however, two identical letters from Henry VIII on 25 June 1534, which authorize Dr Peter Ligham and Dr Gwent (Dean of the Arches) as part of Archbishop Cranmer's metropolitan visitation to 'procure the chapter seale of euery Spirituall incorporacyon that you shall come vnto, and the subscription of euery man of that chapter to be putt to this writynge devysed by vs and oure consaill that conter paine wherof subscrybyd by my lord of Cantorbury ye shall herewith receive'.[54] Indeed, in the well over one hundred of these professions that survive, the signatures of the members of the institution follow the text of each profession, and wax seals are also connected to each document. Many of the signatures appear to be original, though some are written in the same hand.[55] The professions exist for a variety of 'Spirituall incorporyons', both regular and secular. Monasteries, convents, cathedral chapters, colleges, and hospitals are all included. Most of the professions date from 13 June to 22 October 1534. Ten professions from Kent date from December 1534 and January 1535. Corpus Christi College, Cambridge made this profession on 9 March 1535, and the last recorded profession in this form was made at Calais on 27 March 1535.[56] Although the professions of each and every monastery and institution of the realm do not survive, enough of them do survive to suggest that the tendering of this institutional profession was comprehensive. The absence of a profession from a specific monastery should not be taken as evidence that this monastery did not make its profession, but rather that its profession has been lost. Thus, in contrast to parish priests, Henry forced every member of the clergy associated with any institution to make a detailed profession of his succession *and*

[53] See Appendix E, IV for the form of this institutional profession as well as a comparison to the friars' profession.

[54] The letter also commissioned these men to take the subscriptions of every secular priest to the familiar statement against papal authority; Bodleian Library, Ashmole MS 1729, fol. 2ʳ (*LP*, VII 876); Bowker, 'Supremacy and the Episcopate', 229.

[55] The original professions (mixed in with the bishop's oaths of supremacy) are preserved at the National Archives in E25. They are printed in Rymer (ed.), *Foedera*, XIV:487–527 and (alphabetically) in the *Sixth Report of the Deputy Keeper of the Public Records*, App. II:279–306. They are arranged by date in *LP*. See for example, *LP*, VII 921, 1024, 1121, 1216, 1347, 1594.

[56] BL Lansdowne MS 989, fols. 131ᵛ–133ʳ (*LP*, VIII 360); NA E25/23/2 (*LP*, VIII 458).

supremacy, and to confirm it with an oath. The fact that Henry targeted his institutional clergy with a much stronger, more detailed profession is significant. Henry was clearly making an important distinction between his secular clergy and his institutional clergy.

Two final forms of clerical professions survive from the spring of 1534. On 19 April 1534 Thomas Goodrich, Roland Lee, and John Salcot (alias Capon) were consecrated as bishops of Ely, Coventry and Lichfield, and Bangor respectively. Days before their consecration, they swore a new oath to the king that replaced the previous oath new bishops had taken to receive their temporalities from the king. In this new oath, they promised to maintain the 'preemynence and prorogatife' of the king and the jurisdiction of his 'ymperiall Croune of the same afore and ayenst all manner of persons powres and authorites', they recognized the king 'ymmiediat-lye vnder almyghtye god to be chyef and supreme hedd of the churche of England', they offered to maintain and defend all statutes of the realm made against the Pope, and – echoing the oath of succession – they pledged to keep and defend the entire contents of the Act of Succession and all other statutes to be made in confirmation of the same.[57]

In addition to the oath sworn by these new bishops, there is also suggestive evidence that some of the old bishops may have made another new oath to the king in the spring of 1534. On 20 April John Husee wrote to Lord Lisle, 'The bishops of Durham, Winchester, and York are now sent for, to what intent God knoweth. Some thinketh they shall to [*sic*] the Tower.'[58] In May 1534, Bishop Roland Lee wrote to Cromwell:

Plesseyth you to take the payne to speke with thys berer whoo hathe browght the ij[nd] answer frome the Bishope of Chechister whereby and by the informacion of thys berer hee presaue [perceives?] not a littill dissimulacion wiche is not to be forgotten. In Remuneracion of the same it whold Right well agre hee callyd in hys owne person hether ad praestandum Sacramentum [to swear the oath] & is as other Bishopes be.[59]

[57] NA SP1/83, fol. 54[r] (*LP*, VII 427). Goodrich's oath is dated 2 April 1534. Burnet gave a near identical text for Roland Lee's oath; Burnet, *History of the Reformation*, VI:290–1. Lee's oath does not contain a date, but must be sometime between 19 March and 19 April 1534. For the model form of this oath, see NA C82/690, no. 2 (*LP*, VII 1379). For a transcription of the entire text of this oath, see Appendix B, V.
[58] Byrne (ed.), *Lisle Letters*, II:129–30 (*LP*, VII 522).
[59] NA SP1/84, fol. 101[r] (*LP*, VII 759). This letter is undated but it must be after Lee's consecration. Moreover, in the letter Lee said he was travelling toward Syon, which allows us to establish the month as May. *LP*, VII 622 shows that Lee was at Syon on 7 May 1534. Except for *LP*, VII 758 (which clearly belongs at the end of May because of the reference to the London Charterhouse), there is no other evidence that Lee was at Syon at any other time in 1534.

Both of these letters could of course refer to the oath of succession. But they also could refer to a mysterious profession entitled 'The promise of the bishops to renounce the Pope and his bulls'. Whereas the oath made by Goodrich and Lee was an elaboration of the old oath bishops made to the king for their temporalities, updated with clauses on the succession and supremacy, this profession was a detailed rejection of the oath that all new bishops swore to the Pope until the spring of 1534. In addition to a detailed renunciation of their oath to the Pope and all bulls they had received from him, the profession also contained the now familiar clause that 'the Bishop of Rome had and has no more authority or jurisdiction in this your kingdom of England by divine right than any other foreign bishop'.[60] There is no *direct* evidence that anyone ever made this profession, nor is there a date on the profession itself. It does, however, seem to fit here, and there are some tantalizing suggestions that Henry's old bishops may indeed have sworn this oath. In this profession, the bishop promised to turn over to the king all the bulls he had received from the Pope and to hold his bishopric henceforth only from the king. William Rastell, in a fragment that is the basis of much of our information on both John Fisher and Thomas More, claimed that, 'The king caused al his bushopes savinge the bishop of Rochester to surrender al theire bulles to hym, whereby they were ma[de] bushopes, and they toke the king's lettres Pattents to be bushopes [all] onely by hym.'[61] This statement immediately preceded a sentence describing the tendering of the oath of succession to the London clergy in 1534. Furthermore, in a letter dated 29 January (with no year), Bishop Tunstall wrote to Cromwell asking to be excused from handing over his bulls of confirmation to the king in person.[62] These sources suggest the possibility that some of the bishops consecrated before 1534 actually made this profession.[63] Finally, there is evidence that at least some of Henry's bishops took the institutional profession in the summer of 1534, for institutional professions by the bishop of St Davids and the bishop of Bath and Wells survive.[64]

---

[60] NA sp6/3, fols. 63ʳ–64ʳ. This profession will be discussed in greater detail below. Its complete form is transcribed in Appendix C.

[61] Ortroy (ed.), 'Vie du bienheureux martyr Jean Fisher Cardinal, évêque de Rochester', 12 (1893): 253.

[62] BL Cotton MS Cleopatra E VI, fols. 245ʳ–246ʳ (*LP*, x 202). *LP* places this letter in 1536.

[63] If no bishops actually swore this exact profession, it is still significant that the oaths which all bishops swore in February and March 1535 did include a clause renouncing papal bulls addressed to them. See below and Appendix F, 1.

[64] NA E25/85; NA E25/119. The latter document is the profession of the Cathedral of Bath and Wells, which Bishop John Clerk also signed.

The multiplicity of overlapping professions in the spring and summer of 1534 must have created a great deal of confusion. After all, at the same time, the commissioners were administering the oath of succession, the clerical subscription against papal power, the friars' profession, the institutional profession, and at least one new bishops' oath as well. Cranmer himself was puzzled at times, as he revealed in an undated letter to an unidentified member of the central bureaucracy (probably Lord Audley):

> where you have sent forth commissions to justices of the peace to take the same oath [of succession], I pray you send me word, whether you have given them commission to take oaths as well of priests as of other. And if so, then I trust my labours be abbreviate, for in a short time the oaths (hereby) shall be take[n] through all England; which seemeth to me very expedient so to be; trusting this expedition shall discharge your lordship, me, and other of much travail in this behalf; but yet I would gladly know who shall take the oaths at the religious of Syon, which is specially to be observed, and also the charter houses, and observants, and other religious exempt.[65]

And if Cranmer was confused in 1534, any historian writing in the twenty-first century is bound to encounter enigmas when attempting to determine which letters relate to which professions. For example, when on 1 September 1534, the prior of the Charterhouse of Henton wrote to Henry VIII, claiming that he had been 'enstructyd by master Layton of yowr gracis pleasure concernyng the subscrybyng and sealyng of a certeyn profession in wrytyng', we simply do not know if this profession was the oath of succession, the subscription against papal authority, or the institutional profession.[66]

The story of the universities serves as a nice summary of the multiplicity of the professions of 1534. As has been noted, both universities first signed the declaration that the bishop of Rome has no greater authority in England than any other foreign bishop. Cambridge did so on 2 May, Oxford on 27 June. On 31 May Henry wrote to Cambridge University to reassure them that even though he commanded them to give their oaths of succession to the mayor of the town and to the bishop of Ely, he intended nothing against the privileges of the university.[67] Three days later, Lord Audley wrote to the mayor of Cambridge, commissioning him to tender the oath of

---

[65] Cranmer, *Miscellaneous Writings and Letters*, 291–2. The 'religious exempt' were institutions that were exempt from the jurisdiction of the ordinary of their diocese and instead answered directly to a higher power, usually either the monarch or a prelate in Rome.

[66] NA sp1/85, fol. 136ʳ (*LP*, vii 1127), printed in Thompson, *Carthusian Order*, 447–8.

[67] CCCC MS 106, #257 (pg. 566).

succession to the town and university separately.[68] No such letters survive for Oxford, but a similar process must have taken place there as evidenced by Dr London's claim that he 'wasse the second person who toke a corporall ooth in Oxford befor my lord of Lincoln and the mayer, then commission-ars, to maytayne the same [defense of this matrimony] to the vttermost of my power'.[69] Next, the colleges of Oxford and Cambridge were clerical institutions, and five institutional professions survive for Oxford Colleges. Oriel College made their profession on 27 July, Brasenose on 31 July, Bal-liol on 1 August, and Merton and All Souls' on 28 September.[70] The only institutional profession to survive from Cambridge is from Corpus Christi College. This profession is exceptional not only in its isolation, but also in its extremely late date of 9 March 1535.[71] But it is clear that over the course of 1534, the universities first rejected papal authority, then swore the oath of succession, and finally made their institutional professions, the last of which included an acknowledgement of Henry's supremacy.

After the flurry of professions in the spring and summer of 1534, the end of the year closed more quietly. Parliament met again in November and passed the Act of Supremacy, which confirmed that Henry was indeed 'the onely supreme [heed] in erthe of the Churche of England callyd Anglicana Ecclesia'.[72] No profession, however, was attached to this statute, though of course all the institutions and at least some of Henry's bishops had already sworn oaths acknowledging Henry's headship. Parliament also passed a second Act of Succession, retroactively setting the form of the oath of succession and claiming that all oaths of succession taken earlier in the year should be interpreted as this form.[73] This form was essentially the same as the one sent to the commissioners in Sussex on 20 April. Finally, Parliament passed the Treasons Act, which declared that anyone who did 'malicyously wyshe will or desyre by wordes or writinge, or by crafte ymagen invent practyse or attempte, any bodely harme to be donne or commytted to the Kynges moste royall personee, the Quenes, or their heires apparaunt, or to depryve theym or any of theym of the dignitie title or name of their royall estates' was a traitor, and as such, was to be punished with death.[74] The refusal of the oath of succession was not specifically mentioned as treason.

[68] CCCC MS 106, #42 (pg. 123).

[69] NA SP1/77, fol.107ʳ (*LP*, VI 739). *LP* mistakenly places this letter in 1533.

[70] Oriel College: NA E25/102/8 (*LP*, VII 1024(26)); Brasenose College: NA E25/102/7 (*LP*, VII 1024(35)); Balliol College: NA E25/102/3 (*LP*, VII 1121(1)); Merton College: NA E25/102/1 (*LP*, VII 1216(34)); All Souls' College: NA E 25/102/4 (*LP*, VII 1216(32)).

[71] BL Lansdowne MS 989, fols. 131ᵛ–133ʳ (*LP*, VIII 360).

[72] *Statutes of the Realm*, 26 Hen. 8, c. 1, III:492.   [73] *Statutes of the Realm*, 26 Hen. 8, c. 2, III:492–3.

[74] *Statutes of the Realm*, 26 Hen. 8, c. 13, III:508–9.

At the start of 1535, then, only the oath of succession was backed by an act of Parliament. Yet this did not stop Henry from pressing even more professions on his clergy. Once again, Henry first targeted his bishops. Starting on 10 February 1535, Henry made all his bishops and his two archbishops make and sign a new profession. This profession contained familiar elements. The bishops promised faith and obedience to Henry and to his heirs as the supreme head(s) of the English Church, rejected papal authority, pledged never to call the bishop of Rome the Pope, and promised to observe all the laws in the kingdom for the extirpation of papal authority. Yet the profession added new clauses wherein the bishops pledged never to give faith or obedience to the Pope despite any earlier profession, never to enter into a treaty with anyone who was attempting to restore papal jurisdiction, never to appeal to the Pope, to reveal any letters they received from him to the king, never to send letters to the Pope in return without the consent of the king, never to seek or consent to any papal bulls or dispensations, never to seek or keep a dispensation or exception to this profession, and finally to revoke all protestations previously made that were in conflict with this current profession.[75] Virtually all of these professions were made in February and March 1535.[76] Unlike the friars' profession and the institutional profession, this new profession of the bishops was not confirmed by an oath. It was also the first profession since before the Act of Succession not to mention explicitly Henry's marriage to Anne and his new succession.

Also in March 1535, Cromwell wrote the following remembrance to himself: 'to delyuer the othe and profession of the Bisshoppes to the pryor of Augustyne ffreers and the provincyall of the black ffreers to thentent they may practise the obseruacion of the same thorough out all the orders of ffreers'.[77] No evidence exists of the friars actually making this profession, though a modified form of it was made by the Universities of Oxford and Cambridge and their colleges in the autumn of 1535. During the first part of September, Richard Layton and John Tregonwell made a visitation of the University of Oxford. On 12 September Tregonwell wrote to Cromwell to inform him that they had completed their work. He also informed him that they had obtained professions – one from the university and one from

---

[75] These professions are collected in NA E25 and interspersed among the institutional professions of 1534. For the complete text of this profession, see Appendix F, 1.

[76] The exceptions to this statement are the Welsh professions. The bishop of St David's profession (NA E25/84/1) bears the date of 4 April 1534, though it is almost certainly a scribal error and should read 1535. The bishop of St Alsaph's profession (NA E25 4/2) bears the date of 1 June 1535.

[77] NA sp1/91, fol. 58ʳ (*LP*, VIII 345).

each college – and that every scholar had made these professions, as well as taking the oath of succession again.[78] The only profession to survive from this visitation is a copy of the profession of Corpus Christi College, Oxford, made on 9 September 1535.[79] A similar visitation must have taken place at Cambridge at the end of October, for the profession of the University of Cambridge survives from 23 October as does the profession of Gonville Hall made on 25 October.[80] Strangely, professions of this sort also survive from Cobham College, Kent (made on 27 October 1535) and from Worcester Cathedral (made on 16 August 1536).[81] These university professions differed from the bishops' professions made earlier in the year in that they had a new preamble and an altered wording in clause twelve. These new sections made the profession stronger by explicitly turning the profession into an oath and more carefully guarding against taking the profession with equivocation or dissimulation. In addition, these new university professions contained three additional clauses not found in the professions of the bishops: one clause wherein the juror renounced all exemptions, grants, privileges, and gifts conferred by the pope, another wherein the juror professed to be a subject of the king alone, and a third wherein the juror promised not to pay any money to the pope or his representatives. Finally, the professions of Gonville Hall and Cambridge University added yet another clause wherein the juror pledged to observe faithfully the statute of succession.[82] Besides this added clause on the succession, all of the pledges made as part of the visitation of the universities in the autumn of 1535 were essentially the same.[83]

If the bishops and the universities made another profession of loyalty to Henry VIII in 1535, did not the monasteries do so as well? After all, Henry

[78] NA sp1/96, fol. 138ʳ (*LP*, IX 351). For another letter confirming this visitation and the oaths taken during it, see *State Papers, Published under the Authority of His Majesty's Commission*, 1:425–6 (*LP*, VII 1148 – incorrectly put in 1534 by *LP*).

[79] BL Lansdowne MS 989, fols. 134ʳ–136ᵛ (*LP*, IX 306). This is not the original profession but a copy.

[80] The university's original profession is BL Additional Charter 12827. A copy of it is BL Harleian MS 7041, 193–96 (*LP*, IX 666). The profession of Gonville Hall was printed in Fuller, *History of the University of Cambridge*, 164–6.

[81] I have no explanation why Cobham College made this profession. It was a college of secular priests, but to my knowledge, it was not officially part of either university. For Worcester Cathedral, see below.

[82] The additional clause on the succession in the profession of Cambridge University and Gonville Hall was redundant, for both the letters from the visitation at Oxford and the instructions for the visitation at Cambridge indicate that the oath of succession was once again tendered in addition to this profession. See footnote 78 above as well as *LP*, IX 615, printed in Cooper (ed.), *Annals of Cambridge*, 1:375 and *LP*, IX 616. The profession of Worcester Cathedral also included this clause.

[83] There are negligible differences among them. Consult Appendix F, II for the text of this profession where these differences are highlighted.

sent out two commissions to the monasteries in 1535. The purpose of the first, known as *Valor Ecclesiasticus*, was to document church wealth, while the second's purpose was to examine the morals and behaviour of monks and nuns. Some historians of the Tudor period have assumed that Henry indeed made the monasteries swear an oath of supremacy in 1535. Perhaps the earliest historiographical claim of this sort was written in the short annals of a monk of St Augustine's Abbey in Canterbury. Concerning the visitation of the monasteries, he wrote: 'In this visitation, all men vtterly renounced the name of the pope, hys priuilegies and exempt places & c.'[84] Some modern historians have echoed this assertion. David Knowles, for example, claimed: 'In the spring of 1535 commissioners were appointed to require acknowledgment of the king's headship of the Church, and this was usually obtained by administering an oath upon the gospels in general terms of acceptance of the king's headship. All religious houses were visited for this purpose in due course.'[85] Similarly, G. W. Bernard, in his recent magisterial work on the Henrician Reformation, suggested that Henry imposed 'fresh oaths' on certain monasteries in the spring of 1535.[86] Conversely, most of the detailed accounts of the actual visitations of the monasteries in 1535 (Knowles included) do not mention the tendering of an oath of obedience during the process of visitation.[87] Historiographical consensus is thus lacking. I will argue that the claim that the monasteries swore the oath of supremacy in 1535, while not completely unfounded, lacks the necessary documentary evidence to prove its occurrence.

The best evidence for the monasteries taking an oath in 1535 comes from a draft of the commission for general visitation (not *Valor Ecclesiasticus*) in January 1535. In it, the visitors are instructed 'to show and demand an oath of fidelity and obedience to us and our heirs from the same and from anyone else of the said monasteries and from those present and serving at other places'.[88] Of course, an oath of 'fidelity and obedience' was a general term for any oath in which the swearer promised to be 'faithful and true' and 'obedient' to a social superior. While clauses of fidelity were included in circulating professions like the oath of succession, such a description of the oath gives us little idea of its content, for it was possible to swear an oath of fidelity without making any reference to the supremacy or the succession.

---

[84] BL Harleian MS 419, fol. 113ʳ.
[85] Knowles, *Religious Orders*, III:230. This is also the assumption of Thompson, *Carthusian Order*, 467.
[86] Bernard, *King's Reformation*, 162, 166, 168.
[87] Gasquet, *Henry VIII and the English Monasteries*; Woodward, *Dissolution of the Monasteries*; Baskerville, *English Monks and the Suppression of the Monasteries*; Knowles, *Religious Orders*, III:268–90.
[88] NA E36/116, fol. 15ᵛ (*LP*, VIII 76).

The royal injunctions that accompanied this visitation exhorted the monks to observe, keep, and teach 'all and singular contents, as well in the oath of the king's highness' succession, given heretofore by them, as in a certain profession lately sealed with the common seal, and subscribed and signed with their own hands'.[89] This obviously referred to the oath of succession and to the institutional profession made in 1534. The injunctions did not, however, instruct the monks to make another new profession in 1535. They simply commanded the monks to observe all the statutes made or to be made for the extirpation of papal authority and to preach and teach that the Pope's authority was not established by Scripture but rather that the king was supreme under God on earth in England. Moreover, the eighty-six articles of inquisition relating to this visitation contain no reference to an oath or profession of any kind.[90] And in this regard, the injunctions for the visitation of the monasteries contrast sharply with those for the visitation of the universities in the autumn of 1535. Although the first article for the visitation of Cambridge is very similar to the first injunction for the visitation of the monasteries (commanding them to observe the oath of succession and institutional profession *already* sworn), Cromwell issued an additional set of injunctions to the universities, the first of which specified 'that by a writing to be sealed with the common seal of the University, and subscribed with their hands, they should swear to the king's succession, and to obey the statutes of the realm made or to be made, for the extirpation of the papal usurpation, and for the assertion and confirmation of the king's jurisdiction, prerogative, and preeminence'.[91] Thus, despite the fact that a draft of the initial commission spoke of an oath of fidelity, none of the actual instructions or injunctions for the visitation of the monasteries – in contrast to those for the universities – specified the making of a new profession.

The actual general visitation of the monasteries did not commence until the end of the summer in 1535. In the meantime, the commissioners for *Valor Ecclesiasticus* did visit the monasteries. These commissioners sometimes took the opportunity to advocate royal supremacy, observe the monks' response, and report any opposition, but there is no evidence that they ever tendered a specific profession.[92] Yet if the commissioners for *Valor*

[89] Burnet, *History of the Reformation*, IV:217; Wilkins (ed.), *Concilia*, III:789. Wilkins has 'other' instead of 'othe', but this must be an incorrect transcription. Burnet has 'oath'.

[90] These articles are printed in Wilkins (ed.), *Concilia*, III:786–9 and Burnet, *History of the Reformation*, IV:207–16.

[91] The original articles of visitation for Cambridge are *LP*, IX 616. Cromwell's injunctions are printed in Cooper (ed.), *Annals of Cambridge*, I:375.

[92] See for example *LP*, VIII 560 (printed in Thompson, *Carthusian Order*, 457) and *LP*, VIII 968.

Ecclesiasticus did not tender any oath or profession to the monasteries in the spring and summer of 1535, some monasteries certainly anticipated that the regime was about to tender them a new oath of supremacy. The best evidence for this is that John Houghton, Robert Laurence, and Augustine Webster, the priors of the Charterhouses of London, Beauvale, and Axholme respectively, sought an interview with Cromwell in the spring of 1535 to forestall the commission and seek exemption from swearing 'the diabolical decree'.[93] It was only after this interview that the government began pushing an oath of supremacy on these priors and the members of the London Charterhouse.[94] Hence, the whole struggle with the London Charterhouse over the oath of supremacy that started in 1535 was instigated by the Charterhouse itself! The regime responded with an oath only *after* it discovered the obstinacy of the Charterhouse in refusing to swear an oath not yet demanded of them.

The greatest support, however, for the argument that the monasteries were not comprehensively tendered the oath of supremacy or some new profession in 1535 is the fact that not one monastic profession exists from either of the two visitations of 1535. This stands in marked contrast from the bishops' professions, all of which survive, and the university professions, some of which survive. Moreover, when the general visitation of the monasteries finally commenced at the end of July 1535, it proved to be an extensive affair that generated many documents. Copious letters and reports remain from the four visitors: Richard Layton, Thomas Legh, John Ap Rice, and John Tregonwell.[95] Yet in this myriad of letters, nary a mention is made of any profession of royal supremacy. There are a few exceptions to this rule. First, in a letter from Richard Layton to Cromwell on 24 August, Layton wrote that Witham Charterhouse 'hath professide and done althynges accordyng as I shall declare yow at large to morrowe erly'.[96] Second, Thomas Legh wrote that Axholme Charterhouse 'have sealyd the profession concernyng the kyng', while the proctor of Axholme, Thomas Bernyngham also spoke of 'a professione to be assigned wyth owr handis and sealled with owr Covent seall and other lettres'.[97] Yet the

---

[93] Chauncy, *Passion and Martyrdom*, 75 (Chauncy erroneously reported that an oath was attached to the act of supremacy); Knowles, *Religious Orders*, III:231.

[94] The priors were executed that spring, not for refusing to swear an oath of supremacy (though this undoubtedly played a role), but officially for vocally denying royal supremacy, which was in violation of the Treason Act. For the interrogations and trials of the priors, see *LP*, VIII 565, 566, 609.

[95] These letters can be followed in *LP*, VIII–IX. Many of them are printed in Wright (ed.), *Three Chapters of Letters*.

[96] Wright (ed.), *Three Chapters of Letters*, 59 (*LP*, IX 168). Also see Thompson, *Carthusian Order*, 447.

[97] *LP*, X 50, 104, both of which are printed in Thompson, *Carthusian Order*, 451–2.

context of this profession of Axholme was the election of a new prior after the execution of Augustine Webster. Except for the phrase 'concerning the king', there is no indication that this profession had anything to do with the supremacy or succession, though that remains a possibility. When the visitation of the monasteries is compared to the visitation of the universities, these two hints of a monastic profession appear even slighter. The visitation of the universities produced vastly fewer letters, yet in the few extant, it is clear that the universities' profession was worthy of comment. The University of Oxford wrote to Henry VIII, relating how the visitors had required them to renounce papal authority under their common seal and swear fealty to him. At the same time, John Tregonwell wrote to Cromwell, explaining that professions had been taken from the university as a whole and from every college individually.[98] Hence, not only the lack of any surviving monastic professions, but also the comparatively scant references to a monastic profession in the letters of the visitors suggest that the visitors of the monasteries in 1535 did not demand an oath or profession of the supremacy, at least not in any systematic manner. Perhaps because the professions of 1534 had accomplished their purpose, Henry no longer felt that he had to issue another profession to be made comprehensively by all the monasteries of the realm.

Thus, in the spring and early summer of 1535, Henry was pushing the supremacy on his monasteries in an unsystematic manner. The pressure the crown did exert was focused on select monasteries with a history of opposition to Henry, and the acknowledgement required of them was less formal than a solemn oath. This is best illustrated by examining in detail the situation of the Carthusian Abbey of Mountgrace in the summer of 1535. Two monks of Mountgrace had refused the oath of succession in 1534, and the monastery was accordingly monitored closely by the regime.[99] In June 1535 Edmund Lee, the archbishop of York, sent Dr Langridge, the archdeacon of Cleveland, to preach the king's new title and to deliver books on the king's supremacy around Yorkshire. When Langridge stopped at Mountgrace, Prior John Wilson 'received the booke, but he alowed not the thinge, and saide he trusted that none of his broderne wolde alowe anie suche thinges, the saide Archideacon did his best to alure hym, but he coulde not bringe it to pass'.[100] Looking back, Lee confirmed that

[98] *State Papers, Published under the Authority of His Majesty's Commission*, 1:425–6 (*LP*, VII 1148 – incorrectly put in 1534 by *LP*); NA sp1/96, fol. 138ʳ (*LP*, IX 351).

[99] NA sp1/85, fol. 20ʳ (*LP*, VII 932).

[100] BL Cotton MS Cleopatra E VI, fol. 240ᵛ (*LP*, VIII 963), printed in Ellis (ed.), *Original Letters*, ser. 3, II:337–342.

the priors of Mountgrace and Hull 'were sore bent rathre to die, than to yelde to this youre royall style'.[101] So Lee sent a letter to Wilson, and Wilson then had interviews with both Tunstall (the bishop of Durham) and Lee. Lee persuaded Wilson that the 'kinges Majestie was supreme heed immediatly vnder Christ of this Churche of Ingland', and by 9 July, Lee wrote to Cromwell that Wilson 'holdethe hym selfe well content, and full wieselie considerethe that it besemethe not hym to stonde in anie opinion againse so manie, not onlie beeing of good lernynge, but also some of goode livenge'.[102] Although Wilson was convinced, he freely admitted that he had 'muche troble with certyen of his breythern whome by cause they wold not acknolege ther dwtes vnto the kinges Majestie and vtterly expell the bishop of Rome out of ther hartes'.[103] On 13 July the Earl of Northumberland wrote to Henry that Richard Marshall and Jamys Neweye, a priest and lay brother of Mountgrace, had tried to flee to Scotland 'by cause *they wold not be sworne vnto suche articles* as they were bounde according to youre highnes most dradde lawes'.[104] On 20 July Sir Francis Bigod also wrote to Cromwell, recounting how 'the Prior of Mountgrace praide me not to moave ne to vex any of his brethern for he had sente to yower mastership his mynde concernyng boith hym self and his brethern; therfor I wolde ther meddle no farther, yit this I well parsaive by the prior that moste parte of his brether be as yit trators'.[105] Finally, on 8 August Archbishop Lee again wrote to Cromwell, repeating that 'the priour of Mountgrace is yelded', though some of his 'simple brodren' still held needed alluring.[106] After 8 August we hear nothing more of Mountgrace until Thomas Legh visited it in early February 1536 as part of the general visitation of the monasteries. Legh simply reported they were 'ready to fulfil the King's pleasure'.[107] Mountgrace's story makes it clear that the regime was pushing them to recognize Henry's supremacy in the summer of 1535, but it is also significant that the language describing this submission was quite general. They simply 'yielded' or 'conformed'. The only time an oath was mentioned was when Marshall and Neweye fled in order to avoid swearing to 'suche articles'. Yet like the London Charterhouse, these monks probably anticipated the tendering of an oath, for surely if an oath was tendered there

---

[101] Ellis (ed.), *Original Letters*, ser. 3, II:374 (*LP*, x 99).
[102] *LP*, xv 125, printed in Thompson, *Carthusian Order*, 472–4; *LP*, viii 1011, printed in Ellis (ed.), *Original Letters*, ser. 3, II:344. Also see *LP*, xi 75, partially printed in Thompson, *Carthusian Order*, 468.
[103] *LP*, xv 125, printed in Thompson, *Carthusian Order*, 472–4.
[104] *LP*, viii 1038, printed in Thompson, *Carthusian Order*, 468–70. My italics.
[105] *LP*, viii 1069, the relevant part of this letter is printed in Thompson, *Carthusian Order*, 470.
[106] *LP*, ix 49, printed in Thompson, *Carthusian Order*, 471.   [107] *LP*, x 288.

it would have been noted in the other letters documenting Mountgrace's story.

Other select monasteries were pressured into some type of informal acceptance of royal supremacy in 1535. In 1535 John Pysent cryptically wrote to Sir John Alyn that some of the monks of the Sheen Charterhouse 'wyll gladly obbey the kynges grace in thys poynt for as moche as yt ys not agaynst the scrypture off god', but others would rather dye because of 'a lytyll scrypulosyte off conscyence'.[108] Neil Beckett, a historian of Sheen Charterhouse, assumed this referred to the oath of supremacy, but nothing in Pysent's letter explicitly supports the assumption that he was referring to an oath.[109] Syon Abbey, the first place where a subscription to the king's marriage to Anne was tendered, also fell under royal pressure again in 1535. On 4 May 1535, Henry executed Richard Reynolds, a monk of Syon who had denied royal supremacy, but no documentation exists of Reynolds being administered an oath of supremacy.[110] Until January 1536 the sisters and brothers of Syon were subject to a preaching campaign on royal supremacy and pushed to consent to Henry's new title.[111] In spite of the claims of G. W. Bernard, there is no evidence of the government demanding or the inhabitants of Syon actually taking an oath.[112] Indeed, the sisters of Syon seemed to have acquiesced to Henry's supremacy by sitting still after having been told to depart from their chapterhouse if they refused to consent to Henry's title.[113] This was a far cry from a corporal oath or a solemn profession. By contrast, the cathedral monastery of Worcester did swear an oath in almost the exact same form as the one sworn by the

---

[108] NA SP1/85, fols. 125[r] (*LP*, VII 1091 – incorrectly placed in 1534 by *LP*), printed in full in Thompson, *Carthusian Order*, 441–2.

[109] Beckett, 'Sheen Charterhouse', 173. For another compelling yet vague example, see NA SP1/98, fol. 32[r] (*LP*, IX 638).

[110] John Leek, a clerk of Syon, reported that Reynolds had spoken that Katherine was the true queen of England and that he would not accept Henry as the supreme head of the church; *LP* VIII 565. Interrogated by the Lord Chancellor, Reynolds defiantly upheld his rejection of royal supremacy and for this reason was executed under the Treasons Act; *LP*, VIII 661.

[111] Wright (ed.), *Three Chapters of Letters*, 44–6 (*LP*, VIII 1125); Aungier, *History and Antiquities of Syon Monastery*, 435–8 (*LP*, VII 1090, incorrectly placed in 1534 by *LP*); Knowles, *Religious Orders*, III:215–21.

[112] Bernard claimed that in May of 1535, Bedyll 'reported that they hoped to have the king's pleasure concerning oaths obeyed'. The letter Bernard cited in support of this statement (*LP*, VII 622) is clearly from 1534 and refers to the oath of succession, a fact which Bernard himself admitted when discussing the letter in a different context. The same letter cannot be from two different years! See Bernard, *King's Reformation*, 168 and 634 (note 561), 157–8 and 632 (note 468). Bernard also erroneously placed the letter relating to Syon's and Stokesley's subscription to Henry's annulment (NA SP1/82, fols. 11[r]–12[r]) in 1536, despite the fact that the original letter in the National Archives clearly says '4 Jan 1533', which is of course 1534 according to the old calendar. See Bernard, *King's Reformation*, 170, 634.

[113] Wright (ed.), *Three Chapters of Letters*, 48–50 (*LP*, IX 986).

university colleges in the autumn of 1535, but Worcester Cathedral swore it on 16 August 1536, a year after the general visitation of the monasteries.[114] It is not clear why Worcester Cathedral was targeted in 1536,[115] and it is possible that other cathedrals were administered the universities' profession at a later date.[116] In general, however, it is safe to conclude that although Henry continued to demand that specific monasteries acknowledge his title of supreme head of the church in some manner, he did not tender a uniform and methodical profession or oath of supremacy to them after 1534 as he did to the bishops and universities.

After the flood of oaths and professions in 1534 and the continued but more selective use of them in 1535, things began to settle down administratively in 1536. Parliament met again in the spring of 1536 and updated its legislation on the succession and the supremacy. It passed a new Act of Succession, which like the previous one, required all adult English subjects to take a corporal oath for the succession 'by the commaundement of your Majestie or of your heires or successours, at all tymes hereafter frome tyme to tyme when it shall please your Highnes or your heires or successours to appoynt'.[117] The oath attached to this act was similar to the original oath of succession, but it diverged in three ways. First, Henry's new wife Jane Seymour was substituted for Anne. Second, the initial clause swearing fidelity to Henry specified that he was 'supreme hede in erth under God of the Churche of Englonde'. Finally, the oath promised that in the event of a lack of heirs through Henry and Jane, the swearer would be loyal to whomever Henry appointed as his successor.[118] The act then specified that any person doing knight's service to the king should swear this oath. It ended, in contrast to the first Act of Succession, by stipulating that whoever refused this oath was guilty of high treason.

Despite the fact that this new Act of Succession authorized Henry to command all his adult subjects to take the new oath of succession, there is no substantial evidence that anyone actually took this oath. Two

---

[114] The oath is printed in Burnet, *History of the Reformation*, VI:83–5. I have collated it with the universities' profession in Appendix F, II.

[115] In 1535 there was a conflict between some of the brothers of the cathedral and their abbot, Prior More. A few of the brothers even accused More of treason in a letter to Thomas Cromwell. Yet this dispute was over by the spring of 1536, and Prior More was allowed to retire in style, which suggests that this dispute was unrelated to the oath of 16 August. For details on this story, see Knowles, *Religious Orders*, III:342–5. John Noake's claim that the oath of 16 August 1536 was in response to a secret rebellion fomented by the cathedral monastery has no evidence to back it up. See Noake, *Monastery and Cathedral of Worcester*, 225–7.

[116] Bowker, *Henrician Reformation*, 90.   [117] *Statutes of the Realm*, 28 Hen. 8, c. 7, III:661.

[118] *Statutes of the Realm*, 28 Hen. 8, c. 7, III:661–2. See also Appendix D, III for the text of this new oath of succession as well as a comparison to the former oath of succession.

references to it survive. The first, pointed out by Elton years ago, is a few spare leaves from an ancient manuscript Gospel. These leaves contain two oaths, both of which commence with the text of the new oath of succession but then diverge slightly from the text stipulated in the act and from each other.[119] The second reference to this oath comes from Edward Lee's archiepiscopal register of York. On 27 March 1538, Thomas Legh issued an inhibition to the clergy of York Province in lieu of a planned general visitation of the province. In addition to other matters of visitation, all clergy, churchwardens, and two or three people from each parish were to swear fealty and obedience to the king, renounce the pope and his jurisdiction according to the Act of Succession, and subscribe their names. Except for a scant reference concerning a matrimonial dispute from 7 May 1538, no further documentation of this visitation survives, though it evidently was complete by 7 July when the inhibition was relaxed.[120] In the end, Elton was correct in his observation concerning this oath: 'the signs that anyone took notice or action are extraordinarily slight and dubious – nonexistent by comparison with the evidence for 1534'.[121]

In addition to the new Act of Succession, the Parliament of 1536 also passed the Act for Extinguishing the Authority of the Bishop of Rome. This act declared that all ecclesiastical persons (religious or secular), all laymen holding any office or position of authority or holding land from Henry, all persons taking a university degree, and whomever else it pleased Henry to specify must take a new corporal oath against the Pope upon assuming their office, position, or degree. Embedded in the act was the actual form of this new oath. Like the bishops' oath of 1535, this oath did not mention the succession at all. It commenced with two new clauses rejecting the authority and jurisdiction of the Pope and agreeing never to consent but rather to resist such authority and jurisdiction. The swearer then promised to repute and take the king as the '*oonly* supreme hedd in erth of the Church of Englond', the familiar clause updated with the addition of the word 'only'. The final three clauses were direct (though updated and slightly modified) derivations from the first oath of succession and the oath new bishops had been taking since the spring of 1534 upon their consecrations. In these clauses, the swearer pledged to observe and defend all statutes made and to be made for the extirpation of papal authority and corroboration of the king's supremacy; not to attempt or suffer to be attempted

---

[119] BL Additional MS 4507, fols. 4^r–5^r, 7^r–8^r. The divergences are minor. In the first oath, the swearer is bound not to commit any felonies or treason but rather disclose any known cases to the king. In the second, the swearer agrees to pay rent and do service for a manor he holds from the king.
[120] Kitching (ed.,) *Royal Visitation of 1559*, xiv.   [121] Elton, *Policy and Police*, 226.

anything to the damage, derogation, or hindrance of these statutes; and to reject any previous oath made to or in favour of the Pope and his power. Like the new Act of Succession, this act also specified that anyone who refused to take this oath was guilty of treason, the penalty for which was execution.[122]

Unlike the new oath of succession, there is evidence for the tendering of this oath, at least for ecclesiastical persons. First, this was the form of the oath that the London Charterhouse took when they finally capitulated on 18 May 1537.[123] Moreover, all new bishops consecrated after 31 July 1536 took this oath, for many of these oaths are included in Cranmer's archiepiscopal register alongside other documents relating to the election and confirmation of new bishops.[124] It is less clear exactly when new parish priests and other holders of lower benefices began taking this oath, but records of institutions and ordinations contained in episcopal registers indicate that it was being administered by the early 1540s.[125] For example, a typical institution from the 1540s noted that the person being promoted 'undertoke an oath on the holy Gospels of God concerning the renouncing, refuting, and refusing the authority and jurisdiction exercised by the Roman pontiff according to the meaning, force, and effect of the statutes of Parliament'.[126] It is also likely that this oath was tendered regularly at the universities. A copy of the exact oath stipulated by the act (with the marginal note 'and Ireland' often added after the phrase 'the churche of England') follows the heading 'The othe takyn byfore admyttyng any to the college for renounsing thauthoritie of the busshop of Rome' in a British Library manuscript.[127] Furthermore, when condemning Cambridge University's acceptance of Mary's Counter-Reformation, James Pilkington proclaimed: 'As oft as they had anye liuinge in anye college of the universites, as oft as they tooke degree in the scholes, as oft as they tooke any benefice, and when they were made priests or byshoppes, so ofte they sweare and forsweare all that nowe they denye.'[128] Excluding the text of the act itself, there is not much corroborating

---

[122] *Statutes of the Realm*, 28 Hen. 8, c. 10, III:665. For the complete form of this oath and notes comparing it to previous oaths, see Appendix G, 1.
[123] NA E25/82/2 (*LP*, XII (1) 1232), printed in Rymer (ed.), *Foedera*, XIV:588–9.
[124] See for example the oaths of Nicholas Heath (Rochester) or Edmund Bonner (London) in LPL, Cranmer's Register, fols. 259ʳ, 260ᵛ. Identical oaths follow throughout Cranmer's Register. This oath replaced the one sworn by Roland Lee and Thomas Goodrich in the spring of 1534.
[125] GL MS 9531/12 (Bonner's Register), fol. 145ʳ, 171ᵛ; LPL, Cranmer's Register, fol. 388ʳ ff., Hinde, (ed.), *Registers of Cuthbert Tunstall*, 102; Bowker, *Henrician Reformation*, 172–3.
[126] LPL, Cranmer's Register, fol. 388ʳ.   [127] BL Additional MS 39235, fol. 50ᵛ.
[128] James Pilkington, *Of the cause of burning Paul's Church*, quoted in Mullinger, *University of Cambridge*, II:121.

evidence that lay holders of political office took this oath. In a letter
from February 1537 or later, John Butler wrote to Cranmer from Calais:

please it your grace to be aduertysed that at dyuers tymes here tofor I haue openly
declared vnto my Lord deputie, the Mayor, & all other of the kynges Counsell
here the othe of renouncynge the busshopp of Romes pretensid power: which was
stablysshed in the last parlyament of the kynges maiestie holden at Westminster.
But suche othe is ther noon taken, used or spoken of amonge them, for lack
wherof moche papistrye dothe rayne styll, and chiefely amonge them that be
Ruelars. Wherfor your grace myght do the kynges maiestie high service to procure
a Commyssion for to be sent vnto my Lorde deputie, with some other to be ioyned
with him in the said Commyssion that were not of the papisticall sort (which were
hard to be found amonge the Counsell here) to se the said othe put in execution
from tyme to tyme as est [best?] as my officer shalbe admitted, accordinge to the
kinges statute.[129]

We do not know if Butler's experience in Calais was representative of
the rest of the realm. It is possible that lay office holders made this oath
without making any documentary reference to it. Regardless, it is apparent
from episcopal registers and from Pilkington's comment that all persons
promoted to an ecclesiastical benefice eventually took this oath.

One more oath from the Henrician Reformation remains. In 1544 Parliament passed the Act concerning the Establishment of the King's Majesty's
Succession in the Imperial Crown of the Realm. This act began by rehash-
ing the two oaths set forth in the parliamentary session of 1536. Yet because
'bothe the saide Othes mencioned in the saide severall Actes there lacketh
full and sufficent wordes, wherby some doubtes myght arise', this act issued
a new oath 'in lewe and place of those two othes'.[130] The text of this oath
was basically a much expanded version of the oath of supremacy mandated
in the 1536 Act for Extinguishing the Authority of the Bishop of Rome with
the addition of a new preamble and a clause promising fealty and obedience
to Henry and to his heirs and successors as stipulated by the 1536 Act of
Succession. The oath also emphasized Henry's imperial status by stressing
that Henry's supreme headship applied not only to England but also to
Ireland and to his other dominions. The act of 1544 ended by declaring
that the same people formerly required to take the oath attached to the

---

[129] NA sp1/102, fol. 24^r (*LP*, x 292). The letter contains the date 11 February, but has no year. *LP* places
it in 1535 or 1536, but Butler's words demonstrate that the letter cannot be earlier than 1537. Butler
wrote of the oath renouncing the pope 'stablysshed in the last parlyament'. The first oath explicitly
renouncing the pope to be backed by a parliamentary statute was the oath stipulated in the Act for
Extinguishing the Authority of the Bishop of Rome of 1536. Since the parliamentary session of 1536
did not commence until 14 February, Butler's letter from 11 February must be from 1537 or later.
[130] *Statutes of the Realm*, 35 Hen. 8, c. 1. III:956.

Act for Extinguishing the Authority of the Bishop of Rome must now take this oath instead. Cranmer's Register shows that after 1544 some bishops-elect took this new oath at their consecrations. Yet Cranmer's Register also contains examples after 1544 of the old oath for the extinguishing of the authority of the bishop of Rome, which suggests that implementation of this new oath was not uniform.[131]

What conclusions can be drawn from this overview of Henry VIII's use of professions and oaths to secure his succession and supremacy? Throughout this narrative, it has become apparent that three factors affected the power of a device: what kind of device it was, the content of the device, and the extent of its administration. As for the first factor, Henry tendered to his subjects a mixture of oathless subscriptions and formal oaths. It is possible that this was a negligible coincidence, but the clear hierarchy between oaths and promises in the sixteenth century suggests otherwise. It was not a coincidence that the parish clergy were required to make only a simple subscription while the institutional clergy were bound with a solemn oath. Henry knew what he was doing. He must have felt that certain of his subjects needed to be bound more strongly than others. Furthermore, the professions Henry employed after 1534 were stronger not only in being oaths, but also in more explicitly rejecting any kind of equivocation.

The second factor in determining the power of a particular profession was the content of that profession. Here there were three different themes: the recognition of the Boleyn (and later Seymour) marriage and succession, the rejection of papal jurisdiction, and the establishment of royal supremacy. In 1533 and the first part of 1534, Henry focused on the first two issues and separated them into distinct professions. The subscription tendered to Syon in January 1534 exclusively dealt with Henry's marriages. The oath of succession – on the surface at least – referred only to the succession. The statement to which Henry forced all his bishops and secular clergy to subscribe concerned solely the authority of the bishop of Rome. Even though Henry initially separated these issues into different professions, the fact that he circulated professions on both of these issues at the same time (perhaps even tendering them to some subjects simultaneously) shows that the two were interrelated. Indeed, the professions of the friars and the institutional professions of 1534 combined the first two issues and added the third, Henry's supremacy. By 1535 the supremacy clearly had taken precedence since the new profession of the bishops did

---

[131] LPL, Cranmer's Register, fols. 315ᵛ–316ʳ, 326ʳ⁻ᵛ, 328ʳ⁻ᵛ, 331ʳ⁻ᵛ, 332ᵛ, 333ᵛ, 334ᵛ–335ʳ.

not even mention the succession. Likewise in the oath from the statute of 1544, the succession was an afterthought; the vast majority of that particular oath – which Parliament claimed to be a combination of the oaths of succession and supremacy – dealt with the rejection of papal authority and establishment of royal supremacy.

The third factor contributing to the power of an oath was the scope of its administration. In this regard, the oath of succession was by far the most radical of the Henrician professions. Henry tendered this oath to every adult subject in his realm regardless of social status. The administrative effort for such an undertaking in the sixteenth century was massive and unprecedented. The quantity of letters from the summer of 1534 that testify to the confusion which the administration of the oath of succession engendered demonstrate that the regime was indeed in uncharted waters. Yet why expend all this administrative effort for an oath that on the surface made no reference to papal authority or royal supremacy but merely involved the king's choice of a wife and heir? The great scope of the oath of succession suggests that there was something more to its content than met the eye, a theme to which we will return in Chapter 4.

If the oath of succession was radical in scope, what about the oath of supremacy? Another conclusion of this chapter is that the term 'oath of supremacy' is a misnomer. There was no single oath of supremacy. Instead, there was a plethora of professions rejecting papal authority and acknowledging Henry's supremacy circulating after 1534, some confirmed with oaths, some without. Unlike the oath of succession, these professions had no parliamentary backing until 1536, so Henry was free to adapt and modify these professions as he saw fit. Furthermore, when historians refer to 'the oath of supremacy', they sometimes mean the oath tendered to the monasteries during the visitations of 1535. Yet we have seen that it is doubtful that most of the monasteries took an oath in 1535. A few of them may have, but evidence indicates that some kind of informal acknowledgement of Henry's supremacy was much more common. And while any sort of rejection of papal authority and recognition of royal supremacy was radical in content, the acknowledgements of the supremacy were much less radical in scope than the oath of succession. Elton was quite right in his observation that 'the realm as a whole was never sworn to the supremacy'.[132] It was not until the 1536 Act for Extinguishing the Authority of the Bishop of Rome that Henry even bothered to demand that a layman acknowledge

---

[132] Elton, *Policy and Police*, 229.

his supremacy, with the possible exception of Thomas More.[133] And this act required an oath of supremacy from laymen only if they assumed some office or position of authority. This was not particularly radical, for an oath of office was traditionally required for everyone newly assuming a position of authority. Henry simply tacked on clauses about his supremacy to an already established oath. The supremacy then – unlike the oath of succession – was radical in content but not in scope.

But what of those subjects from whom Henry did demand a profession of his supremacy? It is overwhelmingly clear that Henry focused on his clergy. Yet among his clergy, Henry targeted certain groups over others. The bishops were hit hardest in Henry's campaign. If Ambassador Chapuys can be trusted, already in 1533 the regime circulated two different subscriptions to certain bishops, one concerning Henry's desired annulment and the other abrogating papal authority. Bishop Stokesley (along with Syon Abbey) was asked to sign a document on Henry's annulment and remarriage in early 1534, and all the bishops (John Fisher excluded) swore the oath of succession in the House of Lords later that spring. They may have also agreed to the statement that the Pope had no greater jurisdiction in England than any other foreign bishop in Convocation at the end of March, and they certainly signed this statement one or two months later. The new bishops Goodrich, Lee, and Capon swore an oath to the king in April 1534, an oath that explicitly rejected papal authority and acknowledged Henry's supremacy. The rest of the bishops may have been forced to make another profession renouncing the Pope and his bulls at this time as well. In the summer of 1534, some of Henry's bishops took the institutional profession, while every single bishop was again administered a new, more detailed profession on Henry's supremacy in February and March 1535. This means that there were at least six and as many as nine separate professions circulating from 1533 to 1535 that specifically targeted or at least included Henry's bishops! Even though we cannot prove that every bishop made each of these professions, the sheer number and variety of the professions is significant. After the bishops, the universities also received careful royal scrutiny. They gave judgement on Henry's first marriage in 1529, agreed to the statement against papal jurisdiction, swore to the succession, made the institutional profession in 1534, and were hit again in the fall of 1535 with a new profession of the supremacy combined with another tendering of the oath of succession. The professions made by the friars and

---

[133] For a discussion of Thomas More, see Chapter 4.

institutions of the clergy in 1534 were also formidable in that they included an acknowledgement of Henry's royal supremacy and were confirmed with an oath. This was not true of the subscriptions of the non-institutional secular clergy. Established clergy never had to swear to Henry's supremacy unless they earned a university degree or took a new benefice. Henry did not treat all his clergy alike; the scope of the professions of supremacy varied according to the status of the cleric.

CHAPTER 3

The origin and motivation of the Henrician professions

Now that we know how Henry implemented his Reformation of 1534, the next question is: why? Clearly Henry's basic motivation behind administering a variety of subscriptions and oaths in the 1530s was the enforcement of his break with Rome and establishment of his supremacy over the church in England. Yet this explanation does not address the complexity revealed in the previous chapter. Why did Henry tender different kinds of professions of varying strength to different groups of subjects? Why did Henry obsessively target his bishops? Why was there a special focus on the universities? Why did he attach an oath to the professions of the institutions and friaries but not to those of the secular parish clergy?

The simplest answer to these questions is that Henry tendered stronger, more numerous professions to the groups of his clergy that had the most power and a history of resistance to his annulment and supremacy.[1] The bishops of England had wealth, prestige, and jurisdictional power over their diocesan clergy as well as seats in the House of Lords. The universities were centres of cultural authority where the next generation of England's leaders was trained. The friars were the chief preachers of the realm, which gave them influence over the laity, and Syon Abbey and the Carthusian Charterhouses were the wealthiest, most austere, most learned, and thus most influential houses of the realm. As for a history of resistance, the bishops led the opposition to Henry's reforms in the Convocations of 1531 and 1532, while Bishops Fisher and Tunstall were Katherine's chief counsellors and advocates. The Universities of Oxford and Cambridge had proved embarrassingly obstinate in initially refusing to declare that divine law prohibited the marriage of a widow to the brother of her deceased husband.

---

[1] James Murray provided a variation on this reasoning in his explanation for why Archbishop Browne imposed an oath against the papacy only on the cathedral and monastic chapters of his diocese of Dublin in 1537. According to Murray, Browne focused solely on these groups because of their social prominence as educators of others, their influence over parish appointments, and their potential to become ecclesiastical judges; Murray, *Enforcing the English Reformation in Ireland*, 103–4.

Finally, certain institutions such as Syon Abbey, Sheen Charterhouse, and members of the Observant Franciscans were implicated in supporting Elizabeth Barton, the prophetic Nun of Kent who decried Henry's divorce and prophesied against him.[2]

There is, however, another deeper reason why Henry chose to implement his Reformation in the way that he did. The primary *motivation* for the strategy of implementation of the Reformation of 1534 will become apparent when we examine the *origin* of the Henrician professions. A key episode in the origin of the Henrician professions took place in the 1532 clash between Henry and his clergy. On 11 May 1532, right in the middle of Henry's struggle with Convocation over the independent jurisdictional power of the clergy, Henry called into his presence Thomas Audley (Speaker of the House of Commons) and twelve representatives from that house. Edward Hall probably numbered among the twelve. According to Hall, Henry then delivered this speech:

> welbeloued subiectes, we thought that the clergie of our realme had been our subiectes wholy, but now wee haue well perceiued that they bee but halfe our subiectes, yea, and scace our subiectes: for all the Prelates at their consecracion make an othe to the Pope clene contrary to the othe that they make to vs, so that they seme to be his subiectes, and not ours, the copie of bothe the othes I deliuer here to you, requiryng you to inuent some ordre, that we be not thus deluded of our Spirituall subiectes.[3]

Audley and the representatives then returned to the House of Commons, where Audley read to the House the two oaths a new bishop made: one to the Pope, and one to the king.[4]

Although this story is familiar to historians, its full significance has never been realized. Historians usually have glossed over this story as another attempt by Henry to intimidate his clergy into submission, which it certainly was.[5] Yet Hall and John Foxe placed much more weight on this story than modern historians. Hall believed: 'The openyng of these othes was one of the occasions why the Pope within two yere folowyng

---

[2] For the clerical opposition to Henry's reforms in 1531 and 1532, see Scarisbrick, 'Pardon of the Clergy'; Kelly, 'Submission of the Clergy'; Lehmberg, *Reformation Parliament*, 105–60. For the obstinacy of the universities in 1530, see Mullinger, *University of Cambridge*, 1:613–22; Wood, *History and Antiquities*, 11:40–4. For the involvement of certain monastic institutions in the prophecies of the Nun of Kent, see Bernard, *King's Reformation*, 155, 167; Beckett, 'Sheen Charterhouse', 166–8.

[3] Hall, *Hall's Chronicle*, 788.

[4] Hall printed the form of both oaths. They are included here in Appendix A, IV and B, IV.

[5] Kelly, 'Submission of the Clergy', 113–14; Lehmberg, *Reformation Parliament*, 150–1; Scarisbrick, *Henry VIII*, 299.

lost all his iurisdiccion in Englande.'[6] Foxe, who erroneously placed the narrative in 1530 and gave credit to Thomas Cromwell, made an even stronger statement, claiming that the opening of these oaths to the people was '*the* occasion that the Pope lost al his interest and iurisdiction heere in Englande'.[7] Although Foxe's statement is undoubtedly an exaggeration, he and Hall were right to emphasize this episode. The oaths of 1534 and 1535 were, to a great extent, a response to previous oaths sworn by the clergy. The differences among the professions of 1534 and 1535 can be accounted for by the extent to which Henry felt a particular group of subjects had sworn an oath prejudicial to his royal authority. At the centre of this story are the contradictory oaths of a bishop-elect to the Pope and king, so an examination of the origin and context of these oaths is crucial to understanding the motivation behind Henry's particular method of implementing his supremacy in 1534 and 1535.

THE EVOLUTION OF THE EPISCOPAL OATHS TO THE POPE AND TO THE KING

The background behind Henry's confrontation with the representatives from the House of Commons goes back to the Middle Ages and the evolution of the episcopal oaths to the Pope and to the king. According to Robert Barnes (a leading English evangelical in the 1530s) and Thomas Earl (a minister of St Mildred's, Bread Street, whose commonplace book contains various notes on issues of the sixteenth century), new bishops first swore an oath in 759 under Pope Gregory III. This was a simple, five-clause oath in which the bishop-elect swore to keep the faith of the Catholic Church, to abide in the unity of that faith and not consent to the contrary, to seek the profits and honour of the church of Rome, to have no conversation with any bishops who say or do anything against the statutes of the holy fathers, and to oppose these bishops and report them to the Pope.[8] This oath (which we will designate oath A 1) was innocuous enough; there was not even a clause pledging loyalty to the Pope. Yet it is not certain that this oath in its above form was actually sworn. Our sources for this oath are Barnes and Earl, two sixteenth-century English evangelicals, who were certainly biased.

If bishops-elect did take the oath prescribed by Gregory III in the early Middle Ages, this oath was eventually discarded in favour of a stronger,

---

[6] Hall, *Hall's Chronicle*, 789.　　[7] Foxe, *AM* (1583), 1054. My italics.
[8] Barnes, *A supplicacion* (1534), fol. DI^v; CUL MS MM. I. 29, fol. 29^r. See Appendix A, 1 for the actual text of this oath.

more detailed oath. This stronger oath (oath A II) was codified in canon law and had seven clauses. The bishop-elect first swore fidelity to St Peter, to the holy Church of Rome, and to the Pope and his lawful successors. He then promised never to counsel or to do anything that would result in the Pope losing life or limb or being taken in any trap. He pledged to keep the Pope's counsel secret and to defend and maintain the papacy and the rules of the holy fathers. In the final clauses, the bishop-elect agreed to attend a council when summoned, to treat the Pope's legate honourably, and to visit the see of Rome, either personally or by a representative, on a regular basis.[9] The emphasis in this new oath was clearly loyalty to the papacy. According to Barnes, this new episcopal oath was a result of the conflict between the Holy Roman Emperor and the Pope. Oath A I was discarded 'bicause that by it, the bysshoppes were not bounde to betraye theyr prynces, nor to reuelate theyr councelles to the Pope'.[10]

It is not clear if the exact form of oath A II was ever tendered in England, for a preliminary foray into medieval English episcopal registers has not yielded any examples of this form.[11] Instead, an expanded version of oath A II (which we shall call oath A III) was tendered to English bishops and archbishops in the fourteenth century. For example, Archbishop-Elect William Courtenay took oath A III in 1382 upon receiving the pallium, Thomas Arundel took the oath in 1396 when he ascended to the see of Canterbury, and the bishop-elect of St Asaph took this oath during Arundel's archiepiscopate.[12] Oath A III included all the same clauses as oath A II, but some of these clauses were greatly expanded. Furthermore, oath A III contained four new clauses not in oath A II. In these new clauses, the bishop-elect swore to avoid plotting against the Pope in word or deed; to reveal to the Pope anyone he knew to be involved in such a plot; and never to sell, alienate, or give away any of the possessions belonging to the bishopric. The final new clause concerned the papal schism. The bishop-elect swore never to support but rather to persecute the antipope Clement VII and all of his followers.[13] Hence, oath A III continued the trend of oath A II, placing even more emphasis on loyalty to the papacy.

[9] *CIC*, x.2.24.4, Friedberg, II:360. This is the same oath recorded in the *Collectanea satis copiosa* under the heading, 'The prelates olde othe made to the pope'; BL Cotton MS Cleopatra E VI, fol. 53ʳ. Barnes believed (incorrectly) that this oath was the form used by bishops-elect in England in the 1530s. He thus included an English translation of this oath in his *Supplicacion* of 1534, fol. DIᵛ. For the exact form of this oath, see Appendix A, II.

[10] Barnes, *A supplicacion* (1534), fol. DIᵛ.

[11] It is possible that a comprehensive search of all medieval source material will reveal that this oath was sworn in England.

[12] Wilkins (ed.), *Concilia*, III:154–5; LPL, Arundel's Register, fols. 3ʳ, 12ᵛ.

[13] The full text of this oath can be found in Appendix A, III.

The evolution of episcopal oaths to the pope had one more step before arriving at the stage at which it remained until the Henrician Reformation. During the fifteenth century and down to 1534, English bishops and archbishops swore an oath of canonical obedience to the Pope at their consecration. This new oath (oath A IV) was once again different from previous episcopal oaths to the Pope. Oath A IV contained all the same clauses as oath A III (excluding the final clause against the antipope Clement VII), but many of these clauses were simplified as in oath A II. More important, however, was the addition of three new clauses. In the first of these new clauses, the bishop-elect swore to promote, increase, and defend the rights, honours, privileges, and authority of the Church of Rome and the Pope. In the second, the bishop-elect swore to observe and cause all men to observe the rules of the holy fathers and the apostolic decrees, ordinances, sentences, dispensations, and commands. Finally, the bishop-elect swore to persecute all heretics, schismatics, and rebels.[14] In addition to this oath of canonical obedience to the Pope, English bishops-elect swore a simple, two-part oath of canonical obedience to their archbishop at their consecrations.[15] Like their bishops, English archbishops-elect swore oath A IV to the Pope at their consecration, but they also swore another oath to the Pope upon the reception of their pallium.[16] This oath (oath A V) omitted all the new clauses of oath A IV and most of the new clauses of oath A III. In content, it was basically oath A II with the addition of the clause from oath A III on not alienating archiepiscopal possessions.[17] While oath A V was thus a regression from oaths A III and A IV, it must be stressed that archbishops-elect swore oath A V *in addition* to oath A IV. Thus, the general trend in the evolution of episcopal oaths to the Pope was to strengthen the obedience bishops owed to the Pope by increasing the quantity and quality of clauses outlining that obedience.

It is more difficult to reconstruct the evolution of the oaths bishops-elect made to the king for the restitution of their temporalities. These

---

[14] The full text of oath IV, along with notes comparing it to the other episcopal oaths to the Pope, can be found in Appendix A, IV.

[15] In this oath, the bishop-elect promised canonical obedience, reverence, and subjection to his archbishop. He also swore to defend the rights of the Church of Canterbury or York, depending on the province. For a few examples of this oath, see Wood (ed.), *Registrum Simonis de Langham*, 264–5; LPL, Warham's Register, fol. 3ᵛ; LPL, CM 51, #22 (Tunstall).

[16] For specific references to the pallium oath among English archiepiscopal registers, see footnote 12 of the Appendix. Exceptionally, Stephen Patryngton, bishop-elect of St David's under Archbishop Chichele, also took this oath at his consecration instead of oath IV; Jacob (ed.), *Register of Henry Chichele*, 1:24.

[17] The order of the clauses in oath V also differed from oath II. Consult Appendix A, V for the exact form and order of this oath.

oaths were not written down in episcopal registers. Yet a few of them survive in undated manuscripts in the British Library. It is likely that these illustrate the basic form of the oath in the fifteenth century (which we shall call oath B I). This oath was divided into two parts. The first 'oath of renunciation of a bishop' was not an oath at all but rather a proclamation in which the bishop-elect renounced all words in his papal bull of consecration contrary and prejudicial to the king and then asked the king for the restitution of his temporalities. In the second part, the 'oath of fidelity', the bishop-elect swore fealty to the king, promised to be attendant to the king's business and to keep his counsel secret (an echo of the bishop-elect's oath to the Pope), acknowledged that he held the temporalities of his bishopric from the king, and promised to be obedient to the king's commands that pertained to these temporalities.[18] The primary purpose of this oath, then, was to insure that the bishop-elect acknowledged that all the temporalities (land, income, etc.) of his bishopric were granted by the king and not the Pope.[19] The king, not the Pope, was thus his overlord. It was similar to the oath that a vassal to whom the king had granted land would swear upon receiving that land. This oath did not mention the 'spiritualities' of the bishopric. These were bestowed by God through the power of the church and granted specifically by the bishop-elect's papal bulls of consecration. Of course, Henry VIII redefined 'spiritual' as 'sacramental', which meant that the temporalities the bishop held from the king encompassed much more than just land and income and included the bishop's jurisdictional power as well.[20] Hence, the oath of a bishop-elect to the Pope bound him as the vassal of the Pope, while at the same time the oath of a bishop-elect to the king bound him as a vassal to the king.

The oath that a bishop-elect swore to the king was also malleable. It could be changed depending on the situation. The oath of fidelity Cardinal Adrian of Castello made to Henry VII for the bishopric of Bath and Wells demonstrates this principle. This oath (oath B II) had oath B I as its base, but the clauses from oath B I were greatly expanded in B II. These expansions emphasized that Henry VII was Adrian's 'supreme lord'. Oath B II also

---

[18] BL Harleian MS 433, fol. 304^v; BL Cotton MS Vespasian c xiv, fols. 436^r–v. For the full text of this oath, see Appendix B, 1.

[19] The exact clause is, 'I shall knowlage and do the seruices due of the temporalities of my Bisshopriche of C. the whiche I clayme to holde of my said souerayn lord the king, and the whiche he yeveth and yeldeth me'; BL Harleian MS 433, fol. 304^v. The clause is thus ambiguous. Is the bishop-elect claiming to hold the temporalities of the bishopric or the bishopric itself from the king?

[20] For a further discussion of Henry's definition of spiritual, see Ullmann, 'Realm of England is an Empire', 181–200.

contained four new clauses not found in B I. In two of these new clauses, Adrian declared that he would neither attempt nor consent to anything harmful or prejudicial to the king, his heirs, and the privileges, rights, prerogatives, and customs of the realm. If he became aware of any such action, he would let the king know immediately. Significantly, bishops-elect swore the same two clauses to the Pope in their oaths of canonical obedience. Perhaps this part of Adrian's oath to the king was a response to his oath to the Pope. In the other two new clauses, Adrian swore to attend faithfully and diligently to the business committed to him by the king, and to seek papal bulls and apostolic letters pertaining to royal business and send them to the king when he received them. The changes in Adrian's oath thus reflected his special status as a cardinal in Rome. Perhaps Henry VII felt that as a foreigner who resided at the papal curia, Adrian's loyalty might be unbalanced in favour of the Pope. Thus, Henry made Adrian call him his 'supreme lord' and bound him to protect the prerogatives and rights of Henry and England.[21]

Adrian's expanded oath to the king was exceptional. The form of the oath for restitution of temporalities that Henry VIII tendered to Stephen Gardiner (Bishop-Elect of Winchester) and Edward Lee (Archbishop-Elect of York) in 1531 was much simplified. Indeed, this oath (oath B III) was even simpler than oath B I, omitting the clauses from B I on being attendant to the king's business and keeping his counsel secret. Oath B III was, however, stronger in that it eliminated the ambiguity as to whether the bishop-elect held merely the temporalities of his bishopric or the bishopric itself from the king. Oath B III explicitly proclaimed that the bishop-elect held 'the said busshoprick immediately and only of your Hignes'.[22] Yet another form of the oath of a bishop-elect to the king survives from the early 1530s. This oath (oath B IV) is included in the collection of documents known as the *Collectanea satis copiosa* that was put together for Henry VIII by Edward Fox and Thomas Cranmer, and a similar form is copied down in *Hall's Chronicle*. Oath B IV brought back the clauses from oath B I not in oath B III. Oath B IV, however, divided clause one into two parts and then rearranged the order of the clauses. In content, the only novel part of oath B IV was that the bishop-elect swore fidelity to the king 'aboue all creatures' – probably another attempt to prioritize loyalty to the king over

---

[21] Burnet has preserved for us Adrian's oath to Henry VII; Burnet, *History of the Reformation*, IV:5–7. I have included the full text of this oath in Appendix B, II.

[22] For Gardiner's oath, see BL Additional MS 34319, fol. 21ᵛ, printed in Gardiner, *Letters*, 479–80. For Lee's oath, see Rymer (ed.), *Foedera*, XIV:428–9. For the full text of this oath, see Appendix B, III.

loyalty to the Pope.[23] Although there is no evidence that this exact form of the oath was ever taken, it is significant (as we shall see) because it is the form of the oath that Henry believed his bishops swore to him.

HENRY'S AWARENESS OF THE OATHS OF A BISHOP-ELECT AND THE EVOLUTION OF THESE OATHS

Both of the oaths taken by a bishop-elect had thus evolved by the early 1530s to intensify the bonds of loyalty the bishop owed to his overlords: the Pope or king depending on the oath. This dual intensification served to highlight the contradictory nature of these oaths. Yet more important for our purposes than the actual evolution of these oaths is Henry VIII's knowledge of the evolution of these oaths. How much did Henry know? From where did he get the information that led to his speech on 11 May 1532? According to John Foxe, the king's informant was Thomas Cromwell. Foxe wrote that sometime in 1530, before Cromwell was a servant of the king, Cromwell had secured an interview with Henry and presented him with a copy of the two contradictory oaths. These oaths greatly impressed Henry, who then took Cromwell into his service and sent him to Convocation to expose to the bishops their treachery in swearing contradictory oaths. After displaying these oaths in Convocation, Cromwell charged the clergy with *praemunire*, and this led to the struggle between Henry and Convocation in 1531.[24] According to this story, then, Henry was ignorant of these oaths until 1530. Once enlightened by Cromwell, he knew the two oaths only in their contemporary form. Yet Foxe's story has too many holes in it for us to accept it at face value. If Cromwell did enlighten the king in 1530 and the king sent Cromwell to Convocation immediately, why did Henry wait until 1532 to raise the issue to Parliament? Why raise the issue to one body and not the other? Furthermore, why is there no note in the records of Convocation of Cromwell, then a little-known upstart, charging into Convocation, presenting the clergy with the two contradictory oaths, and then accusing the bishops of *praemunire*? Surely this would have created a stir! Furthermore, in a different section of *Acts and Monuments*, Foxe lifted his account of the events of 11 May 1532 directly from *Hall's Chronicle*, without making any reference to the episode with Cromwell in 1530.[25] It therefore seems likely that Foxe was incorrect in his claim that Cromwell

---

[23] BL Cotton MS Cleopatra E VI, fols. 53ᵛ–54ᵛ; Hall, *Hall's Chronicle*, 789. Foxe replicated the oath printed in *Hall's Chronicle* in his retelling of the episode of 11 May; Foxe, *AM* (1583), 1053. For the full text of this oath, see Appendix B, IV.

[24] Foxe, *AM* (1583), 1179.   [25] Foxe, *AM* (1583), 1053.

brought the two contradictory oaths of a bishop-elect to the attention of the king in 1530.

Modern historians have suggested other explanations for the origins of Henry's speech on 11 May 1532. John Guy, while not explicitly endorsing Foxe's version of the event, has emphasized the role of Thomas Cromwell. Specifically, Guy observed that Henry's remark that the clergy were but half his subjects was a favourite phrase of Cromwell and that a catalogue of Cromwell's papers reveals that he had in his possession some form of 'the oaths of the prelates made to the Pope'.[26] George Bernard, by contrast, has noted that according to the Venetian ambassador, in the spring of 1532 the bishops of the realm declared that they could not assent to Henry's divorce without papal consent because they had sworn an oath in their consecrations not to oppose the Pope's wishes. This, argues Bernard, was probably the origin of Henry's speech of 11 May 1532.[27]

A more complete explanation – one that does not necessarily exclude the theories of Guy and Bernard – is that Henry originally learned about the contradictory oaths of a bishop-elect to the king and Pope by reading the *Collectanea satis copiosa*.[28] The *Collectanea* was a collection of writings from Scripture and ancient authors that dealt with royal and ecclesiastical power. It was compiled as part of Henry's effort in 1530 to establish his claim that the realm of England was an empire and thus immune from papal jurisdiction because of the ancient privileges of the realm. (This, of course, was part of Henry's larger campaign to secure an annulment of his marriage to Katherine of Aragon.) As John Guy noted, the compilers of the *Collectanea* 'were seeking to establish three basic principles of English regal power: secular *imperium*, spiritual supremacy and the right of the English Church to provincial self-determination, i.e. national independence from Rome and the papacy'.[29] It is clear that Henry read the *Collectanea*, for marginal notes in his hand are scattered in forty-six places throughout the manuscript. Cromwell also read the *Collectanea*. Indeed, Graham Nicholson, the historian who first alerted the historical community to the importance of the *Collectanea*, has convincingly argued that it was the basis of the famous preamble of the Act of Appeals of 1533.[30]

---

[26] Guy, *Public Career of Sir Thomas More*, 196–7; *LP*, VI 299, pgs. 137 and 139.
[27] Bernard, *King's Reformation*, 65; *Cal SP Venice*, IV 761.
[28] The *Collectanea satis copiosa* is BL Cotton MS Cleopatra E VI, fols. 16–135.
[29] Guy, 'Thomas Cromwell and the Intellectual Origins of the Henrician Revolution', 159.
[30] Nicholson, 'Act of Appeals and the English Reformation', 19–30. For a general analysis of the *Collectanea*, see Nicholson, 'Nature and Function of Historical Argument', 81–92. Nicholson also convincingly argued that Edward Fox, the king's almoner, was the primary compiler of the *Collectanea*; ibid., 114–19.

Yet neither Nicholson nor any other historian has observed that a small section on the oaths of a bishop-elect to the Pope and to the king is nestled in the middle of the *Collectanea*. This section contains the text of the old oath of a bishop-elect to the Pope as prescribed by canon law (oath A II), the standard oath of canonical obedience to the Pope of a bishop-elect in the fifteenth and early sixteenth centuries (oath A IV) with a slight but significant variation, a version of the oath to the king by a bishop-elect (oath B IV), and a short commentary on how to interpret the contradictions between these oaths.[31] The most likely explanation for Henry's speech of 1532 is that Henry and Cromwell both discovered these oaths by reading the *Collectanea* in 1530, but they did not act on them until the spring of 1532 when Henry's bishops claimed that their oath to Pope precluded them from accepting Henry's divorce without papal consent.

Furthermore, when the forms of the oaths in the *Collectanea* are compared to the forms of the oaths Henry presented to Audley as recorded by Hall, it becomes clear that Henry was drawing his knowledge from the *Collectanea*. The second oath recorded in the *Collectanea* was the standard oath of canonical obedience to the Pope prevalent in the early sixteenth century but with three differences. First, whereas in all the other oaths of canonical obedience circulating at the time, the bishop-elect swore to defend the Roman papacy and either 'the regalia of holy Peter' or 'the rules of the holy fathers', the oath in the *Collectanea* exceptionally included both clauses. The form of the oath to the Pope that Henry presented to Audley (as preserved by Hall) also had both clauses. Second, the oath in the *Collectanea* differed from the standard oath of canonical obedience in episcopal registers in that the oath in the *Collectanea* substituted the word 'scitatem' for 'noticiam'. Again, the form of the oath in *Hall's Chronicle* used the word 'knowledge,' which is a literal translation of 'scitatem', not 'noticiam' (fame, acquaintance). Third, the last two clauses of the episcopal oath of canonical obedience were omitted from the form copied in the *Collectanea*, which simply contained the abbreviation 'Etc'. While these two clauses were in the form of the oath in *Hall's Chronicle*, they differed from the form of the oath in episcopal registers in that Hall's clauses were much simpler and abbreviated. All of this strongly suggests that Henry took the oath of canonical obedience (which Hall then copied down) from the *Collectanea*.[32] The same argument applies to the episcopal

---

[31] BL Cotton MS Cleopatra E VI, fols. 53ʳ–54ᵛ.
[32] BL Cotton MS. Cleopatra E vi, fol. 53ʳ⁻ᵛ; Hall, *Hall's Chronicle*, 788–9. See Appendix A, IV of this dissertation for a detailed mapping of the differences between the form of this oath in episcopal registers and the forms contained in the *Collectanea* and *Hall's Chronicle*.

oath to the king for restitution of temporalities. The oath to the king in the *Collectanea* is extraordinary in three ways. It divided the first clause into two sections and then moved the second section to a later part of the oath, it altered the general order of all the clauses, and it included the new words 'above all creatures'. Once again, all these peculiarities were present in the oath to the king that Henry presented to Audley.[33] The fact that the same textual oddities which distinguished the oaths in the *Collectanea* from the standard oaths circulating at the time were replicated in the oaths Henry presented to Audley suggests that the oaths Henry presented to Audley on 11 May 1532 were copies of the oaths from the *Collectanea*. The *Collectanea* was Henry's source.

Yet the relevant section of the *Collectanea* contained more than just the two oaths Henry presented to Audley. The section started with 'The prelates olde othe made to the pope'.[34] This was the original oath as prescribed by canon law (oath A II), a shorter and less detailed oath of canonical obedience. Immediately following this 'olde othe' was the 'new othe of the prelates made to the pope' (oath A IV), a more detailed oath that included three additional clauses. Henry noticed these changes. In the *Collectanea*, someone – presumably Henry since the marginal notes throughout the manuscript are in his hand – underlined four clauses of the 'new othe'.[35] Two of these clauses were the additional ones not in oath A II. These were the clauses in which the bishop-elect swore to defend the rights, honours, privileges, and authorities of the Pope and Roman Church; and to observe and cause to be observed by all men the rules of the holy fathers and the ordinances, sentences, provisions, and commands of Rome. These clauses further explain why Henry brought the contradictory oaths to the attention of Parliament in the spring of 1532 and not earlier. At just the same time as the clergy obstinately refused to submit their ecclesiastical ordinances and laws to royal judgement, Henry produced evidence that the clergy had actually sworn to defend and observe these same ecclesiastical rights, honours, sentences, and ordinances! The fact that these clauses were not in the old oath probably heightened Henry's indignation, for it suggested that these clauses had been deviously added at some point in English history. Here was evidence of the Roman Church having unjustly increased its own power over Henry's clerical subjects! The other two clauses Henry underlined, while not new, were even more significant. In these clauses,

---

[33] BL Cotton MS Cleopatra E VI, fols. 53ᵛ–54ʳ; Hall, *Hall's Chronicle*, 789. The exact wording of the oath in *Hall's Chronicle* varies at points from that in the *Collectanea*. See Appendix B, IV for more information on these slight variations.
[34] BL Cotton MS Cleopatra E VI, fol. 53ʳ.   [35] BL Cotton MS Cleopatra E VI, fol. 53ʳ⁻ᵛ.

the bishop-elect swore never to do in counsel or deed anything contrary or prejudicial to the Pope and to report anyone who contemplated or did such an action to the Pope. At a time when Henry was certainly contemplating acting against the Pope to secure his annulment, these clauses must have struck him as treasonous. If Henry did indeed gain his knowledge of the oaths of a bishop-elect from the *Collectanea*, he was also well aware that the oath of canonical obedience had evolved to intensify the loyalty owed to the Pope, an evolution of which he did not approve.

The section of the *Collectanea* on oaths concluded with a short explanation of how to interpret the contradictions between the oath to the Pope and the oath to the king. It cited two canons, each of which suggested a different interpretation of the contradictions. The first canon was 'One cannot swear an oath in prejudice to the rights of a superior.' If this canon guided the interpretation of the oaths, Henry had nothing to worry about. This canon suggested that all oaths – theoretically including the oath of a bishop-elect to the Pope – were taken with the tacit condition 'if it is not prejudicial to the rights of a superior'. Henry underlined this condition.[36] The other canon, however, suggested a more troubling interpretation. This canon was, 'Whoever swears not to act against someone is able to act against him in his own causes and causes of the church'.[37] The basis for this canon was a letter from Pope Honorius III. One Prince Antiochenus had evidently caused some of his prelates to swear an oath never to act against him. The prelates wrote a letter to Honorius asking what they should do if Antiochenus made any move against them or their churches. Honorius replied that the prelates 'were not held to this oath but were able to stand freely for the rights and honours of this church and also able to defend their particulars against this prince'.[38] If this canon were applied to the two oaths of a bishop-elect, then Henry's bishops could indeed violate their oath to the king and act against Henry if their actions were in defence of the church. This section of the *Collectanea* concluded by asserting that the proper interpretation of the two oaths should be that a clerical subject without violation of any oath sworn beforehand (to the Pope) ought to adhere to his prince in the prince's just causes. Although this interpretation was certainly favourable to the king, it probably did little to set Henry's mind at ease, for Henry was now aware not only of the contradictions between the two oaths of a bishop-elect but also that canon law allowed

---

[36] BL Cotton MS Cleopatra E VI, fol. 54ʳ; *CIC*, x.2.24.19, Friedberg, II:366.

[37] *CIC*, x.2.24.31, Friedberg, II:372.

[38] *CIC*, x.2.24.31, Friedberg, II:372. The letter supporting this canon (and thus this particular quote) was not included in the *Collectanea*. See the following footnote.

two opposing interpretations of these oaths. This was why Henry ordered Parliament 'to inuent some ordre' between the two oaths.[39]

THE POLEMICAL CONTEXT FOR HENRY'S ATTACK ON
THE OATH OF A BISHOP-ELECT TO THE POPE

The immediate source of Henry's information on the contradictory oaths of a bishop-elect and the resulting threat of his bishops placing their loyalty to the Pope above their loyalty to him was the *Collectanea*. Yet the information compiled in the *Collectanea* had not been gathered in a vacuum. Attacks on episcopal oaths of canonical obedience were not new in 1532, and the development of the Reformation only increased these attacks. Indeed, the episcopal oath of canonical obedience suffered criticism throughout the sixteenth century by reformers from various countries. Although these polemics cannot be shown to have influenced Henry directly, they are still important because they demonstrate the wider significance of this issue. By establishing a deeper ideological context from which Henry moved to attack the episcopal oath to the Pope, we are able to understand better the logic behind Henry's actions.

Perhaps the earliest attack on the episcopal oath of canonical obedience came from a Wycliffite writer at the end of the fourteenth century. This anonymous writer commenced his manuscript treatise by transcribing (and translating into Middle English) the episcopal oath to the Pope common in the later Middle Ages, oath A III.[40] The oath is to Urban VI, a detail which, along with the reference to the papal schism dates the manuscript from 1378 to 1389. Although the author opened the treatise by citing Chrysostom's interpretation of Matthew to suggest that all swearing was evil, he spent the body of the treatise arguing why each clause of the bishop's oath to the Pope was wrong. One of the greater arguments that emerged from

---

[39] The section of the *Collectanea* on the interpretation of the two oaths is written in convoluted and abbreviated Latin. Although I believe my summary above is correct, I will include the original Latin so that readers may come to their own conclusions. It is as follows: 'Iuramentum, si quod prestitum fuerit, prout in schedula presentibus annexa continetur, non obligat subditum iurantem, vt aliquid faciat contra ius et preeminentiam regie maiestatis Nam in huiusmodi iuramento inest ex iuris interpretatione tacita conditio, vidlt [videlicet] si non sit in priudicium iuris superioris. vt expresse habetur in textu, et prescribentes in ca. venientes, de iureiurando pro quo etiam facti ca. petitio in eodem titulo ubi habetur que clericus iuras [iuramentas?] cont[ra] aliquem non esse: Nihilomin[u]s cont[ra] eundem agere pot [potuit?] tam pro iure et honore sue ecclie que in casa propria. Quin igitur canones tam fauorabilem iuramenti interpretacionem admittunt in causis predictis multo fortius conâdere [contradere?] videntur vt sine aliqua iuramenti violatione antea prestiti pot [potuit?] debet clericus subditus principi ei in causis suis iustis et pro regni vtilitate adherere pro quorum descusione arma etiam sumere dicti canones clericis permittunt'; BL Cotton MS Cleopatra E VI, fol. 54[r–v].

[40] BL Additional MS 24202, fol. 1[r–v].

this clause-by-clause attack was that the oath to the Pope made the Pope a greater earthly lord than the king. The king's lordship was an ordinance of God but the Pope's lordship was not. Inasmuch as the Pope had any power, it was a ghostly or spiritual power that God alone could defend. The mere act of swearing an oath to the Pope gave to the Pope earthly power, and God had ordained that all earthly power belonged to kings.[41] Thus, by swearing an oath to the Pope, bishops committed treason against all kings, against God's ordinances, and against God himself.[42] Already at the end of the fourteenth century, then, the episcopal oath of canonical obedience was being depicted in derogation of royal authority.

In 1534, that wonder year of Henrician professions, the English evangelical Robert Barnes published an updated version of his *Supplicatyon . . . to the most excellent and redoubted prince kinge henrye the eyght*. Unlike his *Supplicatyon* of 1531, which had only a small section attacking the Pope's power to dispense people from their oaths, the *Supplicacion* of 1534 contained a large diatribe against the episcopal oath of canonical obedience. Like the Wycliffite writer, Barnes first transcribed the text of the episcopal oaths to the Pope (oaths A I and A II in this case) and then proceeded to attack each clause of the oath. Barnes' conclusions were also similar to the tract from the fourteenth century. The oath did not agree with God's word. From where did the Pope get the dignity of a lord? Speaking to the bishops directly, Barnes proclaimed that the 'cause of your othe' was to 'betraye your prynces'.[43] The oath was an excuse for treason, 'for nowe yf he be a traytour, he is to be excused. Why? For he is sworne to it.'[44] Barnes went beyond the Wycliffite writer, however, in that Barnes compared the oath to the Pope directly to the episcopal oath to the king. Barnes reminded the bishops of England:

For the very truthe is, that the kynges grace, and his counsell, consyderyng your othe made to the pope to be preiudiciall to his regall power, causeth you, in your othe afterwarde made vnto hym, to reuoke those thynges that you had afore sworne to the pope, and to declare that his grace and his counsell dyd recken your othe made to the pope to be agaynste hym, therfore he maketh you to revoke it by name, namynge the same othe, & also the same pope.[45]

No one could swear allegiance to two people. The bishops were in a predicament in which no matter what they did, they were perjured. But which of the two oaths would the bishops choose to break? Why, their

---

[41] BL Additional MS 24202, fols. 2^r–v, 4^v, 5^r, 7^r, 9^r, 12^r.

[42] BL Additional MS 24202, fol. 5^r.   [43] Barnes, *A supplicacion* (1534), fol. D3^r.

[44] Barnes, *A supplicacion* (1534), fol. D2^v.   [45] Barnes, *A supplicacion* (1534), fol. D4^r.

oaths to their prince of course! The Pope could always absolve the bishops from their oaths to their prince, 'but of your othe made vnto the Pope, there is no absolucion, neither in heuen, nor erthe'.[46] Thus, in the same year when Henry began circulating professions renouncing the Pope and acknowledging the king's supremacy, Barnes published a treatise that not only reminded Henry of the dangers of the episcopal oath to the Pope but also warned Henry that the bishops could subvert their oath to the king by breaking it and seeking papal absolution after the fact.

And Barnes was not the only one to worry about the Pope's dispensing power in regard to oaths. Thomas Cranmer noted some disturbing canonical trends on oaths in his 'The collection of tenets extracted from the canon law, shewing the extravagant pretentions of the church of Rome'.[47] Cranmer observed that the Pope claimed the power 'to judge which oaths ought to be kept, and which not'. As a result, the Pope 'may absolve subjects from their oath of fidelity, and absolve from other oaths that ought to be kept'. Finally, and perhaps most frighteningly to Henry, the Pope claimed the right to 'excommunicate emperors and princes, depose them from their states, and assoil their subjects from their oath of obedience to them, and so constrain them to rebellion'.[48] If the Pope did indeed have these powers, then the episcopal oath of loyalty to the king was worthless; the Pope could easily subvert it by absolving the bishops of their oath to the king.

The polemical attack on the episcopal oath to the Pope was not limited to England. In his famous 1520 *Address to the German Nobility*, Luther proclaimed: 'The harsh and terrible oaths which the bishops are wrongfully compelled to swear to the pope should be abolished.'[49] Bullinger in his *Decades* called the episcopal oath of canonical obedience to the Pope a 'wicked oath' whereupon a bishop did 'renounce and forsake the friendship of Christ, and humble himself to become the bond-slave and footstool of the pope of Rome'.[50] Conversely, the Council of Trent extended the oath of canonical obedience beyond prelates, decreeing that every person entering into a new benefice must within two months 'promise solemnly and swear that they will preserve in their obedience to the Roman Church'.[51] Clearly, the episcopal oath of canonical obedience to the Pope was an issue of

---

[46] Barnes, *A supplicacion* (1534), fol. EI[v].
[47] Strype dated this manuscript from 1533. Burnet dated it from 1544. See Cranmer, *Miscellaneous Writings and Letters*, 68 (note 1).
[48] Cranmer, *Miscellaneous Writings and Letters*, 69–70.
[49] Luther, *To the Christian Nobility of the German Nation* (1520), 164.
[50] Bullinger, *Decades*, PS, X:141–3.   [51] Schroeder (ed. and trans.), *Canons and Decrees*, 201.

some importance. In this context, Henry's presentation of the two contrary episcopal oaths to Audley and his claim that the oath of canonical obedience 'deluded' him of his 'spirituall subiectes' was not without justification.

RISING TENSION: OATHS OF A BISHOP-ELECT
FROM 1532 TO MARCH 1534

After Henry's speech to Audley on 11 May 1532, Parliament did not immediately 'inuent some ordre' between the oaths of a bishop-elect as Henry had charged. Nevertheless, while the issue was put on the back burner for the rest of 1532, it was not completely forgotten. The first draft of the Act of Appeals, mostly likely written sometime at the end of 1532 or the beginning of 1533, proclaimed that the Pope desired of all English bishops 'a corporall othe of obedience and subieccion to the see Appostolik contrary to their naturall dutie of obedience and alegiance that they shold and own to be to the kinges of this ralme having the imperiall crown of the same'.[52] Perhaps more important was Henry's clash with Archbishop Warham, which actually started before Henry's speech to Audley. On 24 February 1532, Warham publicly declared that he disassociated himself from all acts made or to be made in Parliament since its opening in 1529 which were prejudicial to papal authority or in derogation of the rights, customs, and privileges of the metropolitan church of Canterbury.[53] On 15 March Warham and Henry openly exchanged hot words in the House of Lords. Henry charged Warham with *praemunire* and based his charge on the claim that Warham had consecrated Henry Standish as bishop of St Asaph before Standish had done homage to Henry, taken his oath of fidelity to the king, and sued for the restitution of his temporalities.[54] It probably was not a coincidence that the material for Henry's accusation centered on the oaths of a bishop-elect. In the speech Warham prepared for his defence (which he must have prepared sometime before his death on 23 August 1532), Warham prioritized the episcopal oath to the Pope over the episcopal oath to the king: 'it wer according that a spiritual man shuld first give his othe of obedience to the spiritual hed which is the Pope . . . and not to preferr the temporal Prince to the Pope in a spiritual

---

[52] NA sp2/n, fol. 74[r]; Elton, 'Evolution of a Reformation Statute', 179–80.
[53] Warham's protestation is printed in Wilkins (ed.), *Concilia*, iii:746. In *Concilia*, Wilkins claimed that the protestation is from Warham's Register, but this is not true. I have, however, found a sixteenth-century copy of Warham's protestation among the papers of Robert Beale: BL Additional MS 48022, fols. 142[v]–3[v].
[54] Kelly, 'Submission of the Clergy', 103.

matter'.[55] Moreover, Warham asserted that his own oath to the Pope, especially the clause wherein he swore to observe the apostolic commandments, bound him to consecrate Standish immediately upon receiving the papal bulls. Otherwise, he would have been guilty of perjury. If Warham had to choose between incurring the guilt of perjury for breaking his oath to the Pope or incurring the penalty of *praemunire* for acting without Henry's approval, Warham declared he would accept the latter without hesitation.[56] We do not know whether Henry ever knew of Warham's prepared defence. If so, it would have infuriated him, for Warham not only placed the episcopal oath to the Pope above the episcopal oath to the king but also justified his actions by citing his own oath to the Pope.

Ironically, the same event that prevented Warham from publicly articulating his defence, namely his death, led to the most dramatic display of the contradictions between the oaths of a bishop-elect in the sixteenth century. With Warham gone, Henry needed a new archbishop of Canterbury. Henry's primary concern was to select one who would grant him an annulment of his marriage to Katherine, but the person Henry selected, Thomas Cranmer, had concerns about the episcopal oath of canonical obedience to the Pope. According to John Foxe (who based his account on Cranmer's answer to Bishop Brokes during Cranmer's treason trial under Mary), Cranmer initially refused Henry's summons to return to England from Germany in order to accept the archbishopric because Cranmer considered that 'the means he must have it', notably the oath of canonical obedience to the Pope, 'was clean against his conscience'.[57] When Henry persisted in his desire to make Cranmer archbishop, Cranmer explained to the king that his conscience forbade him to take the archbishopric at the Pope's hand, for Henry was the supreme governor of the church in England. After a few more conversations with Henry, 'the king himself', according to Cranmer, 'called doctor Oliver and other civil lawyers, and devised with them how he might bestow it upon me, enforcing me nothing against my conscience'.[58] Henry then informed Cranmer that he could receive the archbishopric 'by the way of protestation, and so one to be sent to Rome, who might take the oath, and do every thing in my name'.[59]

[55] The draft of Warham's defence is printed in Moyes, 'Warham: An English Primate', 401–14 (*LP*, v 1247). The page numbers for this particular quote are 405–6.
[56] Moyes, 'Warham: An English Primate', 406.
[57] Cranmer, *Miscellaneous Writings and Letters*, 223.
[58] Cranmer, *Miscellaneous Writings and Letters*, 4.
[59] Cranmer, *Miscellaneous Writings and Letters*, 223–4.

Cranmer decided that Henry's recommended course of action was valid, stipulating only that Henry 'should do it *super animam suam*'.[60] Accordingly, on 30 March 1533, in the chapterhouse of the College of St Stephen's at Westminster, in the presence of the notary John Clerk and witnesses Thomas Bedyll, Richard Gwent, and John Cocks, Cranmer made the following protestation:

In the name of God Amen. In the presence of you witnesses here present of authentic character and worthy of faith, I Thomas, bishop-elect of the archbishopric of Canterbury, allege, say and protest, openly, publicly, and expressly with these writings, that since an oath or oaths are accustomed to be sworn by the Archbishop-Elect of Canterbury to the highest pontiff... it is not nor will it be my will or intention by such oath or oaths, no matter how the words placed in these oaths seem to sound, to bind myself on account of the same to say, do, or attempt anything afterwards which will be or seems to be contrary to the law of God or against our most illustrious king of England, the commonwealth of his kingdom of England, or the laws and prerogatives of the same. And that I do not intend by such an oath or oaths to bind myself in any way that prevents me from freely speaking, counselling and consenting to all and singular things concerning the Reformation of the Christian religion, the government of the Church of England, the prerogative of the same Crown, or that prevents me from carrying out and reforming these things in the Church of England which seem to me to need Reformation. And I protest and profess that I will swear the said oaths according to this interpretation and this understanding and not otherwise nor in another way. And furthermore I protest that whatever oath my proctor swore formerly to the highest pontiff in my name, that it was not my intention or will to give him any power by virtue of which he could have sworn any oath in my name contrary or repugnant to the oath sworn by me or to be sworn by me henceforward to the most illustrious king of England. And in case he [my proctor] swore any such contrary and repugnant oath, I protest that he swore it without my knowledge or authority and I want it to be null and invalid. I want these protestations to be repeated and reiterated in all clauses and sentences of the said oaths, and from these [protestations] I do not intend to withdraw nor will I withdraw in any way by anything done or said by me, but I want these to always remain in effect for me.[61]

Immediately after taking this protestation, Cranmer left the chapterhouse and proceeded to the high altar of the same college to receive his consecration at the hands of the bishops of Lincoln, Exeter, and St Asaph. After

---

[60] Cranmer, *Miscellaneous Writings and Letters*, 224.
[61] LPL, Cranmer's Register, fol. 4ᵛ. Strype printed the Latin of this profession in his *Cranmer*, II:683–4. It is also included with a few errors of transcription in Cranmer, *Miscellaneous Writings and Letters*, 560. I have quoted this protestation at length because of its great importance and because no previous historian has bothered to translate the protestation into English.

John Longland, Bishop of Lincoln, read Cranmer his consecration oath (oath A IV), Cranmer declared he would take the oath only according to the protestation he had just made. He then swore the oath. Again, before taking his oath upon reception of the pallium (oath A V), Cranmer reiterated that he swore this oath under the protestations made in the chapterhouse. Finally, a third time, he required those present to bear witness that he took these oaths according to his protestation.[62]

Although Cranmer's use of a protestation allowed him to take his oaths to the Pope in a manner that did not offend his conscience or clash with his oath to the king, this method of swearing was dubious to say the least. The appointment of a proctor to go to Rome to take the oath of canonical obedience before the Pope was not the problem. Proctors often took oaths on behalf of someone else. Because of the distance between Rome and England, English bishops-elect rarely if ever journeyed to Rome themselves to make the oath in the Pope's presence. The making of a nullifying protestation before an oath, however, was quite controversial. Before swearing to the Treaty of Madrid in 1525, Francis I of France had made two secret protestations to the effect that the treaty oath he was about to swear would not bind him, and Francis' actions created an international polemical debate over the validity of a pre-oath protestation.[63] This episode was certainly known in England since Hall made a reference to it in his *Chronicle*,[64] and the controversial nature of a pre-oath protestation was probably the reason why Cranmer did not make the contents of his protestation public.[65] Indeed, when what Cranmer had done became public knowledge during Mary's reign, Reginald Pole blasted Cranmer for entering into his archbishopric 'by a feigned oath, by fraud, and dissimulation'. What else did Cranmer's protestation serve 'but to testify a double perjury, which is to be forsworn afore you did swear? Other perjurers be wont to break their oath after they have sworn, you break it afore'.[66] Thomas Martin agreed, boldly proclaiming at Cranmer's heresy trial: 'Hee [Cranmer] made a protestation one day, to keepe neuer a whitte of that whiche he woulde

---

[62] LPL, Cranmer's Register, fols. 4ʳ–5ᵛ.

[63] For the text of these two protestations, see Champollion-Figeac (ed.), *Cativité du roi François Iᵉʳ*, 300–4, 466–78. An apology for Francis' actions as well as the reponse of Emperor Charles V (who felt cheated by Francis' protestations) are printed in *Pro divo Carolo*, 113–22, 125–82. For background on this episode, see Hauser, 'Traité de Madrid'.

[64] Hall, *Hall's Chronicle*, 712.

[65] Cranmer of course publicly declared three times at his consecration that he took his oaths to the Pope according to his protestation, but the notarial instrument documenting the episode does not state that Cranmer read the actual contents of his protestation (made earlier in the chapterhouse) at his consecration.

[66] Cranmer, *Miscellaneous Writings and Letters*, 538.

sweare the next day, was thys the part of a christian man?'[67] At the same time, the Bishop of Gloucester derisively compared Cranmer to a man who killed another but thought himself safe because he had protested before the deed that it was not his will to kill.[68] Finally, Francis I could at least excuse himself by contending that his oath to the Treaty of Madrid was taken in fear under constraint and force, for Francis was the prisoner of Charles V at the time of the treaty oath. Cranmer, however, could not claim even this 'delusion', for as Pole observed in his letter to Cranmer: 'Whereunto you were not driven, neither *vi*, nor *metu*, as you were not in this your case.'[69] Cranmer's protestation was thus not without controversy.

The controversy surrounding Cranmer's protestation probably served to emphasize to Henry the conundrum of the episcopal oath to the Pope. In order to receive consecration through the instrument of a papal bull, all new bishops had to swear an oath to the Pope. But from 1532 on, Henry was aware that this oath conflicted with the episcopal oath to the king and provided a convenient excuse for episcopal resistance to the Crown. Hence, after 1532 Henry did not allow any of his bishops to take an unqualified oath of canonical obedience to the Pope. Cranmer's case famously illustrated this, but Cranmer was not the only one to make such a protestation during this time. On 17 January 1534, at Cranmer's manor at Lambeth in the presence of numerous witnesses, Christopher Lord (or Bord), Abbot of the Monastery of Newsey, made the exact same protestation before his consecration as suffragan bishop of Sidon as Cranmer had made before his consecration as archbishop.[70] Whether this was at the instigation of Cranmer or Henry, we do not know. Either way, Lord's protestation highlights the fact that the problem of the episcopal oath to the Pope was not going away. Unless Henry wanted his bishops-elect to continue making controversial protestations nullifying their oath of canonical obedience to the Pope, he needed to establish a more lasting precedent. He did this with the Act Restraining the Payment of Annates, which Parliament passed in March 1534. (Annates were the income paid to the Pope by a new bishop or prelate, generally equal to one year's revenue of the benefice.) In addition

---

[67] Foxe, *AM* (1583), 1876.

[68] [Harpsfield?], *Bishop Cranmer's Recantacyons*, 33–4.

[69] Cranmer, *Miscellaneous Writings and Letters*, 539. Also see [Harpsfield?], *Bishop Cranmer's Recanta-cyons*, 46.

[70] A copy of the notarial instrument of this protestation is preserved in the papers of Robert Beale, an Elizabethan lawyer and civil servant; BL Additional MS 48022, fols. 165^v–166^r. Sidon was an area of Phoenicia. After 1291, the bishopric, also known as the suffragan of Tyre, was titular. Lord obviously had no power in Sidon. For another independent source verifying that Lord was indeed consecrated as bishop of Sidon during this time, see Eubel et al., *Hierarchia catholica medii aevi*, III:299.

to forbidding the payment of annates absolutely (a conditional restraint had been in effect for a year), this act outlined a new procedure for the election and consecration of English bishops. No one was to procure any papal bulls for his consecration, the chapter and dean or prior and convent had to elect a bishop of the king's choosing, and the bishop-elect was to make 'a corporall othe to the Kynges Hyghnes *and to none other*'.[71] No longer did English bishops have to swear before almighty God oaths of loyalty to two different powers, powers that had the potential to conflict. They no longer had to choose which oath to break. Henry had solved the problem that had worried him since he had read the *Collectanea*. Or had he? The Act Restraining the Payment of Annates concerned only future bishops. What about all of Henry's current bishops who were sworn to the Pope? How was he to guarantee their loyalty? And what about the rest of his clergy? Were any of them bound by a corporal oath to some power or authority prejudicial to royal will?

THE PROFESSIONS OF 1534 TO 1536 AS A RESPONSE TO PREVIOUS OATHS

The professions of 1534 through 1536 were Henry's final response to the problem of having subjects who had sworn oaths of loyalty to a foreign power. This is most apparent when we examine the content of professions administered exclusively to Henry's bishops. The first episcopal oath of 1534 was the new oath to the king that a bishop-elect took upon his consecration (oath B v). Even though the Act Restraining the Payment of Annates abolished the oath of canonical obedience to the Pope previous bishops had sworn upon their consecration, oath B v was still clearly designed as a response to the bishops' oath of canonical obedience to the Pope. Oath B v was almost twice the size of the old episcopal oaths to the king. In this new oath, the bishop-elect claimed to take both his temporal and spiritual profits of his bishopric 'all onlye of your maiestie and of your heyres kynges of this Realme *and of none other*'. The bishop-elect acknowledged Henry 'ymiediatly vnder almyghtye god to be chyef and supreme hedd of the churche of England', and swore to sustain his preeminence, prerogatives, and imperial jurisdiction 'afore and ayenst all manner of persons powers and authorities whatsoeuer they be'. Most revealingly, the bishop-elect promised never to 'accepte any othe or make any promyse pacte or covenante secreatlye or apertly by any manner of [means] or by any color

---

[71] *Statutes of the Realm*, 25 Hen. 8, c. 20, III:463–4 (quote from 464). My italics.

of pretence to the contrarye of this myne othe or any parte therof'. Finally, the bishop-elect promised to observe and defend the statutes of the realm made against the Pope and made for the surety of Henry's succession. The goal of oath B v was thus to articulate that the bishop-elect owed loyalty solely to the king and not to the Pope. To make this loyalty more secure, it expressly forbade any future oath that contradicted this present oath.[72]

The second episcopal oath of 1534 was the 'profession of the bishops to renounce the Pope and his bulls'. The profession was aimed at Henry's established bishops, and thus it was even stronger in its opposition to the episcopal oath of canonical obedience to the Pope than oath B v. In this profession, the bishop confessed that 'against God and his order which wants all men to be subject to their princes', he had wronged his king by taking an oath to the Pope and swearing 'to be faithful' to him, 'to defend the papacy against all men, your majesty not excepted', and 'to observe his commands, ordinances, decrees, and provisions'. The bishop then admitted that this oath was 'unlawful' and 'unjust'. He declared that this oath was 'broken', 'void', and 'not to be observed', and humbly sought pardon from the king for the offence of swearing to the Pope. After reiterating that the Pope had no power or jurisdiction in England, the bishop renounced his papal bulls and promised to hand over to the king all papal bulls in his possession. More than any other profession of 1534 through 1536, this profession reveals the level of the king's concern over the episcopal oath of canonical obedience to the Pope.[73]

Although Henry's bishops may or may not have taken the 'profession of the bishops to renounce the Pope and his bulls',[74] all of Henry's bishops did unquestionably make a profession to his supremacy in February and March 1535. This profession also contained clauses formulated in response to the oath of canonical obedience to the Pope. In the second clause of this profession, the bishop pledged never to promise or give any fidelity or obedience, 'simply or under oath', to any external power, including the Pope. The profession then lifted a few clauses from the episcopal oath of canonical obedience to the Pope and either caused the bishop to promise the opposite or applied the clauses to the king. For example, the bishop promised 'to defend against all men' the king and his successors. Likewise, the bishop pledged to reveal to the king all papal counsel delivered to him by papal nuncios or letters. These clauses were direct negations of clauses from the episcopal oath to the Pope. After some standard clauses

[72] NA SP1/83, fol. 54[r] (*LP*, VII 427). My italics. For the full text of this oath, see Appendix B, v.
[73] NA SP6/3, fols. 63[r]–64[r]. For the text of this profession in its entirety, see Appendix C.
[74] For a discussion of evidence for its tendering, see Chapter 2.

renouncing papal authority and acknowledging Henry's supremacy, the bishop closed his profession by promising never to seek 'a dispensation, exception, or remedy of law or deed against this my foresaid profession and promise'. Finally, he declared that 'if I made any protestation in prejudice to this my profession and promise, I revoke it now and for all times to come'. In sum, the episcopal profession of supremacy of 1535 negated specific clauses from the oath to the Pope, rejected previous declarations in support of the Pope, and promised neither to make an oath of loyalty to the Pope in the future nor seek any papal dispensation from this current profession.[75]

It is thus apparent why Henry administered so many professions to his bishops between 1533 and 1536. He was worried that their previous oaths to the Pope made them disloyal subjects unwilling to reject papal authority or recognize royal supremacy. This is why all the professions designed exclusively for the bishops responded directly to the episcopal oath of canonical obedience to the Pope. This was also why Henry's bishops were included in the professions not designed exclusively for them, professions such as the oath of succession, the institutional profession, and the declaration that the Pope had no more authority in England than any other foreign bishop. Because they had sworn allegiance to the very person whom Henry opposed, Henry could not be too careful in securing their loyalty. It was best that they be tested and bound multiple times.

If the episcopal oaths of canonical obedience to the Pope explain why Henry placed his bishops at the very centre of his campaign to enforce his Reformation through subscriptions and oaths, how do we explain why Henry bound his institutional clergy with stronger professions (both in form and content) than he did his secular, parish clergy? Less evidence on the origin of these professions survives. It is likely that Henry targeted specific institutions like the universities or Syon Abbey because of their history of opposition to his annulment and their potential for future resistance as centres of influence. Yet the most convincing explanation of the discrepancy between the professions of the institutional and secular clergy is again the likelihood that institutional clergy had sworn an oath prejudicial to Henry's full supremacy.

First, friars and monks had professed allegiance to a foreign authority. Abbots and priors, like bishops, often took an oath of canonical obedience to the Pope directly. The 1534 Act for the Exoneration from Exactions Paid to the See of Rome accordingly forbade abbots and priors from making an

---

[75] For the text of this profession, see Appendix F, 1.

oath to the Pope.[76] The regular friars and monks did not make a specific oath to the Pope, and this probably explains why there is nothing in the text of the professions of the institutions and the friars explicitly in response to an oath to the Pope. Regular friars and monks did, however, vow obedience to their prior or abbot and to their monastic rule. This vow also could conflict with obedience to the king. Recall that Cromwell demanded that Houghton, Laurence, and Webster reject 'obediences to whatever person or *order* they had owed or promised'. Moreover, some monks used their vow of obedience to justify resistance. The convent of Observant Friars at Greenwich refused to take their oath because they believed the clause about the bishop of Rome having no greater authority in England than any other foreign bishop 'was clerely agaynst their professyon and the rules of sayncte Frauncis'.[77] The Cordelier Franciscans of Guernsey used a similar excuse, 'saying howe that they had heretofore made an Othe, whiche othe they wold not change, but rather forsake the Convent and Countrey than to make any outher'.[78] Henry and Cromwell were certainly aware of the potential node of resistance in monastic vows of obedience. One of Cromwell's injunctions for the visitation of the monasteries in 1535 read:

Also, that the abbot, prior, or president, and brethren may be declared by the king's supreme power and authority ecclesiastical to be absolved and loosed from all manner of obedience, oath, and profession by them heretofore (perchance) promised or made to the said bishop of Rome, or to any other in his stead, or occupying his authority, or to any other foreign prince, or person; and nevertheless let it be enjoyned to them, that they shall not promise or give such oath or profession to any such foreign potentate hereafter; and if the statute of the said order religious, or place, seem to bind them to obedience or subjection, or any other recognizance of superiority to the said bishop of Rome, or to any other foreign power, potentate, person, or place, by any ways, such statutes by the king's grace's visitors be utterly annihilate, broken, and declared void and of none effect, and that they be in no case bounden or obligate to the same; and such statutes to be forthwith utterly put forth and abolished out of the books or muniments of that religion, order, or place by the president and his brethren.[79]

---

[76] *Statutes of the Realm*, 25 Hen. 8, c. 21, III:470.

[77] The article from the rule of St Francis that the Greenwich Franciscans cited was as follows: 'Ad hec per obedientiam injungo ministris ut petant a domino papa unum de sancte Romane ecclesie cardinalibus, qui sit gubernator, protector, et corrector istius fraternitatis, ut semper subditi et subjecti pedibus sancte ecclesie ejusdem stabiles in fide catholica paupertatem et humilitatem, et secundum Evangelium Domini nostri Jesu Christi, quod firmiter promisimus observemus'; Wright (ed.), *Three Chapters*, 41–2 (*LP*, VII 841).

[78] Ellis (ed.), *Original Letters*, ser. 2, II:92.

[79] Wilkins (ed.), *Concilia*, III:790; Burnet, *History of the Reformation*, IV:217–18.

In Henry's proclamation of 9 June 1535 enforcing the statutes for abolishing papal authority, he claimed that '*both* the bishops and clergy of this our realm' had renounced papal authority, 'utterly renouncing all other oaths and obedience to any foreign potentate'.[80] Thus, bishops were not the only ones who had made a profession that conflicted with loyalty to Henry.

The institutions that Henry targeted most were the Universities of Oxford and Cambridge. In 1530, the universities had resisted acknowledging that it was against divine law to marry the widow of one's brother, and this probably made Henry suspicious of their loyalty. But also important was the fact that universities were places where oaths had been sworn. The inhabitants of most colleges had to take an oath to follow the statutes of their college.[81] These statutes undoubtedly made references to obedience to the Roman Church and to the Pope. In 1531, after the trial of Nicholas Shaxton, the Vice-Chancellor of the University of Cambridge imposed an oath to renounce a long list of heretical 'errors' on all those taking degrees in divinity from the university.[82] The fact that the oath was abolished within a year indicates its controversial nature. Other oaths were occasionally tendered there as well. Writing from exile, Richard Marshall excused his refusal to preach Henry's supremacy on grounds that it was against Scripture and the doctrine of the church as revealed in the Decretals, 'which I was sworn openly in the University of Oxford to declare and stick unto'.[83] As influential and obstinate institutions where many potentially subversive oaths had been sworn, the universities were places that merited special attention.

The issue of whether an individual had sworn an oath that could conflict with royal authority also explains why Henry made some of his secular clergy take the institutional profession while others, his parish priests, only had to sign an oathless statement against the power of the Pope. Members of secular institutions like cathedrals, colleges, or hospitals usually made an oath to follow the customs and statutes of their institution.[84] Again, the customs and statutes to which these secular priests were sworn may have contained material offensive to Henry. In fact, Henry was so concerned about these statutes that in 1532 he demanded that his clergy submit all of them to a select committee for review and accept the

---

[80] Hughes and Larkin (eds.), *Tudor Royal Proclamations*, 1:230. My italics.
[81] Mullinger, *University of Cambridge*, 1:455.
[82] Porter, *Reformation and Reaction*, 61.   [83] *LP*, x 594.
[84] Any cursory glance at the list of institutions preserved in late medieval and early modern episcopal registers will demonstrate the prevalence of this oath among priests serving at a secular institution. For examples of the forms of these oaths, see Bodleian Library, Rawlinson MS B 167, fols. 110^r–13^r.

abrogation of any of the statutes the committee found in derogation of his royal prerogative.[85] And if these institutional secular priests were sworn to observe a statute prejudicial to royal authority, Henry needed another oath to override the obligations of the previous oath and to ensure that his clergy remained loyal to him. By contrast, secular parish priests typically took no oaths to observe a set of statutes. The only oath they swore upon their institution was an oath of canonical obedience to their bishop. So once Henry gained the obedience of his bishops, the secular parish clergy also owed their allegiance to him through their oath to the bishops. No oath nullifying a previous promise was needed. Conversely, all the orders of friars and some of the monastic orders were outside of episcopal jurisdiction; their superiors resided in Rome. They were exempt from episcopal oversight, which also explains Henry's heightened concern over them.[86]

The only part of the implementation of Henry's Reformation that does not initially fit into the problem of previous oaths is the oath of succession. The oath of succession was administered to all adult males, most of whom had not sworn any oath prejudicial to royal authority. But this may explain why the oath of succession was a weaker profession in content. The main purpose of the oath of succession was, as the text of the oath indicates, to swear allegiance to Henry and his offspring through Anne. It was essentially an enhanced oath of fidelity, and there actually was precedent for the tendering of an oath of fidelity to every adult male in England. The most recent precedent was the oath of allegiance Henry VIII forced all inhabitants of Tournai to swear when he conquered that region in 1513.[87] Yet another oath was even more widespread in late medieval England. According to an Elizabethan manuscript on the court leet (a periodical manorial court), in medieval England 'it was ordeyned that every person of the age of xii yeres and haue beene resident in a place a yeare & a day shalbe sworne to be true and faythfull to the prince and also that the people might be kept in obedience'.[88] As David Martin Jones has observed, this was part of the normal business of the courts leet and tourn (a twice-yearly hundred court under the jurisdiction of a county sheriff).[89] Writing in the early seventeenth century, Sir Edward Coke agreed, adding that these

---

[85] Bray (ed.), *Records of Convocation*, VIII:184–5; Lehmberg, *Reformation Parliament*, 149–50; Kelly, 'Submission of the Clergy', 112–13; Wilkins (ed.), *Concilia*, III:749.

[86] Knowles, *Religious Orders*, III:177.

[87] Mayer, 'On the Road to 1534', 14–15; Cruickshank, *English Occupation of Tournai*, 40. For a draft of this oath, see NA SP1/230, fols. 60ʳ–62ᵛ (*LP*, I (ii) 2319).

[88] CUL MS. GG. VI. 1, fol. 150ʳ.   [89] Jones, *Conscience and Allegiance*, 17.

courts continued to tender this oath in his time. Coke then provided the
text of the oath, which he claimed to take from the works of Bracton and
Britton:

You shall swear, that from this day forward, you shall be true and faithfull to our
Soveregn Lord King _____, and his heires, and truth and faith shall bear of
life and member, and terrene honour, and you shall neither know nor hear of any
ill or damage intended unto him, that you shall not defend. So help you Almighty
God.[90]

Clauses one, two, and seven of the oath of succession seem to be expanded
versions of this oath. Of course, the tendering of this oath in the courts
leet and tourn was a regular affair whereupon each resident of an area was
probably called upon to swear this oath only once or twice in his life, either
when he turned twelve or moved into a new area. Thus, the procedure was
different from the large-scale administrative effort of the oath of succession
to mobilize the entire realm to swear at the same time. Yet the fact that
the entire adult male populace of England had in theory already sworn
fealty to Henry and his heirs remains significant. In this light, the oath of
succession was simply an effort to update the traditional oath of fidelity by
specifying to which heirs Henry's subjects owed loyalty.

Nevertheless, the oath of succession was still designed in part to nullify
previous oaths conflicting with royal authority. The background here is
Henry's struggle with Katherine of Aragon's household in 1533. On 5 July
1533, Henry issued a royal proclamation declaring that his first marriage
had been annulled and that, as a result, Katherine no longer possessed the
title of queen. Anyone who continued to call Katherine queen instead of
the new style 'princess dowager' would be guilty of *praemunire* and suffer
the penalties of imprisonment and loss of lands and goods.[91] This royal
proclamation was met with considerable opposition by Katherine's long-
time servants, for according to Lord Mountjoy, 'they coulde not see howe
the Kynges grace coulde discherge their conscyences to calle her Pryncesse,
they beyng sworne to her as Quene'.[92] By December Henry had decided
to respond to this situation by making Katherine's servants swear a 'newe
oathe' of loyalty to Katherine as princess dowager, replacing the oath to her
as queen. In response, Katherine's servants again argued that they 'myght

---

[90] Coke, *Reports*, 589; Jones, *Conscience and Allegiance*, 269.
[91] Hughes and Larkin (eds.), *Tudor Royal Proclamations*, 1:209–211.
[92] NA SP1/79, fol. 158ʳ (*LP*, VI 1252), *State Papers, Published under the Authority of His Majesty's Commission*, 1:408. Also see BL Cotton MS Otho C X, fol. 213 (*LP*, VI 1253).

not be sworn . . . consydering there first othe made to her as queane, they myght not take the second othe without perjury'.[93]

Eventually, all of Katherine's servants, other than those from Spain, took this new oath, but Henry had learned his lesson. Just in case any other person tried to cite a previous oath as grounds for resisting the Boleyn marriage and succession, the oath of succession explicitly stated that each person give obedience or faith 'not to any other within this Realm [such as Queen Katherine?], nor foreign Authority, Prince, or Potentate; and in case any Oath be made, or hath been made by you to any other Person or Persons, that then you to repute the same as vain and annihilate'.[94] These clauses were significant enough to be replicated without change in all subsequent Henrician oaths of succession, excluding the oath preserved on the leaves of a manuscript Gospel.[95] Even though the majority of Henry's subjects had not sworn an oath to a foreign authority, he wanted to make sure that if they had, their oath would be invalidated by the oath of succession.

The chief problem with interpreting the oath of succession primarily as an updated oath of fealty (with a few clauses thrown in nullifying any previous oaths to a foreign authority) is that this interpretation tends to separate the oath of succession from the clerical professions of 1534 and 1535, whose purpose was to reject papal authority, confirm royal supremacy, and bind the consciences of particular groups of clergy who had a record of having taken oaths conflicting with royal authority. Although the conservative text of the oath of succession seems to warrant such a separation, the events of the 1530s warn us against making so simple a dichotomy. Henry's divorce and remarriage to Anne were intricately connected to his rejection of papal authority. The clerical professions with clauses on both the succession and the supremacy illustrate this connection. Moreover, the oath of succession was being tendered throughout the realm at the same time as the professions against papal jurisdiction and the acknowledgements of royal supremacy. Hence, Geoffrey Elton wrote that the purpose of the oath of succession was to gain the country's adherence 'not so much of the legitimacy of the issue to be expected from the Boleyn marriage, but rather of the major policy which that marriage symbolized – the political revolution and religious schism'.[96] Bernard agreed, arguing that the oath

---

[93] BL Cotton MS Otho C x, fols. 210[r]–212[r] (*LP*, VI 1541). This letter is an original but it is mutilated. A complete copy of the letter is BL Harleian MS 283, fol. 102[r–v], and the letter has been transcribed in *State Papers, Published under the Authority of His Majesty's Commission*, 1:415–17.
[94] *Journal of the House of Lords*, 1:82.   [95] See Appendix D.   [96] Elton, *Policy and Police*, 226.

of succession was made '*in effect*, in support of the break with Rome'.[97] If this is true, why did the text of the oath of succession not include explicit references to papal jurisdiction or royal supremacy? It may be that the regime designed the conservative text of the oath of succession to serve as a sweetener, a sugar coating that masked the bitterness of schism concealed at the core of the oath and made it easier to swallow. Or alternatively, perhaps the regime did not feel it necessary to mention papal jurisdiction or royal supremacy since the majority of the people to whom the oath of succession was tendered had not taken a previous oath that worried Henry, and they generally were not a threat to his new policies. All that he needed was to remind them of the loyalty they owed to their sovereign, a loyalty to which they were bound no matter what policies the sovereign pursued. Either way, the fact that Henry tendered the oath of succession at the same time as other professions rejecting papal authority and acknowledging royal supremacy does suggest that the Henrician regime's true aim with the outwardly mild oath of succession was to secure acquiescence to its Reformation.

To conclude, it might be helpful to place the arguments of this chapter in the general context of the historiography of the Henrician Reformation. There are two primary interpretations of the Henrician Reformation today. One interpretation, originating with John Foxe but more sophisticatedly articulated today by Eric Ives, champions the significance of faction in determining the policies of Henry VIII.[98] Ives and his supporters argue that while Henry was dominant, he was also vulnerable to the manipulation of various court factions.[99] Various factions, in turn, explain the nature of the Henrician Reformation, which (according to this view) was hesitant, oscillating, contradictory, and ineffectual.[100] A very different view is offered by G. W. Bernard. Bernard emphasizes a strong personal monarchy, asserting that faction played little role in the determination of Henrician policy. Henry himself was always in control; his servants were just that, servants.[101] Accordingly, Bernard interprets the Henrician Reformation as

---

[97] Bernard, 'Tyranny of Henry VIII', 119. My italics. Even stronger is C. S. L. Davies' assertion that the oath of succession 'committed the individual not merely to observe the law, but to positive approval of the entire legislation of the Reformation Parliament'; Davies, 'Cromwellian Decade', 185. Davies' comment is too extreme, for, as we shall see, many people did not believe the oath of succession bound them to approve the entire legislation of the Reformation Parliament.

[98] For the origin of the theory of faction in Foxe's *Acts and Monuments*, see Bernard, 'Making of Religious Policy', 321.

[99] Ives, 'Stress, Faction and Ideology', 196–7; Ives, 'Henry VIII', 29–33.

[100] An example of this view of the English Reformation is Haigh, *English Reformations*.

[101] Bernard, *Power and Politics*, 7–10.

being a consistent and unified movement of which the king was the princi-pal architect.[102] The general thrust of this chapter has tended to support the interpretation of Bernard over Ives. Despite the great variety of professions of the Henrician Reformation, a single, unifying rationale underlay them all. The oaths of 1534 and 1535 were designed to invalidate previous bonds of loyalty to a foreign authority and rebind the consciences of English subjects to Henry and his policies. The variations in number, form, and strength of these professions were directly related to the probability that certain subject groups had previously sworn an oath prejudicial to Henry's full supremacy over the church. Furthermore, the principal force behind this policy was Henry himself. Through the *Collectanea*, Henry had full knowledge of the contradictory nature of the oaths of a bishop-elect. It was Henry who brought these oaths to the attention of Parliament, demanding that they invent some order between them. Foxe's story about Cromwell's role in this episode is probably fabricated. Henry was also the person who accepted responsibility for Cranmer taking his oath of canonical obedience with a protestation. This does not mean, however, that councillors like Cromwell, Audley, and Cranmer were not important. As should be clear from the last chapter, they were the ones who directed the actual adminis-tration of the professions of supremacy to the various subject groups of the English populace. Echoing the words of David Loades, Henry decided 'the direction of policy', but councillors like Cromwell were often in charge of finding the 'ways and means' of implementing this policy.[103] The essential point is that there was no discrepancy between the ways and means used to implement policy, that is, the various oaths and subscriptions of the Henrician Reformation, and the policy objectives set by Henry himself.

One objection to this interpretation is that the scope of these two chap-ters has been too limited. First, the temporal focus of this analysis has largely been limited to the first half of the 1530s, a time when Cromwell and Cran-mer were Henry's most influential councillors. Would our interpretation of the Henrician Reformation change if we took a longer view of Henry's reign? It is important to note here that neither the fall of Cromwell nor the conservative reaction of the Six Articles revoked, altered, or challenged the professions of 1534 to 1536. Indeed, the oath established by Parliament in 1544 was totally consistent with the professions of the 1530s. A second, more trenchant objection is that the subject of these two chapters is too limited.

---

[102] For this argument in short form, see Bernard, 'Making of Religious Policy'. For the full articulation of this argument, see Bernard, *King's Reformation*. Bernard's view has recently been popularized in Lucy Wooding's new biography *Henry VIII*.

[103] Loades, *Henry VIII*, 122.

It is indeed true that an analysis of oaths and subscriptions as a means of implementing the reforms of 1534 sheds no real light on the formulations of faith, the dissolution of the monasteries, the end of pilgrimages, the Six Articles, and the acceptance and then restriction of vernacular Scripture – all of which were significant components of the Henrician Reformation. None of these policies were accompanied by professions, and outside the issue of papal authority and royal supremacy, none of the professions in circulation in the 1530s dealt with matters of faith. While this fact does allow the possibility that faction may have played a greater role in the development of these policies, it also supports Richard Rex's argument that the Henrician Reformation was unified and consistent in that its core was always the doctrine of obedience.[104] Henry's greatest concern was the issue of loyalty and allegiance, and his concern with it explains why it was the core theme of all the professions of the 1530s. The other changes of the Henrician Reformation were not as central a concern to Henry, which explains why they were not enforced with oaths. The crux of the Henri-cian Reformation was royal supremacy, and oaths were the primary means through which royal supremacy was implemented.

[104] Rex, 'Crisis of Obedience'.

CHAPTER 4

Responses to the oaths of succession and supremacy

Having used oaths to explore the implementation of the Henrician Reformation (both how it was accomplished and why), it is now time to turn
to the English people's response to that same Reformation. Accordingly,
this chapter asks three questions. First, who took the Henrician oaths of
succession and supremacy, and who refused to take them? Second, why did
individuals choose or refuse to take the Henrician oaths? This question is
particularly important for the oath of succession, for answering it will help
us understand if the English people really did perceive it as rejecting papal
jurisdiction and establishing royal supremacy. Third, for those individuals
who took the oaths, how did they take them?

The more basic question that underlies each of these three specific questions is: What did the English people think of the Henrician Reformation?
This question has a long historiographical pedigree, but it has yet to be
approached through the lens of oaths.[1] Oaths are an especially rich source
of popular perception of the Henrician Reformation because oaths were
also the chief means through which people participated in the Henrician
Reformation. All adult males were given a chance to swear the oath of
succession. At first glance, this might seem like a relatively limited form of
participation. In the eyes of the Henrician regime, the only choice individuals had was whether to swear or refuse the oath. And while choosing
to refuse the oath of succession or supremacy was a particularly active
form of opposition to the Reformation, the decision to swear these oaths
does not necessarily suggest that an individual actively approved of the
Henrician Reformation of 1534. The enthusiastic and the apathetic chose
this option, for it was the path of least resistance, the only way to avoid
the risk of arousing the wrath of the king. Yet not everyone was content
to participate according to these two models. Some chose to swear these

[1] See for example, Scarisbrick, *Reformation and the English People*; Marsh, *Popular Religion*; Shagan,
Popular Politics and the English Reformation.

116

oaths, but they did so on their own terms in ways that did not imply full acceptance of the policies of the Henrician regime. The question of how the English people took their oaths is thus significant not only because it reveals what the people thought of the Henrician Reformation of 1534, but also because it demonstrates the extent to which the English populace actively participated in the Henrician Reformation.

WHO SWORE AND WHY SOME PEOPLE REFUSED TO SWEAR

The overwhelming majority of Englishmen took the oath of succession. For example, John Johnson (alias Antony) reported that 'the moest part or all Kent have taken ther oth acordyng to the kynges commyssyon', saving two Observant friars (Fathers Mychelson and Gam), the vicar of Sittingborne, and his chantry priest.[2] Johnson's comment for Kent is representative of the rest of the realm. Only a handful of Englishmen refused to swear. This is the most striking feature of the response to the oath of succession.

Of more importance than the decision to take or refuse the oath of succession is the question of why people decided to accept or decline the oath. The oath of succession was after all ambiguous. In content the oath of succession was simply a traditional oath of fealty with additional clauses accepting the Boleyn succession and rejecting previous oaths made to anyone who was not king of England. It did not explicitly mention papal authority or royal supremacy. Did most Englishmen swear the oath of succession because they did not perceive it as particularly radical? This seems to have been the reason behind the eventual decision of Houghton and Middlemore (the prior and procurator of the London Charterhouse) to take the oath, for they became convinced 'that no matter of faith was involved and that there was no sufficient occasion for incurring death'.[3] Unfortunately, our information on the London Charterhouse is exceptional; the overwhelming majority of sources on the oath of succession are silent on the rationale underlying the decision to swear this oath. To determine why most Englishmen swore the oath of succession, we will have to rely on inferences derived from the Pilgrimage of Grace (discussed in the next chapter). Yet we can also approach this issue from the opposite side, exploring why the handful of individuals who refused to swear the oath of succession did so. If it can be shown that these individuals rejected the oath because they believed in papal supremacy, then we can reasonably assume that at least some individuals realized that the oath of succession was an

---

[2] NA sp1/88, fol. 146ʳ (*LP*, vii App. 27).   [3] Chauncy, *Passion and Martyrdom* (1570), 61.

effort to enforce Henry's jurisdictional revolution. The motivation behind the refusal to swear the oath of succession is thus crucial to understanding the oath itself.

Of course, it impossible to know the motivation of every person who refused to swear the oath of succession. For example, it is not clear why Dr Nicholas Wilson (Henry's one-time confessor), James Holywell (a scrivener), or Thomas Leighton and Jeffray Hodeshon (two monks of the Mountgrace Charterhouse) initially refused to swear to the succession.[4] Yet we can reconstruct the motives of a few high-profile nonjurors. It is apparent that some of the people who declined to swear the oath of succession did so because they believed that Henry's marriage to Katherine of Aragon was valid. Katherine and her daughter Mary obviously refused the oath for this reason. Katherine had no desire to declare her marriage to Henry illegitimate. Mary did not want to proclaim herself a bastard. We can safely deduce that those associated with these two women – Katherine's Spanish servants, Richard Barker (a priest in Lincoln who was a protégé of Katherine), Mary's maid Anne Husee, and Mary's long-time schoolmaster Richard Featherstone – refused the oath in defense of Katherine and Mary.[5] The king's rejection of his marriage to Katherine was also the sticking point in the London Charterhouse's initial rejection of the oath of succession. Prior Houghton told the commissioners that he did not know how Henry's long-standing marriage to Katherine, which was approved by canon law, could be declared invalid. One Gervase Shelby cited a similar excuse for his refusal to swear the oath:

That his Conscience grevid hym sore to take the oethe . . . Sainge that his grace hath broken the Sacrament of matrimonie, also sainge when his grace went ouer the Sees, that he went to Rome vnto the Pope to haue his fauoure to marie with oure Soueraigne ladie quen Anne, & the Pope wolde gyue hym no licence, nere his councell, Wherfor me thynkith it apittiefull case to be sworne &c[6]

Thus, although we cannot be sure of all the reasons why those who refused the oath of succession made their stand, Henry's renunciation of his marriage to Katherine comes forth as one prominent motive.

[4] For information on the refusal of the oath of succession by Wilson, see Hall, *Hall's Chronicle*, 815; *Statutes of the Realm*, 26 Hen. 8, c. 22, III:527. For Holywell, see NA SP1/92, fol. 171ᵛ (*LP*, VIII 763). For Leighton and Hodeshon, see NA SP1/85, fol. 20ʳ (*LP*, VII 932).

[5] For information on the refusal of the oath of succession by Katherine's Spanish servants, see *LP*, VII 690, 696, 726, 786, 809. For Richard Barker, see Bowker, *Henrician Reformation*, 138. For Husee, see *LP*, VII 530, 662, 1036. For Featherstone, see *Statutes of the Realm*, 26 Hen. 8, c. 22, III:527; Bernard, *King's Reformation*, 574–5.

[6] NA SP1/76, fol. 200ʳ (*LP*, VI 634 – incorrectly placed in 1533 by *LP*). Also see Elton, *Policy and Police*, 279–80.

Disapproval of Henry's divorce was also one of the reasons why Henry's two greatest opponents, Bishop John Fisher and Sir Thomas More, refused to take the oath of succession, though the cases of Fisher and More are complicated by many other possible explanations. What is clear is that the altered succession alone did not offend the consciences of Fisher and More. In a letter to Thomas Cromwell recounting his refusal of the oath, Fisher averred that any prince could with the consent of his commons appoint any successor he wanted. Accordingly, Fisher recounted: 'I was content to be sworn unto that part of the othe ass concernyng the succession. This is a veray trowth, ass God help my sowl att my most neede. All be itt I refused to swear to sum other parcels, bycause that my conscience wold not serve me so to doo.'[7] The author of 'The Life of Fisher', one of our key sources for the events of the early 1530s, confirmed that Fisher was prepared to swear 'some part therof' but not the oath of succession in its entirety unless he could 'frame yt with other condicions and in other sort then it now standeth'.[8] In a letter to his daughter Margaret Roper on 17 April 1534, Thomas More expressed a similar sentiment:

But as for myself in good faith my conscience so moued me in the matter, that though I wolde not denie to swere to the succession, yet vnto the othe that there was offred me I coulde not sware, without the iubardinge of my soule to perpetuall dampnacion . . .

Surely as to swere to the succession I see no perill, but I thought and thinke it reason, that to mine owne othe I loke well my self, and be of counsaile also in the fashion, and neuer entended to swere for a pece, and set my hande to the whole othe.[9]

Clearly, there was something else in the oath of succession besides the succession itself that offended More and Fisher.

But what was it in the oath that so upset More's and Fisher's consciences? William Rastall, a nephew of Thomas More who was also a lawyer, reported that More and Fisher were wrongfully imprisoned 'bycause the othe contaigned more thinges then were warranted by the acte of succession'.[10] According to William Roper, More's son-in-law, More himself wrote that he was committed to the Tower 'for refusing of this oath not agreeable

[7] BL Cotton MS Cleopatra E VI, fol. 172 (*LP*, VII 1563). This letter is printed in Strype, *Cranmer*, II:691–2 and in Bruce, 'Observations on the Circumstances which Occasioned the Death of Fisher', 93–4.
[8] Ortroy (ed.), 'Vie du bienheureux martyr Jean Fisher', 12 (1893): 136.
[9] More, *Correspondence*, 502, 507.
[10] Ortroy (ed), 'Vie du bienheureux martyr Jean Fisher', 12 (1893): 253.

to the statute'.[11] Of course, our main problem here is that the first Act of
Succession did not stipulate the exact form of the oath. Since we do not
know what form of the oath of succession More and Fisher were tendered,
we are unable to make a definitive judgement on what part of the oath
went beyond the act and offended More and Fisher. It is possible and even
likely that More and Fisher were tendered the same form of the oath as
taken in the House of Lords on 31 March or the form of the oath attached
to the Commissioners in Sussex dated on 20 April.[12] The section of these
two oaths that most clearly departs from the Act of Succession is the now
familiar rejection of any previous oath to the Pope or to any other foreign
body. Fisher certainly might have had qualms about this section of the oath
of succession considering his episcopal oath of canonical obedience to the
Pope, but why would More, a layman, have troubled his conscience over
an oath to the Pope that he had almost certainly never sworn?

In answer to this question, Stanford Lehmberg has proposed that in the
oath of succession, the person swore not only to repudiate previous oaths
sworn to the pope or any other foreign authority but also to 'renounce the
power of any "foreign authority or potentate"'.[13] The equivocal wording of
the oath of succession makes Lehmberg's claim hard to substantiate. The
oath reads:

Ye shall swear to bear your Faith, Truth, and Obedience, alonely to the King's
Majesty, and to the Heirs of his Body, according to the Limitation and Rehearsal
within this Statute of Succession above specified, and not to any other within this
Realm, nor foreign Authority, Prince, or Potentate; and in case any Oath be made,
or hath been made, by you, to any other Person or Persons, that then you to repute
the same as vain and annihilate.[14]

The syntax of the oath makes it ambiguous whether one is to *swear* 'not
to any other . . .' or whether one is to swear *to bear obedience* 'not to any
other . . .'. If the clause starting with 'not to any other' is modifying the verb
'to swear', then the person taking the oath is renouncing only a previous
oath to the Pope. If this clause is modifying the verb 'to bear', then the
person taking the oath is renouncing all obedience to the Pope. The rest
of the oath of succession seems to suggest (in opposition to Lehmberg)
that the former interpretation is correct. The clause preceding 'not to any
other' – 'according to the Limitation and Rehearsal within this Statute of
Succession above specified' – is clearly modifying the verb 'to swear', and
the clause following 'not to any other' also refers to the swearing of an

---

[11] Roper, *Man of Singular Virtue*, 81.   [12] Both of these oaths are in Appendix D.
[13] Lehmberg, *Reformation Parliament*, 203.   [14] *Journal of the House of Lords*, 1:82.

oath to the Pope. In the end, however, it is impossible to make a definitive judgement on this. The language of the oath of succession (perhaps by design) is simply too opaque.

Geoffrey Elton observed that another section of the form of the oath of succession administered in the House of Lords that may have offended More and Fisher was the promise to observe 'all other Acts and Statutes made since the Beginning of this present Parliament, in Confirmation or for due Execution of the same [act of succession]'.[15] If More and Fisher interpreted this clause as binding their consciences to all Parliamentary statutes passed since 1529, there was much at which to take offence. For example, the act forbidding papal dispensations and the payment of Peter's Pence of March 1534 referred to Henry as the 'supreme hede of the Church of Englonde', recognizing 'noo superior under God but only your Grace', and it attacked the Pope for his 'usurpacion' and his 'abusyng', 'begylyng', 'pretendyng and perswadyng' the English people 'that he hath full power to dispence with all humayne lawes uses and customes of all Realmes'.[16] Yet Elton's point is mitigated by the fact that the text of the oath from the House of Lords did not simply bind the swearer to 'all other Acts and Statutes made since the Beginning of this present Parliament', but rather to 'all other Acts and Statutes made since the Beginning of this present Parliament, *in Confirmation or for due Execution of the same*'. This qualifying phrase made the oath less inclusive, for was the act against Peter's Pence really 'made in confirmation' of the Act of Succession? Hence, this qualifying phrase makes it less likely that More, a brilliant lawyer well aware of the power of a qualifying phrase, was offended by this section of the oath.

Cranmer provides us with another possible reason why More and Fisher rejected the oath of succession. Cranmer reminded Cromwell 'that my lord Rochester and master More were contented to be sworn to the Act of the king's succession, but not the preamble of the same'.[17] Cranmer then asked Cromwell if Henry would be satisfied to swear them simply to the act and not to the preamble. Elton dismissed this observation, arguing that since More claimed 'the oath went beyond the demands of the act' and 'the act plainly states that an oath to "its whole effects and contents" (which includes the preamble) was required', Cranmer had misunderstood More.[18] Yet Cranmer's letter contained another supposition.

---

[15] Elton, *Policy and Police*, 224. Philip Hughes has put forth a similar interpretation; Hughes, *Reformation in England*, 1:270, nt. 1.
[16] *Statutes of the Realm*, 25 Hen. 8, c. 21, III:464–5.
[17] Cranmer, *Miscellaneous Writings and Letters*, 285–6.   [18] Elton, *Policy and Police*, 223.

While Cranmer admitted he was ignorant of 'the cause of their refusal', he deduced 'it must needs be either the diminution of the authority of the bishop of Rome, or else the reprobation of the king's first pretensed matrimony'.[19] Again, Elton pointed out that the preamble to the oath of succession 'has nothing very anti-papal to say'.[20] This is certainly true, but we cannot so easily dismiss Cranmer's observation, especially since Cromwell wrote back to Cranmer that the king thought:

> that if their othe should be so taken [without the preamble] it were an occasion to all men to refuse the hole or at the lest the lyke, ffor in case they be sworn to the succession and not to the preamble it is to be thought that it might be taken not onelie as a confirmacion of the Bishop of Rome his auctoryte and but also as a reprobacion of the Kinges second mariage.[21]

Why could swearing to the succession without the preamble be taken as a confirmation of the Pope's authority if the preamble was not anti-papal?

One possible answer to this question is that More and Fisher may have been shown a version of the 'preamble' that contained text not in the 'preamble' of the actual statute. It is even possible that the 'preamble' shown to More and Fisher contained references to Henry's supremacy or the infamous clause 'the bishop of Rome had no greater authority in England than any other foreign bishop'. This clause was first raised at the end of March in Convocation. Henry asked his leading prelates to subscribe to it sometime in April or May, and he tendered it to all his secular clergy throughout the summer of 1534. Moreover, on 28 April Cranmer wrote that Mr Roodd 'hath subscribed the book of the king's grace's succession, and also the conclusion *"quod Romanus Episcopus non habet majorem auctoritatem a Deo sibi collatam in hoc regno Angliae quam quivis alius externus episcopus"*'.[22] Since the clergy of the realm were being tendered this clause simultaneously with the oath of succession, it is certainly in the realm of possibility that Fisher, a leading prelate, had this clause attached to his oath of succession. But More was a layman. Would this clause also have been added to his oath of succession? It is perhaps significant that the clergy of London were tendered the oath of succession on 13 April, a week before the rest of the city. The only layman tendered the oath on 13 April was none other than Thomas More, a point which Nicholas Harpsfield astutely emphasized in his *Life and Death of Sr Thomas Moore*.[23] Harpsfield

---

[19] Cranmer, *Miscellaneous Writings and Letters*, 286.   [20] Elton, *Policy and Police*, 223.
[21] NA SP1/83, fol. 88ʳ (*LP*, VII 500).   [22] Cranmer, *Miscellaneous Writings and Letters*, 287.
[23] Harpsfield, *Life and Death of Sr Thomas Moore*, 166. Harpsfield composed this work during the reign of Mary. For independent verification of More being tendered the oath before the rest of the laymen of London, see Chapuys' letter of April 16: *LP*, VII 490.

also contended that More was tendered an oath to the supremacy around this time:

> And albeit in the beginning they were resolued that with an othe, not to be acknowen whether he had to the Supremacie beene sworne, or what he thought thereof, he should be discharged, yet did Queene Anne by her importunate clamour so sore exasperate the king against him that, contrary to his former resolution, he caused the saide othe of the Supremacie to be ministred vnto him; who albeit he made a discrete qualified answere, neuertheless was forthwith committed to the towre.[24]

Harpsfield also referred to the Act of Succession as the 'Statute for the othe of the Supremacie and matrimonie,' which suggests he cannot be trusted completely.[25] Nevertheless, it remains possible that Fisher and More refused to take the oath of succession because their version of the oath or preamble of the act contained references either to Henry's supremacy or to the abrogation of papal authority.

Cranmer's other guess, that it was 'the reprobation of the king's first pretensed matrimony' that offended Fisher and More, has even more evidence in support of it. Although the oath of succession tendered in the House of Lords made no mention of Katherine or Anne, the preamble of the Act of Succession did 'diffyntyuly clerely and absolutely' declare and adjudge the king's first marriage 'to be agaynst the lawes of Almyghty God' and 'of noo value ne effecte, but utterlie voyde and adnychyled'.[26] Moreover, the oath of succession attached to the commission to Sussex, in contrast to the one taken in the House of Lords, did mention Henry's 'most dere & intyerly belouyd lawfull wyff quen anne'.[27] We know that both Fisher and More had problems reconciling their conscience to the argument that Henry's first marriage was against God's law. Roland Lee reported to Cromwell that Fisher was 'Redy to make hys othe for the Succession' and to swear never to meddle more in the validity of the king's first marriage, 'but as for the case of the prohibicion Leviticall, hys conscience is soe kyntt, that he cannot put it of[f] frome hym, what soo euer betyde hym'.[28] Moreover, in both of their trials, Fisher and More were asked whether they would:

> consent, approve, and affirme [the Kinges] Highnes mariage with the moste noble Quene Anne, [that now] is, to be good and laufull; and affirme, saye,

[24] Harpsfield, *Life and Death of Sr Thomas Moore*, 169.
[25] Harpsfield, *Life and Death of Sr Thomas Moore*, 166.
[26] *Statutes of the Realm*, 25 Hen. 8, c. 22, III:472.   [27] See Appendix D, II.
[28] BL Cotton MS Cleopatra E VI, fol. 165 (*LP*, VII 498), printed in Strype, *Cranmer*, II:692–3. This letter is placed in April 1534 by *LP*.

and pr[onounce] thother pretended mariage betwene the Kinges said High[nes and] my Lady Catherine, Princesse Dowager, was and is [unlawful], nought, and of no[none effect] or no?[29]

Fisher responded that he would obey all the parts of the act of succession 'saving allweys his conscience' and swear to them, 'Albe it to answer absolutely to this interrogatorie, ye or nae, he desireth to be pardoned'.[30] More simply avoided the question, replying 'that he did never speke nor medle ayenst the same, nor therunto make no aunswere'.[31] The fact that Fisher and More could not reconcile their consciences with admitting Henry's marriage to Katherine was 'unlawful' does not necessarily mean that this was what offended them in the oath or preamble to the Act of Succession, for again we do not know the exact form of the oath or preamble tendered to them. Nevertheless, it is the most likely option since the Boleyn succession was connected to the invalidity of Henry's first marriage even more intricately than it was connected to the abrogation of papal authority or rejection of oaths to the Pope.

Thus, Houghton, Shelby, Fisher, and More all rejected the oath of succession to some extent because of its implicit or explicit (depending on the form of the oath and one's knowledge of the preamble of the act) condemnation of Henry's marriage to Katherine. This condemnation of Henry's first marriage was still connected to papal authority, for it was the Pope who had granted a dispensation to Henry to marry his brother's widow Katherine. A rejection of Henry's marriage to Katherine as unlawful could thus be seen as a rejection of the papal power of dispensation. A rejection of Henry's marriage to Katherine also accepted that the Archbishop of Canterbury, rather than the Pope, had the authority to give Henry an annulment. In this sense, the oath of succession can be seen as denying 'papal authority in England' and supporting the 'wholesale renunciation in practice of papal authority'.[32] Shelby appears to have almost made this connection, since he cited the fact that the Pope had refused to give Henry a licence to annul his marriage with Katherine. Yet modern historians can make this judgement of the oath of succession because they know what happened after the spring of 1534. Hindsight highlights the connections between the rejection of Henry's marriage to Katherine and Henry's religious schism. This would not have been clear to the average English laymen in 1534. The various clerical professions that combined the oath

[29] *State Papers Published*, 1:432, 436 (*LP*, VIII 867).   [30] *State Papers Published*, 1:432.
[31] *State Papers Published*, 1:436 (*LP*, VIII 867 (iii)).
[32] Lehmberg, *Reformation Parliament*, 197; Knowles, *Religious Orders*, III:177.

of succession with the clauses on papal jurisdiction and royal supremacy would of course make this connection apparent to the clergy, but unless they were involved in tendering these professions to the clergy, the laity would have not had knowledge of this overlap. With the possible exception of Shelby, there is no hard evidence (simply suggestions with Fisher and More) that anyone tendered the oath of succession took it or refused it with the understanding that they were making a value judgement on papal authority and royal supremacy. Knowles was right in his observation: 'Ostensibly, however, and even plausibly to contemporaries, it [the oath of succession] was concerned solely with domestic issues, in particular the (to the lay mind) inextricably tangled question of the divorce, and the purely practical matter of the succession.'[33]

If very few members of the English populace refused the oath of succession, what was the response of the English clergy to their professions of 1534? After all, these professions explicitly rejected papal authority and acknowledged Henry's supremacy. Here, even more than with the oath of succession, we are faced with a paucity of evidence. To start, it is often impossible to tell what oath is being referred to in an offhand reference to an oath from the summer of 1534. For example, when Edward Lord Stourton wrote to Cromwell that in the Charterhouse near Bonham seven monks refused to take the 'othe' until their prior returned from pilgrimage, we do not know whether the oath in question was the oath of succession or the institutional profession, much less why these monks desired to wait for the return of their prior before swearing.[34] Our knowledge of Dr Richard Boorde is exceptional in that we can infer why he refused the oath, and from this can infer that he was probably referring to the institutional profession of 1534. Boorde declared that 'he wuld rather be toren with woeld horsses then to assent or consent to the dyminisshinge of any one iote of the bisshopp of Rome his aucthorite of old tyme . . . More ouer sayenge that if any Iurament & othe shuld be reqired of hym to the contrarie then to flee hys cowntre, and soo hathe he don'.[35] We also know that the Observant Franciscans were particularly hostile to the friars' profession of 1534. Judging from the responses of the brothers at Greenwich, the friars objected to the abrogation of papal authority and jurisdiction.[36] Much information survives on the friars because the Henrician regime harshly persecuted

[33] Knowles, *Religious Orders*, III:177.   [34] NA SP1/84, fol. 172[r] (*LP*, VII 834).
[35] NA SP1/99, fol. 198[r] (*LP*, IX 1066).
[36] Wright (ed.), *Three Chapters of Letters*, 41–3 (*LP*, VII 841). See as well NA SP1/83, pgs. 255–6 (*LP* VII 622); Knowles, *Religious Orders*, III:208–10; Bernard, *King's Reformation*, 156–60.

them for their obstinacy.[37] There are, however, very few references to the responses of the clergy to their professions of 1534. Particularly strange is the lack of information on other places where we would expect the institutional profession of 1534 to have engendered vocal opposition. For instance, there is no information extant from Syon Abbey from May 1534 to April 1535.[38] Likewise, Chauncy's detailed narration of the London Charterhouse skips right from the tendering of the oath of succession in May 1534 to the spring of 1535. Although well over one hundred institutional professions survive from the summer and autumn of 1534, we do not have a profession from Syon, the London Charterhouse, or the Mountgrace Charterhouse.

One possibility is that the king simply decided not to administer the institutional profession to the houses where he knew he would encounter resistance. This possibility is unlikely, for there is external evidence not in Chauncy that the London Charterhouse was tendered the institutional profession. An incomplete table in the British Library contains a list of various clerical institutions with a number following each institution. By comparing the numbers listed after the institution in this document with the surviving profession of that institution, it is clear that the list refers to the number of clergymen who signed the institutional profession at their respective college, hospital, or monastery. (The numbers match up.) In this document, under the heading 'London dioc.' the table reads, 'Nine Carthusians contumaciously refused to take the oath.'[39] As such, it seems that the London Charterhouse was tendered the institutional profession of 1534, but we do not know how they responded except that nine of them declined to take it.

Although this paucity of evidence prevents us from drawing any firm conclusions about the response to the clerical professions of 1534, this same lack of evidence implies that the Henrician regime was not especially harsh in punishing those who refused the clerical professions of 1534. With the exception of Fisher and the houses of Franciscan Observants, the Henrician regime did not come down hard on clerical opposition in the

---

[37] *LP*, VII 856; *LP*, VII 1057; *LP*, VII 1095; NA E36/153, 2–3 (*LP*, VII 1607).

[38] Knowles, *Religious Orders*, III:216. *LP* places multiple letters on Syon in 1534 (such as *LP*, VII 1090), but these are incorrectly dated by *LP*.

[39] BL Cotton MS Cleopatra E VI, fol. 209ᵛ (*LP*, VII 891 (ii)). See also an undated letter from Peter Wattes to Cromwell in which Watts claimed that the monks of the London Charterhouse 'iuged it extreme heresie to swere vnto the maynteynyng of the kynges gracious & helthsome actes in preiudice of the popes poere'; NA SP1/83, fol. 172ʳ (*LP*, VII 577). *LP* placed this letter at the end of April 1534, implying that Watts was referring to the oath of succession. Thompson, however, might also be correct in her assumption that the letter belongs in the autumn of 1534; Thompson, *Carthusian Order*, 385. If the letter was from the autumn of 1534, Wattes was most likely referring to the institutional profession.

summer and autumn of 1534. Indeed, it was not until 1535 – when there is no strong evidence that any clerical institution besides the universities and the London Charterhouse were tendered an oath – that Henry began to enforce his supremacy on the monasteries and crack down on opposition. No statute of Parliament supported the clerical professions of 1534, and it appears that the regime was hesitant to punish those who refused these professions at this time. An alternative explanation is that the clergy simply cooperated docilely in 1534, but this is unlikely considering the clergy's history of dissent and the clearly radical language of the clerical professions of 1534. The most probable explanation is that the regime was using the clerical professions of 1534 to feel out resistance, and that it used the knowledge gained from the clerical responses to the professions of 1534 (that is, who resisted them) to select which institutions and clergymen to take further action against in the later 1530s.

HOW PEOPLE TOOK THE OATHS OF THE HENRICIAN REFORMATION

Our examination of the response to the oaths and professions of 1534 needs to go beyond who took the oaths, who refused, and why they refused. Equally important is *how* people took the oaths, for while Henry's subjects could not control the content of the oaths of the 1530s, they could manipulate the manner in which they swore the oaths. This gave Henry's subjects a certain amount of agency. They could choose to swear the oath in a way that subverted the intentions of the Henrician regime in administering the oath. Furthermore, how they swore the professions of the 1530s gives us an idea of what they thought of these professions. Choosing to swear enthusiastically suggests approval and agreement with the content of the oath. By contrast, choosing to swear reluctantly or with equivocation or dissimulation suggests disapproval of and resistance to the content of the oath.

According to the reports of the commissioners for the oath of succession, most people took the oath of succession with alacrity and devotion. Stephen Gardiner claimed that the commissioners, gentlemen, and clergy of the diocese of Winchester took the oath of succession 'very obediently'.[40] Reynold Lytylprow glowingly described the reception of the oath in the city of Norwich: 'I thynke they wer never sen pepyll off swyche [such] wyll & delygens.' Lytylprow was particularly impressed with those under the age of sixteen: 'I thynke neber [a] man ded se [such diligence] ffor

---

[40] Gardiner, *Letters*, 56.

they wold be swornne off ffre ffors [of free force]', one to two hundred of them even kissing the book 'ffor the safyty [of] ther lobyng myndys'.[41] The commissioners gave similar news from the North of England, a place soon to be infamous for its opposition to the Henrician Reformation in the Pilgrimage of Grace. Sir George Lawson, Treasurer of Berwick, claimed that the inhabitants of his county 'be most willyng diligent & redye to appere & to make ther othes acording to the act of parliament & the kinges commissions'.[42] Sir William Gascoygne, writing from Yorkshire, boasted: 'the people in ther moste humbly maner haith resceved & taken ther othes ebyn according to ther dewties lyke trew subgettes'.[43] Likewise, William Maunsell, Under Sheriff of Yorkshire, wrote to Cromwell that the king's subjects in Yorkshire had taken their oaths 'with as humble obedience & ffeithfull myndes as euer did any subiectes holy'.[44]

The commissioners for the oath of succession, however, were probably biased. It was in their best interests to show how loyal their county was rather than to disclose foot-dragging and risk a reprimand for poor government. Ambassador Chapuys painted a very different picture of how the English people swore the oath of succession. Chapuys wrote that the oath Henry forced upon his subjects to observe the laws against Katherine and Mary in favor of Anne 'has served only to irritate the people more'.[45] He claimed that 'the whole people had given [their oaths of succession] with great ill will'.[46] Of course, Chapuys was even more biased than the commissioners but in the opposite direction. One of Chapuys' main goals was to persuade Charles V to invade England. It made sense for Chapuys to depict the English people as detesting Henry's innovations, for then Chapuys could more easily persuade Charles that the English people would flock to his banner once Charles landed. The truth probably lies somewhere between the reports of the commissioners and Chapuys. Most people probably took the oath of succession simply and sincerely since it was ostensibly rather innocuous, but a small number of them undoubtedly did take it 'with great ill will'.

But what about the oaths of supremacy circulating from 1534 to 1536? How did the clergy of England swear them? As we have seen, information on the response to these oaths is scant, but one remark by Friar John Hylsey (Henry's commissioner to tender the friars their profession) is telling: 'I haue not founde anny rellygyas persons in my vysytacion that hathe utterly

---

[41] NA sp1/88, fol. 148ʳ (*LP*, vii App. 29).   [42] NA sp1/88, fol. 141ʳ (*LP*, vii App. 23).
[43] NA sp1/88, fol. 145ʳ (*LP*, vii App. 26).   [44] NA sp1/88, fol. 143ʳ (*LP*, vii App. 24).
[45] HHS, Staatenabteilungen, England, Berichte, Karton 5, 1534, 22 April. (*LP*, vii 530).
[46] *LP*, vii 690.

denyede and refusyde the othe to be obedyente trew and agreable un to the kynges hyghe pleasure and wyll, yett I haue fownde some that hathe sworne wythe an evyll wyll and slenderly hathe takyn an othe to be obedyent.'[47] What did it mean to take an oath 'wythe an evyll wyll and slenderly'? Hylsey was probably referring to swearing the oath with some kind of machination that allowed the swearer to save his conscience from the full force of the oath. There was a variety of such mitigating methods, some were open – such as the adding of a conditional clause to one's oath or the issuing of a public protestation declaring one's interpretation of the oath – but others were secret – such as simple perjury or the addition of clandestine, internal clauses modifying the content of the oath.

The use of the more open machinations was well established before 1534. It was through these methods that the English clergy resisted Henry's initial attempts to get them to agree to his supremacy. For example, in 1531 when Henry demanded that the Convocation of Canterbury sign a declaration that he was the supreme head of the church in England, Convocation agreed to do so only if the conditional 'as far as it is allowed by the law of Christ' was added to the declaration. Some members of Convocation then issued protestations declaring that they did not interpret this declaration as taking any power away from the Pope.[48] Convocation responded in a similar manner in 1532 when Henry commanded that the clergy submit all their ecclesiastical laws and ordinances to him and accept the derogation of those he found opposed to his supreme authority. Convocation agreed to declare their offending constitutions void as long as they did 'not concern the faith nor reformation of sin'.[49] When Henry refused to accept this, the clergy of Convocation agreed to submit their laws and ordinances to Henry and reject any such law the king felt was contrary to his royal prerogative, 'saving to us always all such immunities and liberties of this Church of England, as hath been granted unto the same by the goodness and benignity of your highness, and of others your most noble progenitors'.[50] Henry again rejected this conditional submission, sending into Convocation a delegation of temporal lords to make sure the clergy signed an unequivocal submission. Although some members of Convocation did indeed sign

---

[47] NA sp1/84, fol. 198ʳ (*LP*, vii 869).   [48] See Chapter 2.

[49] Bray (ed.), *Records of Convocation*, vii:187.

[50] Three drafts of this submission survive, all of which are printed in Atterbury, *Rights, Powers, and Priviledges*, 464–71. The final of these three drafts is printed in Wilkins (ed.), *Concilia*, iii:752–3 and Bray (ed.), *Records of Convocation*, vii:182–3. I have quoted from the version in *Records of Convocation*. It should be noted that Bray, the editor of *Records of Convocation*, incorrectly placed this submission under the date of 19 April 1532.

such a document, the bishops of St Asaph, Lincoln, and London (Standish, Longland, and Stokesley) subscribed only with reservations. Standish subscribed 'provided that our most excellent king permit the provincial constitutions not contrary to divine law and to the law of the realm to remain in execution as before'. Longland added the condition 'that the king permit these other constitutions made by the ordinaries to be followed until the said business be examined'. Stokesley consented as long as the 'said document is neither against divine law nor contrary to general councils'.[51] Finally, Henry himself counselled Thomas Cranmer to take his oath of canonical obedience to the Pope with a protestation nullifying the content of the oath, and we have seen that Cranmer did just this in 1533.

Because the English clergy had experience using conditional clauses and protestations to nullify the content of a profession, it is likely that some of them tried to use the same machinations when taking the various professions of 1534 to 1536. For example, Balliol College, Oxford, attached the following protestation to their institutional profession: 'With the said contents having been made (*praehabita*) with the protestation that we intend to do nothing against the divine law nor against the norm of orthodox faith nor against the doctrine of our sacrosanct mother the Catholic Church.'[52] Similarly, when Edward Feld, the Master of Whittington College, subscribed to the statement rejecting papal authority, he wrote: 'I Edward Feld, Professor of Sacred Theology, remit myself to the opinion and judgement of the Archbishop of Canterbury my ordinary', thereby placing the responsibility for his action on Cranmer and mitigating the burden on his own conscience.[53] According to one version of Chauncy's narrative, the London Charterhouse took the oath of succession with the condition 'as far as was lawful'.[54] Equivocation, that is, the exploitation of the ambiguity of language, may also have been attempted. According to the exiled Carthusian John Suertis, when the sacrist of the Beauvale Charterhouse Nicolas Dugmer was offered an acknowledgement of the royal supremacy and asked how he took the king, Dugmer replied: 'I take him as God and the Holy Church take him: and I am sure he taketh himself none otherwise'.[55] Yet this kind of open use of protestations, conditional clauses, and equivocation is exceedingly rare in the documentation of the oaths and

---

[51] Wilkins (ed.), *Concilia*, III:749.   [52] NA E25/102/3, printed in Rymer (ed.), *Foedera*, XIV:498.

[53] NA E36/63, pg. 102 (*LP*, VII 1025(ii)). Brigden's claim that Feld 'subscribed with the proviso that he blamed Cranmer for this treachery' strikes me as an exaggeration; Brigden, *London and the Reformation*, 226.

[54] Chauncy, *Historia aliqvot* (1550), sig. M4ʳ.

[55] Knowles, *Religious Orders*, III:179, nt. 3. Although he did not cite his exact source, it appears Knowles gathered this information from Le Vasseur (ed.), *Ephemerides ordinis Cartusiensis*, III:265.

professions of 1534 to 1536. The form of the oaths and professions of these years was set in advance, and it is unlikely that many commissioners would have accepted additions to the set text if these additions openly mitigated the force of the professions.

It would have been much easier to get away with secret dissimulation since the commissioners could not know the opinions of the swearers' hearts. The simplest form of secret dissimulation was premeditated perjury: the swearing of an oath that one had no intention of keeping. Bishop Stephen Gardiner defended himself against such an accusation when he wrote to Cromwell: 'I shuld be otherwise taken thenne I am; that is to saye, openly to swere oon thinge and pryvely to worke, saye, or doo otherwise; wherof I was never gylty'.[56] But not everyone's conscience was as clear as Gardiner's. Fisher's servant counselled him to take the oath of supremacy, adding 'me thinketh that is no great matter, for you [*sic*] lordshipp may still thinke as you list'.[57] Hall reported that Nicholas Wilson, Henry's one-time confessor who was put in the Tower at the same time as More and Fisher for refusing the oath of succession, eventually 'dissembled the matter and so escaped'.[58] One John Yong highlighted the difference between the Carthusians who refused the oath and died for their constancy and the dissimulation of the curate of Rye, Sir William Inold. Yong testified 'that as good men as true men & better then the same Inold ys weer hanged within this moneth forasmoch as they wuld not be sworne but the kynges highnes & that the same Inold was sworne & hath done to the Contrary'.[59] The subprior of the monastery of Woburn admitted that the rejection of papal authority 'causede repugnance in my herte'. He initially wanted to refuse the oath (presumably the institutional profession of 1534), but a combination of counsel and threats by his abbot convinced him 'to be contente to swere'. In spite of his oath, the subprior remained in a 'blynde scrupulositie of conscience' which led him to cite writings of the doctors in defence of the Pope and, as he confessed, 'causede me many tymes to modifye my declaracions of your [Henry's] iustlye recognishede Suppremitie and also of the Bishopp of Rome uniust therin vsurpacion thynkynge so to haue excusede my conscience before godde'. The subprior eventually became convinced that through his actions against his oath, he 'endangerede bothe body and

The original Latin reads as follows: 'Et cum accersitum ad se Comissarii regii examinarent, quid sentiret de Rege supremam in causis ecclesiasticis protestatem sibis vendicante, respondit: "Sentio de eo, quod Deus cum sua Sancta Ecclesia sentit, et mihi persuadeo ipsusm non melius sentire de se." Commissarii hac responsione contenti, Patrem libertum dimiserunt.'

[56] Gardiner, *Letters*, 66.   [57] Ortroy (ed.), 'Vie du bienheureux martyr Jean Fisher', 12 (1893): 159.
[58] Hall, *Hall's Chronicle*, 815.   [59] NA sp1/92, fol. 183r (*LP*, VIII 776).

sowle and brought my self in ieopardye'.[60] Indeed, as we saw in Chapter 1, the kind of dissimulated swearing practised by Wilson, Inold, and the subprior of Woburn was almost universally decried by Catholics and evangelicals alike. Committing perjury by swearing to something against one's conscience was certainly believed 'to endanger both body and soul'.

So if some Englishmen practised dissimulation in swearing the oaths of the 1530s, how did they justify it in their consciences? Thomas More provides us with a clue in one of his letters to his daughter Margaret Roper on his refusal to swear the oath of succession:

> And some might hap to frame him self a conscience and thinke that while he did it for feare God wolde forgeue it. And some may peraduenture thinke that they will repent, and be shryuen thereof, and that so God shall remitt it them. And some may be peraduenture of that minde, that if they say one thing and thinke the while the contrary, God more regardeth their harte than their tonge, and that therfore their othe goeth vpon that they thinke, and not vpon that they say, as a women resoned once, I trow, Daughter, you wer by.[61]

In other words, some people believed that God judged them by what they thought, no matter how contrary the words they actually swore were to their hearts. This opinion was clearly divergent from the standard Augustinian belief that 'He lies, moreover, who holds one opinion in his mind and who gives expression to another through words or any other outward manifestation.'[62] This use of dissimulation was first defended by the Spanish theologian Sylvester in his *Summa summarum* of 1515, but the kind of swearing to which More referred was not vocally advocated in England until the use of mental reservation by the English Jesuits after 1580.[63]

Nevertheless, if no one in England in the 1530s openly condoned the practice of swearing one thing with one's words and another with one's mind, some certainly practised it at this time. When the remaining monks of the London Charterhouse finally gave in and swore the oath of supremacy in May 1537, they first prayed to God:

> Nor is it hidden from thee, O God, Thou searcher of hearts, how contrary to the law of our mind is the consent which we are constrained to give . . . We beseech thee therefore of thy inexhaustible goodness and gentleness mercifully to pardon thy servants for the sin which, though heart and conscience resist, we are about to commit with our lips.[64]

---

[60] NA sp1/104, fols. 227ʳ–8ʳ (*LP*, x 1239).   [61] More, *Correspondence*, 521.

[62] Augustine, *Lying (De mendacio)*, trans. Sarah Muldowney, in *St Augustine: Treatises on Various Subjects*, 55.

[63] Sommerville, 'New Art of Lying', 172.

[64] Chauncy, *Passion and Martyrdom* (1570), 121.

When John Stanton confessed to the priest Sir George Roland that 'we be sworn vnto the kynges grace & hath all Redy abiured the pope', Roland replied, 'an othe Losly made may losly be brokyn'. Roland gave the analogy of when a friend makes him share a drink of reconciliation with his enemy. Although he may drink with his enemy, he does not actually forgive his enemy in his heart. Roland concluded: 'And so in lyke wyse vppon this othe concerning the abiuracyon of the pope I wyll not abiure hym in my harte'.[65] The Observant Franciscan Friar Forest infamously confessed that 'he had denyed the busshop of Rome by an othe geuen by his outwarde man but not in thinwarde man'.[66] An anonymous writer from the time of Henry VIII accused Hugh Cook, Abbot of Reading, of using a similar shift. Allegedly, when 'the Spiritualitie wer sworne to take the kynges grace for the supreme hed immedatly next vn[der] god of this church of yngland', Cook took the oath but added 'pretly in his owne conscience these words following of the Temporall church . . . but not of the spirituall church'.[67] Dan Laurance Bloneham used another kind of dissimulation. When his fellow monks of Woburn reported to the Henrician regime that Bloneham claimed that he 'was never sworne to forsake the pope to be owr hed and never wilbe', Bloneham confessed: 'At the first tyme that I whas sworne I dyd not ley my hande apon the booke & kyse yt but whas ouer passyde by resone of mouche company. & afterward sayd onwhysely I whas not sworne'.[68] We do not know if the machinations used by the London Carthusians, Roland, Forest, Cook, and Bloneham were exceptional or merely the tip of a submerged iceberg. Dissimulation is by definition secret. Nevertheless, these examples do demonstrate that not everyone took the professions of 1534 in a straightforward, honest manner.

Obscure monks and parish priests were not the only ones to use dissimulation when making their professions. There are indications that none other than Mary Tudor, the future monarch of England, utilized such shifts. Although Mary's story is so convoluted that we cannot be certain what actually happened, the letters relating to her submission illustrate the variety of ways one could submit while still saving one's conscience. Her story is thus worth a detailed examination.

After Henry received his divorce in 1533, he quickly began trying to get Mary to renounce her title of princess. Mary staunchly resisted.[69] The

---

[65] NA sp1/102, fol. 67[v] (*LP*, x 346).
[66] NA sp1/132, fol. 124[r] (*LP*, xiii 1043). For an excellent contextualization of this episode, see Marshall, 'Papist as Heretic'.
[67] NA sp1/155, fol. 61[r] (*LP*, xiv (ii) 613).   [68] NA sp1/132, fols. 77[r], 78[v]–79[r], 156[r] (*LP*, xiii 981, 1086).
[69] See for example *LP*, vi 1249, 1296, 1558; *LP*, vii 296, 393.

passage of the Act of Succession upped the ante, for now Henry had statutory authorization to tender Mary an official oath and to charge her with misprision of treason if she refused to swear it. Sometime in April 1534 Cromwell wrote a remembrance to himself 'to send the copy of the act of the King's succession to the princess Dowager and the lady Mary, with special commandment that it may be read in their presence and their answer taken'.[70] Also in April pressure was brought to bear on Mary by restricting her to her chamber and imprisoning her maid Anne Husee in the Tower until her maid, under duress, took the oath of succession.[71] Although Chapuys wrote on 19 May that if Mary continued to resist, Henry would bring the penalties of the statute of succession against her, she was evidently not officially tendered the oath at this time.[72] On 1 January 1535, Chapuys recounted:

> The princess has been warned how the king her father, in vigour of the statute that has been lately made more rigorous against those who do not want to swear and acknowledge the second marriage, is going to send and summon for her after the feasts to renounce her title and swear to the aforementioned statute. And under pain of her life she must not give herself the title of princess or call Madame her mother Queen. But even if she should be sent to the Tower or executed – and these are threatened her – she will never change her purpose, and the same fault is presupposed of the said Queen [Katherine].[73]

Chapuys was probably referring to the Treasons Act, which did not actually prescribe a specific penalty for refusing the oath of succession. Nevertheless, sometime at the end of January or the beginning of February, Katherine wrote to Chapuys that she 'had been warned by a person of good authority how the king had resolved . . . to summon the princess his daughter to approve and swear the statutes made against her mother the queen [Katherine] and herself [Mary], and, in case she refused, the king would immediately put her to death, or at least in prison for life'.[74] Again, the king was apparently bluffing. As in 1534, Mary was not administered an oath in 1535 and stood firm in her resistance without any sign of dissimulation.

Matters began to heat up again at the end of 1535 and beginning of 1536. This time Mary began to contemplate dissimulation. At the end of December, Emperor Charles V wrote Chapuys a letter detailing the reasons why Mary and Katherine should continue to avoid swearing to Henry's statutes. Charles also counselled, however, that they should take their oaths

---

[70] *LP*, VII 420.   [71] *LP*, VII 530, 662.   [72] *LP*, VII 690; Loades, *Mary Tudor: A Life*, 89–90.
[73] HHS, Staatenabteilungen, England, Berichte, Karton 7, 1535, 1 January (*Cal SP Spain*, V (I), 122).
[74] HHS, Staatenabteilungen, England, Berichte, Karton 7, 1535, 9 February (*LP*, VIII 189).

rather than lose their lives, while protesting that they did so out of fear. Charles claimed that such a form of protestational swearing would not prejudice their rights, and he promised to see to it that a protestation to this effect would be made for them in Rome.[75] By January 1536, Mary again informed Chapuys that Henry was about to summon her to appear before royal councillors to give her oath. She begged Chapuys' advice. At this time Chapuys told her to stand firm and declare 'that she, being a poor and simple orphan without experience, aid, counsel', or understanding of laws and canons, could not respond to them. Rather she must 'entreat' them to 'intercede with her father the king to have pity on her weakness and ignorance'. She could also argue that it was not customary to swear fealty to queens.[76] Yet Mary did not have to put Chapuys' advice into practice at this time, for Henry again backed down. On 10 February, Chapuys reported that the king had started to treat Mary more favourably. Now that Anne had miscarried, failing to provide Henry with his male heir, Chapuys was unsure whether Henry would continue to press Mary to swear the oath of succession.[77]

By the spring of 1536, Mary felt confident seeking the favour of Cromwell and the king. Katherine had passed away in January, and on 18 May, Henry executed Anne Boleyn. One of the main points of conflict between Mary and Henry was now moot. On 1 June, Mary wrote to Henry, beseeching his forgiveness for general offences and confessing that 'next unto God, I do and will submit me in all things to your goodnes and pleasure to do with me whatsoever shall please your grace'.[78] Mary had chosen her words carefully. She framed them in a way that avoided giving judgement on Henry's first marriage or the king's supremacy. The condition 'next to God' was also significant. On 10 June, she again wrote to the king, begging his forgiveness and submitting to him 'next to Almighty God'.[79] She also wrote to Cromwell that she would do her duty to the king 'God and my conscience not offended'. She claimed:

I have done the uttermost that my conscience will suffer me; and I do neither desire nor intend to do less than I have done. But if I be put to any more (I am

---

[75] *Cal SP Spain*, v (1) 245 (*LP*, ix 1035).

[76] HHS, Staatenabteilungen, England, Berichte, Karton 7, 1536, 21 January (*LP*, x 141).

[77] HHS, Staatenabteilungen, England, Berichte, Karton 7, 1536, 10 February (*LP*, x 282); Loades, *Mary Tudor: A Life*, 93–4.

[78] BL Cotton MS Otho c x, fol. 278 (*LP*, x 1022). The correspondence between Mary, Henry, and Cromwell of 1536 are collected in this manuscript, though many of them are very mutilated. Fortunately, most of them are printed in Hearne (ed.), *Sylloge epistolarum*. This particular letter is on pages 147–8 of Hearne.

[79] Hearne (ed.), *Sylloge epistolarum*, 124–5 (*LP*, x 1109).

plain with you as with my great friend), my said conscience will in no wayes suffer me to consent thereunto. And this point except, you nor any other shall be so much desirous to have me obey the King in all things, as I shall be ready to fullfill the same.[80]

Cromwell evidently believed that Mary had deliberately inserted these conditional clauses so as to maintain her obstinate opinions on Henry's first marriage and his supremacy while ostensibly submitting to the king. Mary retorted:

And whereas I do perceive by your letters, that you do mislike mine exception in my letter to the King's Grace, I assure you, I did not mean as you do take it. For I do not mistrust that the King's goodness will move me to any thing which should offend God and my Conscience. But that which I did write was only by the reason of continual custome. For I have allwayes used both in writing and speaking to except God in all things.[81]

Whether Mary inserted these conditional clauses 'by the reason of continual custome' or by deliberate design, they nevertheless had the consequence of weakening her submission.

Henry, by now well versed in the use of conditional clauses and equivocation, would have none of it. He responded by drawing up a set of 'greate and weightye' questions and articles, demanding that Mary respond to them in writing. In these articles, Mary was to recognize Henry as the sovereign emperor of the realm and accept all his laws and statutes. She was to acknowledge him as 'supreme hedde in erthe vnder chr[ist of the] churche of England' and to renounce the usurped jurisdiction of the bishop of Rome as well as all his laws and decrees. Finally, she was to admit that Henry's marriage to Katherine had been incestuous and unlawful.[82] There was no room for vague, equivocal submissions with conditional clauses in this document. When the royal commissioners (the Duke of Norfolk, the Earl of Sussex, and the bishop of Chichester) disclosed this document to Mary, she angrily refused to sign it.[83]

When Cromwell got word of Mary's refusal, he was exasperated and composed a scathing rebuke, emphasizing Mary's equivocation. Cromwell disclosed that he had often assured the king that Mary would submit 'in all things, without exception and qualification, to obey to his [Henry's]

---

[80] Hearne (ed.), *Sylloge epistolarum*, 125 (*LP*, x 1108).

[81] Hearne (ed.), *Sylloge epistolarum*, 126–7 (*LP*, x 1129).

[82] I believe that BL Cotton MS Otho c x, fols. 257A^r–257B^v (263^r–264^v pencil) is a copy of these articles. Loades, as far as I can tell, agrees; Loades, *Reign of Mary Tudor*, 19.

[83] Loades, *Mary Tudor: A Life*, 101; *LP*, xi 7. The chronology here is somewhat confused. See Loades, *Reign of Mary Tudor*, 19–20.

pleasure and laws'. Cromwell was now ashamed of what he had told Henry about Mary. In frustration, he vented: 'Wherefore, Madam, to be plain with you, as God is my witnes, like as I think you the most obstinate and obdurate woman, all things considered, that ever was.' He decided to give her one last chance. Enclosed with his letter, Cromwell sent to Mary a set of articles to which he desired her subscription, adding 'so as you will in semblable manner conceive it in your heart without dissimulation'. Moreover, he required her to write a letter 'declaring, that you think in heart, that you have subscribed with hand'.[84] Cromwell wanted an unambiguous submission with no hint of dissimulation.

Finally, on 22 June Mary submitted. She subscribed to a set of articles that explicitly recognized Henry as the supreme head of the church, rejected papal authority and jurisdiction, and declared Henry's first marriage incestuous and unlawful.[85] Furthermore, complying with Cromwell's instructions, she wrote an accompanying letter to Henry. This letter was extremely obsequious and servile. In it Mary confessed that she wrote 'of the bottom of my heart and stomack'. She acknowledged that she had offended Henry for not submitting to his just and virtuous laws, and she put herself entirely at Henry's mercy. Concerning the articles to which she had subscribed, she wrote: 'I shall never beseech your Grace to have pity and compassion of me, if ever you shall perceive that I shall prevyly or apertly vary or alter from one piece of that I have written and subscribed, or refuse to confirm, ratifie, or declare the same, where your Majestie shall appoint me.' Finally, she professed to 'put my soul into your direction, and by the same hath and will in all things from henceforth direct my conscience'.[86] On 26 June Mary sent another letter to Henry in which she declared that her heart would 'never alter, vary, or change from that confession and submission which I have made unto your Highness in the presence of your council and other attending upon the same'.[87] For the rest of 1536 Mary continued to submit humbly to Henry and repeatedly profess her devotion. For example, on 21 July she wrote that Henry would always find her 'true, faithfull, and obedient to you and yours, as your Majestie and your lawes have and shall limit unto me without alteration, till the hour of my death'.[88]

---

[84] Hearne (ed.), *Sylloge epistolarum*, 137–8 (*LP*, x 1110). Loades suggests that this letter may never have been sent; Loades, *Mary Tudor: A Life*, 102.

[85] A copy of Mary's submission is BL Harleian MS 283, fols. 112ᵛ–113ʳ. It is printed in Hearne (ed.), *Sylloge epistolarum*, 142–3 (*LP*, x 1137).

[86] Hearne (ed.), *Sylloge epistolarum*, 140–2 (*LP*, x 1136).

[87] Hearne (ed.), *Sylloge epistolarum*, 128–9 (*LP*, x 1203).

[88] Hearne (ed.), *Sylloge epistolarum*, 131 (*LP*, xi 132).

Mary's final submission and her subsequent letters of 1536 suggest that Mary had utterly capitulated to Henry. She had abandoned all forms of equivocation or dissimulation and had submitted herself simply and wholly. But was Mary's capitulation genuine? Her behaviour for the rest of Henry's reign suggested that it was. Mary's household was restored, she found favour at court, and she became friends with Henry's later wives, Jane Seymour and Catherine Parr. If Mary's submission was made with a feigned heart, she threw herself into the role of the penitent daughter with a convincing zeal that appears to have satisfied those around her.

Ambassador Chapuys, however, had a different opinion of Mary's submission. Chapuys reported that Mary signed her submission without reading it, 'which will stand as her best excuse'. Moreover, Chapuys narrated how he 'had previously sent to her the form of the protestation which she must make separately'. At that time, Chapuys had also written that 'if it was permitted of her, she should approve the statutes only as much as she was able to do so in accordance with God and her conscience or that she should only promise not to transgress the statutes, without saying anything about approving them'.[89] Mary had apparently put these strategies into practice with her first submissions. We know, however, that neither the king nor Cromwell would tolerate them. In such a situation, Chapuys had also advised Mary that if she 'was in danger of her life', she must:

yield (*condescendre*) to the will of her father... and to save her life, on which depended the peace of this kingdom and the reformation of great disorders which continually happen here, it was necessary that she bear all things and dissemble for some time, especially as the protestations made and the cruel and truculent violence [expressed against her] preserved her rights inviolable and similarly her conscience, seeing also that nothing to which she would agree was expressly against God or the articles of faith, and [finally] that God regarded the intention more highly than the act.[90]

Chapuys concluded his account of Mary's submission by writing:

After the princess had subscribed as mentioned above, she found herself greatly dejected (*peneuse*), but I immediately relieved her of all doubt, even of conscience, assuring her that not only would the Pope not impute to her any guilt, but he would also hold the whole [business] as very well done... She has also beseeched me to write again to your Majesty's ambassador at Rome to obtain a secret absolution from the Pope, otherwise her conscience cannot be at perfect rest.[91]

---

[89] HHS, Staatenabteilungen, England, Berichte, Karton 7, 1536, 1 July (*LP*, XI 7).
[90] HHS, Staatenabteilungen, England, Berichte, Karton 7, 1536, 1 July (*LP*, XI 7).
[91] HHS, Staatenabteilungen, England, Berichte, Karton 7, 1536, 1 July (*LP*, XI 7). Mary did not receive her secret papal absolution. The Imperial ambassador in Rome (Cifuentes) reported to Chapuys

Chapuys also maintained that Mary's servile missives of the summer and autumn of 1536 were a sham designed to maintain her favour with the king. On 7 and 8 October, Chapuys wrote that Henry, concerned about imperial or papal support of the new rebellion in Lincolnshire, was now forcing Mary to write letters to Charles, Mary of Hungary, and the Pope that 'she had of her own free will, without compulsion or fear of any sort, suggestion, impression, respect, or regard for any person whomsoever, acknowledged, confirmed, and approved the statutes' made against Henry's first marriage and in favour of his supremacy over the church.[92] Chapuys assured Charles V and Cifuentes (Charles' ambassador in Rome) that Mary herself had told him that she wrote these letters for fear of her life and that there was 'no truth whatsoever in them'. Mary had again safeguarded her conscience:

If your Lordship [Cifuentes] does not know of it already, I can tell you that for a long time back Her Highness has, by my advice, applied such a remedy and drawn such protests for the safeguarding of her right that I do not think any more are required. To the protest formerly made the Princess herself has since added, after consulting over the matter with me, certain clauses and words which render all other precautions perfectly useless. Your Lordship, however, must keep profoundly secret in these matters, for should these people hear of our precautionary measures for the future the Princess would not be allowed to live long.[93]

It is thus abundantly evident that Chapuys believed that Mary's submission was dissimulated.

Finally, it is worth pointing out that Mary's submission of 1536 contained no oath.[94] She never swore the oath of succession or any oath of supremacy. Whenever Mary believed Henry was going to administer an oath to her, she had stood firm, resisting absolutely. It was only when the matter of oaths was dropped that she began to use equivocation and conditional clauses. Her final submission, while unequivocal, was not made before God. If Mary's final submission was made with a feigned heart, perhaps this contributed to Mary's willingness to dissimulate and subscribe to the articles. It may even be that Henry and Cromwell deliberately substituted an oathless profession for an oath in order to encourage Mary to submit.

that he would not approach the Pope for it, since if the Pope knew that Mary desired absolution, the French would soon know as well. The French, in turn, would inform Henry, and then Mary's life would be in danger; *Cal SP Spain*, v (II), 106.

[92] *Cal. SP Spain*, v (II), 104, 105, trans. Pascual Gayangos.

[93] *Cal. SP Spain*, v (II), 105, trans. Pascual Gayangos.

[94] Lucy Wooding claimed that 'Before Mary was readmitted to his favour, she was forced to beg his forgiveness for her obduracy, and take a solemn and unremittable oath that her mother had never truly been his wife'; Wooding, *Henry VIII*, 200–1. I have found no evidence of this oath.

Perhaps Henry decided that the propaganda he would gain if Mary made an open, unequivocal submission outweighed the concerns of mitigating the exact form of submission. There is no proof that this was the case. Yet even if Mary's submission was so genuine that she would have still made it if asked to confirm it with an oath, her story illustrates that dissimulation was certainly an option when faced with the oaths and professions of the 1530s. It was counselled by no less than the most powerful monarch in the Christian world, and Henry and Cromwell's response to Mary's initial, vague, and conditional submissions indicates that they were well aware of its practice.

Mary was not the only person of rank to be suspected of dissimulation. Rumours were rampant concerning Henry's bishops. Bishop Roland Lee of Coventry and Lichfield reported that Bishop Robert Sherborne of Chichester used 'not a littill dissimulacion' and recommended that Sherborne be summoned to court to swear the oath in person.[95] Chapuys reported that Bishop Cuthbert Tunstall 'has been forced to swear like the others, although he spoke with certain restrictions and reservations'.[96] The king was certainly suspicious of Tunstall. Once the Act of Succession passed, Tunstall was ordered to come to court to swear the oath of succession in person. At the same time, royal agents ransacked his residence in search of incriminating letters.[97] After Tunstall had sworn, the king wrote a letter accusing Tunstall of looking 'for a newe world or mutation', that is, a time when Henry would be laid low and papal authority re-established in England.[98] The same writer who attacked Friar Forest and Abbot Cook for their use of mental reservation accused Bishop Stokesley of London of the same practice:

I cannot think the contrary but the olde bishop of londen whan he was a lyve, vsed the prety medicine that his felow fryer forest was wont to vse and to work with an inward man and an outward man that is to say to speake one thing with theyr mowth and th[en] another thyng with theyr hart.[99]

Finally, Henry also suspected the influential humanists Thomas Starkey and Reginald Pole (eventually Henry's arch-nemesis) of using dissimulation, though of course Pole never swore any oath to Henry. Starkey wrote to Cromwell: 'loth I wold be that any other man schold hire or perceyue that

[95] NA sp1/84, fol. 101ʳ (*LP*, vii 759). For more on this letter, see page 65.
[96] *Cal SP Spain*, v (1) 58 (*LP*, vii 690).   [97] Chibi, *Henry VIII's Bishops*, 169.
[98] Henry's letter does not survive, but Tunstall's letter in his defence leaves us in no doubt of the content of the king's letter. For Tunstall's letter, see BL Cotton MS Cleopatra e vi, fols. 247ʳ–248ʳ.
[99] NA sp1/155, fol. 60ʳ⁻ᵛ (*LP*, xiv (2) 613).

the kyng schold have me in suspycyon of any dyssymilutyor wyth hym, the wych thyng I perceyvyd.' Starkey pledged to Cromwell: 'to you I am open & playn I promys you, that you schal neuer fynd me faynyd man and of thys one thyng I schal assur you'.[100] Starkey also assured Henry and Cromwell that no matter what Henry had heard, Pole would disclose his mind to Henry on the royal supremacy without dissimulation: 'I boldly haue affyrmyd, both to the kyngys hyghnes so also to Maistur secretory, that hyt [Pole's answer] schalbe vnfaynyd & pure, wythout cloke of dyssymulatyon, of the wych syncere Iugement in you the kyng ys desyouse, *by cause per auentur in some other hys grace hath byn therin deceyuyd.*'[101] Although there is no supporting evidence that any of these bishops or humanists actually used dissimulation, the fact that people – even Henry himself – suspected them of it is nonetheless significant.

Indeed, by the summer of 1535 it seems that Henry and his leading advisors were keenly aware of the practice of dissimulation. This probably helps to explain why Henry tendered all his bishops another profession in February and March 1535. In his proclamation enforcing the statutes abolishing papal authority of June 1535, Henry ordered all his sheriffs to watch their bishops closely to make sure they preached Henry's supremacy 'truly, sincerely, and without all manner cloak, color, or dissimulation'. If any bishop or ecclesiastical person did 'omit and leave undone any part or parcel of the premises, or else in the execution and setting forth of the same do coldly and unfeignedly use any manner sinister addition, wrong interpretation, or painted colors', the sheriffs were to inform the Crown immediately.[102] When Henry tendered the universities their new profession in the autumn of 1535, he added the clause to the oath whereupon the person swore 'persuaded and seduced to this, not coerced by force or fear, nor with any trick or other sinister machination, but from our certain knowledge, with resolved minds and just and voluntary wills, purely, willingly, and absolutely'.[103] This clause was clearly designed to prevent taking the oath with dissimulation. Henry was suspicious. Chapuys was right in his observation at the end of 1534 that 'the king does not trust very much the oath that he has exacted on the validity of his last marriage and the succession'.[104]

We are now better able to answer the question of how people responded to the oaths and professions of 1534 to 1536. The overwhelming majority of

[100] NA sp1/92, fols. 45r–46r (*LP*, VIII 575).
[101] BL Cotton MS Cleopatra E VI, fol. 358r (*LP*, VIII 801). My italics.
[102] Hughes and Larkin (eds), *Tudor Royal Proclamations*, 1:231–2.   [103] See Appendix F, II.
[104] HHS, Staatenabteilungen, England, Berichte, Karton 5, 1534, 19 December (*LP*, VII 1554).

the English people took the oath of succession, probably because there was nothing explicit in the text of the oath on the rejection of papal authority or the establishment of royal supremacy. What little information we have on those who did refuse the oath suggests that they refused it because they were not willing to bind their consciences to the statement that Henry's first marriage to Katherine was unlawful. Although the clerical professions of 1534 unambiguously renounced the papacy and acknowledged Henry's supremacy, there are likewise very few signs of resistance to these professions. This indicates either that the clergy were willing to reject the papacy in favor of Henry's supremacy or that the Henrician regime was unwilling to crack down on those who balked at these professions in 1534. It was probably a combination of both of these reasons. Furthermore, whereas the English people and clergy generally took the oaths and professions of 1534 to 1536, the manner in which some of them took these professions allowed them to comply ostensibly while dissenting in their consciences. Some people made their professions with conditional clauses or equivocal additions. Others dissimulated their true opinions through a variety of devious machinations. We do not know how prevalent these practices were, but the anxiety of the Henrician regime over their use signifies that they were important enough to warrant royal concern.

In sum, it is probable that a substantial amount of Englishmen took the oaths and professions of 1534 to 1536 without believing that these professions bound them to assent to Henry's full Reformation, either by swearing the oaths of supremacy with equivocation or dissimulation, or by swearing the oath of succession honestly but simply according to the words of the oath itself (which did not mention royal supremacy or matters of faith). The vast majority of Henry's subjects had sworn the oaths administered to them, but this did not mean that they had actively consented to all his controversial new policies. In fact, Henry's subjects in the North of England were about to make their disapproval of Henry's Reformation quite clear. And just as Henry had sought to implement and enforce his Reformation through oaths, so did the rebels of the Pilgrimage of Grace seek to implement and enforce their rejection of Henry's Reformation through oaths.

CHAPTER 5

Oaths and the Pilgrimage of Grace

On Monday, 2 October 1536, the clamour of the church bells in the town of Louth, Lincolnshire, shattered the morning peace. A day earlier, the townsmen of Louth had seized the keys of the church treasure house in response to a rumour that the impending royal visitation would lead to the confiscation of their church jewels. Now the appearance of John Henneage, an official of the bishop of Lincoln, had spurred the town into action. When William Moreland, late monk of the dissolved monastery of Louth Park, arrived on the scene, he found that 'a great nombre of the comyners' had seized Henneage and were leading him to the parish church. Moreland and other 'honeste men' thrust themselves into the crowd and 'with force strengthe and also with fayre woordes' managed to rescue Henneage, get him inside the church, and lock the choir door between Henneage and the mob. The crowd, however, refused to disperse and shouted 'that they wold haue hym [Henneage] sworne vnto theim and so at lengthe he was sworne, and after him all other persones whiche had contraried theym the night before were in like maner sworne', including Moreland himself.[1] A short time later, the town bells again rang out when John Frankishe, the bishop of Lincoln's registrar, arrived. The crowd seized Frankishe and forced him and Moreland to burn Frankishe's papers. Much of the rest of the day was occupied with the swearing of oaths. The commons compelled the sixty priests who had gathered at Louth for the royal visitation to swear 'to be true to god, to the king, and to the Commons', and also to ring the common bells in their parishes.[2] The commons likewise summoned the heads of the town to appear at the town hall to swear a similar oath.[3] According to Nicolas Melton (alias Captain Cobbler), 'many other mo[r]e honest men of the paryshe' soon came forth, 'whom they [the commons] swore likewise'.[4] The gentlemen of the region were the final prey. On

---

[1] NA E36/119, fol. 48ᵛ (*LP*, XII (i) 380).
[2] NA SP1/110, fol. 143ʳ (*LP*, XI 970). Also see *LP*, XII (i) 70 (1).   [3] *LP*, XI 854.
[4] NA SP1/110, fol. 134ʳ (*LP*, XI 968).

Monday, the commons brought Sir William Skipwith of Ornsby to Louth 'very rigorosly' and compelled him to take their oath.[5] The next day, the commons forced Sir William Askew, Sir Edward Madeson, his brother John Madeson, Sir Robert Tyrwhit, Thomas Portington, and John Booth to swear 'to be true to god and the king and to doo as they did'.[6] The rebellion in the North had begun.

As the rebellion spread into the counties north of Lincolnshire and adopted the name the 'Pilgrimage of Grace', it grew in numbers and strength, becoming the largest religious and social uprising in England between the Peasants' Rebellion of 1381 and the English Civil War of the 1640s.[7] At one point, anywhere from thirty thousand to fifty thousand men were in the field for the rebels.[8] The revolt was essentially religious and popular, though social and political grievances also played a role in motivating the rebels, and many gentlemen and nobles went along with the commons.[9] To a large extent, the Pilgrimage was a popular reaction against the Henrician Reformation of the 1530s, a reaction in which oaths played a major role.

Historians have long recognized the importance of oaths in the Pilgrimage of Grace, generally factoring oaths into their analyses of the Pilgrimage in two ways. First, historians have stressed that the rebels used oaths to mobilize their ranks, disseminate their message, and solidify support for their movement.[10] Second, historians have analysed the language of the various rebel oaths in order to determine the predominant goals and grievances of the rebellion. They use the pilgrims' oaths to argue that the rebellion was primarily about securing social or constitutional reforms or alternatively (and more persuasively) that it was about resisting the Henrician Reformation.[11] In both of these analyses, however, oaths were explored insofar as they provided information on the Pilgrimage itself.

---

[5] *LP*, xi 854; NA sp1/110, fol. 143ʳ (*LP*, xi 970).

[6] NA sp1/106, fol. 295ʳ (*LP*, xi 568); NA e36/118, fol. 54ʳ (*LP*, xi 853); NA e36/119, fol. 54ʳ (*LP*, xii (i) 380).

[7] Shagan, *Popular Politics*, 89.

[8] Bernard estimated the rebel force at thirty thousand; Bernard, *King's Reformation*, 293. Shagan suggested that it consisted of up to fifty thousand; Shagan, *Popular Politics*, 89.

[9] The above statement seems to be the current historiographical consensus. However much modern historians bicker over the specific motivations of the rebels, the success or failure of the Pilgrimage, and the king's strategy in dealing with the rebels, they now agree that the revolt was predominantly popular and religious. See Bush, *Pilgrimage of Grace*, 17 and *passim*; Shagan, *Popular Politics*, 89–128; Bernard, *King's Reformation*, 293–404.

[10] Bush, *Pilgrimage of Grace*, 12, 29, 83, 114, 145, 224, 227–8, 252, 298, 329, 345; Dodds and Dodds, *Pilgrimage of Grace*, 1:94, 145, 181–2, 184, 199, 217, 221, 227; Hoyle, *Pilgrimage of Grace*, 439–41.

[11] Bush, *Pilgrimage of Grace*, 91–2, 196–7; Dodds and Dodds, *Pilgrimage of Grace*, 1:182; Hoyle, *Pilgrimage of Grace*, 205–7, 209; Bernard, *King's Reformation*, 306–7, 329–30.

Although such discussions are enlightening, this chapter takes a different approach, placing the pilgrims' oaths on centre stage and evaluating them in the context of the previous oaths of the Henrician reformation. It argues that the pilgrims' oaths were primarily a response of the English people to the oath of succession. First, the pilgrims responded to the oath of succession by imitating it. Recognizing that an oath was the best way to secure the loyalty of a potential dissident, the pilgrims administered their oaths in a way that was reminiscent of the oath of succession. Second, the pilgrims' oaths were a response to the oath of succession in that they declared the pilgrims' interpretation of the oath of succession, an interpretation consonant with the wording of the oath of succession but dissonant with the Crown's religious policy. Yet this interpretation was controversial, and a recurring theme in the Pilgrimage of Grace was the relationship between the pilgrims' oaths and the oath of succession. The Pilgrimage of Grace was a battle of oaths.

RESPONSE AS IMITATION: THE ADMINISTRATION OF THE PILGRIMS' OATHS

The rebels of the Pilgrimage of Grace responded to the oath of succession by imitating it, a point that a few historians have recognized but not explored in any detailed manner.[12] This imitation was in the administration of the pilgrims' oaths. In the same way in which Henry sent commissioners throughout his entire realm to administer the oath of succession, so did the rebels of the Pilgrimage of Grace tender their oaths throughout every region that they controlled. Indeed, as the revolt spread, so did the administration of the pilgrims' oaths. On Tuesday, 3 October, William Leache, who had been in Louth a day earlier when the uprising commenced, brought word of the rebellion to the town of Horncastle. Immediately, Leache gathered a force of one hundred men, and they compelled the sheriff and other gentlemen of Horncastle to swear 'for saue garde of ther lyffes that they schuld be true to [god] the kyng and the commons and the ffayth of the church'.[13] On Wednesday, Richard Dylcoke of Humberston arrived in Louth. The rebels at Louth forced Dylcoke to swear their oath and then sent him back to Humberston to raise and summon the people there to do likewise.[14] That same week, the rebels of Lincolnshire stopped the Yorkshire lawyer Robert Aske at Ferriby and required him to swear an oath

---

[12] Fletcher and MacCulloch, *Tudor Rebellions*, 39; Bush, *Pilgrimage of Grace*, 12.
[13] NA sp1/110, fol. 124ᵛ (*LP*, xi 967).   [14] NA sp1/110, fol. 173ʳ (*LP*, xi 974).

to be 'trew to God and the king and the comyn welth'.[15] Aske swore, and by 6 October he was back in the East Riding spreading news of the revolt. The first town to rise north of Lincolnshire was Beverley. A letter had arrived (supposedly from Robert Aske) instructing the town to swear the commons' oath. Accordingly, on Sunday, 8 October, one Richard Newdyke 'made proclamation for euerye man to come in and take his oathe to the comons apon payn of deathe and one Richard Wilson, with the othe in thone hand and a book in the other, swering them'.[16] On Monday, the rest of the town assembled on the green to swear the oath, eventually intimidating the local gentry family – the Stapletons – to swear as well as become their captains.[17] That same day, Aske issued a proclamation ordering men to assemble at Skypwithe Morre to appoint captains and take an oath to be true 'to the king's issue and the noble blood', 'to preserve the church of God from spoiling', and to safeguard 'the commons and their wealths'.[18]

As the revolt spread west and north, the commons continued to administer their oaths. On Sunday, 15 October, 'diuers men' led by Thomas Dockwary and Brian Jobson assembled the whole town of Kendal at Tarney Bankes 'and sware thaym in a crofte by to be trewe to god & the king & their auncyent laudable customes'. The gentlemen of Kendal, especially Sir James Leyborne, resisted the oath at first but were eventually coerced into taking it with the help of a force from the neighbouring town of Dent.[19] A similar process took place in Westmoreland and Cumberland.[20] On 18 October the Earls of Shrewsbury, Rutland, and Huntingdon reported to the Duke of Suffolk that the rebels had reached Doncaster and 'there ronge the common bell and swere the mayre and comons of the same, who right gladly received their othe'.[21] In Northumberland, the administration of the pilgrims' oath diverged from the general pattern, for here it was not the commons but Sir Ingram Percy himself who led the drive to swear the gentlemen of the region.[22] As the major urban centres of the North fell to the rebels, more and more gentlemen took the pilgrims' oath. When Aske's host took the city of York, Aske devised a new oath, the so-called 'oath of honourable men'. He also began to use others in addition to the

---

[15] Aske's narrative is printed in Bateson (ed.), 'Pilgrimage of Grace', 332.

[16] Cox (ed.), 'William Stapleton and the Pilgrimage of Grace', 84 (*LP*, XII (i) 392).

[17] Cox (ed.), 'William Stapleton and the Pilgrimage of Grace', 85–6 (*LP*, XII (i) 392).

[18] Bush, *Pilgrimage of Grace*, 83 (*LP*, XI 622).

[19] NA E36/119, fols. 114^r–115^v (*LP*, XII (i) 914).

[20] NA SP1/117, fols. 43^r–44^v, 50^v–52^v (*LP*, XII (i) 687). See also Dodds and Dodds, *Pilgrimage of Grace*, I:220–2.

[21] NA SP1/108, fol. 169^r (*LP*, XI 774).   [22] Dodds and Dodds, *Pilgrimage of Grace*, I:199–200.

commons as his agents of administration, sending the gentlemen of York who supported the rebellion into the countryside to tender the oath to their friends. A proclamation accompanied this oath declaring that anyone who refused the oath had a twenty-four hour grace period before their goods would be seized.[23] The greatest nobles of the region – including Lord Darcy and the Archbishop of York Edward Lee – took Aske's oath on 21 October when Pontefract Castle surrendered to the rebels. Aske reported: 'the said castell was yelded, and the lordes spirituall and temporall and knightes and escueres ther being swhorn'.[24] After the December pardon of the rebels and the subsequent truce that ended the main phase of the revolt, it was the administration of oaths that signalled the renewal of the uprising. When John Hallom and Sir Francis Bigod decided to raise the commons again in January 1537, one of the first moves Hallom made was to swear Hugh Langdale 'leaste he shulde bewraye theym or saide any worde from theym to the prior of Watton his master being than at london'.[25] Bigod then devised a new form of the commons' oath which he sent throughout the countryside.[26] When George Lumley took the town of Scarborough on 17 January 1537, he spoke 'with the baylyfs & other officers of the towne, and sware theym according to Sir Fraunces Bygods letter'.[27] Thus, the spread of the revolt throughout England was accompanied by the spread of rebel oath-taking.[28] Indeed, with the exception of Hull and some of the residents of Carlisle, every town or region that joined the rebel army in 1536 swore some sort of oath of loyalty to the cause.

The administration of the pilgrims' oaths was comprehensive not only in its geographical scope but also in its social scope. Like the oath of succession, it appears that every male in the regions affected was tendered an oath. Writing on 17 October before he capitulated to the rebels, Lord Darcy reported to the king that the commons 'swere everie man preeste and oodre'.[29] William Breyar confessed that in Beverley a proclamation was made 'that euery man shulde be there sworn . . . & so accordynaly he & euery man there beyng toke the same othe'.[30] Likewise, the Preston husbandman William Nycholson testified that 'there every man toke his

---

[23] *LP*, XII (i) 901; Bateson (ed.), 'Aske's Examination', 572; Dodds and Dodds *Pilgrimage of Grace*, 1:181–2; Bush, *Pilgrimage of Grace*, 114–15.

[24] Bateson (ed.), 'Pilgrimage of Grace', 336; Bush, *Pilgrimage of Grace*, 94.

[25] NA E36/119, fol. 28[r] (*LP*, XII (i) 201).   [26] NA SP1/114, fols. 181[r], 183[r] (*LP*, XII (i) 147.

[27] Milner and Benham (eds.), *Records of the Lumleys*, 40 (*LP*, XII (i) 369).

[28] For more details on the exact timing of the various hosts' oath-taking, see Bush, *Pilgrimage of Grace*, 29, 114–15, 145, 196–7, 224, 227–8, 252–3, 298, 323–4, 345.

[29] NA SP1/108, fol. 144[v] (*LP*, XI 760).   [30] NA SP1/109, fol. 39[v] (*LP*, XI 841).

othe'.[31] Social distinctions were, however, still important in the administration of the pilgrims' oaths. Yet during the Pilgrimage of Grace the typical social roles were turned upside down. The commons clearly led the swearing campaign. They created the original oaths of the rebellion, and they were the chief administrators of the oaths. By contrast, the gentry of the North were generally placed in a more passive role. They had the choice to swear the oath or to refuse it.

And just as Henry VIII added incentives to swear the oath of succession by making the refusal of the oath punishable by confiscation of goods, imprisonment, and (after the spring of 1536) death, the commons often resorted to coercion in order to obtain the oaths of reluctant gentlemen. Sometimes the commons threatened the nonjuror with death. For example, when Sir William Fairfax declined to take the oath in the town of Wakefield on 22 October and took off on horseback, the entire town with a host of six hundred men pursued him all the way to Millthrop Hall. There, the host pulled him out of his bed, intimidated him 'to the great fear and danger of his life', and compelled him to take their oath instantly.[32] Similarly, Lord Darcy reported to Henry VIII that the commons 'threten to put them to deathe' who will not swear and thus 'no resistence hathe been made or can be made against them'.[33] Henry Sais, a servant of Christopher Askew, claimed that one of the rebels said to him: 'if ye do not swere thus to be trewe to god & to the king & to the comens, then shalt lose thy hedde'.[34] Robert Sotheby testified that William Leache declared to the sheriff and gentlemen of Horncastle: 'be sworne to do as we doo or ells it schall cost you your lyffe and as man[y as?] wyll not swere'.[35] The proclamation of the commons of the barony of Kendal ordered that any 'lord that denyeth the lawfull oath, se you that he suffer death at that present time'.[36] Families of those refusing to swear were also subject to intimidation. When the gentleman Nicholas Tempest fled into hiding to avoid the rebel host, a group of the commons seized his child John and threatened to strike off the boy's head if Nicolas did not return and take his oath.[37] Likewise, a new form of the rebel oath circulating in Richmondshire in January 1537 explicitly proclaimed: 'If eney lorde or gentyllman do deny to take thys hothe then to put thaym to dethe & put the next of hys blode in hys place & if he do denny put hym to dethe in lyke case so on after anoder to on of the blode wyll take the hothe.'[38]

[31] NA E36/119, fol. 31ᵛ (*LP*, xii (i) 201 (v)).   [32] Dodds and Dodds, *Pilgrimage of Grace*, 1:237.
[33] NA sp1/108, fol. 144ᵛ (*LP*, xi 760).   [34] NA sp1/109, fol. 200ᵛ (*LP*, xi 879).
[35] NA sp1/110, fol. 124ᵛ (*LP*, xi 967 (i)).   [36] Hoyle and Winchester, 'Lost Source', 129.
[37] Dodds and Dodds, *Pilgrimage of Grace*, 1:210 (*LP*, xii (i) 1014).
[38] NA sp1/114, fol. 201ʳ (*LP*, xii (i) 163).

Although the commons sometimes used death threats to get gentlemen to swear, a more usual method of coercion was the menace of property confiscation. An anonymous gentleman of the region of Holland, Lincolnshire, wrote to Lord Audley that he and other gentlemen were 'constreyned & coacted' to swear by a band of commons because the sheriff had ordered that the goods of all those who refused to swear be seized for the maintenance of the rebel army.[39] This became the official policy of the rebel host under the control of Aske, though Aske ordered 'that no man should spoll no man' unless two members of the rebel council consented and the nonjuror was given twenty-four hours to conform.[40] Numerous examples of the threat of spoilage survive. Lord Monteagle informed Henry VIII that several of his servants and tenants 'be sworn to the said rebellyons' because 'in case they had not byn sworn they wold haue spoyled all theyre howses and goodes'.[41] The commons approached Sir Marmaduke Constable at his house and declared 'how they wold eyther haue him swhorn or els spoll him'.[42] John Dakyn, vicar-general of the diocese of York, originally fled the rebels of Richmondshire, but he returned to his house and swore his oath when he heard the commons were going to destroy his goods.[43] Whether through threats of death or property confiscation, the commons used intimidation to compel reluctant gentlemen to take their oaths.

Of course, it is possible to exaggerate the commons' use of force in their administration of the pilgrims' oaths. First, many witnesses claimed that the gentlemen took their oaths freely and willingly. Philip Trotter deposed that, when William Leache and his band of Lincolnshire commons approached Sheriff Edward Dymmoke, Sir William Sandon, and other gentlemen of Lincolnshire and demanded that they take the rebels' oath, the gentlemen responded 'ffurthwithe withoute any Resistens or Denyall with a good will and so they were sworne accordingly'.[44] A witness to the oath-taking ceremony at Doncaster explained that the inhabitants there swore 'gladly', noting 'that never shepe ranne fastir in a mornyng oute of their folde, then they did to receive the said othe'.[45] There was no way that Sir Ingram Percy could claim that he took the oath under duress since when a single messenger presented him with the commons' oath, the nearest host was over fifty miles away and Percy himself immediately began coercing other gentlemen in the region to swear.[46] After his capture, Robert Aske confessed that 'he sware none but gentlemen and they toke their othe vp willingly,

[39] NA E36/121, fol. 72ʳ (LP, XI 585).
[40] Bateson (ed.), 'Pilgrimage of Grace', 335; Bush, Pilgrimage of Grace, 114.
[41] NA SP1/112, fol. 94ʳ (LP, XI 1232).   [42] Bateson (ed.), 'Pilgrimage of Grace', 338.
[43] Dodds and Dodds, Pilgrimage of Grace, I:201–2.   [44] NA E36/119, fol. 13ʳ (LP, XII (i) 70).
[45] NA SP1/108, fol. 169ʳ (LP, XI 774).   [46] Dodds and Dodds, Pilgrimage of Grace, I:199–200.

as semed to hym, after that they were ones taken & brought in, and saith he offred them that othe voluntary'.[47] Hence, some gentlemen must have taken the rebel oath enthusiastically. This should not be surprising in light of the current historiographical consensus that some of the lords and gentry of the North shared the same grievances as the commons, especially insofar as the grievances related to the Henrician Reformation.[48]

The second reason that stories of forced swearing must be taken with a grain of salt is that it was in the gentry's best interest to claim that they had taken their oaths involuntarily. Much of the details of the Pilgrimage emerged after it was over, when Henry sought information on whom to punish for the rebellion. Many of the participants in the revolt thus attempted to portray their oath-taking as reluctant in order to escape royal wrath. We do not know how many of these reports were coloured in such a manner, but the existence of a few contradictory reports demonstrates that not all of the stories of unwilling but coerced swearers can be trusted. For example, the Earl of Shrewsbury wrote to Lord Darcy that he had heard that Darcy's servant Thomas Grice had compelled Brian Bradford (a servant to Shrewsbury's cousin Henry Savell) and 'put in feare divers oders to be sworne contrary to their myndes and wylles by reason wherof they dare not abyde at home in there owne houses' but had fled to Sheffield, Rotherham, and other places.[49] Grice, however, replied that Bradford 'was sworne wyth his gud wyll openly before sufficaent wit[nesses] and Recorde, for I did reherce vnto hym that ther shuld [be] no man compellyd to swer contraie to thar fre myndes and willes nor ne[ver?] was'.[50] Even more compelling is the story of a late-night oath-tendering in Lancashire. After a few pints at the local alehouse, John Piper, John Yate, and Hugh Parker (only sixteen years old) decided to have a little fun by blackening their faces, dressing in harness, and testing the resolve of a few neighbours who had boasted 'that they wold not be sworn to the commons to dye for it'.[51] According to Robert Banks, who was the group's first victim, John Yate rushed into Banks' house 'and said he must swere to be true to the comons and sayd if he wold not swere he shuld dye'. 'For fear of his liff and of his children', Banks delivered him his harness.[52] By contrast, Yate's deposition

---

[47] Bateson (ed.), 'Aske's Examination', 572. Aske also claimed 'that no man was nother hurt nor wounded to his knowlege, for refusing the othe, nor no other violence offred theym, but that they shulde lose their goodes if they cam not in within xxiiii houres after they were warned'; Bateson (ed.), 'Aske's Examination', 572.

[48] Bush, *Pilgrimage of Grace*, 409–10; Bernard, *King's Reformation*, 321–6.

[49] NA sp1/111, fol. 172^r (*LP*, xi 1112).   [50] NA sp1/111, fol. 173^r (*LP*, xi 1113).

[51] NA sp1/112, fol. 89^v (*LP*, xi 1230).   [52] NA sp1/112, fol. 90^r (*LP*, xi 1230).

mentioned no threats but rather claimed Banks 'was content to be sworn'.[53] The next victim of the group, William Charnocke, stated that Parker, Yate, and Piper 'with force brake his dore, and manasced [menaced] hym to kyll hym' unless he was sworn.[54] Conversely, Parker and Yate contended that Charnocke opened the door for them – they did not break it down – and their testimony makes no mention of threats.[55] Likewise, Percival Saunders (the third victim of the group) claimed that Parker, Yate, and Piper broke down his door, 'clapped a boke to his mouth', and demanded he be sworn. When Saunders refused, 'one of theym tok hym on the backe with a malle and stroke hym down and said if he wold not be sworn he shuld see his own blud befor his own eyes. And so the said percyvall for feare of his liff was sworn vnto theym'.[56] Yate, by contrast, testified that he swore Saunders, Charnocke, and others 'without compulcon of any of theym'.[57] Parker argued that he took part in the whole escapade 'thynking no hurt nor intending noo yll bot thought they had gon to make pastym'.[58] Clearly, both those who tendered the oath and those who took it were trying to present themselves in as favourable a light as possible. What is significant for our purpose is that the dispute centred over whether the oaths that Parker, Yate, and Piper tendered were coerced or not. The conflicting depositions illustrate that not all those who averred that they had taken the rebels' oath unwillingly were necessarily telling the truth.

Finally, the coercion the commons employed in the administration of their oaths was not so overwhelming as to be irresistible. Flight was sometimes an option. Lord Scrope decided to abandon his house and wife rather than to swear to the commons.[59] Likewise, an unidentified man of Dent fled to Sir Marmaduke Tunstall to avoid swearing.[60] Other gentlemen simply held their ground. When Thomas Maunsell, the vicar of Brayton, heard that his brother was in great danger for refusing to swear Aske's oath, Thomas received permission from Aske to tender the oath to his brother in person. Yet when his brother saw Thomas, he 'did smyte at hym [Thomas] and with greate violence did dryve hym out of his house being vnsworne'.[61] Both Sir Ralph Ellerker the younger and the elder refused to swear the commons' oath despite pressure from the Stapleton host.[62] The town of Hull agreed to surrender to the Stapleton host only under the condition that they would not have to take the pilgrims' oath. Stapleton

---

[53] NA sp1/112, fol. 90[r] (*LP*, xi 1230).   [54] NA sp1/112, fol. 89[r] (*LP*, xi 1230).

[55] NA sp1/112, fols. 89[v]–90[r] (*LP*, xi 1230).   [56] NA sp1/112, fol. 89[r]. (*LP*, xi 1230).

[57] NA sp1/112, fol. 90[r]. (*LP*, xi 1230).   [58] NA sp1/112, fol. 89[v]. (*LP*, xi 1230).

[59] *LP*, xi 677.   [60] NA sp1/109, fol. 37[v] (*LP*, xi 841).   [61] NA sp1/113, fol. 55[r] (*LP*, xi 1402).

[62] Cox (ed.), 'William Stapleton and the Pilgrimage of Grace', 85, 89, 97 (*LP*, xii (i) 392).

agreed.[63] Thus, not all gentlemen of the North gave in and swore the rebels' oath when pressured by the commons. This indicates that it was possible to resist the rebels' oath, and thus some degree of consent was involved in the choice of a gentleman to swear.

Despite the above caveats, the general picture that emerges from the Pilgrimage of Grace is one of the commons using force to coerce reluctant gentlemen into taking their oaths. This use of force by the commons in their administration of their oaths demonstrates that, like Henry VIII, the commons believed that a forced oath still had the power to bind a person's conscience. Indeed, once the gentry had taken their oaths, the commons were placated. For example, William Moreland of Louth reported: 'And after the swering of thes gentilmen there was great ioye and moche gladnes made amongs the commons of and vpon the same.'[64] The commons' joy after the gentlemen had taken their oaths indicates that the commons trusted the binding power of oaths, no matter how forced they were. Threats of death and property confiscation were no longer necessary, for now God himself would enforce the loyalty of the gentlemen to the Pilgrimage. The gentlemen's oaths themselves had become powerful means of compulsion. For example, when Captain Poverty sought to gain the support of the town of Kendal for the new uprising at Carlisle in February 1537, he cited Kendal's oath: 'Wherfore we desyre you for ayde and helpe accordyng to your othes and as ye wyll have helpe of us if your cause requyre, as god forbede.'[65] Oaths were powerful, whether taken freely or under threat. William Stapleton's opinion 'that the oathe did no good for it wolde make a man neither better nor yet wourse' was clearly not shared by the majority of the rebels.[66]

In sum, the administration of oaths was integral to the Pilgrimage of Grace, and the pattern of administration mirrored that of the oath of succession. The oath of succession was comprehensive in scope, backed with force, and designed to secure the loyalty of English subjects to the king and his succession. The pilgrims' oaths were also comprehensive in scope, backed with force, and designed to obtain the loyalty of the gentlemen to the commons' cause. Of course, similarity does not necessarily imply imitation. It is conceivable that the rebels of the Pilgrimage of Grace could have employed oaths in the way that they did even if Henry VIII had not

---

[63] Dodds and Dodds, *Pilgrimage of Grace*, I:164, 166.
[64] NA E36/119, fol. 54ʳ (*LP*, XII (i) 380).
[65] Dodds and Dodds, *Pilgrimage of Grace*, II:113 (*LP*, XII (i) 411).
[66] Cox (ed.), 'William Stapleton and the Pilgrimage of Grace', 97 (*LP*, XII (i) 392).

tendered the oath of succession in 1534. After all, the English peasants of 1381 and the German peasants of 1525 had used oaths to raise support for their rebellions and to coerce their social superiors into remaining loyal to their rebellions.[67] Yet oaths played no major role in other popular insurrections of the time such as Cade's Revolt of 1450, the Cornish rising of 1497, the movement against the Amicable Grant in 1525, Wyatt's Rebellion of 1554, and the Rebellion of the Northern Earls in 1569.[68] In the immediate context of sixteenth-century England, then, the rebels' great use of oaths was unique. The pilgrims' temporal proximity to 1534 and the similarity of the administration of their oaths to that of the oath of succession suggest that the pilgrims' oaths of 1536 were an imitation of the oath of succession.

In a sense, the oath of succession both invited and required the pilgrims of 1536 to incorporate oaths into the centre of their rebellion. Henry had taught his subjects that oaths were an ideal means through which to ensure fidelity. By forcing all of them to swear the oath of succession, he had exposed all of them to the power of an oath of loyalty. And oaths were so effective not only because in them God became the enforcer of the promise, but also because anyone could swear them. Oaths were at the same time powerful and easily accessible. Henry's subjects could deploy oaths just as easily as Henry could. After Henry had given such a great example of how to use oaths, Henry should have expected his subjects to respond in kind. Furthermore, the pilgrims' decision to employ oaths as opposed to some other form of compulsion was probably *necessitated* by Henry's administration of oaths. Because Henry had bound his subjects to be loyal to him with an oath – the strongest bond of conscience – the commons had to use an equally strong bond to secure the gentry's loyalty to their cause, lest the gentry turn against the commons and cite their oath to the king as stronger than their bond to the commons. Just as Henry had to employ oaths to cancel out previous oaths of loyalty which his subjects had taken to the Pope, the pilgrims needed to use an oath to emphasize that they were as serious about their pilgrimage as Henry had been about establishing his heirs through Anne Boleyn. The oath of succession had upped the ante.

---

[67] For the role of oaths in the English Peasants' Revolt of 1381, see Dobson (ed.), *Peasants' Revolt of 1381*, 125, 127, 133, 258, 285–6, 290–1. For the role of oaths in the German Peasants' War of 1525, see Scott and Scribner (eds.), *German Peasants' War*, 16–17, 107, 126, 132–3, 138–9, 183, 186, 189, 193, 200, 293, 297, 303–5.

[68] For a further comparison of the roles of oaths in various popular rebellions in medieval and early modern Europe, see Gray, 'So Help Me God', 253–7.

RESPONSE AS INTERPRETATION: THE PILGRIMS' OATHS, THE OATH
OF SUCCESSION, AND LOYALTY TO THE KING

Of course, if an oath was truly binding, this meant that the pilgrims could
not simply imitate the oath of succession; they also had to address the
oath of succession. The consciences of the commons had been bound by
the oath of succession just as much as the consciences of the gentry. The
pilgrims' oaths made sure that the gentlemen (and commons) of the North
stayed loyal to the commons' cause, but what about the loyalty that the
entire realm had sworn to the king? This had to be taken into consider-
ation. As such, the oaths of the Pilgrimage of Grace implicitly declared
the commons' interpretation of the oath of succession. The genius of
the pilgrims' oaths was that they exploited the ambiguities in the oath
of succession so as to allow the pilgrims to maintain that their oaths –
indeed, their uprising in general – was perfectly in line with the fidelity
they had sworn to Henry in the oath of succession. Whereas Henry interpreted the oath of succession as binding his subjects to be loyal to him
and his religious policies, the pilgrims' oaths declared that the commons
interpreted the oath of succession as binding them to be loyal to Henry
if he stayed obedient to God and maintained the church. The Pilgrimage of Grace was thus a struggle over the interpretation of the oath of
succession.

   To start, the content of the various pilgrims' oaths indicates that the commons formulated these oaths in response to the oath of succession. Their
oaths balanced their loyalty to Henry (clearly addressed in the oath of succession) with their opposition to Henry's religious policies (not explicitly
mentioned in the oath of succession and therefore open to interpretation). The Lincolnshire rebels who started the uprising swore to be true
to God, the king, and the commons (or the commonwealth).[69] In this
oath, the swearers declared that they were loyal to the king, not rebels
at all. Yet the fact that the pilgrims also swore to be true to God and
the commons placed limits on their loyalty to the king. It is significant
that the pilgrims swore to God *before* they swore to the king. Moreover,
by swearing obedience to three bodies, the pilgrims declared that God's
policy should coincide with the king's policy, which in turn must coincide
with the commons' policy, for the only way to be loyal to all three of

---

[69] NA E36/121, fol. 72ʳ (*LP*, XI 585); NA SP1/109, fol. 2ᵛ (*LP*, XI 828); NA SP1/110, fol. 124ᵛ (*LP*, XI 967);
NA SP1/110, fol. 134ʳ (*LP*, XI 968); NA SP1/110, fol. 143ʳ (*LP*, XI 970); Bateson (ed.), 'Pilgrimage of
Grace', 332; Bush, *Pilgrimage of Grace*, 12.

these bodies simultaneously was for the three bodies to be in agreement. The pilgrims thus declared their loyalty to the king while at the same time binding their consciences to a particular kind of princely rule, a rule in line with the will of God and the commons. After summarizing the rebels' oath, Lord Darcy remarked: 'For thay be sure as thay say that suche acts against godd the kyng and his commones welthe is not his grace's pleasure.'[70]

The rebels' interpretation of the oath of succession is even clearer in the oaths formulated by the rebels after the revolt had spread outside Lincolnshire. Most of the oaths from this formal stage of the Pilgrimage bound the swearer to be loyal to God, the king, the commons, and 'the church'.[71] The band of commons led by William Leache swore a group of gentleman to 'be true to [god] the kyng and the commons and the ffayth of the church'.[72] The town of Beverley was sworn 'to maynteyn holi church', while the Richmondshire oath of January 1537 proclaimed that all gentlemen must swear 'to manten the profet of hoyle churche wyche wase the howpholldeyng [upholding?] of the crysten faythe'.[73] Some of the oaths from Yorkshire also specified which aspects of God's church the commons were rising to support. In a letter to his son before his capitulation to the rebels, Lord Darcy claimed that the men of Dent, Sedbergh, and Wensleydale swore that 'they will suffer no Spoylls nor Suppression of Abbays, p[ari]che churches nor of the Jewells & ornamentes. Nor also mor money thay will not pay for commissioners nor others'.[74] Some versions of the rebel oath bound the pilgrims 'to resist al them' who did not 'maynteyn holi church' but rather 'willeth the contrary'.[75] The Richmondshire oath explicitly singled out Thomas Cromwell, binding the gentlemen to swear 'to put downe the lorde crowmwell that heretyke & hall hys sekthewyche [sect the which] mayde the kyng put downe prayng & fastyng'.[76] The town of Beverley swore to oppose the 'concellores inventars & procurars' who were attempting 'vtterlye to vndoo boithe the Churche & the commynalte of the reamlme'.[77] This oath also highlights that the maintenance of the church was connected to the maintenance of the commonwealth. Accordingly, some forms of the rebel oath delineated

---

[70] NA sp1/106, fol. 286ʳ (*LP*, xi 563 (2)), quoted in Bernard, *King's Reformation*, 320.
[71] For a typical example, see NA sp1/117, fol. 43ʳ (*LP*, xii (i) 687).
[72] NA sp1/110, fol. 124ᵛ (*LP*, xi 967).
[73] NA sp1/109, fol. 39ᵛ (*LP*, xi 841); NA sp1/114, fol. 201ʳ (*LP*, xii (i) 163).
[74] NA sp1/106, fol. 286ʳ (*LP*, xi 563 (2)), quoted in Bernard, *King's Reformation*, 320.
[75] NA sp1/109, fol. 39ᵛ (*LP*, xi 841).   [76] NA sp1/114, fol. 201ʳ (*LP*, xii (i) 163).
[77] NA sp1/107, fol. 136ʳ (*LP*, xi 645).

specific economic grievances as well.[78] Yet even these economic grievances were connected to the church in that the rebels opposed the exaction of burdensome financial payments as an 'unlawfull act that is against the faith of Christ, the church profitt and the commonwealth'.[79] In general, when the Yorkshire pilgrims expanded on the Lincolnshire oath, they added clauses relating to the church. Thus, when the Yorkshire rebels swore their oaths, they pledged loyalty to a king who would maintain the church, uphold the faith, restore the monasteries, and eject heretics like Thomas Cromwell from his council. At the same time as the rebels were declaring their continual fidelity to Henry – a fidelity solidified in the oath of succession – they were rejecting the recent religious policy of the Crown.

The three fullest forms of pilgrims' oaths support the argument that one of the primary purposes of these oaths was to proclaim the commons' belief that the oath of succession had not bound them to support the religious changes of the 1530s. The oath from Beverley read:

we shall be trewe to god & owr prince & his *lawfull* actes & demandes & that we shall be trew & faithfull to yowe & other, the comyns of the reallme & yowe & them to aide & mantein to the vttermeste of owr power boithe with bodye & goodes ayenste all them that [are?] his concellores inventars & procurars vtterlye to vndoo boithe the Churche & the commynalte of the realme so helpe vs Gode.[80]

The oath Aske composed for Sawley Abbey began:

Ye shall swere to bere trew faith & fauor vnto god his faith & churche matenaunyce and the kynges grace to subdue & expulse all villayn blod from the sayd kynges grace & his privey councell, and to suppress all herises and ther openions to the best of your powres for the comon welth.[81]

Finally, Aske's famous oath of honourable men read:

Ye shall not entre to this our pilgramaige of grace for the commine welthe but oonly for the love ye bere to goddes faithe and church mylitant and the maynetenaunce therof, the preseruacyon of the kinges persone his Issue and the purifieng of the nobilitie and to expulse all vilaynes bloode and evill councesailours against the comen welth of the same, And that ye shall not entre into our said pylgremaige

---

[78] The Richmondshire oath proclaimed that 'no lorde nor gentyllman shall take nothyng of thare tennandes but honle [only] thare Rentes'; NA SP1/114, fol. 201[r] (*LP*, XII (i) 163). Likewise the commons of Kendal forced their gentlemen to swear an oath 'to be trewe to god & the king & their auncyent laudable customes'; NA E36/119, fol. 114[v] (*LP*, XII (i) 914). The Richmondshire and Kendal oaths referred to the exacting and raising of gressums: that is, 'payments that fell due upon change of either tenant or lord'; Bush, *Pilgrimage of Grace*, 256.
[79] Hoyle and Winchester, 'Lost Source', 128–9.   [80] NA SP1/107, fol. 136[r] (*LP*, XI 645). My italics.
[81] NA SP1/109, fol. 110[v] (*LP*, XI 872).

for no peculyar profuyte to our selves ne to do no dyspleasure to no private personne but by counsaile of the commene welthe nor sle nor murdre for no envye but in your hertes to put awaye all feare for the commune welthe. And to take bifore you the crosse of cryste and your hertes faithe to the restitucyon of his churche and to the suppressyon of hertykes opynyons by the holy contentes of thys Boke.[82]

Two features stand out in these oaths. The first is how similar the first two oaths are to a standard oath of fidelity. The juxtaposition of 'faith' with 'truth' and the emphasis on serving to the 'best' or 'uttermost' of one's power were standard clauses in an oath of fidelity, clauses that could have been lifted directly from the oath of succession.[83] The second is that these oaths qualified the pilgrims' fidelity to the king by swearing to maintain and restore the church, and to suppress heretics and expel villain blood. The Beverley oath even added the modifier 'lawful', suggesting the rebels were not bound to be true to the king's unlawful acts and demands. Yet while the pilgrims' oaths restricted their loyalty to Henry, nothing in the pilgrims' oaths contradicted the oath of succession. There was nothing in

---

[82] NA sp1/108, fol. 48ʳ (*LP*, xi 705). This version is printed in Bernard, *King's Reformation*, 330. For another version of this oath with very slight differences see Toller (ed.), *Correspondence of Edward, Third Earl of Derby*, 50–1; Hoyle, *Pilgrimage of Grace*, 457–8. For a more altered version of this oath that adds clauses about the pilgrims being unable to depart the host without licence from their captains and about keeping their communication secret, see NA sp1/109, fol. 248ʳ (*LP*, xi 902), printed in Hoyle, *Pilgrimage of Grace*, 458–9. A miniature historiographical debate exists on whether Aske's oath of honourable men was a departure from the rebels' grievances of Lincolnshire. Hoyle, following Madeleine and Ruth Dodds, suggested that Aske's oath should be read as follows: You shall not enter to this our Pilgrimage of Grace for the commonwealth but only for the love you bear to God's faith and church militant, etc. Aske's goal, then, was to point out that the rebellion was not about tax grievances or the commonwealth but about the church; Hoyle, *Pilgrimage of Grace*, 206–7. See also Dodds and Dodds, *Pilgrimage of Grace*, 1:139. Bernard disagreed. Bernard argued that Aske's oath should be read as follows: You shall not enter to this our-Pilgrimage-of-Grace-for-the-commonwealth for any reason (especially not for any particular profit to yourselves) but only for the love you bear to God's faith and church militant, etc. Bernard claimed: 'What the religious concerns – "but only for the maintenance of God's faith and Church militant" – are being contrasted with is not the commonwealth but rather the later instruction (which Hoyle fails to quote) "not to enter into our pilgrimage for private profit or displeasure to an private person, but by counsel of the commonwealth."' The commonwealth thus remained an integral part of the Yorkshire uprising; Bernard, *King's Reformation*, 229–330. In general, I agree with Bernard's reading of the oath. Both the later section of Aske's oath of honourable men and the other versions of the rebel oath circulating in Yorkshire at this time continue to make references to the commonwealth. Aske was not seeking to cut the commonwealth out of the pilgrims' programme. Hoyle was correct, however, in emphasizing that Aske's concern was not tax grievances but the maintenance of the church. These two opinions can be reconciled if we recognize that the term 'commonwealth' did not refer simply to tax grievances but to the general health of the realm in which the maintenance of the church played a major role. For the rebels, to have a strong commonwealth was to maintain the church.

[83] See Appendix D for the oath of succession.

the pilgrims' oaths against the Boleyn marriage or succession.[84] Indeed, Aske's oath of honourable men expressly bound the swearer to maintain the king's issue. Neither was there anything in the pilgrims' oaths on the Pope or previous oaths of loyalty to foreign powers. The pilgrims' oaths certainly challenged the thrust of the king's religious policy, but the actual text of the oath of succession had not bound Henry's subjects to the specific features of this policy. By swearing an oath that combined fidelity to the king with defence of the church and repression of heresy, the rebels were declaring their interpretation of the fidelity they had sworn to Henry in the oath of succession and binding their consciences to this interpretation. And because the actual text of the oath of succession was conservative, this interpretation was technically valid.

Yet not everyone agreed that the pilgrims' oaths were a valid interpretation of the oath of succession. The commons and their leaders certainly thought the oaths were conciliatory. When Robert Aske was first stopped by the Lincolnshire rebels and commanded to swear, Aske replied 'that he was ons sworn to the Kinges hignes and issue, and that he wold not be sworn agayn to any other intent'. Upon learning the content of the pilgrims' oath, however, he responded, 'in this oth is ther no treson, but standing with his first oth'.[85] When John Hallom tendered the pilgrims' oath to Hugh Langdale, Hallom asked Langdale 'whether there was any thing therin that a man might not lawfully swere'. Langdale replied 'that he thought not'.[86] Yet those who were lukewarm in their support of the rebels used the overlap between the oath of succession and the pilgrims oath as a way of avoiding the latter oath. They argued that since they had already sworn fidelity to the king in the oath of succession, there was no need for them to swear it again in the rebels' oath. When the commons instructed Bernard Towneley, chancellor of the diocese of Carlisle, and his group to swear their oath to 'be true to almyghty god his chyrche the kynges maieste & the comon welthe', Towneley answered that they 'wer bounde to allrede'.[87] Likewise, when William Leache demanded that the sheriff of Lincolnshire Edward Dymmoke take the pilgrims' oath, Dymmoke

---

[84] Some of the pilgrims did of course want to re-legitimize Mary, as the Pontefract Articles make clear. It should be emphasized, however, that this was not part of their oaths. We should also keep in mind that this was after the execution of Anne Boleyn for treason and the re-introduction of Mary into the king's favour. Furthermore, these clauses of the Pontefract Articles were mainly a reaction against the 1536 Act of Succession (to which the pilgrims had not been sworn) rather than the 1534 Act of Succession (to which they had been sworn). This is evident by their bizarre concern that the king not bequeath the throne to Cromwell. See Hoyle, *Pilgrimage of Grace*, 332–3, 347, 351.

[85] Bateson (ed.), 'Pilgrimage of Grace', 332.   [86] NA E36/119, fol. 22ᵛ (*LP*, XII (i) 201 (ii)).

[87] NA SP1/117, fol. 43ʳ (*LP*, XII (i) 687).

responded, 'wherefore should I swear? I am sworn to the king already'.[88] Finally, those who directly opposed the commons interpreted the pilgrims' oath as against their previous oath of fidelity to the king. When the Stapleton host instructed Sir Ralph Ellerker the younger to take the pilgrims' oath, Ellerker refused, claiming 'he was sworne to the Kinges personne, and other oathe he woulde take none without the Kinges pleasure'.[89] Similarly, when the commons commanded Harry Sais, servant of Christopher Askew, to swear to be 'trewe to god & to the king', he was content to swear. But when one of the commons added 'and not to vs?', Sais replied, 'yf ye be trewe to the king or els I wolde be lothe to swere'.[90] Sais recognized that an oath of loyalty to the commons would be lawful only if it did not conflict with the loyalty he owed (and had sworn to) the king.

Perhaps the most mysterious debate over the relationship between the pilgrims' oaths and the oath of succession comes from an untitled, unsigned, and much-mutilated list of propositions. These propositions contained material on Henry's supreme headship, heretical bishops, parliamentary procedure, and English customs. The list of propositions was most likely drawn up as a guide to what was to be discussed at the conference of leading northern divines at Pontefract Castle, since most of the propositions on the list were indeed discussed at the rebel-controlled Pontefract Council at the end of 1536.[91] Among the propositions we find the following:

Item, if one othe be . . . the same may be adnulled or noo. Item, if one othe be made, [an]d after one oder othe to the contrary, and by the latter othe the partie is sw[orn to] repute and take the fyrste othe voyde, wheder it may be soo by . . . lawe or noo. Item, if a kyng by his last w[ill] wyll hys realme after hys deith & in espicially furth of the Right lyne of in heritaunces yeroff, whedder the subiectes of the same realme be bounde by godes lawes to obey & performe the same wyll or noo.[92]

Yet these particular articles were never discussed at the Pontefract conference. Madeleine and Ruth Dodds suggested that the northern clergy chose to ignore these points because they were well aware that their oaths of supremacy had contradicted their oaths of canonical obedience to the

---

[88] NA SP1/110, fol. 124ᵛ (*LP*, XI 967), quoted in Hoyle, *Pilgrimage of Grace*, 440.

[89] Cox (ed.), 'William Stapleton and the Pilgrimage of Grace', 85 (*LP*, XII (i) 392).

[90] NA SP1/109, fol. 200ᵛ (*LP*, XI 879).

[91] Dodds and Dodds, *Pilgrimage of Grace*, 1:342. We know that Aske sent Archbishop Lee a list of propositions to be discussed at Pontefract: *LP*, XII (i), 698 (3), 901 (107), 1022. It is possible that the list discussed in this paragraph was the one Aske sent to Lee.

[92] NA SP1/112, fol. 24ᵛ (*LP*, XI 1182 (2)).

Pope, and they were uncomfortable addressing that contradiction.[93] This may be true. Nevertheless, the fact that the propositions on oaths are immediately followed by a proposition on whether subjects are bound to the will of a king who altered the line of his inheritance implies, in my opinion, that the rebels were primarily referring to the relationship of the pilgrims' oaths to the oath of succession. The writer of this manuscript probably hoped that the northern divines would clarify the exact relationship between these oaths. Alternatively, the writer might be referring to the relationship of the pilgrims' oaths to a new oath Henry VIII was demanding that all the rebels swear, an oath that explicitly repudiated the pilgrims' oaths. (Although this oath was not yet being tendered among the Yorkshire rebels at the time of the Pontefract Conference, the rebels would probably have known of its existence because the Duke of Suffolk had tendered a version of it to the rebels of Lincolnshire in October after the uprising there had collapsed.[94]) Regardless of whether these articles concerned the relationship of the pilgrims' oaths to the oath of succession or to the oath newly devised by the Crown, the articles demonstrate that the relationship of the pilgrims' oaths to an oath of fidelity to the king was a key issue, an issue made more important by the rebels' contentious claim that their oaths did not conflict with their loyalty to the king.

The genius of the pilgrims' oath – that it responded to the Henrician Reformation by combining the fidelity sworn in the oath of succession with a rejection of the recent religious policy – was also its greatest weakness. Once it became apparent that the king did not support the commons or the commons' rejection of the Reformation of the 1530s, it became much harder to maintain that the loyalty the pilgrims had sworn to the commons or commonwealth was reconcilable with the loyalty sworn to the king. This came out in January and February of 1537 when Hallom, Bigod, and others re-ignited local rebellions in repudiation of the king's December pardon. Bigod noted the potential conflict of oaths in a speech he gave on a hillock at Setterington to rouse support for his new uprising: 'And yet the same is no pardon. Also here ye are called Rebells, by the which ye shall knowledge yourself to have doon ageinst the king which is contrarie to your othe'.[95] Bigod's response was to devise and tender a new oath, 'theffect wherof was in all things like the former othe with this addicion: that no man shulde geve counsaill to any man to sitt still untill suche tyme as they

---

[93] Dodds and Dodds, *Pilgrimage of Grace*, 1:342–3.   [94] For more on this, see below.
[95] *LP*, XII (i) 369, printed in full in Milner and Benham (eds.), *Records of the Lumleys*, quotation from 38.

had obteyned their former articles'.[96] In essence, Bigod was asserting that only by refusing the December pardon and staying in the field could the pilgrims remain unperjured and keep their oath to be true to God, the king, and the commonwealth. Other pilgrims, however, construed Bigod's rebellion as being contrary to that same oath. Even though George Lumley was a participant (unwillingly?) in Bigod's rebellion, when the commons of the same rebellion pressured him to occupy Scarborough Castle, Lumley replied, 'he would not be of their counsel to enter into the castle, for it was the King's house, and there had they nor he nothing to do. And their oath was to do no thing against the King'.[97] Similarly, when a messenger arrived in the town of Durham bearing a copy of Bigod's new oath and a letter exhorting them to rise, the officers of the town responded that they had sworn an oath to rise and take up arms only if commanded by the Earl of Westmoreland or by the king, so they would abide by the king's pardon.[98] Indeed, the majority of the gentlemen of the North who had joined the Pilgrimage in October and December 1536 rejected Bigod's logic and stayed loyal to the king in January and February 1537. The split among the pilgrims engendered by Bigod's revolt therefore illustrates the conundrum inherent in the pilgims' oaths: how the commons who had sworn to be loyal to the king in the oath of succession could maintain that loyalty even while opposing the king's religious policy.

What the above examples make clear is that whether or not an individual agreed that the pilgrims' oaths were a legitimate interpretation of the oath of succession, the pilgrims' oaths were clearly considered in light of the oath of succession. Indeed, the various debates about whether the pilgrims' oaths were reconcilable with the oath of succession prove that the pilgrims' oaths were an interpretation of the oath of succession. Both those who supported the Pilgrimage and those who opposed it believed that the pilgrims' oaths were a response to the oath of succession. Even Henry VIII connected the pilgrims' oaths to the oath of succession, though he of

---

[96] Milner and Benham (eds.), *Records of the Lumleys*, 40. The text of Bigod's new oath was as follows: 'Ye shall swere to kepe trewlie all these articles contened in the othe lately gevenn yow by the Commons at ther last assemblyng aswell towchyng crist churche & faithe ther of as the kynges grace & all the faithfull Commons of this realme, Morouer ye shall not counsell or perswade by noo meanes any person spirituall or temporall to set furth or tary at home or yet to take order in this matter or stay but ernestlie & in the name of John to [pre]pare your selfe to batell agaynst all thoyse which are the vndoers of Christ Churche & of the Commons welth & not retorne bake from o[u]r good Jornay whils all o[u]r petioones be graunted soo helpe yow god your holidomme & by this boke. God save the kyng & all the trew commons'; NA SP1/114, fol. 181ʳ (*LP*, XII (i) 147). For a slightly different version of this oath, see NA SP1/114, fol. 183ʳ.

[97] Dodds and Dodds, *Pilgrimage of Grace*, II:70.

[98] Dodds and Dodds, *Pilgrimage of Grace*, II:78; Bush and Bownes, *Defeat of the Pilgrimage*, 223.

course felt that the pilgrims' oaths were completely contrary to the oath of succession. When Henry heard that his commissioners for the subsidy had not resisted the commons of Lincolnshire, he marvelled that they, 'being our sworne seruauntes . . . wold be so fonde to put your self in to their handes and not acording to your dewties'.[99] In a letter to Ellerker and Bowes chastising them and others for becoming party to the commons, Henry claimed that the Pilgrimage was against God's command and the allegiance his subjects had sworn to him: 'ffor god commaundeth them to obeye their prince what soeuer he be yee though he shuld not directe them Justly and their othe of Alleageance whiche passeth all othes and is the foundacion without the Keping of whiche al other othes be but nought and vayne'.[100] The pilgrims' oath was 'nought and vayne' because it contradicted the oath of succession. To Henry, the pilgrims' oaths were an invalid interpretation of the oath of succession.

Henry thus saw the pilgrims' oaths as compromising his subjects' loyalty to him. By swearing oaths to be loyal to each other and to a platform that opposed the king's religious policy, the pilgrims vitiated the allegiance they had sworn to him in the oath of succession. By responding to the oath of succession with their own oath, the bonds of the first oath had been weakened. As such, Henry did not allow the rebels' oaths to stand unchallenged. In the aftermath of the revolt, Henry had his commissioners – the Dukes of Norfolk and Suffolk and the Earls of Shrewsbury and Sussex – tender a new oath to all those involved in the rebellion, an oath that expressly nullified the rebels' oaths. This oath was not originally Henry's idea. When the revolt in Lincolnshire collapsed in mid October, Henry sent Suffolk and Shrewsbury to Lincolnshire to cause the gentlemen to make a submission and cause the commons to perform a set of articles.[101] Suffolk, however, turned these articles into an oath on his own and tendered it to the Lincolnshire rebels, as evidenced by Henry's letter to Suffolk on 22 October:

And wheras you doo signifie vnto vs in your said Letteres that you haue sworn certan gentlimen and others according to the tenor of the commyssion Ye shall vnderstand we remember not that we haue sent vnto you for that purpose any other commyssion thenne certain Articles signed with the our hande, and therfor require you to signifie vnto vs whither you haue ministered that othe according to the said Articles or otherwise.[102]

---

[99] NA sp1/106, fol. 301ʳ (*LP*, XI 569).   [100] NA e36/121, fol. 25ʳ (*LP*, XI 1175).
[101] The articles Henry sent to Suffolk and Shrewsbury do not survive, though they are clearly mentioned as being included in the letters Henry sent to Suffolk and Shrewsbury; *LP*, XI 715, 717.
[102] NA sp1/109, fol. 22ᵛ (*LP*, XI 833).

That same day, Suffolk wrote to Henry VIII that the rebels of Lincolnshire had taken 'their oaths according to instructions'.[103] Although Henry was not the originator of the idea of making the rebels swear a new oath, he quickly approved of it. When he sent the Duke of Norfolk and Lord Admiral William Fitzwilliam up to Doncaster at the end of November to deliver the king's response to the rebel grievances, to issue the king's pardon, and to demand their submission, Henry added: 'And the said Duke of Norfolk, and Lord Admyrall, in cace thise men growe to a submission, not onely cause them, that shal be presente, to receyve suche othe, as the Licolnshir men have sworn and receyved'.[104] Indeed, the original proclamation of pardon for Yorkshire on 2 December seems to have been an exact and thus outdated replication of the proclamation for Lincolnshire, for it declared that all rebels should come to the city of Lincoln and in the presence of Suffolk (lord lieutenant of Lincolnshire) 'submitte them selfes to his highnes Renoncyng their late rebellious othe and taking such a newe Othe as his grace hath prescribed for the same their genrall and free pardon'.[105] Unlike Suffolk, however, Norfolk and Fitzwilliam were not in a position of strength compared to the rebel host. In the end, after Henry grudgingly consented, they ended up proclaiming the king's free pardon without tendering the rebels an oath.[106] But Henry had not abandoned the idea. After the rebels had for the most part dispersed, Henry sent Norfolk and the Earl of Sussex back to the North in February 1537, instructing them to visit all the major areas of the uprising and administer to the rebels the king's new oath. Henry told Norfolk and Sussex to assemble all the gentlemen and notables of the area, and after they had sworn them, to proceed to administer the oath to the commons. Furthermore, after the gentlemen had sworn to the king, the gentlemen were to return to the countryside and tender the new oath to the rest of the commons. Anyone who refused the oath was to be exempted from the king's pardon and, if Norfolk or Sussex were in a position of strength, those who refused the oath were to be apprehended and sentenced to death.[107] As we shall see, this time Norfolk and Sussex carried out Henry's instructions, and the whole of the North again swore another oath to the king.

Unfortunately, we do not know the exact contents of the oath that Suffolk tendered to the Lincolnshire rebels in October, or that Norfolk

---

[103] *LP*, xi 838.
[104] *State Papers, Published under the Authority of His Majesty's Commission*, 1:504 (*LP*, xi 1064).
[105] NA E36/119, fol. 84ʳ.   [106] Dodds and Dodds, *Pilgrimage of Grace*, ii:1–23.
[107] NA SP1/114, fols. 108ᵛ–109ʳ (*LP*, xii (i) 98 (1)); NA SP1/115, fols. 145ʳ⁻ᵛ, 147ʳ–148ʳ (*LP*, xii (i) 302); NA SP1/115, fol. 206ʳ⁻ᵛ (*LP*, xii (i) 362).

and Sussex tendered to the rest of the rebels in February. Three versions
of a draft of an oath to be tendered to the rebels survive along with two
almost identical sets of specific instructions on how to administer this oath,
instructions that parallel the actual oath in many clauses. Some versions of
this oath are stronger than others, but none of them are dated. Bush and
Bownes have assigned each oath to a different time during the uprisings,
but in the end, their assignments lack supportive evidence and their claims
remain pure supposition.[108] Yet no matter what form of the oath was
actually tendered, it is clear that this oath was designed as a response to
the pilgrims' oaths. The instructions for the tendering of Henry's new oath
read:

wher as they haue heretofore within the tyme of this Rebellyon conspired together
and haue made certain othes and promyses contrary to their dueties of alleageance
and to the grete offence of god and their owne constience they shall nowe by their
othes taken before our lieutenante and counsaill swere and make sure faithe and
promise vtterly to refuse and renounce all their said former oothes.[109]

The strongest oath opened with the clause:

ffirst ye shall swere that ye be hertely sorye that ye haue offended the kinges
hieghnes in this Rebellion and that ye shall repute and take all othes heretofore
made to any personne or personnes for or towching the saide Rebellion to be vayne

---

[108] Bush and Bownes claimed that the set of specific instructions on the administration of the oath
(NA E36/118, fols. 61ʳ⁻ᵛ, *LP*, xii (i) 98 (3)) form the content of the oath Suffolk first devised for
the Lincolnshire rebels in October. Their only evidence for this claim, however, is that this 'oath'
is written in the third person. Of course, if this 'oath' is not an oath at all but a set of instructions
on how to tender the oath that summarizes the oath's content (my position), we can account for
the use of the third person without making any claims about it being the oath devised by Suffolk
from the king's articles. Second, Bush and Bownes argued that the strongest and harshest oaths
(NA SP1/113, fols. 117ʳ⁻120ᵛ, *LP*, xii (i) 98 (4–6)) were the ones the king initially ordered Norfolk
to tender to the rebels at the beginning of December in Doncaster in connection with the king's
pardon. These oaths were the ones the rebels never swore because Norfolk was forced to grant the
rebels the king's pardon without a submission. Finally, Bush and Bownes asserted that the weakest
oath (NA SP1/113, fol. 122ʳ, *LP*, xii (i) 98 (7)) was the one Norfolk and Sussex actually administered
to the rebels in February and March 1537. The government toned down this oath in comparison to
the previous oaths, supposed Bush and Bownes, out of fear of inciting the rebels into further revolt
if the rebels found the oath too offensive. See Bush and Bownes, *Defeat of the Pilgrimage*, 369–70.
Although Bush and Bownes' argument does make logical sense, there is no historical evidence to
support it. Nothing in the surviving letters from this period suggests that the oath Henry sent
up with Norfolk at the end of 1536 was any different from the oath tendered to the Lincolnshire
rebels. Nor is there any direct evidence that the government caused Norfolk and Sussex to tender a
weaker oath because they feared further rebellion, though I will argue below from indirect evidence
that Bush and Bownes are right in this claim. Bernard has thus recognized that in the end, it is
impossible to know what forms of the oath were tendered when, or indeed what forms of the oath
were tendered at all; Bernard, *King's Reformation*, 389–90.
[109] NA E36/118, fol. 61ʳ (*LP*, xii (i) 98 (3)). See also an almost identical clause in the other set of
instructions: NA SP1/114, fol. 123ʳ (*LP*, xii (i) 98 (8)).

vnlaufull and of none effect and also that ye haue offended god and his hieghnes in taking of suche othe as youe haue Receyved for that purpos.[110]

Another version of the oath repeated this information but added that the pilgrims' oaths had been 'taken against your dieuties of Alleagiance'.[111] Even the weakest form of the oath still declared: 'And you shall vtterly renounce all such othes as you haue made during the time of this commotion, and repute the same to be voyde and of non effect.'[112] These clauses leave no doubt that Henry felt that the pilgrims' oaths had compromised the loyalty his subjects had sworn to him during the oath of succession. Moreover, all the forms of Henry's new oath included some variation on the standard phrase of fidelity wherein the swearer pledged to be a 'true and ffaythful subgyet vnto the king'.[113] This combination of rejecting their previous oaths and swearing fealty to Henry is reminiscent of the oath of succession, which also contained this combination of clauses. Thus, the fact that Henry had all his subjects swear what was, in essence, another oath of succession (without the actual parts on the succession) suggests that he interpreted the pilgrims' oaths as vitiating the original oath of succession.

The differences between the various forms of the king's new oath do become significant, however, when we consider whether Henry bound the rebels to be loyal simply to him (as in the oath of succession) or whether he bound them to be loyal to him and his specific religious policy (as in the various oaths of supremacy). Some of the forms of this post-rebellion oath have the pilgrims swear to be faithful and true to Henry 'in Erthe Supreme hed of the churche of Englande', while the instructions for the oath and the weakest form of the oath make no mention of Henry's supremacy.[114] Again, the strongest form of the oath binds the swearer to assist, to the best of his power, all the commissioners appointed for the suppression of the monasteries.[115] Other forms of the oath omit any reference to the monasteries. Indeed, the weakest form of the oath does not contain any express allusion to Henry's religious changes. It simply binds the swearer to be faithful to the king, to reject all oaths made in the insurrection, to do no

[110] NA spi/114, fol. 117ʳ (*LP*, xii (i) 98 (4)).   [111] NA spi/114, fol. 120ʳ (*LP*, xii (i) 98 (6)).
[112] NA spi/114, fol. 122ʳ (*LP*, xii (i) 98 (7)).
[113] NA spi/114, fols. 117ʳ, 118ʳ, 120ʳ, 123ʳ (*LP*, xii (i) 98 (4–6, 8)). The weakest form of the oath changed the wording but the sense was the same. It read, 'you shall swere to be true liegeman to the king our souereign lorde henry the eight'; NA spi/114, fol. 122ʳ (*LP*, xii (i) 98 (7)).
[114] For versions of the oath mentioning Henry's supremacy, see NA spi/114, fols. 117ʳ, 118ʳ, 120ʳ (*LP*, xii (i) 98 (4–6)). For the oath and instructions that do not mention Henry's supremacy, see NA spi/114, fols. 122ʳ, 123ʳ (*LP*, xii (i) 98 (7–8)).
[115] For versions of the oath that mention the monasteries, see NA spi/114, fols. 117ʳ, 118ʳ⁻ᵛ (*LP*, xii (i) 98 (4–5)).

treason or felony, not to rise up in commotion again, and to be obedient to the king, his lieutenant, and his laws.[116] These differences are important because the suppression of the monasteries was a major grievance of the rebels. The rebel oath summarized by Lord Darcy even included a clause in which the rebels bound themselves to suffer no spoiling or suppression of the monasteries.[117] The royal supremacy was also a hot issue, though the rebels never swore an oath about it and were not in complete agreement over it.[118] Some of these forms of the king's new oath thus would have been more offensive to the rebels' consciences than others.

Which form of the oath, then, did the kings' commissioners administer to the pilgrims? Madeleine and Ruth Dodds guessed that they tendered the weakest form of the oath since that was the simplest.[119] Bush and Bownes agreed, claiming that the regime feared the stronger oaths 'might incite further revolt'.[120] Bernard, conversely, has proposed that the stronger oath was most likely tendered because it was more in agreement with the tone of the instructions sent to Sussex and Norfolk, and with Henry's insistence on the suppression of the monasteries.[121] There is no way we can know for certain which form of the oath Henry's commissioners administered. Yet if we examine the responses of the pilgrims to this new royal oath, they suggest that the weakest form of the oath was indeed used. According to the reports of the commissioners, the response of the pilgrims to the administration of this new oath to the king was overwhelmingly positive. On 7 February Norfolk reported that he had tendered the oath to the Ridings of Yorkshire and the city of York itself, 'not fyndyng ani man makyng any maner of yll cowntenaunce against the same'.[122] On 28 February the Earls of Sussex and Derby and Sir Anthony Fitzherbert informed Henry that the gentlemen of Lancashire swore their new oaths 'with as good willes prompt, redy and g[. . . as?] was possible', and that 'they wolld defend and maytein their said othe'. The commons of Lancashire, the commissioners continued, 'ioyously' and 'with most gl[ad] and redye mynde toke their said othe contynually praying for your highnes and cursing all other that were of contrary myndes'.[123] The same earls wrote to Norfolk that the men of Lancashire took their oaths and could not be more sorrowful of their offences or glad of the earls' coming.[124] Finally, Sir Anthony Brown observed that Henry's subjects in Ryedale and Tynedale took the oath

---

[116] NA sp1/114, fol. 122ʳ (*LP*, xii (i) 98 (7)).   [117] NA sp1/106, fol. 286ʳ (*LP*, xi 563 (2)).

[118] Shagan, *Popular Politics*, 101–6.   [119] Dodds and Dodds, *Pilgrimage of Grace*, ii:101.

[120] Bush and Bownes, *Defeat of the Pilgrimage*, 370.   [121] Bernard, *King's Reformation*, 390–1.

[122] NA sp1/115, fol. 206ʳ (*LP*, xii (i) 362).   [123] NA sp1/116, fol. 131ʳ⁻ᵛ (*LP*, xii (i) 520).

[124] NA sp1/116, fol. 253ʳ⁻ᵛ (*LP*, xii (i) 632).

obediently.[125] Even if the commissioners exaggerated the pilgrims' enthusiasm in taking the oath, the willingness of the pilgrims to take a new oath to the king suggests that the commissioners administered the weakest version of the oath.[126] The rebels had risen, in large part, for the defence of the monasteries, and any oath that included a clause about maintaining the king's commissioners in support of the monasteries' suppression would most likely have engendered more opposition among the rebels. That the pilgrims complied with the tendering of the new oaths is a strong indication that the content of the oath was not particularly harsh.

If the rebels were tendered the weakest form of Henry's new oath, then they won the battle over the interpretation of the oath of succession. Unlike the stronger forms, the weakest form of the new oath pronounced no judgement on the pilgrims' oaths. The swearer simply pronounced the pilgrims' oaths 'voyde and of non effect', but did not have to declare them to be unlawful, offensive to God, or against their duties of allegiance. Nowhere in the weakest form of Henry's new oath did the swearer acknowledge that he had rebelled or acted in a way that violated the oath of succession. And since the weakest form of Henry's new oath contained nothing specific on Henry's religious policy, the interpretation of the oath of succession to which the pilgrims had bound their consciences in their pilgrims' oaths (to be loyal to Henry but not to his religious policy) was not actually threatened by this new oath. Although the swearer did have to declare the oaths he had sworn in the Pilgrimage to be void, he was still free to hold this interpretation, for, as in 1534 after the oath of succession, his conscience was bound simply to be obedient to Henry. Of course, this raises questions about Henry's motivation. Why would Henry administer to his subjects another vague and ambiguous oath that did not explicitly bind them to his new religious policy, when the vague and ambiguous nature of the oath of succession had allowed the participants in the uprising to swear the pilgrims' oaths in good conscience in the first place? Had not Henry learned his lesson? Or perhaps Henry had learned his lesson but there was nothing he could do about it. Perhaps this was a subtle admission by the Crown that the regime was not strong enough in 1537 to risk tendering a detailed, explicit – and thus potentially more offensive – oath in support of Henry's

---

[125] NA sp1/116, fol. 178ʳ (*LP*, xii (i) 552).

[126] Of course, we must take these reports with a grain of salt, for it was in the best interest of local officials to claim that people in their regions had cooperated enthusiastically with royal orders. Nevertheless, although it is possible (and even likely) that the commissioners for Henry's new oath exaggerated the degree of enthusiasm with which most pilgrims took their oaths, it is unlikely that these commissioners would have hidden outright refusal to swear or rebellion.

religious policies to a huge group of subjects who had just powerfully expressed their discontent. Henry may have comforted himself by the fact that the weakest version of the oath still bound the swearer to resist any future 'commotion rebellion or insurrection contrary to the kinges peax' and to be true to Henry and 'all his lawes and preceptes as a true leigemen ought to be'.[127] So according to a straightforward interpretation of this clause, the pilgrims were now bound to be true to the Act of Supremacy and the Act of Suppression. Yet as these last chapters have shown, interpretation was not always a straightforward exercise. When oaths became common weapons, the refuge of a varied interpretation became a common defence. Thomas More was certainly right when he exclaimed: 'Mary trouth it is that a mannes oth receyueth interpretacyon.'[128]

The oaths of the Pilgrimage of Grace were the English people's response to the oath of succession. First, they were a response by imitation. Far from cheapening oaths, Henry's tendering of the oath of succession to all his male subjects in 1534 led to an escalation in their use and valuation among his subjects. Henry had taught his subjects that an oath was the strongest bond on an individual's conscience, and his subjects internalized this lesson, using oaths to ensure the loyalty of potential opponents. As the rebellion spread, so did the administration of oaths, and it is apparent that the commons sought to tender their oaths to all adult males with whom they came in contact. Like Henry, the pilgrims used oaths as a form of compulsion. Again, like Henry, the pilgrims were willing to use threats of death and property confiscation to coerce the gentry into taking their oaths, thereby indicating that the commons believed that an oath extorted through force or fear was still binding on an individual's conscience. The oaths of the Pilgrimage of Grace were the photo-negative of the oath of succession; the picture was the same but the agency reversed. Those who had previously accepted the oaths were now the ones administering the oaths. The commons of the North of England thus responded to the oath of succession by appropriating the very device that made the oath of succession so powerful, namely an oath.

Second, the English people responded to the oath of succession by using their pilgrims' oaths to declare their interpretation of the oath of succession and to bind their consciences to such an interpretation. The pilgrims' oaths demonstrated that while the commons believed themselves bound to be true to the king, the oath of succession had not bound them to be obedient to the king's recent religious policy. If Henry had intended (as Elton argued)

---

[127] NA sp1/114, fol. 122ʳ (*LP*, xii (i) 98 (7)).   [128] More, *Dialogue concerning Heresies*, 281.

the oath of succession to bind his subjects 'not so much [to] legitimacy of the issue to be expected from the Boleyn marriage, [as to] the major policy which that marriage symbolized – the political revolution and the religious schism', then the oath of succession had failed.[129] While a few of the participants in the uprisings of 1536 posited that the pilgrims' oath conflicted with their oath to the king, the majority of the participants – especially the commons who took the oath enthusiastically – believed that the content of the pilgrims' oaths with their insistence on maintaining the holy church was perfectly consonant with the oath of succession. Indeed, the pilgrims' oaths were, in a sense, a qualification of the oath of succession, a declaration that the loyalty sworn to the king in the oath of succession must also involve loyalty to the commonwealth, God, and his church. Of course, not everyone agreed that this was a correct interpretation of the oath of succession, and Henry himself was especially adamant that the pilgrims swear a new, unqualified oath of loyalty to him. Yet the willingness of the pilgrims to swear this new oath suggests that it did not challenge the interpretation of the oath of succession that they had declared in their pilgrim oaths.

Finally, this chapter has reinforced the basic premise of this book, that oaths were central to the Henrician Reformation. The episcopal oath of canonical obedience to the Pope was the spark that caused the Henrician state oaths of 1534 and 1535. Henry used these oaths to implement his initial Reformation, that is, his abrogation of papal authority and establishment of royal supremacy over the church in England. Oaths were also crucial to the English people's response to the Henrician Reformation. The English people participated or resisted the Henrician Reformation either by swearing in a specific way (enthusiastically or deceptively) or, as this chapter has shown, administering and swearing their own oaths as a response to the Henrician Reformation. And just like his response to the bishops' oath of canonical obedience to the Pope, Henry reacted by tendering the rebels another oath. The Henrician Reformation was thus a war fought with oaths.

---

[129] The quotation is from Elton, *Policy and Police*, 226.

CHAPTER 6

Oaths, evangelicals, and heresy prosecution

The last four chapters of this book have examined the role of oaths in the enforcement of and resistance to royal supremacy. While royal supremacy was central to the Henrician Reformation, it was not of course the only plank in Henry's religious policy. In addition to implementing Erastian (royal supremacy and the dissolution of the monasteries) and Erasmian (the publication of the Bible in English and a campaign against 'abused' images and relics) reforms, Henry's church continued the tradition of heresy prosecution, a tradition in which oaths played a prominent part. This chapter will explore the role of oaths in English heresy trials from the late 1520s to the death of Henry VIII. In doing so, it shifts our focus from the relationship between the Henrician regime and religious conservatives to the relationship between the regime and evangelicals – those who in the reigns of Henry's daughters would adopt the label 'Protestant'.[1] The argument of this chapter is that while some Henrician bishops continued to use oaths in a traditional manner to bolster their suppression of heresy and some evangelicals subverted the bishops' goals by committing perjury in the traditional Lollard manner, matters were not so simple. Some early evangelicals disingenuously manipulated oaths in order to demonstrate their orthodoxy and win the support of the English people. Yet as Henry's reign

---

[1] The term 'Protestant' has fallen into disuse among historians of the Henrician Reformation. First, as Diarmaid MacCulloch has pointed out, such usage is anachronistic. When an Englishman used the term 'Protestant' under Henry VIII and Edward VI, he referred to those German princes and their subjects who opposed Charles V's religious policy. No matter how similar their doctrines were to German Protestants, Englishmen did not refer to themselves as 'Protestant' until the reign of Mary Tudor; MacCulloch, *Boy King*, 2. Other historians dislike the term because they believe it falsely institutionalizes and defines a group of religious movements that in reality were rather fluid and amorphous during Henry's reign; Marshall and Ryrie (eds.), *Beginnings of English Protestantism*, 4–6. Most historians now prefer the vaguer term 'evangelical' to describe the religious dissidents in Henry's reign who previous historians referred to as Protestant. According to Peter Marshall, two beliefs defined evangelicalism: first, a fervent biblicalism that rejected 'unwritten verities' and sought to reform the church based on Scripture alone; second, a rejection of purgatory and a strong belief in justification by faith alone; Marshall, *Religious Identities*, 7.

progressed, other evangelicals abandoned this strategy, instead favouring oathless, equivocal recantations. And although the Henrician regime generally opposed equivocal recantations, Edmund Bonner seems to have tacitly allowed the disappearance of oaths from the process of heresy prosecution in his diocese. When surveyed as a whole, the occurrence or absence of oaths during the trials of Henrician evangelicals reveals the extent to which the eradication of heresy was not simply a matter of top-down coercion but (as Alec Ryrie has maintained) more akin to a business negotiation wherein both sides yielded significant concessions.[2]

THE TRADITIONAL ROLE OF OATHS IN THE PROSECUTION OF HERETICS

In the trials of evangelicals the Henrician regime often employed oaths in a traditional manner. Traditionally, English authorities utilized three kinds of oaths in their attempts to suppress heresy. First, the usual opening procedure of an ecclesiastical court in a heresy trial was the tendering of an oath to the defendant. This oath was originally called the oath *de veritate dicenda* (to speak the truth), but because this kind of oath was used in other kinds of trials besides heresy where the bishop proceeded *ex officio mero* (by office alone), it became commonly known as the *ex officio* oath.[3] When taking this oath, defendants swore to answer truthfully every question posed by the court, and they typically swore this oath before they had seen the articles prepared against them.[4] For example, in Archbishop Warham's prosecutions of Lollards in 1511 and 1512, Warham forced each suspect 'to swear on the holy gospels of God by him corporally touched to answer faithfully the articles written below objected to him by the office of the said most revered father'.[5] This same oath was used against the evangelical Thomas Bilney. During his heresy trial of 1527, Cardinal Thomas Wolsey 'made the said Master Thomas Bilney swear to respond fully and faithfully ... to all articles and errors preached and set forth by him ... without any mingling of falsity or omission or qualification of the

---

[2] Ryrie's argument will be examined in more detail below.
[3] In an *ex officio* trial, the judge could initiate the trial based on 'common fame', and during the trial he acted as the prosecutor, judge, and jury. In these cases the oath *de veritate dicenda* was of even more importance since it was the only way to gather evidence against the defendants in the absence of witnesses.
[4] Levy, *Origins of the Fifth Amendment*, 23–4; Helmholz, 'Privilege and the *Ius Commune*', 18, 32.
[5] LPL, Warham's Register, fol. 169ʳ. This exact quote is from the examination of William Carder. For the tendering of the *ex officio* oath in the heresy trials of the Coventry Lollards, see McSheffrey and Tanner (eds.), *Lollards of Coventry*, 73, 77, 88, 92, 102, *passim*.

truth."[6] Of course, a variation of this oath could also be used outside the formal *ex officio* procedure in other kinds of examinations of suspected heretics. Sir Thomas More certainly employed this kind of oath in his examinations of evangelicals. For example, when John Birt wrote a letter to the suspected heretic George Constantine to 'go bakke wyth the trouth', More argued that Birt was encouraging Constantine to commit perjury, 'for Byrt wyste well I were not lykely to leue and beleue hym [Constantine] at hys bare worde'.[7] Furthermore, some variation of this oath was also administered to evangelicals such as Richard Webbe, George Gower, and Antony Dalaber.[8]

The second traditional oath in heresy prosecutions was the oath of purgation. If a defendant denied the charges levelled against him and no firm outside proof existed of his guilt, he was sometimes allowed to 'purge' himself by swearing an oath to his innocence and then calling a certain number of compurgators to swear an oath affirming the truth of his purgation oath.[9] This kind of oath was rarely utilized in trials of Henrician evangelicals.[10] One reason was because a defendant had to find a number of compurgators of his own rank, and this was not always easy. When Robert Barnes, a doctor of divinity, attempted to purge himself of charges of heresy before Wolsey, he was unable to do so because Wolsey required that Barnes call forth six to ten other doctors of divinity to attest to Barnes' innocence. Yet only two doctors of divinity were present at the sermon at which Barnes supposedly preached heretically.[11] A more important reason behind the scarcity of the oath of purgation in evangelical heresy trials was that bishops were usually able to establish the guilt of the heretic either by the witness of others or by evidence gathered through the examination of the heretic, thereby excluding purgation as an option. Authorities usually

---

[6] GL MS 9531/10 (Tunstall's Register), fol. 130[v]. The entire process against Bilney from Tunstall's Register is printed in Foxe, *AM* (Townsend), vol. iv, Appendix. Henceforth, I will cite only the original from Tunstall's Register.

[7] More, *Confutation of Tyndale's Answer*, 19–20.

[8] For Webbe, see More, *Confutation of Tyndale's Answer*, 814–15. For Gower, see NA sp1/70, fols. 163[r–v] (*LP*, v 1176); Brigden, *London and the Reformation*, 191. For Dalaber, see Foxe, *AM* (Townsend), v:425–6.

[9] 'Infamatus, contra quem crimen probari non potest, debet se purgare iuramento de veritate, compurgatores vero de credulitate'; *CIC*, x.5.34.5, Friedberg, ii:870–1. 'De testibus, illi vero, qui ad purgandam infamiam inducuntur, id solum tenetur iuramento firmare, quod veritatem credunt eum iuramento dicere, qui purgatur'; *CIC*, x.5.34.13, Friedberg, ii:875. Levy, *Origins of the Fifth Amendment*, 5–6.

[10] For a couple of examples of canonical purgation (one successful and one not) in 1540, see CUL EDR G/1/8 (Goodrich's Register) in *CAP*, vol. vii, part 4, fols. 3[r]–4[r].

[11] Barnes, *A supplicacion* (1534), sig. H4[v].

resorted to oaths of purgation as a last resort, and we shall see a couple of extraordinary examples of them below.

The final and most common traditional oath in heresy trials was an oath of abjuration. Indeed, in its technical definition, an abjuration is simply 'a renunciation on oath'.[12] The actual content to which the heretic swore varied. This usually depended on the judge, for the author of the abjuration was typically the heretic's ordinary, the bishop or the bishop's commissioner. A few abjurations were relatively minimal. For example, the abjurations of two simpletons from the diocese of Rochester in 1538 and 1540 consisted solely of a confession of specific heresies followed by a statement (complete with an oath) that for all the heresies mentioned, 'I vtterlye renounce forsake and abiure as God shall helpe me and this holye Evangelyste'.[13] Similarly, Bishop John Fisher had the evangelical Thomas Batman swear a single-clause oath in his abjuration of 1534, and Archbishop Edward Lee imposed a near-identical oath on the sacramentarian Denise Johnson in 1540. After renouncing their heresies, both Batman and Johnson swore never to hold, believe, preach, or defend their heresies.[14] In most abjurations, however, the content to which a heretic swore was more extensive. Evangelicals under the episcopates of Cuthbert Tunstall, Stephen Gardiner, and Edward Lee (Denise Johnson excluded) supplemented their oaths never to hold, believe, preach, or defend heresy by also swearing never to conceal heresies or heretics from the church or associate with suspected heretics but rather to detect them to their ordinaries.[15] An oath to fulfil one's penance was another common addition to abjurations.[16] Some ordinaries added yet more oaths to the abjurations they imposed on heretics. For example, William Clyff, Archbishop Lee's vicar general, had the Dutch merchants Lambert Sparrow and Giles Vanbeller, as well as Richard Brown (the vicar of North Cave), swear an additional oath never to 'vse rede teach kepe

[12] *Oxford English Dictionary*, 2nd edn, s.v. 'Abjuration'.

[13] KAO DRc/R7 (Hilsey's Register) in *CAP*, vol. VIII, part 8, fols. 195[v], 200[r]. The two heretics, John Foster and John Churchyard, were not evangelicals. Foster's heresies included rejecting that God created him (for he was born of his father and mother), that Christ died (for Christ is alive), and that God is not in a true Christian's heart (for God cannot part himself). Churchyard was guilty of believing that children of Christian parents do not need to be baptized, for as soon as they are born they have life, and as soon as they have life, they will go to heaven.

[14] Centre for Kentish Studies, Maidstone, DRB/A/R/1/13, Microfilm Z3 (John Fisher's Register), fol. 127[r]; BI Register 28 (Edward Lee's Register), in *CAP*, vol. I, part. 14, fol. 141[v].

[15] The exact formula of these oaths varied. For examples, see GL MS 9531/10 (Tunstall's Register), fol. 137[r]; Hinde (ed.), *Registers of Cuthbert Tunstall*, 35–6; Chitty (ed.), *Registra Stephani Gardiner*, 31–2; BI Register 28, in *CAP*, vol. I, part. 14, fols. 82[v]–83[r], 90[v], 100[r].

[16] Hinde (ed.), *Registers of Cuthbert Tunstall*, 35–6; Chitty (ed.), *Registra Stephani Gardiner*, 32; CUL EDR G/1/8 (Goodrich's Register) in *CAP*, vol. VII, part 4, fol. 5.

bye or seel any bookes volumes or queres any workes callid Luthers or any oder mannys bookes or his hereticall sect or of anie odre conteighnyng heresie in them or prohibited by the Lawes of holy church'.[17] By contrast, William Meye, Thomas Goodrich's commissioner general, imposed on the Anabaptist Humphrey Turnor a simpler two-part oath in 1540.[18] Although the exact content of the oaths varied according to the ordinary, it is clear that it was standard practice to include some kind of oath in the heretic's abjuration, and the overwhelming majority of abjurations from the 1520s and 30s (both Lollard and evangelical) contained some kind of oath.

Ecclesiastical authorities employed the oaths *de veritate dicenda*, of purgation, and of abjuration because such oaths added spiritual muscle to the Henrician authorities' campaign against heresy. The oath *de veritate dicenda* and the oath of purgation guarded against heretics lying about their past and current heretical beliefs, and the various oaths of abjuration sought to prevent heretics from continuing to hold heretical beliefs at their abjurations and into the future. In essence, these oaths made sure that evangelicals could not survive a heresy trial and continue to hold their heresy without committing perjury. To escape execution, evangelicals who held opinions their ordinaries deemed heretical had to perjure themselves either by taking the oath *de veritate dicenda*, falsely denying the heterodox articles against them, and then swearing an oath of purgation that they were innocent of heresy or, if purgation was not an option because of the overwhelming evidence against them, by abjuring their beliefs and swearing an oath in their recantations against their consciences.[19] And because it was widely believed that God would severely punish perjury in this life and the next, these oaths meant that the already difficult decision of choosing between renouncing one's beliefs or being burned at the stake was even more tortuous.

THE EARLY EVANGELICAL RESPONSE TO HERESY OATHS

So how did Henrician evangelicals respond to oaths administered in heresy trials? According to Thomas More, early English evangelicals were much more likely to commit perjury – either by denying their heretical activities

---

[17] BI Register 28, in *CAP*, vol. I, part 14, fols. 83ʳ, 90ᵛ, 100ʳ.

[18] CUL ᴇᴅʀ ɢ/1/8, in *CAP*, vol. VII, part. 4, fol. 5ʳ. Turnor swore not to conceal or be conversant with heretics but rather to detect them and to fulfil his penance.

[19] This of course assumes that the heretics had not changed their minds concerning their true beliefs. It was always a possibility that during the trial, the church authorities were able to convert the heretic back to orthodoxy, thereby allowing the defendant to swear his abjuration oath in good conscience.

under oath or by abjuring their heretical beliefs with an oath against their consciences – than they were to honour their oaths and face the penalties for their beliefs and practices:

> Nor yet so moche as any constaunce in theyr doctrine, but & yf they were ones founde out and examined, we se them alwaye fyrst redy to lye and forswere them selfe yf that wyll serue. And whan that wyll not helpe but theyr falshed and periury proued in theyr faces, than redy be they to abiure & forsake it, as longe as that may saue theyr lyues. Nor neuer yet founde I any one, but he wolde ones abiure thoughe he neuer entended to kepe his othe. So holy wolde he be & so wyse therwith, that he wolde with periury kyll his soule for euer, to saue his body for a whyle.[20]

More argued that this willingness to commit perjury was a result of their erroneous beliefs: *because* their doctrine was false, their behaviour was also deceptive. He expanded: 'And syth they be fallen frome god and hys true faith, they haue no greate care of trouth, nor be very scrupulouse in the lendynge of an othe tyll they neede in lyke case to be payed agayne.'[21] More then supported his claims by giving specific examples of evangelical perjury. He narrated how Richard Webbe and Robert Necton, after being detected for heresy, secretly agreed on how they would answer More's questions in order to make sure their stories were consistent. Necton, however, lost his cool and sent More word of their agreement unbeknown to Webbe. When More examined Webbe the next day, Webbe 'answered on his othe many a false answere'.[22] Likewise, More noted how Richard Bayfield was willing to break his abjuration oaths. Bayfield had first abjured in 1528, and it is clear that his abjuration included an oath to renounce his heresies and never to return to them, and an oath on the Gospels to fulfil whatever penance was adjoined to him.[23] Yet before fulfilling his penance, Bayfield fled beyond the seas and began smuggling Tyndale's books into England. When captured and detected for heresy a second time, More declared that Bayfield 'was well contente to haue forsworen yt agayne' and abjured if that would have saved his life.[24]

More's allegation that early English evangelicals responded to heresy oaths by committing perjury is not far-fetched. After all, this was the response of many Lollards. Anne Hudson has stated that approximately

---

[20] More, *Dialogue concerning Heresies*, 422.   [21] More, *Dialogue concerning Heresies*, 266.

[22] More, *Confutation of Tyndale's Answer*, 814.

[23] We can deduce this because these oaths were mentioned in the articles administered against Bayfield in 1531, articles Bayfield admitted were true; Foxe, *AM* (Townsend), iv:682, 684.

[24] More, *Confutation of Tyndale's Answer*, 18. John Foxe, however, denied that Bayfield was willing to abjure a second time; Foxe, *AM* (Townsend), iv:681–2, 688.

ninety-eight per cent of Lollards tried for heresy abjured.[25] Lollard abjurations typically included oaths.[26] Since many of these Lollards later relapsed,
it is safe to assume their initial recantations were feigned and thus perjured.
Indeed, the historiographical consensus is that most Lollards were willing
to take the oaths administered to them in their heresy trials and then disre-
gard them.[27] Lollards were of course not identical to evangelicals, but Alec
Ryrie has posited that the tendency of Lollards to abjure and recant their
beliefs when detected for heresy probably informed the early evangelical
practice of the same.[28] Richard Rex has argued the opposite, contending
that early English evangelicals 'scorned hypocrisy' and were more willing
than Lollards to choose death over recantation.[29] Yet even if we discon-
nect Henrician evangelism from Lollardy, it is still possible to assert that
Henrician evangelicals responded to the oaths administered to them in
heresy trials by committing perjury. Ryrie went so far as to suggest that
the oath theory of evangelicals like Thomas Becon and John Bale provided
evangelicals with a ready excuse to break their abjuration oaths.[30] Susan
Brigden has also declared that she believes More's accusations about the
early English evangelical response to heresy oaths. Brigden pointed out
that the evangelical George Gower, after being forced to take an oath to
tell the truth by Bishop Stokesley and More, later admitted to Thomas
Cromwell that he had responded falsely and committed perjury.[31] Perhaps
the strongest accusation of evangelical duplicity came from the historian
S. R. Maitland. Maitland called attention to the lies of George Joye and
Antony Dalaber.[32] Joye's deception was not technically perjury, but Dalaber's story deserves special attention because Dalaber himself proclaimed
it and John Foxe included it in all four versions of his *Acts and Monuments*.

The setting was Oxford in 1528. Dalaber, a student at the university who
had received heretical books from Master Thomas Garret, helped Garret

---

[25] Hudson, *Premature Reformation*, 158.

[26] For some specific examples, see BL Harleian MS 421, fols. 7ʳ–8ʳ, 10ʳ⁻ᵛ, 27ʳ⁻ᵛ, 29ʳ, 81ʳ⁻ᵛ, 83ʳ, 84ʳ,
85ʳ–86ʳ, 88ʳ, 91ʳ, 129ʳ–130ʳ, 146ʳ⁻ᵛ, 154ʳ⁻ᵛ, 173ʳ–174ʳ, 175ʳ–176ᵛ, 183ʳ–184ʳ; LPL, Warham's Register,
fols. 159ʳ, 161ʳ⁻ᵛ, 175ʳ⁻ᵛ; McSheffrey and Tanner (eds.), *Lollards of Coventry*; Tanner (ed.), *Heresy
Trials in the Diocese of Norwich*.

[27] Hudson, *Premature Reformation*, 373; Aston, *Lollards and Reformers*, 110–11.

[28] Ryrie, *Gospel and Henry VIII*, 80–1.   [29] Rex, *Lollards*, 131–2.

[30] Ryrie, *Gospel and Henry VIII*, 76–8. I disagree with Ryrie on this point. Becon and Bale certainly
counselled the breaking of an evil oath, but this was a standard part of oath theory stretching back
to the Middle Ages. It was not an evangelical novelty. Furthermore, the overall thrust of Becon's
and Bale's treatises (as explored in Chapter 1 of this book) was to increase the sanctity of oaths. For
those who respected oaths, the best response to an evil oath was not to take it and then break it, but
rather to avoid taking it in the first place.

[31] Brigden, *London and the Reformation*, 191; NA SP1/70, fols. 163ʳ⁻ᵛ (*LP*, v 1176).

[32] Maitland, *Reformation in England*, 1–14.

escape out of Oxford when Garret became suspected of heresy. Garret was soon apprehended and brought back to Oxford. Distraught, Garret picked the lock of his chamber, found a young man to guide him to Dalaber's new room, and in the guide's presence exposed to Dalaber the narrative of his capture and how he was undone for heresy. Dalaber quickly realized Garret's error of talking in front of the guide, dismissed the guide, lent Garret some clothes, and sent him off to escape in exile to Germany. The guide told all, and Dalaber was brought before the authorities. Anthony Dunstan, a monk of Westminster and prior of the students, asked Dalaber whether he had seen Garret and whether he knew where Garret went. Dalaber responded that Garret had stopped by his place to borrow a hat and shoes on his way to a Shrovetide celebration at Woodstock. Dalaber admitted to his readers: 'This tale I thought meetest, though it were nothing so.'[33] Shortly thereafter, Dalaber's lie escalated into perjury. He was brought before Master Cottisfords, Dr Higdon, and Dr London and made to lay his right hand on a Mass book, swear that he 'should truly answer unto such articles and interrogatories' as they offered him, and kiss the book.[34] After his oath, Dalaber repeated his false story. The commissioners eventually brought forth the guide who testified of Garret and Dalaber's meeting. Dalaber denied the guide's story, confessing to his readers: 'for I thought my "nay" to be as good as his "yea", seeing it was to rid and deliver my godly brother out of trouble and peril of his life'.[35] Dalaber's story did not hold water. He and Garret ended up abjuring in 1528, though both returned to their heresies.

The evidence examined thus far suggests that early English evangelicals responded to the oaths tendered to them in heresy trials in a straightforward manner. There was nothing complicated about their perjury. They simply lied under oath or falsely swore abjuration oaths in order to save their lives or the lives of their brethren. This was certainly a form of resistance to the Henrician authorities, but it was a game played according to the authorities' own rules. The authorities gave those in trouble for heresy the choice between honest abjuration, death, or perjury. The evangelicals discussed above accepted these choices, electing the third option. Yet not all early English evangelicals were content to play by these traditional rules. Although these evangelicals did not hesitate to commit perjury, they were well aware that oaths were held in high esteem by the general populace. They manipulated their oaths not only to escape punishment

---

[33] Foxe, *AM* (Townsend), v:425.   [34] Foxe, *AM* (Townsend), v:425–6.
[35] Foxe, *AM* (Townsend), v:426.

for heresy but also to present an image of themselves as orthodox victims
unjustly oppressed by a corrupt and deceitful church hierarchy. Whether a
premeditated strategy or an improvised response, this kind of manipulation
of oaths implies that the early evangelical practice of oath-taking was more
than just an effort to save their lives: it was sometimes a propaganda device.

One of the best examples of this phenomenon is the 1527 heresy trial
of Thomas Bilney. The trial records (preserved in Bishop Tunstall's Register) make it clear that Bilney committed perjury. When the trial commenced, Cardinal Wolsey first asked Bilney whether he had sworn an oath
in Wolsey's presence months earlier not to preach or defend Lutheran
opinions. Bilney responded that he had sworn such an oath 'but not
judicially'.[36] Bilney probably meant that the oath he had sworn was not
part of a formal, legal abjuration, so if convicted of heresy this time, he
could not be judged as re-lapsed.[37] Wolsey then tendered Bilney the *ex
officio* oath; Bilney was now bound to respond truthfully to the questions
and articles administered to him. After Bilney submitted an ambiguous
written response to the articles held against him, Bishop Tunstall (Wolsey
had been called away on official business) began calling forth witnesses
who testified under oath that Bilney had preached heresy. At first (also
under oath), Bilney simply denied these accusations. His only evidence
for this denial, according to Thomas More, was his own oath: 'that by
other meanes than the onely othe of the partye that is accused, sweryng
alone agaynst them all'.[38] About halfway through the trial, however, Bilney
switched his strategy and suddenly claimed that he could not remember
what he had preached, requesting the trial be halted for a time.[39] Bilney's
abrupt amnesia was almost certainly feigned since he had never displayed
memory problems before and indeed provided a detailed report of his sermons in private letters to Tunstall.[40] The combination of his initial denial
of the testimony of multiple witnesses with his sudden assertion of forget-
fulness suggests that Bilney was lying under oath. Thomas More recognized
this: 'must it not nedes be that in his [Bilney's] denyenge in verture of his
othe, the thynges which they coulde not but byleue true, they must nedes
therwith beyleue hym all that wyle to lye & be periured?'[41]

Yet Bilney was not willing to forswear himself on all occasions merely to
escape punishment. If so, he would have simply sworn whatever abjuration
oath Tunstall administered to him with little resistance or few qualms of

[36] GL MS 9531/10 (Tunstall's Register), fol. 130ᵛ.   [37] Walker, 'Saint or Schemer?', 233.
[38] More, *Dialogue concerning Heresies*, 276.
[39] GL MS 9531/10 (Tunstall's Register), fol. 134ʳ; Walker, 'Saint or Schemer?', 220–1.
[40] Walker, 'Saint or Schemer?', 221.   [41] More, *Dialogue concerning Heresies*, 277.

conscience. Instead, over and over again, Bilney refused to abjure, even when the evidence against him was overwhelming. For almost a week he denied Tunstall's admonitions to abjure, answering 'let justice be done' or stating that 'he wants to stand by his conscience'.[42] Finally, when pressed with the ultimate threat of death, Bilney capitulated. Even then, his abjuration was extraordinary. Bilney condemned the specific heresies of which he was accused and convicted (mostly a rejection of the cult of the saints but also of merit-based salvation and the authority of a corrupt Pope), admitted that whoever taught them should be excommunicated, promised never to preach these heresies, and sealed his abjuration with an oath.[43] What Bilney did not do, however, was admit that he had preached or held these heretical opinions himself. More immediately picked up that this abjuration was singular; it was 'a forme of abiuracyon, wherof I neuer sawe the lyke, nor in so playne a case neuer wolde were I the iudge, suffer the lyke here after'.[44] The historian Greg Walker has seconded More's opinion, highlighting that Bilney's fellow heretic Thomas Arthur admitted to preaching heresy in his abjuration.[45] In fact, the content of Bilney's abjuration was not as exceptional as More claimed. In his classic compendium of canon law, William Lyndwode stated that purgation could sometimes involve abjuration, and as More himself admitted, this kind of purgation abjuration occasionally included an oath by which the accused rejected the opinions of which he was suspected as false, declared he did not believe them, and that he never would believe or teach them.[46] This is essentially what Bilney swore. Yet this kind of abjuration was reserved for instances when the defendant could be proved only suspect of heresy, when heresy itself could not be legally established. Bilney's abjuration was exceptional because he was clearly *convicted* of heresy, yet he still won a favorable abjuration.[47]

Bilney won such an abjuration because his use of oaths – while perjurous – was consistent and hence powerful. From the very beginning Bilney had admitted that the articles levelled against him were heretical. He did not try to argue that point.[48] But whenever someone accused him of preaching these heretical articles, Bilney denied it with an oath. Bilney protected the value of his oath and prevented opening himself up to charges

---

[42] GL MS 9531/10 (Tunstall's Register), fol. 131ʳ⁻ᵛ.   [43] GL MS 9531/10 (Tunstall's Register), fol. 135ʳ.
[44] More, *Dialogue concerning Heresies*, 271.   [45] Walker, 'Saint or Schemer?', 224–5.
[46] Guy, 'Elizabethan Establishment and the Ecclesiastical Polity', 142–3; More, *Debellation of Salem and Bizance*, 116.
[47] For a clear statement that Bilney was judged convicted of heresy, see GL MS 9531/10 (Tunstall's Register), fol. 131ʳ.
[48] GL MS 9531/10 (Tunstall's Register), fol. 130ᵛ; Walker, 'Saint or Schemer?', 233.

of perjury by refusing Tunstall's initial requests to make a normal abjuration, for if Bilney had made a normal abjuration in which he confessed to holding heretical opinions, Bilney would have admitted his perjury of denying the accusations of heresy brought against him by witnesses. By standing by his oath again and again, Bilney was able to present an image of himself as truthful and thus exploit his judges' high valuation of oaths in order to cause them to doubt (at least a little) whether he actually preached the heretical opinions charged against him. This was why he won a favorable form of abjuration. More recognized this: 'but as clerely as his faute was proued, and by as many, yet wolde he [Bilney] not to dye therefore confesse hym self fauty, but alway stode styll vpon it in vertue of his othe *that all they belyved hym*'.[49]

In addition to securing himself a favorable abjuration, Bilney's strategy regarding oaths had the added benefit of winning him and other English evangelicals popular support. It was a propaganda coup. Until Thomas More published his *Dialogue concerning Heresies* four years later, the English public was not aware of Bilney's manipulation of oaths during the trial itself (which of course was never proven perjurous anyway). The only public part of his heresy trial was his abjuration. In his abjuration, Bilney seemed suspiciously orthodox. He condemned the articles against him as heretical but did not admit to having ever preached them. Why then was he persecuted? Based on his abjuration alone, the church did not have much of a case. Greg Walker was surely right in his conclusion:

> On the issue of the abjuration it can only be inferred that the oath was taken, pious lie included, because it allowed Bilney to maintain the fiction that he was an orthodox Catholic who was condemned for views which he did not hold, in order to silence him. And the value for Bilney of such a fiction was the embarrassment which it caused the authorities and the popular sympathy which it aroused for the defendant himself, his fellow evangelicals and their cause.[50]

Bilney was not the only one to use the strategy of declaring his innocence by oath (probably falsely) and then appealing to others for justice. Thomas Phillips made use of the same tactic. Phillips was a London pointmaker and a chief reader in the Lollard sect of 'known men' in the 1520s who later developed significant evangelical connections. At the end of 1529 and beginning of 1530 he was tried for heresy. He admitted to possessing a vernacular translation of the New Testament and answered equivocally to an article on the Eucharist, but to the rest of the heresies charged to him

---

[49] More, *Dialogue concerning Heresies*, 271. My italics.
[50] Walker, 'Saint or Schemer?', 234.

(the rejection of purgatory, pilgrimages, fasting, vows, Holy Days, prayer to the saints, auricular confession, and pardons) Phillips responded that he 'beleveth tharticle not to be trewere nor any parte therof'.[51] More considered Phillips' responses to be false. More claimed that in Phillips, he found 'no trouth, neyther in his worde nor his othe'.[52] Phillips, however, stood by his oath and continued to deny the heresies charged to him. One Stacy was brought as a witness against Phillips, but Stacy later protested that he had testified out of fear, thereby invalidating his testimony and preventing Bishop Stokesley from proving Phillips' heresy. Stokesley eventually entreated Phillips to submit 'and to swear never to hold any opinion contrary to the determination of holy church'.[53] Phillips replied that he would read to himself the form of the abjuration given to him by Stokesley. But when Stokesley demanded that Phillips read the abjuration 'openly', Phillips refused and appealed to the king as supreme head of the church. The bishop again asked him to abjure. Phillips answered that 'he would be obedient as a christian man should, and that he would swear never to hold any heresy during his life, nor to favour any heretics'.[54] Twice more Stokesley exhorted him to read the abjuration conceived for him by the church. Phillips refused, saying that 'he would forswear all heresies, and that he would maintain no heresies, nor favour any heretics'.[55] Finally, Stokesley excommunicated Phillips and sent him back to the Tower where Phillips remained for four years. The king ignored his appeal. Three years after his trial, Phillips petitioned Parliament. He complained that nothing had been proven against him in court; he was held prisoner only upon the suspicion of common fame. He declared that he was innocent and that it was an affront to his conscience that he 'shuld abjure as though there were no defference betewne an innocent and a nocent, betewne one gyltye and one not gyltye'.[56] On 7 February 1534, Phillips' petition came before the House of Lords. Two days later, they dismissed it as beneath their dignity to consider.[57] The Commons, however, took a greater interest in the petition, and it eventually led to the repeal of the heresy legislation of 1401.[58]

In Phillips' trial, then, we see a similar pattern. Phillips probably did lie under oath in denying the specific heresies charged to him, but he stuck by his position, which made it difficult for Stokesley to prove any heresy against him without witnesses. Phillips was willing to abjure, but not *openly*, which demonstrates his concern for his public image. Instead Phillips proclaimed

---

[51] Foxe, *AM* (Townsend), vol. v, Appendix, no. 2.   [52] More, *Apology*, 126.
[53] Foxe, *AM* (Townsend), v:29.   [54] Foxe, *AM* (Townsend), v:30.
[55] Foxe, *AM* (Townsend), v:30.   [56] Foxe, *AM* (Townsend), vol. v, Appendix, no. 2.
[57] *Journal of the House of Lords*, 1:65–6.   [58] Lehmberg, *Reformation Parliament*, 186–7.

that he would swear an oath against all heresies, but he was never willing to admit publicly to holding any specific heretical positions. This was, in essence, what Bilney had sworn, but Stokesley (unlike Tunstall) was loath to let Phillips get off with such a mild submission. He would not accept Phillips' offer. Furthermore, Phillips' offer to swear this oath was probably a ploy designed to convince others that he was orthodox while at the same time taking advantage of the vagueness and ambiguity of the term 'heresy'. What was heretical to Stokesley and the London populace was not necessarily heretical to Phillips, so Phillips' oath had the dual purpose of projecting an orthodox image of himself while saving his conscience.

Nicholas Shaxton, a master at Cambridge, played a similar game, but in Shaxton's case, the ecclesiastical authorities were willing to play along. During Lent of 1531 Shaxton was accused of holding three heresies: first, that he preached that it was evil and dangerous to declare publicly that there was no purgatory, but it was not damnable to doubt its existence; second, that he preached that no matter how much one fasted, prayed, and abstained from evil company, thoughts, and sights, it was impossible for a man to remain chaste unless he received a gift from God; finally, that he prayed during Mass that the burden of celibacy might be lifted from the clergy, and they might be allowed to wed. During his initial examinations, Shaxton refused to forsake these points. At length, a compromise was reached. Bishop Nix of Norwich reported that 'to avoid *open* abjuration', Shaxton was content to swear an oath devised by the vice-chancellor of the University of Cambridge.[59] Nowhere in this oath did Shaxton admit that he had held or preached heresy. The oath, however, was extremely strict and comprehensive in its rejection of Protestant doctrine and included clauses explicitly accepting the Roman Catholic interpretation of both purgatory and celibacy.[60] Shaxton's oath worked. A letter survives, probably from the vice-chancellor of Cambridge to an anonymous lord, in which the writer vouched for the orthodoxy of Shaxton because Shaxton was willing 'to swere to such an othe as I dede excogytate for quyetnes in theis trobyllows tymes'.[61] Shaxton was eventually promoted to bishop of Salisbury, though he resigned upon the passing of the Six Articles. In 1546 he infamously abjured at Paul's Cross for holding sacramentarian opinions, though this abjuration did not include an oath. The fact that Shaxton continued to hold evangelical doctrines after swearing his oath in 1531 suggests that

---

[59] Foxe, *AM* (Townsend), IV:680. My italics.
[60] For the exact form of Shaxton's oath, see Foxe, *AM* (Townsend), IV:680.
[61] The letter is printed in Foxe, *AM* (Townsend), vol. V, Appendix, no. XVII (*LP*, V 271).

he was willing to commit perjury. His main concern was to escape an open abjuration. He did so by swearing an oath refuting the very heretical opinions he held without actually admitting to holding them.

Many early English evangelicals, then, responded to the oaths administered to them in heresy trials by committing perjury. They inherited from their Lollard predecessors a willingness to lie under oath and to renounce their beliefs. Yet not all of them were willing to swear on the authorities' own terms. Evangelicals like Bilney, Phillips, and Shaxton consistently and strategically proclaimed under oath that they did not hold the heretical opinions charged to them, and then they swore oaths decrying the same heresy of which they were charged (and almost certainly guilty). The benefit for them of such a strategy was that it allowed them to portray themselves as orthodox victims unjustly prosecuted for heresy, targeted only because they made anti-clerical statements. This coincides with Ethan Shagan's claim that anti-clericalism was a 'point of contact' between religious radicals and the populace at large: 'Evangelicals co-opted the genre of popular anticlericalism as a means of legitimating their complaints and winning support among their conservative neighbours.'[62]

And their propaganda probably worked, at least to an extent. After all, Richard Rex has shown that the English populace of London sympathetically interpreted Richard Wyche's execution in 1440 – which the authorities claimed was for heresy – as an unjust vendetta for Wyche's anti-clerical statements.[63] It was therefore not inconceivable that the English populace might buy into the propaganda of evangelicals like Bilney, Phillips, and Shaxton. Thomas More, for one, was worried that the degree of public sympathy for persecuted evangelicals was extensive enough to warrant explicit rebuttals. For example, at the beginning of his *Dialogue concerning Heresies*, More admitted that the people of London spoke and wrote that Bilney was forced to abjure for heresies he did not hold because of the 'malyce and enuye' of the friars, and because he had decried the clergy's 'pompe & pryde and other inordynate lyuynge'.[64] More continued:

And surely syr quod he some folke that thynke this dealynge of the clargye to be thus (and good men to be myshandlyd for declarynge the trouth, and the scrypture selfe to be pulled owt of the peoples handys, lest they shold perceyue the trouth) be ledde in theyr myndys, to dowte whyther Luther hymselfe (of whose oppynyons or at the lest of whose workys all these busynesse bygan) wrote in dede so euyll as he is borne in hande.[65]

---

[62] Shagan, *Popular Politics*, 146–7.   [63] Rex, 'Which is Wyche?', 88–106.
[64] More, *Dialogue concerning Heresies*, 28.   [65] More, *Dialogue concerning Heresies*, 29.

Similarly, the lawyer Christopher St Germain wrote: 'certayne it is that there is a great rumour amonge the peple, that it is so, & that spiritual men punysshe nat heresye onely for zele of the fayth, and of a loue & a zele to the people... but that they do it rather to opresse them that speketh any thynge agaynste the worldlye power or ryches of spyrytuall men'.[66] It should be emphasized that at least some of the sympathy persecuted evangelicals received was a result of the perception of them as orthodox, a largely inaccurate perception that some evangelicals were able to strengthen through their clever and perjurous use of oaths.

Of course, the abjuration oaths of Bilney and Shaxton were not a complete victory for evangelicals. Although not as desirable as a standard abjuration, the ecclesiastical authorities still gained much from these milder abjurations. First, the authorities avoided, at least for a time, executing these evangelicals and potentially turning them into martyrs. Second, they gained positive propaganda in their own campaign against heretical doctrine. Through these oaths, the authorities were able to make suspected heretics clearly and openly decry the heresy to which they were charged. Even if the suspects did not admit their guilt, they did publicly admit that the doctrines of which they were accused (and probably guilty) were wrong and thus anyone who did hold them was worthy of guilt. Finally, these oaths allowed the authorities to burden evangelicals with the sin of perjury if their abjurations were less than sincere. In an era where the dominant discourse was that perjury was a grave offence against God, this could pose a problem for the consciences of the abjured. For example, according to Hugh Latimer and John Foxe, Bilney was thrust into 'anguish and agony' after his first trial and 'pierced with sorrow and remorse for his abjuration'.[67] Greg Walker has surmised that 'it was his [Bilney's] decision to ground his defense upon subtlety and untruth rather than a straightforward exposition of the evangelical position which so tormented him'.[68] Walker may be right, for during his execution speech Bilney did apologize for his commission of perjury and ask for prayers from his auditors because of it, though he did not explicitly connect his perjury to his heresy trial of 1527.[69] Beyond the peril perjury posed to the consciences of the abjured evangelical, it was also a dangerous card to play in the game of public

---

[66] Saint Germain, *Treatise concernynge the Diuision betwene the Spirytualtie and Temporalitie*, 191. For More's rebuttal of this, see his *Apology*, 111–16. It is also probable that the attack on the unjust proceedings in heresy trials in the 1532 Supplication of the Commons was partly a result of the success of Protestant propaganda. See Gee and Hardy (eds.), *Documents Illustrative*, 151–2.

[67] Foxe, *AM* (Townsend), IV:641–2.   [68] Walker, 'Saint or Schemer?', 233.

[69] *LP*, V 372 (3), printed in Foxe, *AM* (Townsend), vol. IV, Appendix, no. 3.

relations. It worked initially precisely because people trusted the evangelicals' oaths and took them at their word that they did not hold heretical doctrine. Yet if it came out that they were perjurers – and Thomas More did his best in the early 1530s to propagate this view – their lying could easily create a popular backlash that would benefit the ecclesiastical authorities. In sum, even though the abjurations of evangelicals like Bilney and Shaxton were more favourable to evangelicals than traditional abjurations, the ecclesiastical authorities still got the better end of the deal.

OATHS AND HERESY TRIALS IN LATER HENRICIAN ENGLAND

It was these factors that likely contributed to a subtle shift in evangelical strategy in the 1530s and early 1540s. First, evangelicals began to preach and defend their 'heretical' doctrines more openly. This undoubtedly was in part a result of the safer atmosphere of the mid 1530s created by Henry's patronage of evangelically minded men like Thomas Cromwell and Thomas Cranmer. Yet evangelicals also began to preach their views even during their prosecutions for heresy, a dangerous practice. Second, evangelicals began to shy away from direct perjury: that is, lying under oath. They still dissimulated and deceived the authorities through equivocation, but their practice of this rarely included an oath. Finally, evangelicals started to turn the tables on their Catholic persecutors and accuse them of being deceptive perjurers.

This transition is first evident in the heresy indictment of Hugh Latimer in 1532. Like other evangelicals in trouble for heresy at this time, Latimer refused to admit that he had preached heresy. He insisted that he was orthodox. Unlike Bilney or Shaxton, however, Latimer did not employ oaths to convince others of his orthodoxy. Instead, he relied on slippery language and on manipulation of the king's growing antipathy towards the papacy. Latimer was summoned to appear before Bishop Stokesley in January 1532 to answer to the charges of preaching heresy. Throughout his examinations in the winter of 1532 (about which very little is known), it appears that Latimer consistently asserted that he had not condemned Catholic practices or doctrines but merely abuses of them.[70] On 11 March 1532, Latimer was summoned before the Convocation of the Clergy of Canterbury. Three times they demanded that he subscribe to a document of articles. Three times Latimer refused.[71] The articles, preserved in Tunstall's Register, do not specify that Latimer held heretical beliefs at all. They

---

[70] Chester, *Hugh Latimer*, 76.   [71] Bray (ed.), *Records of Convocation*, VII:179.

are simply a list of positive beliefs on the existence of purgatory, the cult of the saints, the efficacy of pilgrimages, the binding nature of vows of chastity, the power of good works to earn merit, the continuity of Apostolic succession, the efficacy of the sacraments to communicate the merits of Christ's Passion, the usefulness of images, and a few other side issues.[72] It seems as though Convocation was offering to Latimer a similar deal offered to Bilney and Shaxton. If Latimer's sole goal was to project an image of himself as orthodox without admitting his heresy, he should have signed these articles.

According to the Spanish ambassador in England, Latimer then appealed to the Privy Council, before which he 'propounded heresy enough'. Next, Latimer appealed to the king himself. When brought before the king to dispute with the bishops, Henry noticed that one of the primary articles against Latimer was that he had preached that the Pope was not the sovereign chief of the church. This article pleased Henry, who ordered Latimer to be released on the condition that he preach a sermon retracting some of his less orthodox opinions.[73] On 21 March Latimer again appeared before Convocation. Probably on account of the intervention of the king, the bishops of Convocation decided that they would absolve Latimer from excommunication if he subscribed to articles eleven and fourteen, two innocuous and uncontroversial articles on the power of bishops to inhibit preachers and the usefulness of consecrations and benedictions of the church. Latimer submitted and admitted that he had erred in preaching against the aforesaid articles. Yet his submission was shifty:

My Lords, I do confess, that I have misordered myself very farre, in that I have so presumptuously and boldly preached, reproving certain things, by which the people that were infirm hath taken occasion of ill. Wherefore I ask forgiveness of my misbehaviour; I will be glad to make amends; and I have spoken indiscreetly in vehemence of speaking, and have err'd in some things, and in manner have been in a wrong way (as thus) lacking discretion in many things.[74]

Latimer admitted that he erred in 'discretion' and preached 'indiscreetly', but he did not admit to preaching heresies. In response, Stokesley, sitting in for Archbishop Warham, 'delayed the oath to subscribe to the aforesaid articles' until 10 April when Latimer was to appear before Warham. Then (it is not clear whether this happened on 21 March or 10 April) Latimer subscribed voluntarily to the selected articles eleven and fourteen and was

---

[72] GL MS 9531/10 (Tunstall's Register), fol. 142ᵛ, printed in Foxe, *AM* (Townsend), vol. VII, Appendix, no. 6.
[73] *Cal SP Spain*, IV (2) 664 (*LP*, V 148).   [74] Wilkins (ed.), *Concilia*, III:747.

told to appear on 15 April.[75] The records do not indicate that he took any oath. At this stage, Latimer had refused to admit to preaching heresy, he had avoided signing any orthodox articles that offended his conscience (unlike other evangelicals), and he had evaded swearing any oath.

Latimer was not out of hot water yet. He had foolishly written a letter to his opponent Master Greenwood declaring that he had not preached any errors, nor admitted them publicly, but rather he would continue to preach as he always had.[76] In other words, Latimer had exposed his equivocation. On 19 April, Latimer appeared before Convocation and was ordered "to swear an oath to answer faithfully next Monday'. It is quite possible that Convocation was trying to use an oath to ensure that Latimer did not equivocate this time. Latimer must have realized his danger, for instead of swearing this oath *de veritate dicenda*, Latimer responded that he had appealed to the king. Archbishop Warham ignored this response and again told him he must 'appear [that is, be present] to swear the oath'.[77] The appeal to the king did not work quite so well for Latimer this time; the king communicated that he wanted Latimer to be judged by Warham and Convocation. Accordingly, Latimer appeared before Convocation again on 22 April and confessed his equivocation:

That where he had aforetime confessed, that he hath heretofore erred, and that he meaned then it was onely error of discretion, he hath sythens better seen his own acts, and searched them more deeply, and doth knowledge, that he hath not erred only in discretion, but also in doctrine; and said, that he was not called afore the said lords, but upon good and just ground, and hath been by them charitably and

---

[75] The records of Convocation are confusing here and deserve to be quoted in full: 'et postea differebat dominus locum tenens iuramentum ad subscribendum articulis praedictis, et ad praestandum se coram reverendissimo decimo quinto Aprilis . . . Et tunc, praedictus Latimer, exceptis articulis undecimo et decimo quarto subscripsit voluntarie et assignavit sua manu propria unde praedictus Latimer fuit absolutus a sentencia excommunicationis, et monitus ad comparendum decimo quinto Aprilis, ad audiendumulteriorem processum etc., quorum articuluorum verus tenor exprimitur articulatim'; Bray (ed.), *Records of Convocation*, VII:180; Wilkins (ed.), *Concilia*, III:747. Gerald Bray, the editor of the *Records of Convocation*, kept Latimer's subscription under 21 March. Most historians, however, have assumed that the 'tunc' meant that it happened on 10 April. There has also been disagreement over the definition of 'exceptis'. Alan Chester asserted that Latimer signed all the articles on 10 April; Chester, *Hugh Latimer*, 80. Robert Demaus claimed that on 10 April, Latimer signed all the articles except the eleventh and fourteenth, which he claimed Latimer had signed on 21 March; Demaus, *Hugh Latimer*, 139–40. Harold Darby and Susan Wabuda, by contrast, declared that Latimer signed only articles eleven and fourteen on 10 April; Darby, *Hugh Latimer*, 76; Wabuda, 'Equivocation and Recantation', 231. All of these statements – though opposing – are based solely on the records of Convocation. I agree with the interpretation of Darby and Wabuda that Latimer signed only articles eleven and fourteen, though it is not clear whether he did so on 21 March or 10 April.

[76] Latimer, *Sermons and Remains*, 356–7.

[77] Bray (ed.), *Records of Convocation*, VII:181–2; Wilkins (ed.), *Concilia*, III:748.

favourably intreated. And where he had afore time misreported of the lords, he knowlegeth, that he hath done yll in it, and desired them, humbly on his knees, to forgive him: and where he is not of ability to make them recompence, he said, he would pray for them.[78]

So this time around, Latimer admitted that he had erred in doctrine. Yet his submission was still favourable and extraordinary. The records of Convocation admit that Latimer was then 'received into grace upon the special request of the king'.[79] Latimer did not specify what heretical doctrines he had preached, he made no formal abjuration, and he was not required – despite Warham's threats – ever to swear an oath. Latimer had equivocated and admitted to preaching heretically, but he had not perjured himself.

The master of this technique was Edward Crome. Crome was first in trouble for heresy in March 1531. Henry ordered Crome to recant his opinions, and the bishops drew up a set of fourteen positive articles of orthodox Catholic belief that Crome was to read in a sermon at Paul's Cross.[80] These articles were clearly designed as a propaganda device to make Crome reject evangelical heresy in the presence of the London populace. At his recantation sermon Crome prefaced these articles by proclaiming: 'There be some men that do say I have been abjured, and some say that I am perjured, but the truth is, that I am neither abjured, nor yet perjured.'[81] Indeed, Crome was technically correct. The fourteen articles included neither an admittance of having held heretical opinions nor an oath of abjuration. Crome was thus offered an even sweeter deal than Bilney or Shaxton. But even then, Crome was not content to play his assigned role. After reading each article, Crome glossed each one in such a way as to deny their content without actually putting forth a heretical opinion.[82] Crome was in trouble again in 1541 for an Advent sermon of the previous year in which he had, among other things, denounced the Mass. Henry had Bonner draw up an explicit yet oathless recantation in which Crome admitted his errors and reaffirmed proper Catholic doctrine.[83] Crome dutifully read the

[78] Wilkins (ed.), *Concilia*, III:748.   [79] Bray (ed.), *Records of Convocation*, VII:183.
[80] These articles were very similar to the ones drawn up for Latimer a year later. They are preserved in GL MS 9531/10 (Tunstall's Register), fol. 138ᵛ, printed in Foxe, *AM* (Townsend), vol. v, Appendix, no. 16.
[81] Wabuda, 'Equivocation and Recantation', 230.
[82] For the exact words of Crome's sermon, including his glosses, see Strype, *Ecclesiastical Memorials*, vol. III, Appendix, 19–27. For a nice evaluation of this sermon, see Wabuda, 'Equivocation and Recantation', 230.
[83] The abjuration is GL MS 9531/12 (Bonner's Register), fol. 25ʳ⁻ᵛ, printed in Foxe, *AM* (Townsend), vol. v, appendix, no. 16.

recantation, but he read it in the third person and did not integrate it into his sermon. Richard Hilles reported:

Now when the Sunday came, on which he was to recant, he preached a godly discourse, and at the end of it told the people that he had received a written document from the king's majesty which he was ordered to read to them. And after he had read it, he committed the congregation to God in a short prayer, and so went away: whereas the king certainly intended him to receive that writing as a specimen of the doctrine which he was to follow in his sermon.[84]

In the words of Susan Wabuda, Crome 'preached reform as usual, and presented the articles of submission as if they were a list of doctrines that Henry wanted announced'.[85] On 11 April 1546, Crome preached a sermon attacking transubstantiation and putting forth a commemorative interpretation of the Mass. Once again, Crome was ordered to recant. Once again, he made an oathless recantation which was ambiguous, adding at the end of his sermon: 'Worshipful audience, I come not hither to recant nor yet am I commanded to recant nor God willing I will not recant yet.'[86] Henry finally had enough. He applied extreme pressure on Crome and on 27 June 1546, Crome preached another recantation sermon in which he espoused an unambiguously orthodox interpretation of the Mass and admitted to his previous equivocation:

I dyd not nor intended not to sette foorthe the same with a symple mynde according to the true sense and meaning of them but having one meanynge secreatelye in myne harte knowinge in my conscience the sense and meanyng of thartycles to be contrarie to the same, I dyd vse collusion and color of my hole proceding concernynge the declaration of the saide Articles whereby I might appeare boothe to mantayne myne owne former evyll opynyon and neverthelesse to satysfie my promysse in setting foorthe of Thartycles aforesaide.[87]

Crome's use of equivocation has been well documented by Susan Wabuda. What Wabuda has not noticed, however, is that none of Crome's machinations included oaths. Oaths were absent from all his recantations, and there is no record of Crome being asked questions on oath.

The new kind of evangelical strategy was not limited to Latimer and Crome. As Susan Brigden has demonstrated, Robert Barnes, Thomas Garret, and William Jerome used the same kind of machinations in their

---

[84] Robinson (ed. and trans.), *Original Letters*, 215.

[85] Wabuda, 'Equivocation and Recantation', 234.

[86] Wabuda, 'Equivocation and Recantation', 235. For the actual recantation, see GL MS 9531/12 (Bonner's Register), fol. 101ᵛ, printed in Foxe, *AM* (Townsend), vol. v, Appendix, no. 16.

[87] GL MS 9531/12 (Bonner's Register), fol. 101ᵛ, printed in Foxe, *AM* (Townsend), vol. v, Appendix, no. 16; Wabuda, 'Equivocation and Recantation', 236.

recantations of 1540. They read the recantations prepared for them but then followed or preceded these recantations with sermons in which they taught the very same evangelical doctrine of which they were recanting![88] Their goal was clearly designed to subvert the authorities' attempt to use their recantations as a means to disseminate conservative doctrine. Indeed, one of their supporters noted 'howe gayly they had all handled the matter, both to satisfie the recantacion and also in the same sermons to utter out the truth, that it myght sprede without let of the worlde'.[89] For these connived and janus-faced recantations, Henry himself ordered that they be imprisoned in the Tower, and they were soon executed as part of the fall of Thomas Cromwell. Yet even in their equivocation, Barnes, Garret, and Jerome did not commit perjury, for oaths were not part of their recantations.

Thus far, oaths have been significant in the heresy trial of later Henrician evangelicals only insofar as they were absent. Latimer, Crome, Barnes, Garret, and Jerome did not commit perjury, but neither did they use oaths to manipulate public opinion. A slightly different picture appears in the trials of Anne Askew and Robert Wisdom.

In 1545 Askew was prosecuted under the Act of Six Articles for sacramentarian doctrine. In her examinations before a jury, before the Lord Mayor of London, and before Bishop Bonner of London, Askew consistently responded equivocally. She refused to answer incriminating questions outright but gave responses that were neither technically heretical according to the letter of the law nor contrary to Protestant doctrine.[90] Askew could get away with giving partial and equivocal responses to the questions asked of her because there is no record of the authorities ever tendering her the *ex officio* oath, which would have bound her to respond to *all* questions truthfully. Eventually, Bonner drew up a recantation for her to sign that explicitly stated that the communicant received the corporeal body of Christ during the Eucharist. Two accounts of this subscription survive. The recantation preserved in Bonner's Register indicates that Askew subscribed absolutely, while Askew herself claimed that she had subscribed with the qualification that she consented to the recantation only so far as it agreed with God's word and the true Catholic Church, a qualification that according to her

---

[88] Brigden, 'Popular Disturbance', 265–6. For the primary sources behind this story, see Gardiner, *Letters*, 164–75; GL MS 9531/12 (Bonner's Register), fol. 37ʳ; Foxe, *AM* (Townsend), v:433 and Appendix, nos. 7 and 8; BL Cotton MS Cleopatra E V, fols. 405ʳ–406ʳ.

[89] Gardiner, *Letters*, 174; Brigden, 'Popular Disturbance', 266.

[90] Askew, *First examinacyon*; Hickerson, 'Ways of Lying', 55, 59; Hickerson, 'Negotiating Heresy', 785–90.

interpretation of Scripture and the true church nullified the content of the recantation.[91] We do not know if Askew was telling the truth here, but it is nonetheless significant that Askew felt it necessary to refute the rumour (undoubtedly fuelled by her subscription) that she had renounced her beliefs. She did so by claiming that she had subscribed conditionally.[92]

Askew's use of equivocation and her attempt to portray herself as not having renounced her sacramentarian beliefs have been expertly examined by Megan Hickerson.[93] Yet what Hickerson has not explored is the role of oaths in Askew's story. Contrary to Robert Parsons' allegation in 1604, neither the recantation preserved in Bonner's Register nor the one embedded in Askew's own account contained an oath.[94] By contrast, Askew did employ oaths in her apology in order to demonstrate to her readers the veracity of her own version of the events. She proclaimed 'as sure as the lorde lyueth' that she never meant to recant, she took 'the same most mercyfull God . . . whych hath made both heauen and earthe, to recorde' that she held 'no opynyons contrarye to hys most holye worde', and she again took 'hym to witnesse' that she had and would until the end of her life 'vtterlye abhorre' the evil opinions contrary to God's blessed verity.[95] The sharp contrast between Askew's oathless trial and abjuration and her oath-laden defence of her conduct during her trial and abjuration is striking. It suggests that Askew was well aware of the power of an oath; she was hesitant to swear them as part of her strategy of equivocation but she had no qualms about using oaths to validate the narrative of events that she had prepared for fellow evangelicals.

Robert Wisdom, parish priest of St Margaret's in Lothbury, recanted his errors at Paul's Cross on 14 July 1543, along with Robert Singleton and the great evangelical propagandist Thomas Becon. Unlike Barnes, Crome, or Askew, Wisdom did not employ any techniques of equivocation. Indeed, the author of Wisdom's recantation, Bishop Stephen Gardiner, pre-empted

---

[91] GL MS 9531/12 (Bonner's Register), fol. 101ʳ; Askew, *First examinacyon*, fols. 35ᵛ–39ʳ; Askew, *Lattre examinacyon*, fols. 51ᵛ–52ᵛ.

[92] Askew wrote a manuscript account of her 1545 trial and recantation and her 1546 ordeal while in prison again in 1546 for heresy. The purpose of her writing was 'to satisfie your expectation, good people'; Askew, *First examinacyon*, fol. 1ᵛ. She was evidently aware that some of her fellow evangelicals had heard that she had apostatized, and she wrote her story to refute that rumour. Askew's manuscript eventually found its way into the hands of John Bale on the Continent. Bale published Askew's account in two parts in 1547. Askew was burned at the end of 1546 for heresy after refusing to recant or give the names of fellow evangelical gentlewomen. Bale's publication and elucidation of Askew's trial and death has the distinction of being the first English Protestant martyrology.

[93] Hickerson, 'Ways of Lying', 50–65.

[94] For Parsons' allegation, see Nichols (ed.), *Narratives of the Days of the Reformation*, 307–8.

[95] Askew, *Lattre examinacyon*, fols. 51ᵛ, 54ʳ, 55ʳ.

such a move by placing the following words in Wisdom's recantation: 'howesoever I haue counterfett before, thyncke not that I counterfett nowe, for I declare vnto you playnely what I am'.[96] Wisdom admitted that he had wrongly preached against free will, prayers to the saints, and the charity of public ministers for putting people into prison for preaching the truth. Indeed, establishing the falsity of evangelicals and their doctrine in contrast to the truth of the conservative doctrine of the established Henrician Church was clearly one of the goals of Gardiner in writing Wisdom's recantation. Gardiner made Wisdom declare: 'I knowledge my self to have offended the true doctryne of oure Religion and to have spoken therein untruyle.' Wisdom confessed that he had 'untruyly' 'slaundered comon justyce', for he knew 'noo man partycularlye to have been persecuted for the truyth'. Garret and Jerome had been executed for their 'false and untrue doctryne'. Wisdom concluded by exhorting his audience to 'folowe the truythe taughte us' by England's prelates.[97] Despite all this rhetoric of truth, Wisdom did not seal his abjuration with the ultimate attestation of truth, an oath.

Wisdom's unequivocal betrayal of the truth bitterly grieved his conscience. In 1545 he penned a revocation of his recantation in which he narrated the events leading up to his recantation and vehemently decried his recantation. He averred that he was 'ernestlie repentaunte and sorye of that gret slaunder and occasion of evill that he then comytted aginste the congregation of god'.[98] His recantation had been made out of fear of death, but now he was determined to proclaim again 'the trouthe of gods worde', even though he recognized 'that this my revocation shall cooste me my life'.[99] Obviously, Wisdom felt that his duty to preach evangelical truth now trumped his fear of punishment. Much of Wisdom's revocation was concerned with defending the real 'truth' of Scripture. Unlike his recantation, oaths played an important rhetorical role in Wisdom's defense. First, like Askew, Wisdom used oaths as proof of the truth of his revocation. When he dealt with the part of his recantation in which he had admitted to having counterfeited in his preaching, Wisdom denied this and swore 'afore god and our lord Jesus Christe that shall in his gloryouse kingdome Iudge the quicke and deade' that he had always preached the truth and

[96] GL MS 9531/12 (Bonner's Register), fol. 43ʳ, printed in Foxe, *AM* (Townsend), vol. V, Appendix, no. XII; Wabuda, 'Equivocation and Recantation', 228.
[97] GL MS 9531/12 (Bonner's Register), fol. 43ʳ, printed in Foxe, *AM* (Townsend), vol. v, Appendix, no. 12.
[98] Emmanuel College, Cambridge MS 261, fol. 88ʳ.
[99] Emmanuel College, Cambridge MS 261, fol. 90ʳ⁻ᵛ.

the gospel of Scripture.[100] At the end of his revocation, Wisdom again swore: 'And I testify to all men by this boke that I will vnfainedlie the same to be taken iuste devised by the byshope of winchester and for feare of dethe consented vnto subscribed and redde by me vnfaithfull and wicked wretche.'[101]

Second, in Wisdom's revocation we see that Bishop Bonner actually employed an oath to convince Wisdom to recant. According to Wisdom, after his initial denunciation for heresy, Bonner summoned him and asked him to confess. Wisdom refused, pointing out that Bonner was not his ordinary and had no jurisdiction over him. When neither threats nor flattery worked, Bonner began 'to swear unto me by God and by his faith and by his baptism, that if I would confess myself faulty, he would dismiss me so free that I should never more hear of it, nor never more be troubled for it'.[102] This kind of oath seems to have been part of Bonner's general strategy, for he made a similar promise to Askew's cousin Christopher Brittain.[103] Although Wisdom thought 'baptism a great oath, and believing that a bishop never would have been perjured', he still refused to submit.[104] Bonner again swore a similar oath. Finally, Wisdom's uncle scared him with an exposition on the horrors of imprisonment and convinced him to submit. Wisdom recounted:

I hearing this and afraid of these perils, agreed unto them especially touching the Bishop's oath, made first to me, and now again unto them; and so came before the bishop and confessed, and wrote whatsoever the bishop's scribe bade me, and then delivered it unto the bishop. This bill (for all his baptism) the Bishop of London laid up in store.[105]

Bonner then passed on Wisdom's submission to Gardiner, who used it as evidence against Wisdom. Bonner's betrayal of his oath gave Wisdom ample opportunity to expostulate on the perjury of his captors. Wisdom declared that there was more truth in 'a womans talle...then in the byshoppe of londons othe that sticked not to periure his baptisem so he might deteine me'.[106] Such deception was not limited to Bonner but was common among England's conservative prelates: 'They care neither

---

[100] Emmanuel College, Cambridge MS 261, fol. 107[r].
[101] Emmanuel College, Cambridge MS 261, fol. 130[r].
[102] Emmanuel College, Cambridge MS 261, fol. 92[v].
[103] Askew, *First examinacyon*, fol. 18[v]. Bonner seems to have kept his promise concerning Askew in 1545 since she was initially set free with a favourable abjuration; Hickerson, 'Negotiating Heresy', 774, 783.
[104] Emmanuel College, Cambridge MS 261, fol. 92[v].
[105] Emmanuel College, Cambridge MS 261, fol. 93[r].
[106] Emmanuel College, Cambridge MS 261, fol. 124[v]. See a similar declaration on fol. 101[v].

for perjury nor for other mischief, so they may deface the truth and put preachers to silence.'[107] Their perjury was just one proof of 'their paynted hypocrisie falsly called religion where in deade yt ys but an owtwarde glisteringe falslie pretensed holynes'.[108] Evangelicals had now come full circle from Thomas More's allegations; now it was an evangelical who was accusing the ecclesiastical authorities of perjury, and then arguing that this perjury invalidated their piety. In fact, Wisdom's accusations were just the beginning. Under the reign of Mary Tudor, evangelicals commonly roasted their prelates for their perjury in acquiescing to the restoration of papal authority after having taken the Henrician oaths of supremacy.[109]

It is understandable that evangelicals like Wisdom sought to paint their conservative persecutors as perjurers, for such a picture had obvious worth as propaganda. It is also easy to explain why later Henrician evangelicals practised equivocation: it allowed them to escape the flames without fully rejecting evangelical doctrine. Indeed, in some cases it even allowed them to publicize evangelical doctrine. What is less clear, however, is why the prosecutions of Latimer, Crome, Barnes, Garret, Jerome, Askew, and Wisdom did not include any of the oaths traditionally administered in heresy trials. One possible solution, recognizing that all the oathless trials examined above (Latimer's excepted) happened after 1534, would be to ground the absence of traditional oaths in the legal changes brought about by the 1534 Heresy Act. The Heresy Act of 1534 does partially explain the disappearance of the *ex officio* oath, for according to the statute ordinaries were no longer allowed to prosecute heresy on their own authority (*ex officio mero*). In order for bishops to proceed against a suspect, the suspect had to be indicted by a secular court or be accused by two or more witnesses.[110] This meant that when an ordinary proceeded against a person suspected of heresy, he already possessed substantial evidence against the suspect. It was not as necessary to force suspects to provide the evidence of their own guilt by asking them questions under oath. But as we have seen in Askew's case, ordinaries still might want to examine the suspect to gain further evidence, and there is nothing in the Heresy Act that prevented them from tendering the suspect some kind of oath *de veritate dicenda*. Indeed, the Privy Council did administer this oath to Latimer in 1546 as part of its investigation against Crome.[111] Moreover, the Heresy Act does

[107] Emmanuel College, Cambridge MS 261, fol. 93ᵛ.
[108] Emmanuel College, Cambridge MS 261, fol. 95ʳ.
[109] Foxe, *AM* (Townsend), VI:682–3; VII:160; VIII:112; BL Lansdowne MS 389, fols. 29ʳ–32ʳ, printed in Strype, *Ecclesiastical Memorials*, Appendix to vol. III, 123–6.
[110] *Statutes of the Realm*, 25 Hen. VIII, c. 14, III:454–5.   [111] *LP*, XXI (1), 823.

not provide any illumination into the disappearance of oaths of abjuration. Hence, the Heresy Act is an insufficient explanation for the disappearance of traditional heresy oaths.

A more likely explanation is that Edmund Bonner deliberately excluded oaths from the heresy prosecutions in his diocese of London. After all, the oathless recantations of Crome, Barnes, Garret, Jerome, Askew, and Wisdom all happened in Bonner's diocese. Other recantations preserved in Bonner's Register, those of Thomas Becon, Robert Singleton, and John Heywood, are also missing abjuration oaths.[112] This stands in marked contrast to the abjurations made in the 1530s and 40s contained in registers of Edward Lee, John Hilsey, Nicholas Heath, and Thomas Goodrich, all of which included traditional abjuration oaths.[113] The evidence therefore points to Bonner. And if we examine the published recantations of Alexander Seton and William Tolwyn, we get hints of why Bonner pursued such a policy. Seton declared that Bonner could 'haue compelled me, accordyng to the Ecclesiastical lawes of this Realme to abiure & also might haue extremly punyshed me for the same offences' but he was 'and is contented with this onely penaunce, (that is to say) that I make here this open declaracyon unto you of my sayde offences, & that I do not hereafter prech or teach' any heresy against the holy church again.[114] Similarly, Tolwyn stated in his recantation: 'I haue found such charytable goodnes and mercy in my Lorde byshop of London, vpon my submission and sute vnto him, that vpon only this declaration here made of my offens vnto you, with promyse that I wyll endeuer my selfe to the best of my power to lyue' as a Catholic, never to preach or teach any heresies, and to detect heresies and their maintainers, 'his lordshyp is content to respyt the rest of my penaunce, and vpon my good deseruynge and doyng accordyng to my seyd promyfe to forgyue all togyther'.[115] In other words, Bonner was most likely prescribing milder forms of recantations without oaths to suspected heretics in his diocese as an attempt to convince those with tender consciences to accept his deal and recant!

This insight supports Alec Ryrie's contention that rather than being a bloodthirsty and oppressive regime as depicted by John Foxe, the Henrician prelacy much preferred recantations to burnings and exploited these recantations as a form of propaganda, though of course Ryrie's axiom that 'any

---

[112] GL MS 9531/12 (Bonner's Register), fols. 43ʳ–44ᵛ, 61ʳ, 62ᵛ.
[113] BI Register 28, in *CAP*, vol. I, part. 14, fols. 82ᵛ–83ʳ, 90, 100ʳ, 141ᵛ; KAO ᴅʀᴄ/ʀ7 in *CAP*, vol. vIII, part 8, fols. 195ᵛ, 200ʳ; CUL ᴇᴅʀ ɢ/1/8, in *CAP*, vol. vII, part. 4, fol. 5ʳ.
[114] Seton and Tolwyn, *Declaracion made at Poules Crosse*, sig. ᴀ3ᵛ.
[115] Seton and Tolwyn, *Declaracion made at Poules Crosse*, sig. ʙ3ʳ.

process of recantation involved the swearing of an oath' does not hold.[116] It is true that Bonner's policy of allowing recantations without oaths made these recantations weaker in that they were not made with God as witness, but they were still of great propaganda value for the conservative prelacy in that the person suspected of heresy *publicly* admitted to holding specific evangelical tenets, denounced these tenets as heretical, and then praised the benevolence and mercy of the prelacy. For propaganda purposes, it mattered less that the recantation was before God and more that it was before men. Of course, the use of equivocation during a recantation would lessen its propaganda value significantly, but the conservative prelacy (namely Bonner and Gardiner) appears to have been less likely to allow equivocal recantations than oathless recantations. The equivocal recantations of Latimer, Barnes, and Crome were not approved by the prelacy. Latimer and Crome were eventually caught equivocating and had to confess and retract their equivocation in 1532 and 1546 respectively, while the recantations of Barnes, Garret, and Jerome in 1540 were completely rejected, and they were burned at the stake. Indeed, despite the claims of Eamon Duffy and Megan Hickerson that the ecclesiastical authorities (particularly Bonner) allowed ambiguous, equivocal submissions, the recantations that were hand prepared by the prelates in Henry's reign were actually designed to preclude equivocation.[117] We have seen that this was the case with Wisdom, and Crome was likewise made to declare in 1541 that he was 'resolued and fully perswadid in his harte and conscience' to remain loyal to his new-found orthodoxy.[118] Askew may have got away with equivocation in 1545, but it was she not Bonner who made this public. The recantation set down by Bonner for posterity did not contain the conditional phrase Askew supposedly added but rather denied it by commencing: 'to thentent the woorlde may see what credence ys nowe to be gyven vnto the same woman whome shorte tyme hathe moost dampnablye altered and chaunged her opynyon and beleaf and therefore rightfullie in opyn Courte arrayned and condempned'.[119] Thus, Bonner's willingness to allow oathless recantations

[116] Ryrie, *Gospel and Henry VIII*, 76, 82–4.
[117] Duffy, *Fires of Faith*, 140–1, 144–6, 167. For Hickerson, see below.
[118] GL MS 9531/12 (Bonner's Register), fol. 25ʳ, quoted in Ryrie, *Gospel and Henry VIII*, 82.
[119] GL MS 9531/12 (Bonner's Register), fol. 101ʳ. By contrast, Megan Hickerson has suggested that Bonner cooperated with Askew's equivocal recantation in 1545; Hickerson, 'Negotiating Heresy', 774–95. Hickerson was correct in her assertion that Bonner was aware of Askew's equivocation in 1545 and let her go, but it is not clear that he let her subscribe conditionally. Moreover, Bonner did not make Askew's recantation public until 1546. (The wording of this clause quoted above suggests that Bonner set forth his version of Askew's recantation in 1546 as a justification for her forthcoming execution.) Thus, Bonner never *publicly* supported Askew's equivocation. He may have been prepared to tolerate it, but he was not prepared to publicize it.

but not equivocal ones demonstrates the extent to which he was willing to compromise.

Of course, Bonner would not have omitted oaths from evangelical recantations if he did not believe that such an omission would more easily convince them to recant. Although there is no direct evidence of evangelicals declaring to the authorities that they would submit only if their recantations were oathless, it is possible – even probable – that this was part of the strategy of some later Henrician evangelicals, for this explains Bonner's policy. Furthermore, it is clear that evangelicals like Barnes, Crome, and Askew did not want to be perceived as rejecting evangelical doctrine. This was why they equivocated. Yet if they sealed their recantations with an oath, they would have placed more emphasis (at least in the eyes of those who accepted the church's traditional teaching on the sanctity of oaths) on the recantations themselves rather than the equivocal statements they added in an effort to subvert the original meaning of their recantations. Finally, evangelicals undoubtedly had no desire to commit perjury. Besides the obvious benefits of avoiding a serious sin, there were real propaganda advantages to steering clear of perjury. Not only did it allow them to deny the accusations of Thomas More, but it lent more credence to their own burgeoning claims (manifested above in allegations of Robert Wisdom) that the conservative prelates were the real perjurors.[120] Moreover, it was during the first half of the 1540s that the first two full-length English evangelical works on oaths were printed: *A Christen exhortacion vnto customable swearers* (1543) by John Bale and *An Inuectyue agenst the moost wicked and detestable vyce of swearing* (1543) by Thomas Becon, who himself made oathless recantations before and after the publication of his book. These works emphasized the gravity of the sin of perjury. It was thus extremely convenient for evangelicals making recantations to evade an oath, for then they were not open to the charge of perjury if and when they went back on their recantation and began preaching evangelical doctrine. Not swearing a recantation oath allowed evangelicals to avoid contradicting their propaganda against perjury with incongruous practice. It is therefore quite conceivable that evangelicals began to refuse to recant under oath as a matter of principle.

But what a principle! Was it not inconsistent for evangelicals to have little problem practising equivocation and dissimulation in their heresy processes but shun practising dissimulation under oath? Did English evangelicals

---

[120] Wisdom was not of course the only evangelical to make such an argument. William Tyndale, for example, employed similar arguments: Tyndale and Frith, *Works of the English Reformers*, 1:487–8.

actually advocate that oathless dissimulation was licit but perjury illicit? They never openly taught this doctrine. In public, evangelicals took the moral high ground on oaths and condemned perjury. Concerning general, oathless dissimulation, they either avoided discussing it or condemned it as wrong. The exception to this rule was William Tyndale, who taught that to dissemble and deceive for the good of one's neighbour was not only licit but commendable, even if sealed with an oath: 'To persuade him that pursueth his neighbour, to hurt him or slay him, that his neighbour is gone another contrary way, is the duty of every Christian man by the law of charity, and no sin; no, though I confirmed it with an oath.'[121] The more radical Henrician evangelicals who chose to go into exile after the passage of the Six Articles rather than to compromise their beliefs naturally took a harder line on general dissimulation. John Bale wrote of Tolwyn's recantation:

For if he belieueth, that [by] denyenge the verite with mouthe onlye, he ys out of that parell of sowle so longe as he styll retayneth yt in hys hart, he is sore deceyued ... Manye are now in englande which walke vndre these subtile shadowes, but yf they thynke so to auoyde the daungers of gods indygnacion, they sore deceyue themselues.[122]

George Joye likewise proclaimed:

Trewth it is, that it is all one thynge, not to defende the trewth and to denye the trewth ... Let men beware how they dissemble with the trewth in this worlde, lest in soche an vngodly securite they pluke the synne of the holy ghost into theyr bosoms ... No, not so did daniel, for he knewe that the trewe religion and worship must be farre from a colourable dissembling without any lying shyftis of hypocricie.[123]

Yet Alec Ryrie has convincingly argued that exiled evangelicals like Bale and Joye were more radical than the majority of Henrician evangelicals and thus cannot be taken as representative.[124] The majority of early English evangelicals, especially ones like Barnes, Latimer, and Crome who all made use

---

[121] Tyndale and Frith, *Works of the English Reformers*, II:293–4.

[122] Bale, *Yet a course at the Romyshe foxe*, fol. 3ᵛ–4ʳ, quoted in Wabuda, 'Equivocation and Recantation', 239–40. It should be noted that despite the fact that Tolwyn's abjuration did not include an oath (and Bale faithfully printed Tolwyn's abjuration), Bale still acted like it did. Bale attacked Bonner for 'so cruellye exactinge soche a shamefull profession and abhomynable othe as thys is here'; Bale, *Yet a course at the Romyshe foxe*, fol. 14ʳ.

[123] Joye, *The exposicion of Daniel*, fols. 33ʳ, 84ᵛ, quoted in Ryrie, *Gospel and Henry VIII*, 70. It is worth noting that despite this quote, Joye did not hesitate to lie when attempting to flee England in order to escape persecution. Indeed, he unashamedly confessed this dissimulation; Joye, *Letters whyche Johan Ashwell*, fol. D2ʳ.

[124] Ryrie, *Gospel and Henry VIII*, 93–112.

of it, were silent on the theme of non-perjurous dissimulation.[125] Nevertheless, although they never officially taught that one could honourably equivocate as a form of dissimulation in times of trouble as long as it was not confirmed with an oath, this was what they did in practice. In this regard, late Henrician evangelicals were similar to the Catholic recusants at the end of Elizabeth's reign described by Alexandra Walsham. In all their public, printed works, these recusants took a strong line against dissimulation and outward conformity with Protestantism, for they had to reconcile their teachings on this subject with their propaganda that the Church of England was completely heretical and depraved. Yet in their unprinted casuistic manuals for priests and in private interactions, recusant priests sometimes allowed conformity with Protestant worship as a means to escape persecution.[126] Although the issue for Henrician evangelicals was public recantations as opposed to church attendance, their practice suggests that they were also willing to tolerate a certain degree of compromise with the regime as long as it did not clash with their open propaganda. In the latter years of Henry's reign, however, that compromise stopped at the commission of perjury.

The general findings of this chapter have supported Alec Ryrie's argument that 'Recantation in this period was not merely a process by which reformers submitted to the regime . . . it involved an element of negotiation.' Both the Henrician regime and persecuted evangelicals made compromises.[127] Yet by narrowing our focus to the role of oaths in heresy prosecutions, we have refined Ryrie's conclusions. Some ecclesiastical authorities continued to employ the traditional oaths *de veritate dicenda*, of purgation, and of abjuration in a way that presented evangelicals on trial for heresy with only three choices: honest abjuration, perjury, or death. Some early evangelicals responded in the traditional Lollard way, by dissimulating under oath and thus committing perjury. As Henry's reign progressed, however, oaths disappeared from the heresy prosecutions of many notable evangelicals. Bishop Bonner in particular seems to have been willing to drop abjuration oaths as an incentive to induce evangelicals to recant. And evangelicals, while still generally more willing to recant than endure the flames, weakened their recantations both by using equivocation and avoiding sealing their recantations with an oath. Instead, evangelicals employed oaths to demonstrate their steadfastness to their evangelical

---

[125] It is commonly known that Latimer preached harshly against all forms of lies. See Latimer, *Sermons by Hugh Latimer*, 500–3. This sermon, however, was given under Edward VI when times had changed.

[126] Walsham, *Church Papists*, 29–30, 70–1.　　[127] Ryrie, *Gospel and Henry VIII*, 88.

brethren and, in the case of Wisdom, to accuse the conservative prelates of being the real perjurors. When Henry's reign is viewed chronologically, the ecclesiastical authorities were becoming more willing to compromise and evangelicals less willing.[128] The latter pattern continued in the reign of Mary Tudor, while the former did not. Under Mary, many evangelicals (now more accurately called Protestants) refused to dissimulate at all, regardless of whether such dissimulation encompassed perjury. The ecclesiastical authorities, while still perhaps willing to allow ambiguous recantations in certain select cases, generally re-inserted oaths back into the process of heresy prosecutions.[129] Yet during the reign of Henry, the prosecution of heresy and resistance to this prosecution was more a process of negotiation than it was one of simple enforcement and defiance.

[128] My argument that evangelicals were growing less willing to compromise at the end of Henry's reign fits well with Thomas Freeman's recent claims: Freeman, 'Over Their Dead Bodies', 17.

[129] For the revival of the *ex officio* oath under Mary, see Levy, *Origins of the Fifth Amendment*, 76–7. For examples of abjuration oaths under Mary, see BL Harleian MS 421, fols. 81^{r-v}, 83^r, 84^r, 85^r-86^r, 88^r, 91^r, 146^{r-v}, 154^{r-v}, 173^r-174^r, 175^r-176^v, 183^r-184^r.

Conclusion

The argument of this book is that oaths were crucial to the English Reformation. The Henrician regime implemented and enforced its Reformation with oaths, and the English people resisted, negotiated, and acquiesced to this same Reformation through oaths. Oaths were the primary point of contact between the regime and people during the Henrician Reformation. The task of this conclusion is to explore the political and theological ramifications of this argument. In particular, the central question of this conclusion is how the massive employment of oaths during the Henrician Reformation affected the English Crown, the nature of oaths, and the English people. The answer to this question is ambiguous. While the Henrician regime's extensive use of oaths strengthened the authority of the Crown in the short term, in the long term it empowered the English people and set in motion a process that eventually led to a devaluation of oaths.

Two historiographical contexts are relevant here. The first context is the historiography of the effects of the Reformation in general on the power of the Crown. Summarizing the state of the field, Alan Smith and Kevin Sharpe have observed that, in the end, the Reformation may have undermined the authority of the Crown by empowering Parliament and by linking religious uniformity to political loyalty. While Parliament was generally subservient to the Crown during Henry's reign, the fact that Henry secured all his major reforms through Parliament legitimized its authority and set the stage for Parliament's challenge of the crown in the seventeenth century. Similarly, Henry's efforts to combine religious and political authority in the person of the king meant that those subjects who opposed the religion of the established church eventually opposed the royal authority that undergirded this religion.[1] These points notwithstanding, the current weight of opinion is that, in the short term at least, the Henrician Reformation augmented the power of the Crown. First, Henry's dissolution

---

[1] Smith, *Emergence of a Nation State*, 87–9; Sharpe, *Selling the Tudor Monarchy*, 476–7.

of the monasteries and appropriation (and then sale) of their lands filled the royal coffers. Second, the declaration of royal supremacy increased the Crown's jurisdictional and administrative power by eliminating the competing authority of the Pope in England, by bestowing the Crown direct control over English clergy, and by giving the Crown access to a highly structured system of organization that could be exploited for propaganda and administrative purposes. Finally, and most importantly, the doctrine of royal supremacy sanctified the Crown. It imbued the king with sacral authority that gave him dominion over not only his subjects' bodies but also their souls and consciences.[2] Indeed, this notion of sacred monarchy is integral to the widely popular confessionalization thesis of Heinz Schilling and Wolfgang Reinhard which, among other things, argues that the Reformation and Counter-Reformation increased the power of the state and strengthened social discipline.[3]

In this context, my argument that the Henrician regime implemented and enforced its Reformation through oaths seems to support the argument that the Reformation increased the power of the Crown. After all, oaths were forms of spiritual coercion. They gave the Crown access to the power of God, an omniscient and omnipotent being. Oaths were the perfect test of loyalty or orthodoxy, for they made God both the proctor and grader of the exam. Oaths also served as bonds cementing the juror's future behaviour and beliefs. Once a person swore to be loyal to Henry and his heirs, to take action against all who opposed the Crown, or never to hold heretical beliefs again, God became the guarantor of the juror's future loyalty and orthodoxy. After a person had made a sworn promise, any subsequent action or utterance against the juror's oath would call down the wrath of God, if not in this life, then in the next. Oaths thus increased the power of the Crown by allowing it to appropriate the power of God and use this power for its own means.

Yet the second historiographical context relevant to the use of oaths during the Henrician Reformation casts a shadow of doubt on this conclusion. This context is the debate over how the nature of oaths changed during the early modern era. Christopher Hill, Keith Thomas, and C. John Sommerville have argued that oaths became secularized in the sixteenth and especially the seventeenth century. Shorn of their divine power, oaths lost

---

[2] Smith, *Emergence of a Nation State*, 29, 87–90; Sharpe, *Selling the Tudor Monarchy*, 475–6; Jones, *Conscience and Allegiance*, 25.

[3] Reinhard, 'Reformation, Counter-Reformation, and the Early Modern State', 123–8; Schilling, 'Confessional Europe', 655–67; Schilling, *Religion, Political Culture and the Emergence of Early Modern Society*, 209, 232–8.

their efficacy.[4] Edward Vallance and David Martin Jones have countered, contending that while the plethora of state oaths of the seventeenth century did engender a new casuistry that could weaken the efficacy of oaths, the majority of the English people continued to consider oaths serious bonds of real spiritual power.[5] John Spurr has taken the opposite approach, arguing that the decline narrative is wrong not because oaths continued to be sacred but because they were never particularly sacred in the first place. According to Spurr, there existed a whole demi-monde of people who delighted in profane swearing, thereby thumbing their nose at the belief that God would punish perjury.[6]

The debate over the decline of oaths raises a significant question for our research: did the Henrician regime's employment of oaths lead to a decline in their sanctity and therefore their efficacy? This question is especially pertinent because many of the factors that Hill, Thomas, and Sommerville claimed caused the decline of oaths – the imposition of a substantial penalty on those who refused to swear, the administration of contradictory oaths, and the practice of equivocation, mental reservation, and perjury – were all present during the Henrician Reformation. Moreover, since the power of oaths depended on the belief that God was the enforcer of oaths, and since the Henrician regime sought to shore up its own authority by using oaths to harness this divine capacity, the authority of the regime itself was, to some extent at least, connected to the sanctity of oaths. If the spiritual power of oaths was somehow undermined, then the royal power buttressed by oaths was equally cast on shaky ground.

The first factor that potentially undermined the divine power of Henrician oaths was the fact that the regime backed these spiritual bonds with temporal punishments. If a convicted heretic refused to swear an oath of abjuration, he or she could be burned. Those who refused the oath of succession were guilty of misprision of treason, the penalty for which was perpetual imprisonment and loss of land and goods. After 1536, the refusal of the oath of succession was treason, the penalty for which was execution. Furthermore, Richard Rex has theorized that Henry administered the oath of succession to the laymen of London on the same day as he executed Elizabeth Barton and her followers because he wanted the executions to intimidate his subjects into taking the oath of succession.[7] Hence, these

---

[4] Christopher Hill, *Society and Puritanism*, 382–419; Thomas, *Religion and the Decline of Magic*, 76–8; Sommerville, *Secularization of Early Modern England*, 140–3.

[5] Vallance, 'Protestation, Vow, Covenant and Engagement', 408–24; Vallance, *Revolutionary England*, 115, 128–9, 165–8; Jones, *Conscience and Allegiance*, 166–8.

[6] Spurr, 'Profane History of Early Modern Oaths', 37–63; Spurr, 'Perjury, Profanity and Politics', 45–6.

[7] Rex, 'Execution of the Holy Maid of Kent', 218–19.

oaths were to a great extent forced, and oath theory taught that forced oaths were not necessarily binding.

This then begs the question: did the Henrician regime sabotage the effectiveness of its oaths by coercing them through the use of force? Emperor Charles V and Ambassador Chapuys certainly thought so. We have already seen that Charles counselled Mary to take an oath to Henry rather than forfeit her life. Charles knew from his experience with Francis I over the Treaty of Madrid that Mary could later wiggle out of her oath by claiming that she had sworn out of fear and compulsion. Chapuys applied the same reasoning to the oath of succession in general:

> The King himself could not show better the invalidity of his own statute than by compelling, as he was actually doing, people to swear to it, which was a compulsory act much condemned by the best jurists, whose authority I then and there quoted. I said further [that] I maintained that the rudest people in England had been heard to say that evidently the statute had no force at all, since they were called upon and obliged to swear beforehand a thing which had not yet been examined and tried . . . People swore because they dared not offer opposition, the penalty being forfeiture of life and property, and no one in these times wished to become a martyr; besides which, several reconciled themselves to the idea, by the notion that oaths taken by force, against morality (*bonnes meurs*), were not binding, and that even if the oath was a true and legitimate one they could contravene it more honourably than the archbishop of Canterbury there present, who, the day after swearing fidelity and obedience to the Pope, had issued a summons against the Queen.[8]

Henry was probably aware of this argument, since the institutional professions of supremacy in 1534 stipulated that the monk or friar taking the oath swear 'most freely' (*libentissime*). Yet the oath of succession had no such qualifier. As such, it is possible that Chapuys was right that the English people did not consider their consciences bound by the oath of succession because it was forced. The rebels' use of oaths during the Pilgrimage of Grace, however, demonstrates both that they did consider their consciences bound by the oath of succession (that is why they had to respond to it with their own oath) and that they themselves put faith in the power of forced oaths in that they compelled many gentlemen to take their oaths under duress. The participants in the Pilgrimage of Grace, then, still considered a forced oath to contain spiritual power.

The second factor that could have weakened the spiritual power of oaths was the Henrician regime's administration of oaths that contradicted

---

[8] *Cal SP Spain*, v (1) 58, trans. Pascual Gayangos.

previous oaths. Henry tendered oaths to his bishops that nullified their previous oaths to the Pope. Likewise, in the oath of succession of 1534, jurors swore to repute any previous oath made to a foreign authority as 'vain and annihilate'.[9] Finally, the oath Henry administered to the rebels in the Pilgrimage of Grace seeking pardon directly annulled the pilgrims' oaths. When faced with such conflicting oaths, it is possible that people concluded that God must not pay attention to oaths. If God really valued the majesty of his name, should he not have punished those who dared to commit perjury by swearing an oath against their previous oath? Yet the fact that both the regime and the pilgrims of grace responded to an offending oath by administering another oath shows that they still believed in the power of oaths. Oaths in the Henrician Reformation were like nuclear weapons in the Cold War. The proper response to the fact that your enemy had developed a similar nuclear weapon to the one you possessed was not to abandon nuclear weapons, concluding they had lost their efficacy. Rather, it was to develop more powerful and numerous nuclear weapons to one-up your enemy. Similarly, the response of the Henrician regime and the pilgrims of grace to the fact that their enemy had sworn an oath that contradicted a previous oath was not to abandon oaths, concluding they lost their efficacy. Rather, it was to administer another, stronger oath that either invalidated the previous oath or forced a favourable interpretation on the previous oath. Oaths engendered more oaths. Hence, one ramification of the employment of oaths in the Henrician Reformation was the continued and even increased administration of oaths by later regimes, lest their new policies somehow lack the spiritual muscle of their predecessors' old (and sometimes opposing) policies.

The third and final factor that could have invalidated the spiritual power of oaths was the use of dissimulation. We do not know the extent of dissimulated swearing, but we do know that it was practised by both conservatives who opposed royal supremacy and evangelicals who disagreed with conservative theology. This certainly undercut the effectiveness of oaths and thus weakened the authority of the regime that relied upon them. Nevertheless, it is surely significant that later Henrician evangelicals dissimulated but often avoided doing so under oath, thereby implicitly admitting that they respected the special status of oaths. And even the actual commission of perjury by early evangelicals like Bilney, Phillips, and Shaxton implied that the general public held oaths in high esteem. Bilney, Phillips, and Shaxton committed perjury in a consistent and

---

[9] *Journal of the House of Lords*, 1:82.

calculated way in order to present an image of themselves as basically orthodox and honest, but this image would have never gained traction unless the English people trusted the oaths of these evangelicals. Hiding your heterodoxy behind oaths of orthodoxy works only if the people around you cannot see through your cloak of oaths. Finally, we should recognize that no real ideological justification existed in England in the 1530s for utilizing shifts like equivocation and mental reservation when taking an oath. Conservatives and evangelicals alike condemned such shifts as perjury. Eventually, the continued use of oaths by subsequent English governments led Roman Catholic casuists (under Elizabeth) and some Protestant casuists (during the Civil War, Interregnum, and Glorious Revolution) to advocate equivocation and mental reservation as ways to *avoid* perjury without capitulating to the government.[10] Whether or not equivocation and mental reservation were technically perjury, they certainly weakened the bonds of oaths. Yet the very fact that casuists felt the need to justify these practices and exclude them from the category of perjury shows that they felt that many people still considered oaths sacred. If everyone believed, like Peter Norris of Middlewich, that 'oathes were but words, wordes were but wynde and wyde is mutable', then there would have been no need for casuistry.[11]

It therefore seems that the majority of people in Henrician England still considered oaths to be spiritually formidable, though it is also true that at least some of Henry's subjects undermined the spiritual efficacy of oaths by dissimulating. But an oath's ability to access the power of almighty God was not the only characteristic that made them useful to the Henrician regime. Oaths were also a form of propaganda. The action of publicly taking an oath exerted a kind of social pressure on those witnessing the event, especially if the juror was of high status or influential in some other way. It is not a coincidence that the administration of the oath of succession started out at the top of society and trickled its way down the social ladder. The proclivity to imitate one's superior was a means by which the Henrician regime achieved conformity. And even if a person took an oath equivocally, the juror's action still provided an example to others, for they were probably unaware of the juror's dissimulation. Bonner definitely grasped this, realizing that the social currency of an open recantation justified the omission

---

[10] Zagorin, *Ways of Lying*, 186–220; Carrafiello, 'Robert Parsons and Equivocation', 671–80; Tutino, 'Between Nicodemism and "Honest" Dissimulation', 534–53; Sommerville, 'New Art of Lying', 159–84; Vallance, 'Protestation, Vow, Covenant and Engagement' 408–24; Vallance, *Revolutionary England*, 128–9.

[11] Quoted in Hindle, 'Keeping of the Public Peace', 234.

of the standard oaths of abjuration from the recantation. Although these recantations lacked the spiritual muscle of an oath, they still possessed great propaganda value in that a suspected heretic publicly condemned the heresy of which he was suspected. In a sense, then, the social pressure of oaths depended not so much on the fact that they were made before God (the definition of an oath) but rather that they were made before men. This is why the English people's participation in the Henrician Reformation was so important. As more people participated in the Reformation by swearing oaths, the pressure on the rest of English society to acquiesce increased as well.

The social power of oaths was also reinforced by their perceived spiritual power. The general public's belief in the sacred nature of oaths created a form of social pressure on the juror himself, for even if the juror's own conscience was not grieved by perjury, his neighbours knew that perjury was wrong. Andy Wood has recently argued that the Henrician regime relied on the readiness of its subjects to transmit to the regime the seditious speech of others. People were willing do this, wrote Wood, because seditious speech offended both their 'loyalty to the crown' and their 'sense of conscience'.[12] What Wood omitted to point out was that it was the device of an oath that both cemented the English people's loyalty to the Crown and placed a bond on their consciences. Henrician oaths thus created watchdogs of one's neighbours. When someone spoke or acted in a way contrary to his oath, his neighbours chastised him for it and, sometimes, reported him to the authorities. When Dr Benger of Wingham affirmed the authority of the Pope at the table of the archdeacon of Canterbury in 1535, the archdeacon and other observers reminded him that such an affirmation was against their oath, and then they communicated the discussion to Cranmer.[13] Likewise, when Master Brown, the parson of Chesterton, showed his fellow priest Thomas Arundell a prophecy contrary to Brown's oath of supremacy, Arundell promptly informed Cromwell.[14] Indeed, the only reason we know that anyone dissimulated when taking a Henrician profession is because the dissimulators eventually engaged in careless conversation with their neighbours, who then snitched on them. Dr John London's claim to Thomas Bedyll that he 'wold not be so vnwise to say to thys yong man [London's kinsman] any wordes soundyng contrary to myn own p[rov]en and corporall othe' tells us more about the social pressures of

[12] Wood, '"A Lyttull Worde ys Tresson",' 844.
[13] Cranmer, *Miscellaneous Writings and Letters*, 300–2.
[14] NA sp1/88, fol. 49ʳ (*LP*, vii 1624).

perceived perjury than it does about the genuineness of Dr London's oath of succession.[15]

The thrust of this conclusion thus far has been to argue that the spiritual and social power of oaths increased the authority of the English Crown. Henrician oaths created both an internal weight on the juror's conscience and an external social pressure on the juror's speech and behaviour, and both of these forces helped to secure the loyalty and orthodoxy of the English people to the king and his church. When we broaden our gaze beyond Henry's reign, however, the Henrician regime's use of oaths did more to empower its subjects than it did to strengthen its own authority. The Henrician regime's employment of oaths educated the English people on the uses and advantages of oaths. The tendering of the oath of succession taught the people a lesson, a lesson they then acted upon in the Pilgrimage of Grace by administering their own oaths in imitation of the oath of succession. Likewise, the large amount of propaganda on the duty to keep one's oath (much of it coming from clergy sympathetic to royal supremacy) taught the English people about the spiritual power of an oath. And once the English people had been schooled in how and why to use oaths, what was to stop them from using oaths to their own advantage? After all, the beauty of oaths was that anyone could swear them. No licence or commission was required. Oaths gave everyone access to the highest power, a power higher than the Crown. Whatever cause an individual espoused, once he or she had sworn an oath to it, that cause became a matter of eternal significance. Since a person's soul was more valuable than any earthly matter, keeping one's oath (whatever it was) now trumped all other allegiances.

In practice, there were three ways in which oaths empowered the English people. The most active way by which people appropriated the power of oaths was simply by swearing oaths of their own volition, either oaths of their own devising or oaths devised by others but not intended for or required of the people. Such oaths were not necessarily subversive to the English Crown. The Elizabethan bond of association is a good example. Elizabeth's Privy Council issued and encouraged this oath. Although the Council intended that only justices of the peace and gentlemen should take the bond, popular enthusiasm was so high for the measure that many townsmen swore the oath themselves, binding their own consciences to defend Elizabeth and, in the event of her assassination, hunt down her assassins.[16] The bond thus gave townsmen a role in the political process not

[15] NA sp1/77, fol. 107ʳ (*LP*, vi 739).   [16] Cressy, 'Binding the Nation', 218–24.

intended for them. The English people also used oaths to advance their own causes against their neighbours. Steve Hindle has noted, for example, an increase in the late sixteenth and early seventeenth centuries of the practice of swearing the peace. What happened was that an individual, usually one of low or middling social status, would appear before a magistrate and swear an oath that he believed that his life or body was in danger from another. This oath, as a grave act placing the fate of the juror's soul in danger if it was false, was enough to cause the magistrate to place a recognizance on the person accused of harassing the juror, in effect coercing this person to cease harassing the juror lest the person suffer serious financial consequences.[17] Finally, the English people used oaths to oppose the policies of the Crown. The most notable examples here are of course the oaths of the Pilgrimage of Grace, but the Scottish National Covenant and the various Parliamentary oaths of the 1640s, while not originating among the lower order of society, still show that oaths could be used to galvanize popular resistance to the king or his policies.[18] Whether in opposition to royal policies, to those who would thwart royal policies, or to a private enemy, the practice of swearing oaths allowed the English people to play a role in the political process and to further their own objectives.

The second way that oaths empowered the English people was by providing them with a strong ideology from which to draw when resisting the established church and state. As Ethan Shagan has reminded us, resistance requires legitimacy, and in a conservative society like early modern England, it was far from easy to legitimize resistance to one's lawful sovereign.[19] Alec Ryrie has seconded this axiom, pointing out that during the Reformation, 'opposition was principally a matter of conscience', but conscience dictated obedience to those authorities God had ordained, and it forbade rebellion.[20] The standard teaching on oaths, however, provided a ready-made ideology that could legitimize resistance while still keeping the moral high ground of conscience. People could (and did) argue that they must resist their lawful superiors in order to avoid committing perjury or taking the name of the Lord in vain. The sanctity of oaths and majesty of God's name became a shelter for their consciences. Once someone swore an oath about an issue, keeping that oath became a matter of being obedient to God, and obedience to God trumped all other forms of obedience. For example, during the reign of Mary Tudor, many English Protestants argued

---

[17] Hindle, 'Keeping of the Public Peace', 218–27.
[18] For overviews of the oaths of the 1640s, see Jones, *Conscience and Allegiance*, 104–69; Vallance, *Revolutionary England*, 51–129.
[19] Shagan, *Popular Politics*, 88.   [20] Ryrie, *Age of Reformation*, 123.

that they could not accept the authority of the Pope because to do so would
violate their oaths of supremacy, and to violate a lawful oath was to sin
against God. Consider Cranmer's explanation to Queen Mary about why
he refused to have the bishop of Gloucester as his judge:

> But forasmuch as in the time of the prince of most famous memory King Henry the
> Eighth, your grace's father, I was sworn never to consent that the Bishop of Rome
> should have or exercise any authority or jurisdiction in this realm of England;
> therefore, lest I should allow his authority contrary to mine oath, I refused to
> make answer to the Bishop of Gloucester, sitting here in judgement by the Pope's
> authority, lest I should run into perjury.[21]

Many more examples from Mary's reign could be cited.[22] The point is that
the ability to swear an oath gave the English people the means to take any
kind of personal opinion and turn it into a matter of principle, specifically
the extremely high principle of not dishonouring God by committing
perjury.

   If swearing oaths provided people with a powerful ideology from which
to resist the policies of those in authority, the ideology of oaths also provided the English people with a justification not to swear the state oaths
which became common in the sixteenth and seventeenth centuries. A good
example here is Edmund Bonner's refusal to swear the Elizabethan oath
of supremacy in 1564 when Bishop Robert Horne administered it to him
a second time. (After 1563, the second refusal of the oath of supremacy
was treason.) The clerk who documented Bonner's response noted (among
Bonner's other arguments on the legality of Horne's status as bishop) that
in reference to the oath of supremacy, 'the defendant in his conscience
and lerning thinketh he ought not to give: forasmuch as he cannot give it
without committing of deadly sin'. Bonner continued: 'the said oath, like
as all other oaths, ought to have three companions, appointed in Scripture
to be *veritas, judicium, et justicia*'. The oath of supremacy, claimed Bonner,
did not have these three companions, so he could not take it, trusting that
the queen 'myndeth not her subjects to ronne into perjury, but to keep
to their conscience and bounden duty'.[23] Later that year, Bonner wrote a
letter to Elizabeth in which he elaborated on his reasons for not taking the

---

[21] Cranmer, *Miscellaneous Writings and Letters*, 447. For a confirmation of this episode according to
   the Catholic version of Cranmer's trial, see [Harpsfield?], *Bishop Cranmer's Recantacyons*, 31. This
   extremely rare book is a reprint of a Latin manuscript preserved in the Bibliothèque Nationale de
   France, Paris.
[22] Foxe, *AM* (Townsend), VI:682–3, 688; VII:151, 154, 156, 160, 677–8; Cranmer, *Miscellaneous Writings
   and Letters*, 226, 454; Hooper, *Later Writings*, 566; Ridley, *Works*, 369–70.
[23] BL Harleian MS 421, fol. 5[r–v], printed in Strype, *Annals of the Reformation*, vol. 1, part 2, 5–6.

oath. He contended that an oath could be sworn 'without danger of eternal salvation' only if it had three companions, 'namely truth of conscience, judgement of discretion or deliberation, and justice; so that what is sworn is lawful and just'. Bonner then cited Romans 14:23 that 'all that is not from faith is sin' and observed that 'he who acts against his conscience is considered to build to hell'. He concluded by asserting that he was certain that Elizabeth did not want to ensnare her subjects in 'deadly sin or perjury'.[24] In essence, Bonner was arguing that for him, the oath of supremacy lacked truth, judgement, and justice because he was not personally convinced in his conscience of the truth of Elizabeth's supremacy, and to swear to something of which one was unsure was perjury and a mortal sin. Abbot John Feckenham made similar claims in 1566 when he refused to swear the oath of supremacy.[25]

Even more elaborate arguments were constructed by Puritans in the 1580s and early 1590s, when they foiled the attempts of the Court of High Commission and the Court of Star Chamber to investigate the *classis* movement by refusing to swear the *ex officio* oath. Puritans argued that the *ex officio* oath lacked judgement. Because the defendant was tendered his oath to answer all subsequent questions truthfully before he knew the content of these questions, he was unable to judge whether the questions (and therefore the oath) were lawful. To swear such a general oath in ignorance, argued the Puritans, would be against Scripture, for was the *ex officio* oath not like Herod's general oath to Herodias to give to her whatever she wanted before he knew what she wanted?[26] In a similar vein, Puritans argued that the *ex officio* oath was a vain oath. Since the information sought by the authorities could be gathered through the testimony of witnesses without an oath of the defendant, the *ex officio* oath was unnecessary. Unnecessary oaths were vain oaths, and vain oaths were against the word of God, reasoned Puritans.[27] Summing up this and other arguments against the *ex officio* oath, Thomas Cartwright wrote:

wee fynde oure selves much moved in conscience to refuse it [the *ex officio* oath] in that [it is] aboute a dutie of Gods worshippe (such as is an oath whearein whosoever taketh his name in vaine shall not be guiltlesse) desiringe for warrant

---

[24] Inner Temple Library, Petyt MS 538, vol. 47, fols. 2^r–v.

[25] NA sp12/36, fol. 45^r–v; Horne, *Answeare Made by Rob. Bishoppe of Wynchester*, fols. 6^v, 91^v.

[26] For the scriptural references, see Matt. 14 and Mark 6.

[27] For these two arguments as well as many other Puritans' arguments against the *ex officio* oath, see Gray, 'Conscience and the Word of God: Religious Arguments against the Ex Officio Oath', *Journal of Ecclesiastical History*, forthcoming.

and securitie to oure consciences, some proofe oute of the worde of God by the mouthe of his servants the ministers yett are not thearein satisfied.[28]

The foundation of the resistance arguments of Marian Protestants like Cranmer, Elizabethan recusants like Bonner, and Elizabethan Puritans like Cartwright was the basic theory of oaths described in Chapter 1. To swear against truth, justice, or judgement was to sin gravely. This was an ideology designed to ensure the majesty of God's name and protect the sacredness of oaths. It was, in fact, the same ideology upon which the Henrician regime depended in order to prevent its subjects from taking the oaths of succession and supremacy falsely or lightly. Hence, the same ideology of the sanctity of oaths that lent spiritual power to the Henrician regime's attempt to enforce its Reformation eventually empowered those who disagreed with the religious policies of the Crown by allowing them to justify their resistance by conscience.

The fact that oaths legitimized resistance *by conscience* is significant. Indeed, the third and final way in which oaths empowered the English people was by making an individual's conscience the ultimate judge of matters of controversy. Historians have warned us about reading our modern notions of conscience back onto the early modern era. In the sixteenth century, there was no such thing as the subjectivity or relativity of conscience. Two consciences that came to opposing conclusions could not be equally valid. The validity of one's conscience was not based on the sincerity of one's opinion but rather on the degree to which one's conscience corresponded to divine law.[29] Take the common example of Thomas More's citation of conscience when he refused to swear the oath of succession. More was not saying that his subjective conscience had the right to believe whatever it wanted to believe.[30] In the words of David Martin Jones, both More and his opponents 'agreed that conscience followed the law, not the individual's determination. The issue between More and his interlocutors was whether Rome or Westminster possessed the requisite authority to determine that law'.[31] What was true for the issue of conscience was also true for the issue of oaths. Technically, individuals were not free to decide whether an oath was valid (and therefore binding) or not. If an oath was sworn in truth, judgement, and justice, it was binding. The problem, of course, was that the religious pluralism that came out of the Reformation meant that there were different views on what constituted truth, judgement, and justice. By

---

[28] Cartwright, *Cartwrightiana*, 31.   [29] Walsham, 'Ordeals of Conscience', 32–3.
[30] Bernard, *King's Reformation*, 148.
[31] Jones, *Conscience and Allegiance*, 37. See also Cummings, 'Conscience of Thomas More', 3–7.

extension, there were different views on which oaths were lawful. Who, then, was to decide which oaths were binding?

Despite attempts by the authorities to prescribe for the people the legality or illegality of a particular oath, the actual administration of oaths placed an emphasis on the individual juror's conscience as the final judge. Oaths, in theory at least, always involved the consent of the juror. The individual administered the oath had to make a choice as to whether the oath was lawful or not, that is whether the content to which he was asked to swear was true and godly. Once an oath was administered to a person, it forced this person to decide for himself the relevant issue (be it the succession, the supremacy of the church, or the definition of heresy), a decision the person could have avoided and dismissed as above his judgement if not for the oath. It was not that the administration of oaths made the individual's subjective conscience the final authority in determining truth – that remained God's revelation, variously interpreted of course – it was that the administration of oaths obliged and therefore empowered the juror's own conscience to decide which interpretation of this authority he thought most true. The fact that oaths empowered the individual to cast his vote in issues of controversy is significant, for as Norman Jones has asked, 'How could obedience be maintained in a community which arrogated to the individual conscience the right to make decisions?'[32]

Furthermore, the administration of oaths empowered the particular consciences of the English people in that it was the juror as an individual who was ultimately responsible for consequences of his oath. If he broke his rightful oath or swore a wrongful oath, it was his own soul that stood in danger of eternal damnation. If we return to our example of Thomas More, we can clearly see how oaths vested authority and responsibility in an individual's conscience. More wrote to Dr Nicholas Wilson of the oath of succession:

> levyng every other man to there owne consyence my selff will withe goode grace folow myne. For ageynste myn own to swere were perell of my dampna[cion] and what myne awne shalbe to morowe my selff can not be suer and whether I shall haue fynally the grace to do accordyng to myne owne consyence or not hangythe in Goddys goodnes and not in myne.[33]

More may have based his conscience on 'the generall counsail of Christendome',[34] but it was he as an individual who would suffer in hell

---

[32] Jones, *English Reformation*, 186.
[33] More, *Correspondence*, 532–3; quoted in Cummings, 'Conscience of Thomas More', 13.
[34] More, *Correspondence*, 506; Bernard, *King's Reformation*, 148.

if his conscience made the wrong decision about the oath of succession. Oaths, though designed to be bonds that glued society together, in a sense isolated a person from society by holding the individual accountable before God for what he swore.

Thus, by forcing a person to make his *own* decision and by teaching a person that this decision affected his *own* salvation, oaths were the training grounds of individualism. Oaths were designed to bind an individual's conscience, but the very fact that they acted on the *individual* conscience meant that in the long run, they shifted emphasis from social passivity to individual agency. The more you ask me my opinion on a matter (and administering an oath to me does just that), the more I think my opinion matters. When I am held accountable to God for my opinion, I really think it matters. The more I think my opinion matters, the more likely I am to express it or act on it even when I am not asked. Like the doctrine of priesthood of all believers and new accessibility of the Bible, which empowered people to *discover* for themselves what was right by reading the word of God,[35] the mass administration of oaths during the Reformation eventually empowered people to *decide* for themselves what was right and then act on these decisions in their own ways, ways not necessarily in harmony with the policy of the Crown.

The Henrician regime's prolific employment of oaths therefore had an ambiguous legacy. Oaths allowed the Henrician regime to appropriate the power of God in its efforts to coerce its subjects into obedience and orthodoxy. The mass tendering of oaths also created a form of social pressure on English subjects. In the short term, this spiritual and social power of oaths strengthened the Crown. In the long term, however, the Henrician regime's implementation of its Reformation through oaths backfired, for it invited its subjects to participate in the political process while at the same time giving them an example of how to manipulate a higher authority to their own ends. Oaths were a powerful but egalitarian instrument. They could be used by anyone for a large variety of purposes. Whenever an indiscriminate expedient is introduced into an established game, the result is a levelling of the playing field. So it was with oaths.

---

[35] For further reflections on the importance of the Bible and the doctrine of the priesthood of all believers as causes of the individualization of conscience, see Jones, *English Reformation*, 184–6; Klinck, *Conscience, Equity, and the Court of Chancery*, 264–5.

Appendix

The purpose of this appendix is to allow the reader to trace the development of oaths over time and to see how various oaths are related to each other. The appendix is divided into sections based on the kind of oath presented. Within each section, the alpha-numerals in parenthesis indicate parallel passages shared by other oaths in that section. Italicized and underlined text is also used to highlight connections between oaths. The exact meaning of the use of italicized and underlined text is explained at the beginning of each section or oath, and it varies depending on the oath.

A: THE OATHS OF A BISHOP-ELECT TO THE POPE

I. Oath to Gregory III in 759[1]

I byshopp of (N) do swere to my lord the pope that I shall keep the ffaithe of the Catholique Churche

And that I wyle abydd yn the vnytity of the said ffayth and not consent for any mans pleasure to contrary the same

I do Bynd me in faith full promyss to seale the honnor commodity and proffites of the churche of Rome

And yf any Bysshop or Byshopres say or doo agaynst the old statutes of holy fathers with him or them I shall have no conversatyon

But rather by all meanes forbydd the same and shall trewly geve warning therof vnto my Lord the pope.

So God shall me helpe all sayntes and holy dom.

---

[1] The text of this oath is taken from Thomas Earl's Commonplace book: CUL MS MM. I. 29, fol. 29ʳ. Robert Barnes also gives a very similar text of this oath in his *Supplicacion* of 1534, fol. DIᵛ.

II. Oath of a bishop-elect as prescribed by canon law[2]

(1) Ego N. episcopus ab hac hora in antea fidelis ero sancto Petro, sanctaeque apostolicae Romanae ecclesiae, dominoque meo Papae C. eiusque successoribus canonice intrantibus.

(2) Non ero neque in consilio neque in facto, ut vitam perdat aut membrum, vel capiatur mala captione.

(3) Consilium quod mihi aut per se, aut per literas, aut per nuncium manifestabit, ad eius damnum nulli pandam.

(4) Papatum Romanae ecclesiae et regulas sanctorum Patrum adiutor ero ad defendendum et retinendum, salvo ordine meo, contra omnes homines.

(5) Vocatus ad synodum veniam, nisi praepeditus fuero canonica praepeditione.

(6) Legatum apostolicae sedis, quem certum legatum esse cognovero, in eundo et redeundo honorifice tractabo, et in suis necessitatibus adiuvabo.

(7) Apostolorum limina singulis annis aut per me aut per certum nuncium meum visitabo, nisi eorum absolvar licentia.

Sic me Deus adiuvet et haec sancta evangelia.

III. Oath to the Pope used in England in the later Middle Ages[3] *(text not underlined but in italics indicates words not in oath II or IV; text that is both italicized and underlined indicates words not in oath II but in oath IV)*

(1) Ego Willelmus, episcopus olim Londoniensis, in archiepiscopum Cantuariensem electus, *promitto et juro*, quod ab hac hora inantea, *quamdiu vixero*, fidelis et obediens ero beato Petro, sanctaeque apostolicae Romanae ecclesiae, et domino meo Urbano, *divina providentia* papae sexto, suisque successoribus canonice intrantibus:

(2) non ero in consilio, *consensu*, vel facto, ut vitam perdant aut membrum, aut capiantur mala captione;

(3) consilium *vero*, quod mihi *credituri sunt* per se, aut per nuncios, sive per literas, nulli *manifestabo* ad eorum damnum, *me sciente*;

---

[2] The text of this oath is taken from *CIC*, x.2.24.4, Friedberg, ii:360. This is the same oath recorded in the *Collectanea satis copiosa* under the heading 'The prelates olde othe made to the pope'; BL Cotton MS Cleopatra E VI, fol. 53ʳ. Barnes believed (incorrectly) that this oath was the form used by bishops-elect in England in the 1530s. He thus included an English translation of this oath in his *Supplicacion* of 1534, fol. DIᵛ.

[3] The text of this oath is taken from William Courtenay's oath to the Pope upon becoming archbishop of Canterbury in 1382. It is printed in Wilkins (ed.), *Concilia*, iii:154–5. The same oath, translated into Middle English, is included in the late fourteenth-century Lollard tract attacking this oath; BL Additional MS 24202, fol. 1ʳ⁻ᵛ. Moreover, Thomas Arundel took this oath (with differences in wording in clauses 1, 7, and 11) when he became archbishop of Canterbury in 1396, and the bishop-elect of Worcester took it as well while Arundel was archbishop; LPL, Arundel's Register, fols. 3ʳ, 12ᵛ.

(4) papatum Romanum, et *regalia sancti Petri* adjutor ero ad retinendum, defendendum, *et recuperandum, salvo ordine meo*, contra omnem hominem, *ac honorem et statum ipsorum, quantum in me fuerit, conservabo, ipsisque adhaerebo, et pro posse favebo*;

(6) legatos et nuncios sedis apostolicae *benigne in terris meis archiepiscopatus suscipiam, et dirigam, et defendam, securumque ducatum praestabo eisdem*, ac in eundo et redeundo honorifice tractabo, et in suis necessitatibus adjuvabo, *nec, in quantum in me fuerit, permittam eis aliquam injuriam fieri vel inferri, et quibuscunque, qui contra praemissa vel eorum aliquod conarentur aliquid attemptare, quantum potero me opponam, eosque pro posse impediam*;

(8) *offensiones et damna praedicti domini nostri papae, et dictae Romanae ecclesiae, quantum potero, evitabo, nec ero in consilio, vel in facto, seu tractatu, in quibus contra ipsum, vel eandem Romanam ecclesiam aliqua sinistra vel praejudicialia machinentur*;

(9) *et si talia a quibusvis procurari novero vel tractari, impediam hoc pro posse; et, quanto citius potero, commode significabo alteri, per quem possit ad eorum notitiam pervenire.*

(5) Vocatus *ex quacunque causa* ad synodum, *seu ad eos* accedam, nisi praepeditus fuero canonica praepeditione, *eisque obedientiam et reverentiam debitas exhibebo et praestabo*.

(7) Apostolorum limina, *Romana curia existente citra vel ultra montes*, singulis *trienniis* visitabo, aut per me, aut per nuncium meum, nisi *apostolica* licentia remaneam.[4]

(10) *Possessiones ad mensam mei archiepiscopatus pertinentes non vendam, nec donabo, neque impignorabo, neque de novo infeudabo, vel aliquo modo alienabo, inconsulto Romano pontifice.*

(11) *Item, Robert, olim Basilicae duodecim apostolorum dicto Gebennensi, nunc antipapae, qui se Clementem septimum nominat, Johanni olim tit. sancti Marcelli dicto Ambiavensi, Geraldo, olim tit. sancti Clementis dicto majoris monasterii presbyteris, dictae ecclesiae cardinalibus, perditionis filiis, justo Dei judicio, auctoritate apostolica condemnatis, et eorum sequacibus, ac dantibus eis vel eorum alteri auxilium, consilium, vel favorem, cujuscunque fuerint praeeminentiae, ordinis, religionis, conditionis, seu status, etiamsi pontificali, regali, vel reginali, vel quavis alia praefulgeant dignitate; etiamsi fuerint Romanae ecclesiae cardinales, seu aliis quibuscunque per ecclesiam denotatis, vel inposterum denotandis, quamdiu extra gratiam et communionem sedis praedictae permanebunt, non dabo quovismodo, per me vel alium, directe vel indirecte, publice vel occulte, auxilium, consilium, vel favorem, nec ab aliis,*

---

[4] This exact wording of this phrase varied.

quantum in me fuerit, et impedire potero, dari permittam, sed eos secundum posse meum, donec convertantur, juxta processus apostolicos, et prout justum fuerit, persequar.

Sic me Deus adjuvet, et haec sancta Dei evangelia.

IV. The standard oath of canonical obedience to the Pope of a bishop-elect in the fifteenth and early sixteenth centuries[5] *(normal text is where this oath overlaps with oath III; underlined text is more similar to oath II than to oath III; italicized text is new, that is, not in oath II or III)*

(1) Ego *Guillermus, Archi*episcopus *Cantuarien.* ab hac hora inantea fidelis et obediens ero beato Petro, sanctaeque apostolicae Romanae ecclesiae, ac domino nostro domino Julio, papae secundo, suisque successoribus canonice intrantibus;

(2) Non ero in consilio, aut consensu, vel facto, ut vitam perdant, aut membrum, seu capiantur, *aut in eos manus violenter quomodolibet ingerantur, vel injuriae aliquae inferantur, quovis quaesito colore*;

(3) Consilium vero, quod mihi credituri sunt per se, aut per nuncios, seu literas, ad eorum damnum, me sciente *nemini* pandam;

(4) Papatum Romanum et regalia sancti Petri adjutor eis ero, ad retinendum & defendum contra omnem hominem:[6]

(6) Legatum apostolicae sedis in eundo et redeundo honorifice tractabo, et in suis necessitatibus adjuvabo;[7]

(12) *Jura, honores, privilegia, et auctoritatem Romanae ecclesiae, domini nostri papae, et successorum praedictorum conseruare, defendere, augere, et promovere curabo*;

---

[5] The text of this oath is taken from Archbishop William Warham's consecration oath: LPL, Warham's Register, fol. 2[v], printed in Wilkins (ed.), *Concilia*, III:647. (I have kept Wilkins' expansions of Latin abbreviations and added punctuation because they make the text more legible.) This also seems to be the same oath – with negligible differences in wording – taken by all archbishops and bishops at their consecration in fifteenth- and sixteenth-century England. For example, the same oath was taken by Reginald Pecock, Bishop-Elect of St Asaph in 1444 (Lambeth Palace Library, Stafford's Register, fols. 15[v]–16[r]); by Cuthbert Tunstall, Bishop-Elect of London in 1522 (LPL, CM 51, #23); and by Thomas Cranmer, Archbishop-Elect of Canterbury in 1533 (LPL, Cranmer's Register, fols. 1[v]–2[r]). This is also the basic form of the oath – with a slight modification noted below – in the *Collectanea satis copoisa* (BL Cotton MS Cleopatra E VI, fol. 53[r–v]) and translated into English in Hall, *Hall's Chronicle*, 788–9. Finally, this is the form of the oath taken by Archbishop Stafford in 1443 upon his reception of the pallium: LPL, Stafford's Register, fols. 4[v]–5[r]. Stafford's oath is exceptional because the rest of the forms of the pallium oaths I have encountered are like either oath III or oath V.

[6] The version of this oath in the *Collectanea satis copiosa* and in *Hall's Chronicle* adds the phrase 'et regulas sanctorum patrum' after 'Papatum Romanum' and before 'et regalia sancti petri'.

[7] Although the actual text in this clause is included in both oaths II and III, it lacks the expansion of oath III and thus is closest to oath II. Hall's translation of the oath does not include 'et in suis necessitatibus adjuvabo'.

(8) Nec ero in consilio, facto, vel tractatu, in quibus contra ipsum *dominum nostrum*, vel eandem Romanam ecclesiam aliqua sinistra vel praejudicialia *personarum, juris, honoris, status, et potestatis eorum* machinentur;

(9) Et si talia a quibuscunque procurari novero vel tractari, impediam hoc pro posse, et, quantocius potero, commode significabo *eidem domino nostro*, vel alteri, per quem ad ipsius noticiam pervenire possit:[8]

(13) *Regulas sanctorum patrum, decreta, ordinationes, sentencias, dispositiones, reseruationes, provisiones, et mandata apostolica totis viribus observabo, et faciam ab aliis observari*;

(14) *Haereticos, scismaticos, et rebelles domino nostro, et successoribus praedictis pro posse prosequar, et impugnabo*;

(5) <u>Vocatus ad sinodum veniam, nisi praepeditus fuero canonica praepeditione;</u>[9]

(7) Apostolorum limina, Romana curia existente citra, *singulis* annis, ultra vero montes, singulis *bienniis* visitabo aut per me, aut per meum nuncium, nisi apostolica absolvar licentia;[10]

(10) Possessiones vero ad mensam meam pertinentes non vendam, nec donabo, nec impugnorabo, nec de novo infeudabo, vel aliquo modo alienabo, *etiam cum consensu capituli ecclesiae meae*, inconsulto Romano pontifice:[11]

Sic me Deus adjuvet, et haec sancta Dei euangelia.

V. The archiepiscopal oath upon the reception of the pallium in the fifteenth and sixteenth centuries[12] *(text in normal font is identical to oath IV; text in italics is like oath III; all the text, excluding the order of the clauses and the final clause, comes from oath II)*

(1) Ego Guillermus, Archiepiscopus Cantuarien. ab hac hora inantea fidelis et obediens ero beato Petro, sanctaeque Romanae ecclesiae, et domino

[8] The oath in the *Collectanea satis copiosa* substituted 'scitatem' for 'noticiam'. Hall's translation of the oath uses the English word 'knowledge', which again demonstrates that his source was the *Collectanea*.

[9] Although the actual text in this clause is included in both oaths II and III, it lacks the expansion of oath III and thus is closest to oath II. The version of this oath in the *Collectanea satis copiosa* simply reads: 'vocatus ad synodum venia etc.'. This means that clauses (7) and (10) are not included in the oath in the *Collectanea satis copiosa*, though it is probable that the 'etc.' referred to them.

[10] The oath in *Hall's Chronicle* varies here. It reads: 'the lightes of the Apostles I shall visite yerely personally, or by my deputie'.

[11] The oath in *Hall's Chronicle* varies here. It reads: 'I shall not alien nor sell my possessions, without the Popes Counsaill: so God me helpe and the holy Euangelistes.'

[12] The text of this oath is from William Warham's oath upon his reception of the pallium: LPL, Warham's Register, fol. 3^r, printed in Wilkins (ed.), *Concilia*, III: 647–8. This same oath (with slight differences noted below) was sworn by Archbishops-Elect Langham, Chichele, and Cranmer upon their reception of the pallium. See Wood (ed.), *Registrum Simonis de Langham*, 115; Jacob (ed.),

meo, domino Julio, papae secundo, suisque successoribus, canonice intrantibus;

(2) *Non ero in consilio, aut consensu, vel facto, ut vitam perdant, aut membrum, seu capiantur mala captione*;

(3) Consilium vero, quod mihi credituri sunt per se aut nuncios, seu literas, ad eorum damnum, me sciente neminii pandam;

(4) Papatum romanum, et regulia sancti Petri adjutor eis ero ad retinendum et defendendum, *saluo meo ordine*, contra omnem hominem:

(6) Legatum apostolicae sedis in eundo et redeundo honorifice tractabo, et in suis necessitatibus adjuvabo;

(5) Vocatus ad sinodum veniam, nisi praepeditus fuero canonica praepeditione;

(7) Apostolorum limina, Romana curia existente citra, singulis annis, ultra vero montes, singulis bienniis visitabo per me, aut per nuncium meum, nisi apostolica absolvar licencia;[13]

(10) *Possessiones vero ad mensam mei Archiepiscopatus pertinentes non vendam, neque donabo, neque impignorabo, neque de novo infeudabo, vel aliquo modo alienabo, inconsulto Romano pontifice*:

Sic me Deus adjuvet, et haec sancta Dei euangelia.

B: THE OATHS OF A BISHOP-ELECT TO THE KING IN RESTITUTION FOR TEMPORALITIES

I. The basic form of the oath of a bishop-elect for the restitution of temporalities in the fifteenth century[14]

Sacramentum de renunciatione Episcopi:

(1) I renunce all the Wordes comp[ri]sed in the popes bull made vnto me of this Busshopriche of B the whiche be contrarie & preiudiciell to the King our souerayn lord and to his Coroune,

---

Register of Henry Chichele, 1:17; LPL, Cranmer's Register, fol. 5ʳ⁻ᵛ. Exceptionally, Stephen Patryngto, Bishop-Elect of St David's under Chichele, also took this oath instead of oath IV; Jacob (ed.), *Register of Henry Chichele*, 1:24.

[13] This phrase was quite variable. Langham swore to visit Rome every three years if he resided beyond the mountains, and every two years if he resided on this side of the mountains. Chichele just swore to visit Rome every three years. Stephen Patryngton, Bishop-Elect of St David's under Chichele and Cranmer, like Warham, swore to visit Rome every two years if he was beyond the mountains, but every year if he was on the Italian side of the Alps.

[14] The text of this oath is taken from BL Harleian MS 433, fol. 304ᵛ. An oath that uses many synonyms but is the same in structure and content is BL Cotton MS Vespasian C XIV, fols. 436ʳ⁻437ʳ.

(2) And of that I putte me humblement in his grace praying to haue restitucion of the temporaltes of my Churche of C

Sacramentum de fidelitate Episcopi:

(3) Also I shalbe feithfull & true and feith & trouth shall bere to the king oure souerayn lord and to his heires kinges of England of lyff & lymme and of ertheth worship forto lyve & dye ayenst all people,

(4) And diligently I shalbe attendant vnto the kinges nedes and besorgnes [*sic*] after my witte and power

(5) And the kinges Counsell I shall kepe and layne

(6) And truly I shall knowlage and do the seruices due of the temporalites of my Bisshopriche of C. the whichce I clayme to holde of my said souerayn lord the king, and the whiche he yeveth and yeldeth me

(7) And to his commaundementes that to me atteyneth and belongeth for my temporaltees, I shalbe obbeisaunt,

As god me help and his seintes

II. *Cardinal Adrian's oath of fidelity to Henry VII for the bishopric of Bath and Wells*[15] *(text in italics has no precedent in oath 1)*

(1) Expressè renuncio, et in hiis scriptis manu et sigillo meis in praesentiâ notariorum et testium subscriptorum munitis, totaliter cedo omnibus et quibuscumque verbis, *clausulis et sententiis,* in bullis apostolicis michi factis de praedicto episcopatu Bathoniensi et Wellensi contentis et descriptis, quae sunt *vel quovis modo in futurum esse poterunt* praejudicialia sive dampnosa praefacto serenissimo regi, *domino meo supremo, haeredibus suis de corpore suo legittime procreatis Angliae regibus,* coronae *aut regno suae majestatis juribusve, consuetudinibus, aut praerogativis ejusdem regni, et quoad hoc me integraliter submitto et pono in gratiâ suae celsitudinis.*

(2) Humillime supplicans suam majestatem, dignetur michi concedere temporalia dicti episcopatûs Bathoniensis et Wellensis *quae recognosco tenere a suâ majestate tanquam a domino meo supremo*

(3) Et ego idem Adrianus cardinalis praedictus juro ad haec sancta Dei evangelia per me corporaliter tacta, quod ab hâc die in antea, vitâ meâ naturali durante, ero fidelis et verus ligeus, ac fidelitatem in ligeantiâ meâ pure et sincere servabo; Fideleque et verum obsequium secundum optimum posse meum faciam et impendam serenissimo principi Henrico ejus nominis septimo, Dei gratiâ Angliae et Franciae regi ac domino Hiberniae *domino meo supremo,* et haeredibus suis de corpore suo legittime procreatis

---

[15] Burnet, *History of the Reformation,* IV:5–7.

Angliae regibus, *contra quas cumque personas cujuscumque statûs, gradûs, praeeminentiae aut conditionis extiterint.*

(8) *Nec quicquam faciam aut attemptabo fierive aut attemptari consentiam, quod in dampnum, incommodum, aut praejudicium, ipsius serenissimi regis aut haeredum suorum praedictorum, jurium, libertatum, praerogativarum, privilegiorum et consuetudinum sui incliti regni, quovis modo cedere poterit.*

(9) *Sed omne id quod jam scio, vel imposterum cognoscam inhonorabile, dampnosum aut praejudiciale suae serenitati, aut regno suo, seu contrarium honori aut securitati suae majestatis, aut haeredum suorum praedictorum, non solum impediam ad extremum potentiae meae, sed etiam cum omni possibili diligentiâ id ostendam et significabo, ostendive aut significari faciam eidem serenissimo regi, omni favore, metu, promisso aut jurejurando cuicumque personae aut quibusque personis cujuscumque statûs, gradûs, ordinis, praeeminentiae conditionisve extiterint, antehac per me factis aut interpositis seu imposterum fiendis aut interponendis, penitus sublatis et non obstantibus.*

(4) Honorem insuper suae majestatis ad extremum potentiae meae servabo.

(5) *Parliamentis quoquo et aliis conciliis suae celsitudinis cum in ejus regno fuero diligenter attendam*; consilium quod sua serenitas *per se seu literas aut nuncium suum* michi manifestabit, nemini pandam, *nisi hiis quibus ipse jusserit: et si consilium meum super aliquo facto majestas sua postulaverit, fideliter sibi consulam, et quod magis suae serenitati videbitur expedire, et conducere juxta opinionem et scire meum, dicam et aperiam, atque id si sua serenitas mandaverit pro posse meo diligenter faciam.*

(10) *Causas insuper et negotia omnia suae serenitatis mihi commissa, seu imposterum committenda, in curiâ Romanâ prosequenda, pertractanda et solicitanda, fideliter, accurate et diligenter, cum omnimodâ dexteritate prosequar, pertractabo et solicitabo.*

(11) *Bullasque ac alias literas apostolicas validas et efficaces, in debitâ juris formâ, super eisdem causis et negotiis impetrari expediri et obtineri absque fraude, dolo aut sinistrâ quâvis machinatione quantum in me erit, cum omni effectu enitar, operam dabo et conabor: ac easdem taliter expeditas, cum eâ quam res expostulat diligentiâ, suae serenitati transmittam, aut per alios transimitti, tradi et liberari curabo.*

(6) Et faciam servitia quoque et homagia pro temporalibus dicti episcopatûs, quae recognosco tenere a suâ celsitudine tanquam a *domino meo supremo*, fideliter faciam et implebo.

Ita me Deus adjuvet et sancta Dei evangelia.

III. Stephen Gardiner's oath at Hampton Court on 29 November 1531[16]
(words in italics have no precedent in oath 1)

(1) I Steven Gardener Principall Secretarie to your highnes, and clerk, busshop of Winchester renounce *and clerely forsake* all *such clauses* wordes *sentences and grauntes* which I haue or shall haue herafter of the Popes holines of the busshoprick of Winchester that in any wise is or may be preiudiciall to your highnes *your heires Successours dignitie or estate roiall, knowleging my self to take and hold the said busshoprick immediately and only of your highnes,*

(2) Most lowly beseching your grace the same for restituicion of the temporalities of the said Busshoprick,

(3) Promising as afore that I shalbe faithfull true and obedient subiect to your said highnes your heires and successours during my life

(6) And the seruice and other thinges due vnto your highnes for the restituicion of the said Temporalities of the said busshoprick, I shall truly do and performe

So help me god and the holie Evangelistes.

IV. Oath from Collectanea satis copiosa *and* Hall's chronicle[17] *(words in italics are new; of the words not in italics, clauses 3, 4, and 5 are from oath 1, while clauses 1, 1b, 2, and 6 are more similar to oath III)*

(1) I A. B. clerke vtterly renounce and clerely forsake all suche clauses wordes sentences & grauntes whiche I haue or shall haue hereafter of the popes holynes of and for the Archbishopriche or bishopryche of N. that in any wyse *haue bene is or herafter* may be *hurtfull or* preiudi-ciall to youre highnes your heires, successours, dignite priuileges or estate Royall.[18]

(3) And *ferthermore I doo swere that* I shall be faythefull and trewe, and faithe and treuthe I shall bere vnto you my soueragne lorde and kyng And to youre heires kinges of the same, of life and lymme and erthelie worship

---

[16] BL Additional MS 34319, fol. 21ᵛ. A modernized version is printed in Gardiner, *Letters*, 479–80. Edward Lee took this same oath (with negligible differences) for the archbishopric of York in 1531. See Rymer (ed.), *Foedera*, XIV:428–9.

[17] BL Cotton MS Cleopatra E VI, fols. 53ᵛ–54ʳ; Hall, *Hall's Chronicle*, 789. The oath in *Hall's Chronicle* varies slightly from that in the *Collectanea*. The text above is taken from the *Collectanea* with the slight variations in *Hall's Chronicle* noted in the footnotes below.

[18] The oath in *Hall's Chronicle* is missing 'Archbishopriche or'. It also substitutes 'I Ihon Bishop of A.' for 'I A. B.'.

aboue all creatures for to lyve and die with you and yours agaynste all people.[19]

(4) And diligentlie I shal be attendaunte vnto all your nedes and busynes after my witte and power[20]

(5) And youre counsaill I shall kepe and layne[21]

(1b) Knowleding myself to take and holde the said Archbishopriche or bishopryche immediatlye and onely vpon your grace.[22]

(2) Moste lowly beseching the same for restitution of the temporalties of the said Archbishopriche or bishopryche.[23]

(6) *promysyng as afore that I shal be faythfull trewe and obedient subgyet to your said highnes heires and successours during my lyfe* and the seruyces and other thinges due vnto your highnes for the restitution of the temporalities of the said Archbishopriche or bishopriche I shall treulie do *and obedientlie* performe.[24]

So helpe me god and thes holy Evangelies.[25]

V. Oath of a bishop-elect to the king from April 1534 to 1536[26] (text in italics has no precedent in previous oaths of a bishop-elect to the king)

(3) Ye shall say and swere as followith I shal be faithfull and true and faith and trouth I shall bere vnto your maiestie and to your heyres kynges of *this Realme* And with lyef and lyme and erthely honor for to lyue and dye as your faithfull subiecte ayenste all parsons *of what degree estate or condicion so euer they be*

(12) *And I shall preferr mayntayn and sustayne the ho[nour] suertie right preemynence and prorogatife of your maiestie and of your heyres kynges of this Realme and iurisdicion of your ymperiall Croune of the same afore and ayenst all manner of persons powres and authorites whatsoeuer they be*

---

[19] Hall substitutes 'And Also' for 'Furthermore' and 'to' for 'unto' and does not have the words 'and kyng'.

[20] Hall substitutes 'to' for 'unto' in this clause.   [21] Hall has 'holde' instead of 'layne'.

[22] This clause in Hall reads: 'knowlegyng my self to hold my bishopricke of you onely'.

[23] This clause in Hall reads: 'besechyng you of restitucion of the temporalities of the same'.

[24] Hall substitutes 'before' for 'afore', 'to' for 'unto', and 'for the same bishopric' for 'of the said Archbishopric or bishopriche'.

[25] Hall has 'so God me helpe and all sainctes'.

[26] 'This is the othe that euery person elected or presentid to any archebisshopriche or Bishopriche within this Realme or within any other the kynges domynyons shold swere to the kynges maiestie'; NA sp1/83, fol. 54^r (*LP*, vii 427). The text of the oath itself shows that it is the oath of Thomas Goodrick, Bishop-Elect of Ely. For the oath of Roland Lee upon taking the bishopric of Coventry and Lichfield – which is almost identical to this oath – see Burnet, *History of the Reformation*, vi:290–1.

(8) And I shall not wetyngly do or attempte nor to my power suffer to be done or attemptid any thyng or thynges priuilye or apertly that may be to the dymynycion or derogacion of your Croune of this Realme or of the lawes lib[er]ties rightes and prorogatives belongyng to the same

(13) *But put my hole effectuall endevour from tyme to tyme as the case shall require to advaunce and encrease thesame to my wytt and vttermost of my power. And in no wyse herafter I shall accepte any oath or make any promyse pacte or covenante secreatlye or apertly by any manner of [means] or by any colour of pretence to the contrarye of this myne othe or any parte therof.*

(4) And I shal be diligently attendaunte to your maiestie and to your heyres Kynges of this Realme in all your *commaundmentes* causes and Busyneses[27]

(14) *And also I knowlege and recognyse your maiestie ymmiediatlye vnder almyghtye god to be chyef and supreme hedd of the churche of England*

(6) and clayme to haue the Busshopriche of Elye holy and all onelye of your gyft and to haue and to hold the proffetes temporall and *Spirituall of the same* all onlye of your maiestie and of your heyres Kynges of this Realme *and of none other*

(15) *And in that so[rt] and none other I shall take my restitucion out of your handes accordyngly, vtterlye renounsynge any other sute to be had therfore to any other creature levynge or here after to be excepte excepte [sic] your heyres.*

(16) *And I shall to my wytt and vttermoste of my powre obserue kepe maynteyne and defend all the statutes of this Realme made ayenste reseruacions and prouysions of the Busshop of Rome called the pope of any the Archebusshopriches or Busshopriches of this Realme or of other within your domynyons.*

(17) *And also I shall obserue fulfyll defend maynteyne and kepe to the vttermost of my powre all the hole effectes and contentes of the statute made for the suertie of your succession in the croune of this Realme and all clauses and articles mencioned and conteyned in the said statute and also other statutes made in confirmacion or for the due execucion of the same.*

(18) *And all thynges I shall do with out colour fraude or any other vndue meane aye[nst all] persones powres and auctorities of the worlde what so euer the[y] be, And in no wise for any m[anner of] cause colour respecte or pretence*

---

[27] This seems to be a mix of clauses 4 and 7 from oath B 1.

priuilie or apertly I shall move do or attempte or to my powr[e suffer any] thyng
or thynges to be done or attempted to the contrary herof.

So helpe me god all sainctes and the hollye Evanngelistes.

C: THE PROMISE OF THE BISHOPS TO RENOUNCE THE POPE AND HIS BULLS[28]

(1) Ego N. Archiepiscopus vel episcopus pure sponte et absolute coram vestra Regia Maiestate Angliae, confiteor, quod contra deum et ordinationem eius, qua vult omnes homines suis principibus et Regibus esse subiectos et subditos, et subinde etiam contra vestram celsitudonem, meum solum ac supremum dominum in terris, grauiter deliqui precipue in eo quod episcopum Romanum (quem papa vocant) loco summi domini mei habui et reputaui et in eo quod iuramentum prestiti, semper illi, me fore fidelem, et quod iuraui, me, papatam eius contra omnem hominem (vestra Maiestate minime excepta) defensurum quod que iuraui me mandata illius, ordinationes, decreta et prouisiones obseruaturum et eiusmodi cetera me fasturum, que in dicto iuramento continentur.

(2) Quod sane iuramentum, illegitimum et iniustum et in in [*sic*] vestri Maiestatis potestatem a deo collatam, iniuriosum esse indico, et profiteor, et proinde illud detestor, irritumque et inane esse censeo, et minime obseruandum duco

(3) Quocirca vestram illustrissimam Maiestatem supplex et ex animo deprecor ut has grauissimas offensas mihi ante pedes vestrae Maiestatis prostrato remittere ac condonare dignetur

(4) Preterea confiteor dictum Romanum episcopum non plus autoritatis, aut iurisdictionis habuisse aut habere in hoc vestro regno Angliae de iure diuino: quam alium quemuis externum episcopum.[29]

(5) Et si quam maiorem auctoritatem ac iurisdictionem, in hoc vestro regno exercuit, tam iniuste vsurpauit quia illam a deo se accepisse profitebat et praecedebat quam a deo verum non accepit.

(6) Et ob id merito tale potestate, in hoc vestro regno vsurpata priuatus est.

(7) Et quod papatum autoritatem et iurisdictionem, quam in hoc vestro regno exercuit, et vsupauit, a deo non accepitum pro virili mea defendam contra omnem hominem atque ob id euis mandata, decreta ordinationes

---

[28] NA sp6/3, fols. 63ʳ–64ʳ.
[29] The original text read 'quam alius quivis externus episcopus' and has been corrected by someone (presumably a contemporary) to 'quam alium quemuis externum episcopum'.

prouisiones et cetera similia posthac me non obseruaturum, nec me eisdem
vllo modo paritutum in verbo pontificio promitto

(8) Ceterum omnibus bullis ac breuibus cuiuscumque tenoris fuerint,
a quocumque Romane pontifice, mihi aut ecclesiae meae concessis, atque
omnibus priuelegijs et indultis in eisdem contentis, expresse in his scriptis renuncio, recognoscens me tenere Archiepiscopatum vel episcopatum
meum, iura, iurisdictionem ac possessiones ad eamdem pertinentia de vestra sola Maiestate cui me fidelem et pro omnia obedientem sub deo fore,
profiteor protestor atque promitto,

(9) Quotcumque autem et quascumque bullas originales aut breuia orig-
inalia mihi aut ecclesiae meae a quocumque Romane pontifice concessas
aut concessa, habere et consequi potero: intra quadraginta dies nunc immediate sequentes, illuc deferri curabo, quo vestra Maiestas iusserit, illicque
relinqui seruanda vel cancellanda secundum vestrae illustrissimae Maiestatis beneplacitum.

(10) Et quotcunque bullarum aut breuium transcripta que in regestis
meis inserta, ita alijs actis intermixta sunt, vt ab inuicem seperari non
possunt quamprimum commode fieri possit cancellanda curabo.

(11) Que vero sine preiudicio aliorum monumentorum extrahi et separari
possint: intra quadraginto dies praedict[es] illuc transmitti faciam, quo
vestra Maiestas iusserit, vt praedict[um] est.

(12) Humillime prouolutus in genua postulas a vestra illustrissima Regia
Maiestate vti dignetum fut vestro diplomate, vestro que Regio magno que
sigillo, mihi et ecclesiae meae talia priuilegia et indulta concedere qualia
in dictis bullis continentur, vt nos episcopalia omnia, quam habemus a
vestrae Maiestatis bonitate accepisse gaudeamus et a vestra Maiestate integre
pendere, et eidem soli sub deo seruire teneamur.

D: THE OATHS OF SUCCESSION

In general, text in italics has no precedent in earlier oaths of succession;
italics signify something new; For oath I, text in italics is not in oath II

I. *The oath of succession of 1534 as recorded in the* Journal of the House of Lords[30]

(1) Ye shall swear to bear your Faith, Truth, and Obedience, alonely to the
King's Majesty,

---

[30] *Journal of the House of Lords*, 1:82.

(2) and to the Heirs of his Body,

(3) according to the Limitation *and Rehearsal* within this Statute of Succession *above specified*,

(4) and not to any other within this Realm, nor foreign Authority, *Prince*, or Potentate;

(5) and in case any Oath be made, or hath been made, by you, to any other Person or Persons, that then you to repute the same as vain and annihilate;

(6) and that, to your Cunning, Wit, and uttermost of your Power, without Guile, Fraud, or other undue Means, ye shall observe, keep, maintain, and defend, this Act *above specified*, and all the whole Contents and Effects thereof, and all other Acts and Statutes made *since the Beginning of this present Parliament*, in Confirmation or for due Execution of the same, or of any thing therein contained;

(7) and thus ye shall do against all Manner of Persons, of what Estate, Dignity, *Degree*, or Condition soever they be, and in no wise do or attempt, *nor to your Power suffer to be done or attempted*, directly *or indirectly*, any Thing or Things, privily or apertly, to the Let, Hindrance, Damage, or Derogation thereof, or of any Part of the same, by any Manner of Means, or for any Manner of Pretence or Cause.[31]

So help you God and all Saints.

II. *The oath attached to the commission to Sussex on 20 April 1534*[32]

(1) Ye shall swere to bere ffayth troyth & obedyence alonlye to the Kynges mayestye

(2) and vnto his heyres of his bodye *of his most dere & intyerly belouyd lawfull wyffe quen Anne begoton & to begoton And fferther to the heyres of our Sayd Soueraygn lord*[33]

(3) Accordyng to the lymytacion in the Statute *made for Suerte* of *his* Successyon *of the Croun of the Realme mencyoned and conteynyd*[34]

---

[31] While the text in italics in this clause is omitted from oath B II, it is in the oath of succession stipulated by the act of Parliament from November 1534.

[32] A copy of this commission is BL Harleian MS 7571, fol. 25ᵛ. This oath is also exceedingly similar to the oath as recorded in the act of November 1534 ratifying the oath of succession; *Statutes of the Realm*, 26 Hen. 8, c. 2, III:493. It is also like the oath Cromwell tendered George Cotes on 2 September 1535; NA SP1/96, fol. 59ʳ. Differences between these three oaths will be noted in the footnotes below.

[33] Cotes' oath and the oath from the November statute substitute the word 'to' for 'vnto'. Cotes' oath adds the word 'and' between 'bodye' and 'of' in this clause.

[34] Cotes' oath and the oath from the November statute read 'in the Crown of this Realme' instead of 'of the Crown of the Realme'.

(4) & nott to any other within the Realme nor fforen auctoryte or potentate,[35]

(5) And in case any othe be made or hath byn made by youe to any other person or persons that then youe to repute the same as vayn and adnychillate,[36]

(6) And that to your connyng wytt & vttermoste of your powre without Guyle ffraude or other vndue mean ye shall obserue kepe mayntayn & defend the *sayd* act of Successyon & all the hole effectes & contentes thereof and all other Actes & Statutes made in Confymacion or for due execucion of the same or of any thing therein conteynyed[37]

(7) And this ye shall doo ayenst all maner of persons of what Estate dyngnyte or Condycion so euer they be And in no wyse do or attempte dyrectly any thing or thinges prively or apertly to the lett hynderance damage or derogacion therof or of any part of the same by any maner of meanes or for any maner of pretence[38]

So helpp ye god all sayntes *& the holy Euangelystes.*

III. *The oath of succession from the Act of Succession of 1536*[39]

(1) Ye shall swere to bere faith truth and obedience all onely to the Kynges Majestie, *supreme hede in erth under God of the Churche of Englonde, duryng his lyfe*

(2) And to his heires of his bodye of his moste dere and entierly beloved laufull Wife *Quene Jane* begoten and to be begoten *and procreated*, and further to the heires of our said Soveraigne Lorde,

(3) Accordynge to the lymytacion in the Statute made for suretie of his succession in the Crowne of this Realme, *in the parliament begonne and holden at Westmynster in the viij day of June in the xxviij yere of the Kynges moste gracious reign,*

(8) *And also for lack of such heires, to suche person and persones as the Kynges Highnes shall lymytt and apoynte to succede to the Crowne, by vertue and auctorite of the same acte,*

---

[35] Cotes' oath and the oath from the November statute have 'this Realm' instead of 'the Realme'.

[36] Cotes' oath and the oath from the November statute omit the word 'other' in this clause. Cotes' oath also has 'repute' instead of 'to repute'.

[37] Cotes' oath omits 'counyng wytt & vttermost of your'. The oath from the November statute omits the word 'due'.

[38] The oath from the November statute and Cotes' oath add 'degree' after the word 'dignitie', add 'nor to your power suffer to be don or attempted' after the word 'attempte', and add 'or indirectly' after 'directly'. Thus, in these two oaths this clause is like oath D I rather than oath D II.

[39] *Statutes of the Realm*, 28 Hen. 8, c. 7, III:661–2.

(4) And not to eny other within this Realme, nor forayne auctorite power or potentate,

(5) And in case eny other othe be made or hath be made by you to eny persone or persones that then ye to repute the same as vayne and adnychilate;

(6) And that to your connyng witt and uttermoste of your power, without gile fraude or other undew [meanes] ye shall observe kepe mayntene and defende the said acte of succession, *made in the said parliamente begon and holden at Westmynster in the said viij day of June in the said xxviij yere of the Kynges most royall reign,* and all the hole effects and contentes therof, *and all thynges that shal be done by the Kynges Highnes by auctorite of the same,* and all other actes and statutes made in confirmacion or for execucion of the same or of eny thyng therin conteyned;

(7) And this ye shall doo ayenst all maner of persones of what estate degre or condicion so ever they be, and in no wise do or attempte, nor to your power suffre to be doon or attempted directly or indirectly, any thing or thinges privelye or appertly to the lett hydraunce damage or derogacion therof or of eny parte of the same, *or of eny thing or thynges that shal be done by the Kynges Highnes by vertue or auctorite of the said acte,* by any manere of meanes or eny manere of pretence:

So helpe you God all Seyntes and the holy Evangelistis.

IV. The oaths copied down on the spare leaves of a manuscript Gospel[40]

(1) Ye shall swere and beare faith and truth and obedyence all onely[41] to the Kinges Majestie supreme hed in erthe under God of the Church of Englond duryng his life[42]

(2) And to his heires of his bodye of hys most and enterely belovyd laufull late Wife Quene Jane begotten,[43] and further to the heires of our said Soueraign Lorde,

(3) Accordyng to the lymytacyon yn the Statute made for the suertye of hys Successyon yn the Crowne of thys Realme mencioned and conteyned, *according to the Statue and Lawes in that behalf made*[44]

---

[40] BL Additional MS 4507, fols. 4ʳ–6ʳ, 7ʳ–8ʳ. There are two oaths copied in this manuscript. They commence the same but depart at the end. See below.

[41] The second version of this oath (fols. 7ʳ to 8ʳ) substitutes 'alonly' for 'all onely'.

[42] The second version of this oath is missing 'supreme hed in erthe under God of the Church of Englond duryng his life'.

[43] The second version of this oath adds 'and to be begotten' here.

[44] This clause is more similar to oath D II than oath D III. The last bit of text in italics is not in the second version of this oath.

(9a) *And you shall doo no felonye, nor treasones, nor consent therunto; and if you here or knowe of any, you shall shewe the Kyng and his Councell thereof*[45]

(9b) *And also shall bere faith and truth to our said Soveraign Lorde his heires and pay all suche rent and do such servyce as is due to his grace for the Manour of B – that ye hold of our said Soveraign Lorde,*[46]

So God you helpp and all Saynts Etc.

E: INSTRUCTIONS FOR THE VISITATION OF THE FRIARS, THEIR PROFESSION, AND THE PROFESSION OF THE OTHER CLERICAL INSTITUTIONS IN 1534

For the two sets of instructions, the italicized text is not contained in the other set of instructions. The text underlined in the instructions has no parallel in the actual profession of the friars. In the actual professions of the friars and other clerical institutions, the text in italics is not contained in the other profession.

I. General instructions to the friars[47]

(1) Primum vt omnes et singuli fratres vnius cuiusque cenobii intra regnum Angliae in domo sua capitulari (vt vocât) personaliter praesentes vna congregentur. Deinde vt seorsum et separatim singuli examinentur super quibus visum fuerit.

(2) *Vt fiat inquisitio atque vt* singuli rationem reddere rogantur suae erga Regem nostrum Henricum eius nominis octavam fidei et obedientiae.

(3) Vt vniversi et singuli iurisiurandi sacramento obstringantur vti integram perpetuamque fidem et obedientiam praestent erga eundem Regem nostrum cum Anna Regina vxore eiusdem, et erga sobolem ex eadem Anna tam progeneratam quam progenerandam.

(4) *Vt iureiurando omnes et singuli obligentur praedista omnia populo notificare, praedicare, suadere vbicumque datibur Locus et occasio.*

(5) Vt confirmatum ratumque habeant quod praedictus Rex noster Henricus sit caput ecclesiae in Anglia prout tam in conuocatione cleri quam in parliamento decretum est et ratificatum.

(6) Vt confiteantur episcopum Romanum qui in suis bullis papae nomen vsurpat a summi pontificis principatum sibi arrogat nihilo maioris dignitatis habendum esse, quam caeteros quosuis episcopos in sua quenque dioecesi.

---

[45] This clause is in only the first oath.   [46] This clause is in only the second oath.
[47] BL Cotton MS Cleopatra E IV, fol. 11^{r-v} (*LP*, VII 590).

(7) Vt ne quis eorum pro concione priuatim vel publice habenda eundem episcopum Romanum appellare velit nomine papae, aut summi pontificis, sed nomine episcopi Romani vel ecclesiae Romanae *neque orare pro eo tanquam papa, sed tanquam episcopo Romano pro vt praedictum est.*

(8) *Ne quis eorum omnium in vlla vel priuata vel publica concione quicquam ex sacris scripturis desumptum ad alienum sensum detorquere praesumat sed quisque Christum eius que verba et facta omnia simpliciter, aperte, syncere, et ad amussim sacrarum scripturarum et vere catholicorum doctorum praedicet.*

(9) *Vt diligens fiat inquisitio quot et qui in quoque cenobio conciona-tores sint, deinde vt singulae singulorum conciones seuere examinentur, sint ne catholicae et orthodoxae,* ~~an non~~ *ac vere Christiano concionatore dignae, an non: quodsi catholicae et orthodoxae inuenientur, tunc admittur, approben-turque, sin minus, euestigio comburantur*

(10) Moneantur omnes et singuli quotquot sunt concionaturi vt in suis orationibus et comprecationibus de more faciendis, primum omnium Regem tamquam caput supremum ecclesiae Anglicanae deo et pop-uli precibus commendent. Deinde Reginam Annam cum sua sobole et tum demum Archiepiscopum Cantuariensem cum caeteros cleri ordinibus prout videbitur.

(11) Vt quicquid auri aut argenti facti celatique, et quicquis aliorum bonorum mobilium cuiuscumque generis aliquod cenobium possidere aut habere comperietur, proferre et ostendere rogantur, atque etiam verum minimeque mendacem elenchum seu catalogum rerum omnium et singu-larum tradant.

(12) Vt omnia et singula cenobia ac fratres in eisdem aut poy [unsure of word – MS mutilated] quovis viuentes sese et successores suos conscientia ac iurisiurandi sacramento obligent, et suo quique conuentuali sigillo in domibus suis capitularibus date confirment, quatenus omnia et singula praedicta fideliter obseruent.

II. *Instructions for the visitations of the Franciscan Observants*[48]

SEQUUNTER ARTICULI COMMISSIONIS, GENERALIUM VISI-TATORUM REGNJ ANGLIAE DEPUTATORUM

(1) Jn primis quod omnes et singuli fratres cuiuscumque coenobij in domo sua capitularj congregentur. Deinde singuli seorsum et separatim disquirantur super sequentibus:

---

[48] Vocht (ed.), *Acta Thomae Mori*, 208–9, reprinted with kind permission of Publications of the Institute for Economics of Leuven University / Librairie Universitaire Ch. Uystpruyst.

(2) Primo quod cogantur exhibere fidem et obedientiam Domino nostro Regi Henrico.

(3) Jtem vniversi et singuli iuramento astringantur praestare integram fidem erga ipsum regem Henricum, dominam reginam Annam et sobolem ex ipso rege et ipsa regina Anna tam procreatam quam procreandam.

(4b) *Jtem quod confiteantur matrimonium ipsius regis cum ipsa regina Anna esse verum et legittimum.*

(5) Jtem quod confirmatum et ratum habeant, quod praedictus rex sit caput supremum ecclesiae Anglicanae prout in convocatione cleri et parlamenti decretum est et ratificatum.

(6) Jtem vt confiteantur Episcopum Romanum qui in suis bullis nomen Papae vsurpat, et summi Pontificis principatum sibi arrogat, nihil maioris dignitatis aut authoritatis habendum esse quam ceteros quosque Episcopos in sua quaque diocesj, et ipsum non esse caput ecclesiae vniuersalis.

(7) Jtem ne quis publice vel occulte vocare vel nominare debeat vel audeat Episcopum Romanum nomine Papae aut summi pontificis, sed tantum nomine Episcopi Romanj vel ecclesiae Romanae

(8b) *Jtem si contingat aliquem praedicare, praedicet contra vsurpatiuj Episcopi Romanj potestatem.*

(9b) *Jtem fratres minores de obseruantia, profiteantur regulam b. ffranciscj obseruare sub obedientia regis et non Episcopi romanj. Accipiantque Georgium vorby, prouincialem fratrum Augustinentium pro suo generalj ministro.*

(10) Jtem vt omnes et singuli concionatores et in suis orationibus ex more faciendis primum omnium regem nostrum tanquam supremum caput Ecclesiae Anglicanae Deo et populo commendent. Deinde reginam Annam cum sua sobele. Demum Dominum Archiepiscopum Cantuariensem cum ceteris cleri ordinibus.

(12b) *Jtem nec Ministrj fratrum Minorum obseruantinorum vel conuentualium nec prouincialis patrum Carmelitarum, neque prouincialis cuiuscumque ordinis nec aliquis alius suos fratres aut eorum aliquos visitare praesumat, priusquam frater Georgius Vrobij, prouincialis aeremitarum sancti Augustinj, et frater Joannes Helsey prouincialis fratum praedictorum generales visitatores omnium praedictorum ordinum iuxta regnum Angliae a domino nostro rege henrio ordinati visitauerint [et] certiorem reddiderint.*

(11) Et quicquid auri vel argenti vel quorumcumque mobilium cuiuscumque generis aliquod monasterium seu coenobium habere vel possidere compererint, ipsorum cathalogum sine mendacio ostendere cogantur.

III. Profession of the friars[49]

(2) Quum ea sit non solum Christianae religionis & pietatis ratio sed nostrae etiam obedientiae regula vt Domino nostro Henrico eius nominis octavo cui uni & soli post Christum Jesum seruatorem nostrum debemus universa non modo omnimodam in Christo et eandem sinceram integram perpetuamque animi devotionem fidem, observantiam honorem cultum, reverentiam praestemus. Sed etiam de eadem fide & observantia nostra rationem, (quotienscumque postulabitur) reddamus, & palam omnibus (si res poscat) libentissime testemur

(3) Noverint vniversi ad quos praesens scriptum pervenerit quod nos Priores & conuentus fratrum videlicet minorum ordinis sancti Francisci Fratrum praedicatorum ordinis sancti Dominici Fratrum Heremitarum sancti Augustini et Fratrum carmelitarum ordinis beatae Mariae virginis etiam Prior ordinis Cruciferorum in Civitate Londonie vno ore & voce atque vnanimi omnium & singulorum consensu & assensu hoc scripto nostro sub sigillis nostris comunibus in domibus nostris capitularibus dato pro nobis & successoribus nostris omnibus & singulis imperpetuum prof-itemur testamur ac fideliter promittimus & spondemus, nos dictos Priores & conventus & successores nostros omnes & singulos integram inuiolatam sinceram, perpetuamque fidem observantiam & obedientiam semper praes-taturos erga Dominum Regem nostrum Henricum octavum

(4b) *et erga Serenissimam Reginam Annam vxorem eiusdem et erga castum sanctumque matrimonium nuper non solum inter eosdem juste & legittime contractum ratum & consummatum sed etiam tam in duabus convocationibus cleri quam in parliamento Dominorum spiritualium & temporalium atque communium in eodem parliamento congregatorum & praesentium determina-tum et per Thomam Cantuariensem Archiepiscopum solemniter confirmatum et erga quamcumque aliam ejusdem Henrici Regis nostri uxorem post mortem praedictae Annae nunc vxoris eius legittime ducendam et erga sobolem dicti domini Regis Henrici ex praedicta Anna legittime tam progentiam quam pro-generandam* et erga sobolem dicti domini Regis ex alia quacumque legittima vxore post mortem ejusdem Annae legittime progenerandam

(4) et quod haec eadem populo notificabimus praedicabimus & suade-bimus ubicumque dabitur locus & occasio

(5) Item quod confirmatum ratumque habemus semperque & perpetuo habituri simus quod praedictus Rex noster Henricus est caput ecclesiae Anglicanae

---

49 NA c54/402, m 33d; Rymer (ed.), *Foedera*, xiv:487–9 (*LP* vii 665). This particular profession was made on 17 and 20 April 1534.

(6) Item quod Episcopus Romanus qui in suis bullis papae nomen vsurpat et summi pontificis principatum sibi arrogat nihilo majoris neque auctoritatis aut jurisdictionis habendus sit quam caeteri quivis Episcopi in Anglia vel alibi gentium in sua quisque dioecese

(13) Item quod soli dicto dominio Regi & Successoribus suis adhaerebimus atque ejus *decreta ac proclamationes insuper omnes Angliae leges atque etiam statuta omnia in parliamento & per parliamentum decreta confirmata stabilita & ratificata perpetuo* manutenebimus Episcopi Romani legibus decretis & canonibus si qui contra legem divinam & sacram scripturam esse inuenientur imperpetuum renunciantes[50]

(8) Item quod nullus nostrum omnium in vlla vel priuata vel publica concione quicquam ex sacris scripturis desumptum ad alienum sensum detorquere praesumet sed quisque Christum eiusque verba & facta simpliciter aperte sincere & ad norman seu regulam sacrarum scripturarum et vere catholicorum atque orthodoxorum doctorum praedicabit catholice & orthodoxe[51]

(10) Item quod vnusquisque in suis orationibus & comprecationibus de more faciendis Primum omnium Regem tanquam supremum caput ecclesiae Anglicanae deo & populi precibus commendabit Deinde Reginam cum sua sobole tum demum Archiepiscopum Cantuariensem cum caeteris cleri ordinibus prout videbitur[52]

(12) Item quod omnes & singuli praedicti Priores & Conventus & successores nostri conscientiae ac iusiurandi sacramento nosmet firmiter obligamus quod omnia & singula praedicta fideliter imperpetuum observabimus.

In cuius rei testimonium huic instrumento vel scripto nostro Communia sigilla nostra appendimus & nostra nomina propria quisque manu subscripsimus.

IV. The standard profession of non-Mendicant clerical institutions from 1534[53]

(2) Quum ea sit non solum Christianae Religionis et pietatis ratio, sed nostrae etiam obedientiae Regula Domino Regi nostro Henrico eius nominis

---

[50] This article has no precedent in the instructions for the visitation of the friars.
[51] This clause is not in the profession of the prioress and convent of the priory of Dartford, Kent, made on 14 May 1534; NA E25/39/2 (*LP* VII 665.3), Rymer (ed.), *Foedera*, XIV: 490–1.
[52] This clause is not in the profession of the prioress and convent of the priory of Dartford, Kent, made on 14 May 1534; NA E25/39/2 (*LP* VII 665.3), Rymer (ed.), *Foedera*, XIV: 490–1.
[53] The text of this profession is taken from the profession of the dean and chapter of St Paul's Cathedral made on 20 June 1534; NA E25/82/1, printed with slight variations in Rymer (ed.), *Foedera*, XIV:493–4 (*LP*, VII 865).

octavo (cui vni et soli post Christum Jesum servatorem nostrum debemus vniversa) non modo omnimodam in Christo, et eandem synceram, integram, perpetuamque animi devotionem, fidem, et observantiam, honorem, cultum, et reuerentiam praestemus, sed etiam de eadem fide, et observantia nostra, rationem (quotienscumque postulabitur) reddamus, et palam omnibus (si res poscat) libentissime testemur,

(3) Nouerit vniversi ad quos praesens scriptum peruenerit, quod Nos Decanus et Capitulum Ecclesiae Cathedralis divi Pauli Londoniae, Londoniensis Dioecesis, vno ore et voce, atque unanimi omnium consensu et assensu, hoc scripto nostro sub Sigillo nostro communi in domo nostra Capitulari dato, pro nobis et successoribus nostris omnibus et singulis imperpetuum profitemur, testamur, ac fideliter promittimus et spondemus nos dictos Decanum & Capitulum et Successores nostros omnes et singulos integram, inviolatem, synceram, perpetuamque fidem observantiam, et obedientiam semper praestaturos erga Dominum Regem nostrum HENRICUM octauum et erga Annam Reginam uxorem eiusdem, et erga sobolem eius ex eadem Anna legittime tam progenitam quam progenerandam,

(4) et quod hec eadem populo notifiscabimus, praedicabimus, et suadebimus vbicumque dabitur locus et occasio,[54]

(5) Item quod confirmatum ratumque habemus, semperque et perpetuo habituri sumus, quod praedictus Rex noster Henricus est caput Ecclesiae Anglicanae,

(6) Item quod Episcopus Romanus, qui in suis bullis Papae nomen vsurpat, et summi pontificis principatum sibi arrogat, non habet maiorem aliquam jurisdictionem collatem sibi a deo in sacra scriptura in hoc Regno Angliae, quam quivis alius externus Episcopus,[55]

(7) *Item quod nullus nostrum in vlla sacra concione priuatim vel publice habenda, eundem Episcopum Romanum apellabit nomine Papae, aut summi pontificis, sed nomine Episcopi Romani, vel Ecclesiae Romanae, et quod nullus nostrum orabit pro eo tanquam papa, sed tanquam Episcopo Romano.*[56]

(13) Item quod soli dicto domino Regi et Successoribus suis adhaeribimus, et eius Leges ac Decreta manutenebimus, Episcopi Romani

---

[54] Compare to clause 3 of the friars' profession. The institutional profession is missing the section on Henry's marriage to Anne having been declared legitimate by Parliament, Convocation, and the Archbishop of Canterbury.

[55] Although the basic meaning remains the same, the wording of this clause varies among the different institutional professions of 1534. The second half of this clause sometimes reads: 'nichilo maioris dignitatis habendis sit quam ceteris Episcopi in sua quisque diocesi'.

[56] This clause has no parallel in the friars' profession, but it is the seventh article of the instructions for the visitation of the friars.

Legibus, Decretis, et canonibus, qui contra legem diuinam, et sacram scripturam, aut contra iura huius Regni esse invenientur, imperpetuum renunciantes,[57]

(8) Item quod nullus nostrum omnium in vlla vel priuata vel publica concione quicquam ex sacris scripturis desumptum, ad alienum sensum detorquere praesumet, sed quisque Christum, eiusque verba & facta simpliciter, aperte, syncere, et ad normam seu Regulam sacrarum scripturarum & vere catholicorum atque orthodoxorum doctorum praedicabit catholice et orthodoxe,

(10) Item quod vnusquisque nostrum in suis orationibus et comprecationibus de more faciendis, primam omnium Regem tanquam supremum Caput Ecclesiae Anglicanae, deo et populi precibus commendabit, Deinde Reginam Annam cum sua sobole, tum demum Archiepiscopos Cantuariensem et Eboracensem cum caeteris cleri ordinibus prout videbitur

(12) Item quod omnes et singuli praedicti Decanus et Capitulum et Successores nostri, conscientiae et iurisiurandi sacramento nosmet firmiter obligamus, quod omnia et singula praedicta fideliter imperpetuum observabimus.

In cuius Rei testimonium huic scripto nostro commune Sigillum nostrum appendimus, et nostra nomina, propria quisque manu subscripsimus.

F: THE PROFESSIONS OF BISHOPS AND UNIVERSITIES IN 1535

The italicized text in the bishops' profession denotes text not found in the professions from the universities. Likewise, the italicized text in the professions from the universities denotes additions to or changes from the standard bishops' professions. The text underlined in the professions from the universities indicates a phrase that varies among the surviving professions from the universities. The exact variations are then explained in the footnotes.

I. The standard bishops' profession of 1535[58]

(1) Ego Rolandus Coventrensis et Lichfeldensis Episcopus pure sponte et absolute in verbo Pontificio profiteor ac spondeo illustrissimae vestrae regiae Majestati singulari ac summo domino meo et Patrono henrico dei

---

[57] This is an abbreviated form of clause 13 of the friars' profession.
[58] This is Roland Lee's profession from 27 February 1535; NA E25/36; printed in Rymer (ed.), *Foedera*, XIV: 549–50; Wilkins (ed.), *Concilia*, III:781–2.

gratia Angliae et franciae Regi, fidei defensor, domino hiberniae, atque in
terris ecclesiae Anglicanae supremo immediate sub christo Capiti.

(2) Quod posthac nulli externo Imperatori, Regi, Principi aut Praelato
nec Romano Pontifici (quem Papam vocant) fidelitatem et obedientiam
verbo aut scripto simpliciter vel sub juramento promittam aut dabo vel
dari curabo;

(3) sed omni tempore casu et conditione partes vestrae regiae Majestatis
ac successorum vestrorum sequar et observabo, et pro virili defendam
contra omnem hominem, quem vestrae Majestati aut successoribus vestris
adversarium cognoscam vel suspicabor. Solique vestrae regiae Majestati,
velut supremo meo Principi fidelitatem et obedientiam sincere et ex animo
praestabo,

(4) Papatum romanum non esse a Deo in sacris litteris ordinatum profiteor: sed humanitus traditum firmiter affirmo et palam declaro ac declarabo,
et vt alii sic publicent diligenter curabor.

(5) Nec tractatum cum quocunque mortalium privatim aut publice
inibo aut consentiam, quod Pontifex Romanus aliquam auctoritatem vel
jurisdictionem amplius hic habeat aut exerceat, aut ad vllam posthac
restituatur.

(6) Ipsumque Romanum Episcopum modernum aut ejus in illo Episcopatu successorem quemcunque, non Papum, non summum Pontificem,
non vniversalem Episcopum, nec sanctissimum domimum, sed solum
Romanum Episcopum *et fratrem* (vt priscis Episcopis mos erat) scienter
publice asseram.

(7) Juraque hujus regni *municipalia* pro extirpatione et sublatione Papatus et auctoritatis ac Iurisdictionis dicti Romani Episcopi quandocunque
edita siue sancita pro viribus scientia et ingeniolo meis ipse firmiter
observabo: et ab aliis sic obseruari, quantum in me fuerit, curabo atque
efficiam.

(8) Nec posthac ad dictum Romanum Episcopum appellabo aut
appellanti consentiam, nec in eius Curia pro iure aut iustitia agam,
aut agenti respondebo nec ibidem accusatoris vel rei personam
sustinebo.

(9) Et si quid dictus Episcopus per nuncium vel per litteras mihi significaverit (qualecunque id fuerit) illud quamcitissime commode potero,
aut vestrae regiae Majestati, aut vestris a secretis Consiliariis aut vestris
successoribus, seu eorum a secretis Consiliariis significabo, aut significari
faciam.

(10) Ipseque Litteras aut Nuncium ad eundem Romanum Episcopum
nec ad eius curiam mittam aut mitti faciam, nisi vestra Majestate conscia

et consentiente, aut vestro successore, quod dictae Litterae vel nuncium ad illum deferatur.

(11) Bullas brevia aut rescripta quaecunque pro me vel aliis ab Episcopo Romano vel eius Curia non impetrabo vel vt talia a quouis impetrentur non consulam. Et si talia pro me inscio aut ignorante generaliter vel specialiter impetrabuntur vel alias quomodolibet concedentur eis renunciabo & non consentiam nec vtar eisdem vllo modo. At eas vestrae Majestati aut Successoribus tradi curabo.

(12) Praeterea in vim pacti profiteor et promitto, ac in verbo *pontificio* spondeo, quod contra hanc meam praedictam professionem et sponsionem nulla dispensatione, nulla exceptione, nullo iuris vel facti remedio me tuebor. *durante vita mea naturali,*

(13) Et si quam protestationem in praejudicium huius meae professionis et sponsionis feci Eam in praesens et in omne tempus futurum reuoco et eidem renuncio per praesentes litteras, quibus meum proprium & *Episcopatus mei nomen propria* manu subscripsi *& Sigillum meum majus apposui in perpetuam fidem & testimonium praescriptorum.*

II. *Professions of the universities and colleges from the autumn of 1535*[59]

(1b) *Invictissimo ac pientissimo*[60] in Christo principi *et* domino nostro, Henrico Octavo[61], Dei gratia Angliae et Franciae regi, fidei defensori, domino Hiberniae, ac in terris supremo ecclesiae Anglicanae[62] sub Christo capiti. *Vestri humiles subditi et devotissimi oratores*[63] *Willielmus Buckenham, Magister sive Custos Collegii dicti Gonville Hall, Cantabrigiae, et ejusdem loci Socii,*[64] *reverentiam et obedientiam, tam excellenti et praepotenti principi*

---

[59] The base text of this profession is that of the master and fellows of Gonville Hall, Cambridge made on 25 October 1535; printed in Fuller, *History of Cambridge*, 164–6. I have collated this profession with the four other surviving professions: Corpus Christi College, Oxford on 9 September 1535 (BL Lansdowne MS 989, fols. 134ʳ–136ᵛ (*LP*, IX 306)); Cambridge University on 23 October 1535 (BL Additional Charter 12827); Cobham College, Kent on 27 October 1535 (NA E25/32, printed in Rymer (ed.), *Foedera*, XIV:554–5); and Worcester Cathedral Abbey on 16 August 1536 (printed in Burnet, *History of the Reformation*, VI:82–5).

[60] The Worcester Cathedral oath substitutes 'Illustrissimo et potentissimo' for 'Invictissimo ac pientissimo'.

[61] The Cobham College oath adds an extra 'Domino' before 'Henrico Octavo'.

[62] The Cambridge University oath and the Cobham College oath add 'immediate' here after 'Anglicanae' and before 'sub'.

[63] The Cambridge University oath varies slightly here, reading 'humiles et deuoti subditi et oratores'.

[64] This phrase of course varied depending on what college was making the profession.

debitas et condignas cum omni subjectione et honore.[65] *Noverit*[66] *majestas vestra regia quod nos magister et socii predicti,*[67] *non vi aut metu coacti,*[68] *dolove*[69] *aut* aliqua alia sinistra machinatione, ad haec inducti sive seducti,[70] sed ex nostris certis scientiis,[71] *animis deliberatis, merisque et spontaneis voluntatibus; pure, sponte et absolute, in verbo sacerdotii,*[72] *profitemur, spondemus ac ad sancta Dei Evangelia, per nos corporaliter tacta,*[73] juramus vestrae illustrissimae[74] *regiae*[75] majestati, *singulari ac summo domino nostro et patrono, Henrico Octavo, Dei gratia, Angliae et Franciae regi, fidei defensori, et domino Hibernaie, ac in terris ecclesiae Anglicanae supremo immediate sub Christo capiti;*

(2) Quod posthac nulli externo imperatori, regi, principi aut prelato, nec Romano pontifici, quem papam vocant, fidelitatem, aut obedientiam[76] verbo vel scripto, simpliciter vel sub juramento, promittemus aut dabimus vel dari curabimus;

(3) Sed omni tempore, casu, et conditione, partes vestrae regiae majestatis, ac successorum vestrorum sequemur et observabimus, et pro virili[77] defendemus contra omnem hominem quem[78] vestrae majestati aut successoribus vestris adversarium cognoscemus et suspicabimur. Solique vestrae regiae majestati, velut supremo nostro principi, *et ecclesiae Anglicanae capiti, ac successoribus vestris,*[79] fidelitatem et obedientiam sincere et ex animo praestabimus.[80]

---

[65] Instead of 'subjectione et honore', the oaths of Cambridge University, Corpus Christi College, Cobham College, and Worcester Cathedral have 'subjectionis honore'.

[66] The Cobham College oath and the Corpus Christi College oath add the word 'praeexcellentissimae' here. The Cambridge University oath adds the word 'excellentissimae'.

[67] This phrase varies depending on the oath. For example, the Cambridge oath says the whole university of Cambridge while the Corpus Christi College oath notes the president and scholars of the college.

[68] The Cobham College oath and the Cambridge oath are missing 'coacti'.

[69] The Cambridge and Cobham College oath read 'dolo, vel' instead of 'dolove aut'. The Worcester Cathedral oath reads 'dolore'.

[70] The Corpus Christi College oath is missing 'sive seducti'.

[71] The Cobham College oath has 'conscientiis' instead of 'scientiis'.

[72] The Cobham College oath has 'fidelitatis' instead of 'sacerdotii'. The Cambridge oath has 'sacerdotum et fidelitatus'. The Corpus Christi College oath has 'sacerdotii respective et fidelitate nostra'. The Worcester Cathedral oath omits the whole phrase 'in verbo sacerdotii'.

[73] The exact word order of this phrase varies among the professions, though all of them except the Corpus Christi College oath specify that the oath is sworn touching the holy Gospels of God.

[74] The order of 'vestrae' and 'illustrissimae' varies according to the profession.

[75] The Corpus Christi College oath is missing 'regiae'.

[76] The Corpus Christi College oath is missing 'aut obedientiam'.

[77] The Cambridge, Cobham, and Worcester oaths have 'viribus' instead of 'virili'.

[78] The Corpus Christi College oath adds the word 'eidem' here.

[79] The Cambridge, Cobham, and Corpus Christi oaths do not contain the phrases 'ac successoribus vestris'. The Worcester Cathedral oath has an even longer clause: 'quem etiam supremum in terris ecclesiae Anglicanae sub Christo caput agnoscimus et acceptamus, et successoribus vestris'.

[80] The Cobham College oath and the Cambridge oath contain the additional phrase 'et per praesentes praestamus' here.

(4) Papatum Romanum non esse a Deo in sacris litteris ordinatum profitemur, sed humanitus traditum constanter[81] affirmamus, et palam declaramus ac declarabimus, et ut alii sic publicent diligenter curabimus.

(5) Nec tractatum cum quoqunque mortalium privatim aut publice inibimus, aut consentiemus,[82] quod pontifex[83] Romanus, aliquam authoritatem et jurisdictionem, amplius hic habeat aut exerceat, aut ad ullam posthac restituatur;

(6) Ipsumque[84] Romanum episcopum modernum, aut ejus in illo episcopatu, successorem quemcunque, non papam, non summum pontificem, non universalem episcopum, nec sanctissimum dominum, sed solum Romanum episcopum, *vel pontificem*, ut priscis mos erat, scienter publice asseremus;

(7) Iuraque *ac statuta*[85] hujus regni pro extirpatione et sublatione papatus, et auctoritatis ac jurisdictionis dicti Romani episcopi,[86] quandocunque edita sive sancita, edendaque sive sancienda,[87] pro viribus, scientia, et ingeniolis nostris ipsi firmiter observabimus, et ab aliis sic observari (quantum in nobis fuerit) curabimus atque efficiemus;

(8) Nec posthac ad[88] dictum Romanum episcopum appellabimus, aut appellanti[89] consentimus; nec in ejus curia pro jure aut justitia agemus, aut agenti[90] respondebimus, nec ibidem accusatoris vel rei personam sustinebimus;

(9) Et si quid dictus episcopus per nuncium vel per literas nobis[91] significaverit, qualecunque id fuerit, illud quam citissime commode poterimus, aut vestrae regiae majestati, aut vestris a secretis consiliariis aut vestris successoribus, seu eorum a secretis consiliariis[92] significabimus aut significari faciemus

(10) *Nosque* literas aut nuncium ad eundem Romanum episcopum, *vel ejus curiam*[93] nec mittemus nec mitti faciemus, nisi vestra majestate conscia

---

[81] The Cambridge oath omits the underlined phrase and substitutes 'constitutumque' in its stead.
[82] The Worcester oath is missing 'aut consentiemus'.
[83] The Worcester oath substitutes 'episcopus' for 'pontifex'.
[84] Fuller has 'episcopumque' here, but it must be a mistranscription on his part.
[85] The Corpus Christi College oath is missing the underlined words.
[86] The Cobham College oath has 'Pontificis' here instead of 'episcopi'.
[87] The underlined phrase is not in the Worcester Cathedral oath or the Cobham College oath.
[88] The Gonville oath omits the word 'ad'.
[89] The Corpus Christi oath adds the words 'vel ut appellitur' here.
[90] The Cobham College oath adds words 'consentimus nec' here.
[91] The Worcester Cathedral oath is missing 'nobis'.
[92] The underlined phrase is not present in the Gonville oath. It is negligibly different in the Cobham College oath.
[93] The Cobham College oath is missing the underlined phrase.

et consentiente, <u>aut vestro successore</u>,[94] quod dictae literae vel nuncius ad illum[95] deferatur.

(11) Bullas brevia aut rescripta quaecunque pro nobis vel aliis ab episcopo Romano vel ejus curia non impetrabimus, vel ut talia a quovis impetrentur non consulemus, et si talia pro nobis insciis aut ignorantibus generaliter vel specialiter impetrabuntur, vel alias quomodo libet concedentur, eis renunciabimus, et non consentiemus, nec utemur <u>eisdem ullo modo</u>,[96] at eas vestrae majestati aut successoribus vestris tradi [97] curabimus

(14) *Exemptioni vero qua Romano episcopo vel summo quem vocant*[98] *pontifici, aut ipsi quocumque nomine appelletur, ejusve Romanae ecclesiae mediate vel immediate sumus vel fuimus, ipsiusque concessionibus, privilegiis, largitionibus & indultis quibuscumque*[99] *expresse in his scriptis renunciamus,*[100]

(15) *Et soli vestrae majestati* <u>*vestrisque successoribus*</u>[101] *nos subditos et subjectos*[102] *profitemur, ac nos* [103] *subjiciemus, et* <u>*nos*</u>[104] *solummodo subditos fore spondemus*[105]

(16) *Nec eidem Romano* <u>*pontifici*</u>,[106] *vel ejus nunciis, oratoribus, collectoribus, aut legatis, ullam procurationem, pensionem, portionem, censum, aut quamcunque aliam pecuniarum summam quocunque nomine appelletur, per nos aut interpositam personam vel personas solvemus,* <u>*nec*</u>[107] *solvi faciemus:*

---

94 The Cambridge oath is missing 'aut vestro successore'.
95 The Cobham College oath is missing 'illum'.
96 Instead of the underlined phrase, the Worcester Cathedral oath has 'iisdem ullo pacto seu modo'.
97 The oaths of Cobham College and Cambridge University add the word 'quamcitissime' here.
98 The Corpus Christi oath is missing 'quem vocant'.
99 The Cambridge oath adds the words 'nostram exemptionem tangentibus et concerventibus' here, while the Corpus Christi oath adds the words 'dictam exemptionem respicientibus vel conceneistibus'.
100 The Worcester Cathedral oath has a substantial variation on clause 14. Clause 14 of the Worcester oath reads: 'omnibusque dicti Romani episcopi concessionibus, privilegiis, largitionibus et indultis cujuscumque naturae seu qualitatis existant, ac sub quocumque verborum tenore concessae fuerint, a dicta sede Romana directe vel indirecte, mediate vel immediate aut alias qualitercumque dicti Romani episcopi auctoritate largitis sive consensis quibuscumque publice et expresse in his scriptis renunciavimus, easque irritas et inanes esse volumus'.
101 The oaths of Cobham College and Corpus Christi College do not have the underlined phrase. The oath of Cambridge University has 'tanquam supremo ecclie Anglicane sub christo capiti' instead of the underlined phrase. The Worcester Cathedral oath has the phrase 'velut supremo nostro principi et ecclesiae Anglicanae capiti et successoribus vestris' here.
102 The Worcester Cathedral oath adds the word 'fore' between 'subjectos' and 'profitemur'.
103 The Worcester Cathedral oath adds the words 'ac successores nostros' between 'nos' and 'subjiciemus'.
104 The oaths of Cambridge University and Corpus Christi College are missing the word 'nos' here.
105 The Cobham College oath adds the words '& per praesentes declaramus' here.
106 The oaths of Cambridge University, Cobham College, and Worcester Cathedral have 'episcopo' instead of 'pontifici'.
107 The Gonville Hall oath reads 'aut' instead of 'nec'.

(17) *Statutumque de successione vestra regia in Parliamento vestro editum,*[108] *ac omnia ac singula in eodem contenta, juxta*[109] *formam et effectum ejusdem fideliter observabimus.*[110]

(12) Praeterea in vim pacti profitemur et spondemus, ac in verbo *sacerdotali et sub fidelitate*[111] *vestrae majestati debita et nostra coram Deo conscientia*, promittimus, quod contra hanc nostram praedictam professionem et sponsionem, nulla dispensatione,[112] nulla exceptione, *nulla appellatione, aut provocatione*, nullove juris vel facti remedio nos tuebimur

(13) Et si quam protestationem in praejudicium hujus nostrae professionis et sponsionis[113] fecimus, eam in praesens et in omne tempus futurum revocamus, et eidem renunciamus per praesentes literas, quibus propris manibus[114] nostra subscripsimus,[115] *et eas nostri communis sigilli apprehensione, et notarii publici infra scripti signo et subscriptione committi, curavimus.*[116]

G: POST-1535 HENRICIAN OATHS OF SUPREMACY

I. The oath of supremacy as prescribed by the Act Extinguishing the Authority of the Bishop of Rome of 1536[117]

(1) He from hensforth shall utterly reounce refuse relinquissh or forsake the Bisshopp of Rome and his auctorite power and jurisdiccion;

[108] Instead of 'editum', the Worcester Cathedral oath contains the expanded phrase: 'tento apud Westmonasterium anno regni vestri 28'.
[109] The Worcester Cathedral oath adds the word 'vim' here.
[110] The oaths of Cobham College and Corpus Christi College do not include clause 17 on the Act of Succession.
[111] Instead of the underlined words, the oath of Cobham College has 'in verbo fidelitatis', the oath of Cambridge University has 'in verbo sacerdotii et sub fidelitate', and the oath of Worcester Cathedral has 'ac sub fidelitate'.
[112] The professions of Cobham College and Cambridge University are missing the words 'nulla dispensatione'.
[113] The Worcester Cathedral oath is missing 'et sponsionis'.
[114] The Worcester Cathedral oath and the Cobham College oath add the word 'nomina' here.
[115] The oath of Cambridge University is missing 'quibus propris manibus nostra subscripsimus'.
[116] The oath of Cobham College is missing 'et eas nostri communis sigilli apprehensione, et notarii publici infra scripti signo et subscriptione committi, curavimus'. The oaths of Cambridge and Worcester have this phrase with extremely slight variations.
[117] The text is taken from *Statutes of the Realm*, 28 Hen. 8, c. 10, III:665. The same oath (in the second rather than the third person) is BL Additional MS 39235, fol. 50ᵛ, which is labelled 'The oath takyn byfore admyttyng any to the college for renounsing thauthoritie of the busshop of Rome'. 'And Ireland' is often added in the margin after 'England' in the version from BL Additional MS 39235. This was also the oath sworn by the London Charterhouse on 18 May 1537 (NA E25 82/2 [*LP*, VII (i) 1233], printed in Rymer (ed.), *Foedera*, XIV:588–9). Finally, this oath – minus the first clause – was taken by many bishops-elect at their consecration. See for example LPL, Cranmer's Register, fols. 259ʳ (Heath), 260ᵛ (Bonner).

(2) And that he shall never consent nor agree that the Bisshopp of Rome shall practise excercise or have any manere of auctorite jurisdiccion or power within this Realme or any other the Kynges Domynions, but that he shall resist the same at all tymes to thuttermost of his power;

(3) And that fromhensforth he shall accepte repute and take the Kynges Majestie to be the *oonly* supreme hedd in erth of the Church of Englond;

(4) And that to his connyng wytt and uttermost of his power, without gile fraude or other undewe meane, he shall observe kepe mayntene and defende the hole effectes and contentes of all and singuler actes and Statutes made and to be made within this Realme, in derogacion extirpacion and extinguysshment of the Bisshopp of Rome and his auctorite, and all other Actes and Statutes made and to be made in reformacion and corroboracion of the Kynges Power of supreme heed in erth of the Churche of Englonde;[118]

(5) And this he shall doo ayenst almanere of personnes of what estate dignytie degre or condicion they be, and in no wise do nor attempte, nor to his power suffer to be doon or attempted directly or indirectly, any thing or thinges prively or apertly to the lett hyndraunce damage or derogacion therof or of any parte therof by any manere of meanes or for eny manere of pretence;[119]

(6) And in case any oth be made or hath be made by hym to eny person or persones, in mayntenance defence or favour of the Bisshopp of Rome or his auctorite jurisdiction or power, he repute the same as vayne and adnychilate

So helpe hym God All Seyntes and the Holy Evangelistes.

II. Oath prescribed by the Act concerning the Establishment of the King's Majesty's Succession in the Imperial Crown of the Realm of 1544[120] *(normal text is from oath g 1; italicized text is new)*

(7) *I Robert, archebusshop of Yorke electe, havinge nowe the vale of darkness of the usurped power, auctorite, and jurisdiction of the see and busshope of Rome clerely taken away from myne yeis, do utterly testify and declare in my conscience, that nether the see, nor the busshope of Rome, nor any foraine potestate hath nor ought to have any jurisdiction, power, or auctorite within this realme, nether by God's lawe, nor by any juste lawe or meanes;*

[118] Compare this clause to clause 16 of oath B v and to clause 6 of the various oaths of succession.

[119] This clause is identical to clause 7 of the oath of succession.

[120] The text of this oath is taken from Wilkins, *Concilia*, III:870–1. Its text is essentially the same as the oath in *Statutes of the Realm*, 35 Hen. 8, c. 1, III:956–7. It is also in many episcopal registers from the 1540s.

(1) *And though by sufferance and abusions in tymes past, they aforesaid have usurped and vendicated a fayned and unlawfull power and jurisdiction within this realme, which hath been supported tyll few yeares past; therefore because yt might be denied and thought thereby, that I toke or take it for juste and good, I therefore do now clerely and frankely* renounce, forsake, refuse, and relinquishe that *pretended* auctorite, power, and jurisdiction *both of the see and* busshope of Rome, *and of all other forayne powers,*

(2) And that I shall never consent nor agree that the *foresaid see or* busshope of Rome, *or any of their successours* shall practice, exercise, or have any manner of auctorite, jurisdiction, or power within this realme, nor any other the kynge's realms or dominions; *nor any forayne potestate, of what estate, degree, or condition soever he be*, but that I shall resist the same to th'uttermost of my power;

(8) *And that I shall bear faith, all trought*[121] *and true allegiance to the kynges majestye, and to his heires and successors declared, or hereafter to be declared by auctorite of th'acte made in the session of the parliament holden at Westmynster the 14th day of January, in the xxxv. yere, and in the saide acte made in the xxviii. yere of the kynges majesty's reigne;*[122]

(3) And that I shall accept, repute, and take the kings majestye, *his heyres and successors, when they or any of them shall enjoy his place*, to be th'only supreme heade of the church of England *and Ireland in earthe under God, and in all other his highness's dominions*;

(4) And that with my *body*, connynge, wytte, and uttermost of my power, without gyle, fraude, or any other undue meanes, I shall observe, keape, mainteine, and defende *all the king's majesty's styles, titles, and rights, with these* effects and contents *of th'actes provided for the same*, and all other actes and statutes made or to be made within this realme *in and for that purpose*; and the derogation, extirpation, and extinguisshment of *the usurped and pretended auctorite, power, and jurisdiction of the see and* busshope of Rome, *and all other forayne potentates or potestates as afore; and also as well the said statute made in the said xxviii. yere, as the statute made in the saide session of the parliament holden in the xxxv. yere of the kinges majesty's reign, for establishment and declaration of his highnes sucsession*, and all actes and statutes made and to be made in confirmation and corroboration of the kinges *majesties* power and supremacy in earthe of the churche of England *and of Ireland, and other his grace's dominions, I shall also defende and mayntene with my body and goods, withe all my witte and power*;

---

[121] 'Trought' is mistranscription by Wilkins. As the version of the oath in *Statutes of the Realm* makes clear, the word should be 'trouth'.
[122] This clause is an edited amalgamation of clauses 1–3 of oath D, III.

(5) And this I shall do against all maner of persons, of what estate, dignity, degree, or condition they be; and in no wyse doe or attempte, nor to my power suffre or knowe to be done or attempted, directly or indirectly, any thinge or thinges prively or apertly to the let, hindraunce, damage, or derogation *of any of the said statutes*, or any part thereof by any manner of meanes, or for *or by* any manner of pretence;

(6) And in case any oathe hath been made by me to any person or persons in mayntenaunce, defence, or favour of the bishop of Rome, or his authority, jurisdiction, or power, *or against any the statutes aforesaid*, I repute the same as vayne and adnihilate;

(9) *I shall wholly observe and keepe this oathe.*

So helpe me God, all saintes, and the holy evangelistes.

Bibliography

MANUSCRIPTS

BODLEIAN LIBRARY, OXFORD

Ashmole MS 750. Fifteenth-century manuscripts, including a homily against covetousness and swearing.

Ashmole MS 1729. Historical miscellany, including a letter to Peter Ligham from Cranmer.

Rawlinson MS B 167. Miscellany, including transcriptions of ecclesiastical oaths by Richard Smith.

BRITISH LIBRARY

Additional Charter 12827. Oath of supremacy of the University of Cambridge from 1535.

Additional MS 4507. Collections of Thomas Madox, including later Henrician oaths of succession.

Additional MS 24202. Lollard tracts, including one against the episcopal oath of canonical obedience.

Additional MS 34319 Arundel's book of ordinances, including Stephan Gardiner's oath to the king.

Additional MS 38656. Subscriptions of the top clergy of England against papal authority.

Additional MS 39235. Wodehouse papers, including a later Henrician oath of supremacy.

Additional MS 48022. Robert Beale's manuscripts.

Cotton MS Cleopatra E IV. Papers relating to the monasteries in the reign of Henry VIII.

Cotton MS Cleopatra E V. Papers relating to the Reformation.

Cotton MS Cleopatra E VI. Papers relating to religious matters during the sixteenth century.

Cotton MS Otho C X. Documents from the reign of Henry VIII, including letters from Mary.

Cotton MS Vespasian C VII. Acta inter Angliam et Hispaniam.

Cotton MS Vespasian C XIV. Miscellany, including various oaths of office.

Harleian MS 160. Miscellany, including various oaths of office.

Harleian MS 283. Original letters, including a copy of Mary Tudor's submission.

Harleian MS 419. John Foxe's manuscripts.

Harleian MS 421. John Foxe's manuscripts.

Harleian MS 433. Official documents from the reigns of Edward V and Richard III, including oaths of office.

Harleian MS 785. Law miscellany, including various oaths of office and a coronation oath.

Harleian MS 2143. Abstracts of trials in the Star Chamber.

Harleian MS 6848. Ecclesiastical papers, including examinations of Elizabethan Separatists.

Harleian MS 6849. Parliamentary papers, including examinations and trials of Puritans and Separatists.

Harleian MS 6873. Miscellany, including various oaths of office.

Harleian MS 7041. Miscellany, including a copy of the oath of supremacy of the University of Cambridge.

Harleian MS 7042. Elizabethan documents, including examinations and trials of Puritans and Separatists.

Harleian MS 7571. Miscellany, including a copy of a commission to tender the oath of supremacy in Sussex.

Lansdowne MS 105. Miscellany, including an Elizabethan Parliamentary bill against vain swearing.

Lansdowne MS 155. Miscellany, including various oaths of office.

Lansdowne MS 389. John Foxe's manuscripts.

Lansdowne MS 621. Collection relating to the Court of Chancery, including various oaths of office.

Lansdowne MS 762. Miscellany, including various oaths of office.

Lansdowne MS 989. Bishop Kennett's collection, including an oath of supremacy of Corpus Christi College.

Royal MS 9 A XIV. Theological tracts, including various oaths of office.

CAMBRIDGE UNIVERSITY LIBRARY

MS. GG. VI. Treatise on the court leet.

MS II. I. 39. Thomas Wygenhale's *Speculum iuratoris*.

MS MM. I. 29. Commonplace book of Thomas Earl, minister of St Mildred's, Bread Street.

CORPUS CHRISTI COLLEGE, CAMBRIDGE

MS 106. Documents relating to the University of Cambridge.

EMMANUEL COLLEGE, CAMBRIDGE

MS 261 Letters of the martyrs and Robert Wisdom's revocation of his recantation.

GUILDHALL LIBRARY

MS 9531/10. Tunstall's Register.
MS 9531/11. Stokesley's Register.
MS 9531/12. Bonner's Register.

HAUS-, HOF- UND STAATSARCHIV, VIENNA

Staatenabteilungen, England, Berichte, Kartons 5 and 7: Chapuys' letters to Charles V, 1531–6.

INNER TEMPLE LIBRARY

Petyt MS 538, vol. 47. Ecclesiastical documents, chiefly from the reign of Elizabeth I.

KENT HISTORY AND LIBRARY CENTRE, MAIDSTONE

DRB/A/R/1/13, Microfilm z3. John Fisher's Register.

LAMBETH PALACE LIBRARY

Arundel's Register.
Cranmer's Register.
MS CM 51, #22 and #23. Tunstall's oaths of canonical obedience to his metropolitan and to the Pope.
Stafford's Register.
Warham's Register.

THE NATIONAL ARCHIVES, KEW

C54. Oaths of supremacy of friars.
C66/663. Henrician patent rolls.
C82/690, no. 2. Model form of a new bishop's oath to the king from 1534.
C254/179. Oaths of supremacy and office during Elizabeth's reign.
DL41/1182. Subscriptions to the oath of succession from Lancashire.
E25. Oaths of supremacy of clerical institutions and bishops.
E36. Exchequer: miscellaneous books.
SP1. State papers, domestic, Henry VIII.
SP2. Letters and papers, Henry VIII, folios, 1516–39.
SP6. Theological tracts of Henry VIII.
SP11. State papers, domestic, Mary I.
SP12. State papers, domestic, Elizabeth I.

CALENDARS OF MANUSCRIPTS

Brewer, J. S., R. H. Brodie, and James Gairdner, eds. *Letters and Papers, Foreign and Domestic, of the Reign of Henry VIII, Preserved in the Public Record Office, the British Museum, and Elsewhere.* 2nd edn 1920. 21 vols. in 37. Reprint, Vaduz: Kraus Reprint, 1965.

Brown, Rawdon, G. Cavendish Bentinck, and H. F. Brown, eds. *Calendar of State Papers and Manuscripts, Relating to English Affairs, Existing in the Archives and Collections of Venice, and in Other Libraries of Northern Italy.* London: Longman Green, 1864–1947.

Gayangos, Pascual, ed. *Calendar of Letters, Despatches, and State Papers, relating to the Negotiations between England and Spain Preserved in the Archives at Simancas and Elsewhere.* Vols. IV and V. London, 1879–88.

Gilson, J. P., ed. *Catalogue of Additions to the Manuscripts in the British Museum in the Years MDCCCXI-MDCCCXV.* London, 1925.

EARLY MODERN PRINTED SOURCES

Askew, Anne. *The first examinacyon of Anne Askewe, latelye martyred in Smythfelde, by the Romysh popes vpholders, with the Elucydacyon of Johan Bale.* Wesel, 1546.
The lattre examinacyon of Anne Askewe, latelye martyred in Smythfelde, by the wycked Synagoge of Antichrist, with the Elucydacyon of Johan Bale. Wesel, 1547.

Atterbury, Francis. *The Rights, Powers, and Priviledges, of an English Convocation, Stated and Vindicated in Answer to a Late Book of Dr. Wake's, Entituled, The Authority of Christian Princes over their Ecclesiastical Synods asserted, &c. and to Several Other Pieces.* London, 1700.

Bale, John. *A Christen exhortacion vnto customable swearers. What a ryght & lawfull othe is: whan, and before whom, it owght to be. Item. The maner of sayinge grace, or geuynge thankes vnto God.* Antwerp, 1543?
(ps. Johan Harryson) *Yet a course at the Romyshe foxe. A dysclosynge or openynge of the Manne of synne, Contayned in the late Declaracyon of the Popes olde faythe made by Edmonde Bonner bysshopp of London. Wherby wyllyam Tolwyn was than newlye professed at paules crosse openlye into Antichristes Romyshe relygyon agayne by a new solempne othe of obedience, notwythstandynge the othe made to hys prynce afore to the contrarye.* Antwerp, 1543.

Barnes, Robert. *A supplicacion vnto the most gracyous prynce H. the. viij.* 1534.

Becon, Thomas (ps. Theodore Basille). *An Inuectyue agenst the moost wicked and detestable vyce of swearing.* 1543.

Bicknoll, Edmond. *A Swoord agaynst Swearyng, conteining these principal poyntes. 1 That there is a lawful vse of an oth, contrary to the assertion of the Manichees and Anabaptistes. 2 Howe great a sinne it is to sweare falsly, vainely, rashly, or customably. 3 That common or vsual swearing leadeth vnto periurie. 4 Examples of Gods iuste and visyble punishment vpon blasphemers, periurers, and such as haue procured Gods wrath by cursyng and bannyng, whiche we call execration.* 1579.

Carpenter, Alexander. *Destructorium viciorum.* Paris, 1521.

Chauncy, Maurice. *Historia aliqvot nostri saecvli martyrum cum pia, tum lectu iucunda, nunquam antehac typis excusa.* Mainz, 1550.

Chertsey, Andrew. *The crafte to lyue well and to dye well.* 1505.

    Ihesus. The floure of the commaundementes of god with many examples and auctorytees extracte and drawen as well of holy scryptures as of other doctours and good auncient faders, the whiche is moche vtyle and prouffytable vnto all people. 1510.

Coke, Edward. *The reports of Sir Edward Coke Kt. late Lord Chief-Justice of England, And one of His Majesties Covncil of State. Of Divers Resolutions and Judgements given upon solemn Arguments, and with great Deliberation, and Conference of the most Revered Judges, and Sages of the Law; of Cases in Law which never were Resolved or Adjudged before; And the Reasons and Causes of the said Resolutions and Judgements.* 1658.

Cosin, Richard. *An Apologie for svndrie proceedings by Iurisdiction Ecclesiasticall, of late times by some chalenged, and also diuersly by them impugned. . . . Whereunto . . . I haue presumed to adionie that right excellent and sound determination (concerning Oaths) which was made by M. Lancelot Androwes.* 1593.

Doleman, R. [William Allen, Sir Francis Englefield, and Robert Parsons?]. *A conference abovt the next svccession to the crowne of Ingland, diuided into two parts.* Antwerp, 1595.

Downame, John. *Foure treatises, tending to disswade all Christians from foure no lesse hainous then common sinnes; namely, the abuses of Swearing, Drunkenesse, Whoredome, and Briberie.* 1608.

Gardiner, Stephen. *De vera obedientia. An oration made in Latine, by the right Reuerende father in God Stephan bishop of Winchestre, now Lorde Chauncelour of Englande. With the Preface of Edmonde Bonner than Archideacon of Leicestre, and the kinges Maiesties Embassadour in Denmarke, and now bishop of London: touching true obedience, Printed at Hamburgh in Latine, in officinal Francisci Rhodi Mense Januario, 1536. And now translated in to Englishe, and printed estsones, in Rome, before the castle of .S. Angel, at the signe of .S. Peter. In nouembre, Anno do. M. D. Liii.* Wesel?, 1553.

Hawes, Stephen. *The conuercyon of swerers.* 1509.

Hearne, Thomas, ed. *Sylloge epistolarum, a variis Angliae principibus scriptarum.* In *Titi Livii Foro-Juliensis vita Henrici Quinti, regis Angliae.* Oxford, 1716.

Horne, Robert. *An Answeare Made by Rob. Bishoppe of Wynchester, to a Booke entituled, 'The Declaration of svche Scruples, and staies of Conscience, touchinge the Othe of the Supremacy', as M. Iohn Fekenham, by wrytinge did deliuer vnto the L. Bishop of Winchester, with his Resolutions made thereunto.* 1566.

Joye, George. *The exposicion of Daniel the Prophete gathered oute of Philip Melanchton, Johan Ecolampadius, Chonrade Pellicane & out of Johan Draconite. &c.* Antwerp, 1545.

    The letters whyche Johan Ashwell Priour of Newnham Abbey besydes Bedforde, sente secretly to the Byshope of Lyncolne, in the yeare of our Lord M.D.xxvii. Where in the sayde pryour accuseth George Joye that tyme beyng felow of Peter college in Cambrydge, of fower opinyons: wyth the answere of the sayde George vn to the same opynyons. 1548.

Morice, James. *A briefe treatise of Oathes exacted by Ordinaries and Ecclesiastical Iudges, to answere generallie to all such Articles or Interrogatories, as pleaseth them to propound. And of their forced and constrained Oathes ex officio, wherein is proued that the same are vnlawfull.* Middelburg, 1590?

Peraldus, Gulielmus. *Summarium summe virtutum et vitiorum per figuras.* Lyons?, 1500.

Pro divo Carolo, eivs nominis Romanorum Imperatore Inuictissimo, pio, felice, semper Augusto, Patrepatriae, in satisfactionem quidem sine talione eorum quae in illum scripta, ac pleraque etiam in uulgum aediat fuere, Apologetici libri duo nuper ex Hispaniis allati cum alijs nonnullis, quorum catalogos ante cuiusque exordium reperies. 1527.

Rotuli Parliamentorum; ut et petitiones, et placita in Parliamento. 6 vols. London, 1767–77.

Rymer, Thomas, ed. *Foedera, conventiones, literae, et cujuscunque generis acta publica, inter reges Angliæ, et alios quosvis imperatores, reges, pontifices, principes, vel communitates, ab ineunte sæculo duo-decimo, viz. ab anno 1101, ad nostra usque tempora, habita aut tractata; ex autographis, infra secretiores Archivorum regiorum thesaurarias, per multa sæcula reconditis, fideliter exscripta.* 2nd edn. 20 vols. London, 1726–35.

Seton, Alexander, and William Tolwyn. *The declaracion made at Poules Crosse in the Cytye of London, the fourth sonday of Aduent, by Alexander Seyton, and mayster Willyam Tolwyn, persone of S. Anthonynes in the sayd cytye of London, the yere of our lord god M.D.XLJ. Newly corrected & amended.* 1542.

White, Christopher. *Of oathes: their obiect, forme, and bond: the pvnishment of perivrie, and the impietie of papall dispensations.* 1627.

Wilkins, David, ed. *Concilia Magnae Britanniae et Hiberniae, a synodo Verolamiensi A.D. CCCCXLVI ad Londinensem A.D. [MD]CCXVII.* 4 vols. London, 1737.

MODERN EDITIONS OF PRIMARY SOURCES

Aquinas, Thomas. *Summa Theologiae.* Vol. xxxix, *Religion and Worship.* Edited and translated by Kevin D. O'Rourke. New York: McGraw-Hill, 1964.

Augustine. *St Augustine: Treatises on Various Subjects.* Edited by Roy J. Deferrari. Washington, DC: The Catholic University Press, 1952.

'Sermon 180'. Translated by Edmund Hill. In *The Works of Saint Augustine: A Translation for the 21st Century*, part 3, vol. v, *Sermons on the New Testament (148–183).* Edited by John E. Rotelle, 314–23. New Rochelle, NY: New City Press, 1992.

Bale, John. *Select Works of John Bale.* Edited by Henry Christmas. Parker Society, 1. Cambridge University Press, 1849.

Banks, Mary Macleod, ed. *An Alphabet of Tales: An English 15th Century Translation of the 'Alphabetum Narrationum' of Etienne de Besançon.* English Early Text Society, o.s., 126. London: Kegan Paul, Trench, Trübner & Co., 1904.

Barnum, Priscilla Heath, ed. *Dives and Pauper.* Early English Text Society, o.s., 275. London: Oxford University Press, 1976.

Barrow, Henry. *The Writings of Henry Barrow 1587–1590*. Edited by Leland H. Carlson. London: George Allen and Unwin, 1962.

Bateson, Mary, ed. 'Aske's Examination', *English Historical Review* 5 (1890): 550–73.

'The Pilgrimage of Grace'. *English Historical Review* 5 (1890): 330–45.

Beauvais, Vincent of. *Speculum quadruplex sive speculum maius*. Vol. III, *Speculum morale*. 1624. Reprint, Graz: Akademische Druck, 1964.

Biblia Latina cum glossa ordinaria: Facsimile Reprint of the Editio Princeps Adolph Rusch of Strassburg 1480/81. Introduction by Karlfried Froehlich and Margaret T. Gibson. Turnhout: Brepols, 1992.

Biblia sacra iuxta Vulgatam versionem. Edited by Robert Weber. Stuttgart: Württembergische Bibelanstalt, 1969.

Bond, Ronald B., ed. *Certain Sermons or Homilies (1547) and A Homily against Disobedience and Wilful Rebellion (1570): A Critical Edition*. University of Toronto Press, 1987.

Bradford, John. *The Writings of John Bradford*. Edited by Aubrey Townsend. Parker Society, 5. Cambridge University Press, 1848.

Brandeis, Arthur, ed. *Jacob's Well, An English Treatise on the Cleansing of Man's Conscience*. Early English Text Society, o.s., 115. London: Kegan Paul, Trench, Trübner & Co., 1900.

Bray, Gerald, ed. *Records of Convocation*. 20 vols. Woodbridge: Boydell, 2005–6.

Tudor Church Reform: The Henrician Canons of 1535 and the Reformatio Legum Ecclesiasticarum. Woodbridge: Boydell, 2000.

Bullinger, Henry. *The Decades of Henry Bullinger*. Translated by H. I. Edited by Thomas Harding. Parker Society, 7–10. Cambridge University Press, 1849–52.

Burnet, Gilbert. *History of the Reformation of the Church of England*. Edited by Nicolas Pocock. 7 vols. Oxford: Clarendon, 1865.

Byrne, Muriel St Clare, ed. *The Lisle Letters*. 6 vols. University of Chicago Press, 1981

Calvin, John. *Institutes of the Christian Religion*. Edited by John T. McNeill. Translated by Ford Lewis Battles. Louisville, NY: Westminster John Knox, 1960.

Cartwright, Thomas. *Cartwrightiana*. Edited by Albert Peel and Leland Carlson. London: George Allen and Unwin, 1951.

Champollion-Figeac, Aimé, ed. *Cativité du roi François Ier*. Paris: Imprimerie Royal, 1847.

Chauncy, Maurice. *The Passion and Martyrdom of the Holy English Carthusian Fathers: The Short Narration (1570)*. Edited by G. W. S. Curtis. Translated by A. F. Radcliffe. Introduction by E. Margaret Thompson. London: Society for Promoting Christian Knowledge, 1935.

Chitty, Herbert, ed. *Registra Stephani Gardiner et Johannis Poynet*. Canterbury and York Society, 37. Oxford University Press, 1930.

Cooper, Henry Charles, ed. *Annals of Cambridge*. 5 vols. Cambridge: Warwick and Co., 1842.

Coverdale Bible of 1535. Introduced by S. L. Greenslade. Folkestone: Dawson, 1975.

Cox, J. Charles, ed. 'William Stapleton and the Pilgrimage of Grace.' *Transactions of the East Riding Antiquarian Society* 10 (1902): 80–106.

Cranmer, Thomas. *Miscellaneous Writings and Letters of Thomas Cranmer.* Edited by John Edmund Cox. Parker Society, 16. Cambridge University Press, 1846.

Diekstra, F. N. M., ed. *Book for a Simple and Devout Woman: A Late Middle English Adaptation of Peraldus'* Summa de Vitiis et Virtutibus *and Friar Laurent's* Somme le Roi. Groningen: Egbert Forsten, 1998.

Dobson R. B., ed., *The Peasants' Revolt of 1381.* London: Macmillan, 1970.

Ellis, Henry, ed. *Original Letters, Illustrative of English History.* Series 2 (4 vols.), 3 (4 vols.). London, Harding and Lepard, 1827; Richard Bentley, 1846.

Foxe, John. *Acts and Monuments (1583)... The Variorum Edition.* [online]. Sheffield: HriOnline, 2004. www.hrionline.shef.ac.uk/foxe/.

Foxe, John. *Acts and Monuments of John Foxe; with a Life of the Martyrologist, and Vindication of the Work.* Edited by George Townsend. 8 vols. New York: Ams Press, 1965.

Friedberg, Aemilius, ed. *Corpus Iuris Canonici.* 2 vols. 1879–81. Reprint, Union, NJ: Lawbook Exchange, 2000.

Gardiner, Stephen. *Letters of Stephen Gardiner.* Edited by James Arthur Muller. Cambridge University Press, 1933.

    Obedience in Church & State: Three Political Tracts by Stephen Gardiner. Edited and translated by Pierre Janelle. Cambridge University Press, 1930.

Gee, Henry, and William John Hardy, eds. *Documents Illustrative of English Church History.* London: Macmillan, 1914.

Greenwood, John. *The Writings of John Greenwood 1587–1590, Together with the Joint Writings of Henry Barrow and John Greenwood.* Edited by Leland H. Carlson. London: George Allen and Unwin, 1962.

Greenwood, John and Henry Barrow. *The Writings of John Greenwood and Henry Barrow, 1591–1593.* Edited by Leland H. Carlson. London: George Allen and Unwin, 1970.

Hall, Edward. *Hall's Chronicle; containing the History of England, during the Reign of Henry the Fourth, and the Succeeding Monarchs, to the End of the Reign of Henry the Eighth, in which are Particularly Described the Manner and Customs of Those Periods.* London: J. Johnson et al., 1809.

[Harpsfield, Nicholas?]. *Bishop Cranmer's Recantacyons.* Edited by Lord Houghton. Introduction by J. Gairdner. Philobiblon Society Miscellanies 15 (1877–84).

Harpsfield, Nicholas. *The Life and Death of Sr Thomas Moore, Knight, Sometymes Lord High Chancellor of England, Written in the Tyme of Queene Marie.* Edited by Elsie Vaughan Hitchcock. Early English Text Society, o.s., 186. London: Oxford University Press, 1932.

Hill, Richard. *Songs, Carols, and Other Miscellaneous Poems, from the Balliol MS. 354, Richard Hill's Commonpace-Book.* Edited by Roman Dyboski. Early English Text Society, e.s. 101. London: Kegan Paul, Trench, Trübner & Co., 1907.

Hinde, Gladys, ed. *The Registers of Cuthbert Tunstall Bishop of Durham 1530–59 and James Pilkington Bishop of Durham 1561–76.* Surtees Society, 161. Durham: Andrews & Co., 1952.

Hooper, John. *Early Writings of John Hooper.* Edited by Samuel Carr. Parker Society, 20. Cambridge University Press, 1843.

   Later Writings of Bishop Hooper, Together with His Letters and Other Pieces. Edited by Charles Nevinson. Parker Society, 21. Cambridge University Press, 1852.

Hughes, Paul L., and James F. Larkin, eds., *Tudor Royal Proclamations.* 3 vols. New Haven, CT: Yale University Press, 1964–9.

Hutchinson, Roger. *The Works of Roger Hutchinson.* Edited by John Bruce. Parker Society, 23. Cambridge University Press, 1848.

Idley, Peter. *Peter Idley's Instructions to His Son.* Edited by Charlotte D'Evelyn. Boston: D. C. Heath, 1935.

Jacob, E. F., ed. *The Register of Henry Chichele Archbishop of Canterbury, 1414–1443.* 4 vols. Oxford: Clarendon, 1943–7.

Jerome. S. *Hieronymi Presbyteri Opera, Pars I, 7: Commentariorvm in Mathevm.* Corpus Christianorum Series Latina, 77. Turnhout: Brepols, 1969.

Journal of the House of Lords. Vol. 1. London, 1802.

Kitching, C. J., ed. *The Royal Visitation of 1559: Act Book for the Northern Province.* Surtees Society, 187. Gateshead: Northumberland Press, 1975.

Le Vasseur, Leon, ed. *Ephemerides ordinis Cartusiensis.* 5 vols. Monstrolii, 1890.

Latimer, Hugh. *Sermons and Remains of Hugh Latimer.* Edited by George Elwes Corrie. Parker Society, 28. Cambridge University Press, 1845.

   Sermons by Hugh Latimer. Edited by George Elwes Corrie. Parker Society, 27. Cambridge University Press, 1844.

Laurent, Dominican. *The Book of Vices and Virtues: A Fourteenth Century English Translation of the 'Somme le roi' of Lorens d'Orléans.* Edited by W. Nelson Francis. Early English Text Society, o.s., 217. London: Oxford University Press, 1942.

Lloyd, Charles, ed. *Formularies of Faith Put Forth by Authority during the Reign of Henry VIII. viz Articles about Religion, 1536. The Institution of a Christian Man, 1537. A Necessary Doctrine and Erudition for any Christian Man, 1543.* Oxford: Clarendon Press, 1825.

Luther, Martin. *To the Christian Nobility of the German Nation.* Translated by James Charles M. Jacobs and James Atkinson. In *The Christian in Society I,* edited by James Atkinson. Vol. XLIV, *Luther's Works.* Philadelphia: Fortress Press, 1966.

McSheffrey, Shannon, and Norman Tanner, eds. *Lollards of Coventry, 1486–1522.* Camden Society, 5th series, 23. Cambridge University Press, 2003.

Mannyng, Robert. *Robert of Brunne's 'Handlyng Synne', AD 1303, with Those Parts of the Anglo-French Treatise on Which It Was Founded, William of Wadington's 'Manuel des Pechiez', Re-Edited from Mss. in the British Museum and Bodleian Libraries.* Edited by Frederick J. Furnivall. Early English Text Society, o.s., 119. London: Kegan Paul, Trench, Trübner & Co., 1901.

Milner, Edith, and Edith Benham, eds. *Records of the Lumleys of Lumley Castle.* London: George Bell and Sons, 1904.

Mirk, John. *Mirk's Festial: A Collection of Homilies.* Edited by Theodore Erbe. Early English Text Society, e.s., 96. London: Kegan Paul, Trench, Trübner & Co., 1905.

More, Thomas. *The Apology.* Edited by J. B. Trapp. Vol. ix, *The Complete Works of St. Thomas More.* New Haven, CT: Yale University Press, 1979.

The Confutation of Tyndale's Answer. Edited by L. A. Schuster et al. Vol. viii, *The Complete Works of Thomas More.* New Haven, CT: Yale University Press, 1973.

The Correspondence of Sir Thomas More. Edited by Elizabeth Frances Rogers. Princeton University Press, 1947.

The Debellation of Salem and Bizance. Edited by John Guy et al. Vol. x, *The Complete Works of Thomas More.* New Haven, CT: Yale University Press, 1987.

A Dialogue concerning Heresies. Edited by Thomas M. C. Lawler et al. Vol. vi, *The Complete Works of St. Thomas More.* New Haven, CT: Yale University Press, 1981.

Nelson, Venetia, ed. *A Myrour to Lewde Men and Wymmen: A Prose Version of the* Speculum Vitae, *ed. from B.L. MS Harley 45.* Heidelberg: Carl Winter, 1981.

Nichols, John Gough, ed. *Narratives of the Days of the Reformation, Chiefly from the Manuscripts of John Foxe the Martyrologist; with Two Contemporary Biographies of Archbishop Cranmer.* Camden Society, 77. Westminster: J. B. Nichols and Sons, 1859.

Ortroy, F. van, ed. 'Vie du bienheureux martyr Jean Fisher Cardinal, évêque de Rochester'. *Analecta Bollandiana* 10 (1891): 121–365; 12 (1893): 97–283.

Owen, Dorothy, and David Smith, eds. *Church Authority and Power in Medieval and Early Modern Britain: The Episcopal Registers.* 9 vols. Brighton: Harvester Press Microform, 1986.

Pocock, Nicolas, ed. *Records of the Reformation; the Divorce 1527–1533. Mostly Now for the First Time Printed from MSS. in the British Museum, the Public Record Office, the Venetian Archives and Other Libraries.* Oxford: Clarendon, 1870.

Reynes, Robert. *The Commonplace Book of Robert Reynes of Acle: An Edition of Tanner MS 407.* Edited by Cameron Louis. New York: Garland, 1980.

Ridley, Nicholas. *The Works of Nicholas Ridley.* Edited by Henry Christmas. Parker Society, 39. Cambridge University Press, 1843.

Roberts, Alexander, and James Donaldson, eds. *The Ante-Nicene Fathers: Translations of the Writings of the Fathers down to A.D. 325.* 10 vols. Grand Rapids, MI: Wm. B. Eerdmans, 1950–.

Robinson, Hastings, ed. and trans. *Original Letters Relative to the English Reformation, Written During the Reigns of King Henry VIII, King Edward VI, and Queen Mary: Chiefly from the Archives of Zurich.* Parker Society, 53. Cambridge University Press, 1846–7.

Roper, William. *A Man of Singular Virtue: Being a Life of Sir Thomas More by His Son-in-Law William Roper and a Selection of More's Letters.* Edited by A. L. Rowse. London: Folio Society, 1980.

Ross, Woodburn O., ed. *Middle English Sermons: Edited from British Museum MS. Royal 18 B. XXIII.* Early English Text Society, o.s., 209. London: Oxford University Press, 1960.

Saint Germain, Christopher. *A Treatise concernynge the Diuision betwene the Spiry-tualtie and Temporalitie.* Edited by J. B. Trapp. Vol. IX, *The Complete Works of St. Thomas More.* New Haven, CT: Yale University Press, 1979.

Schaff, Philip, ed. *A Select Library of the Nicene and Post-Nicene Fathers of the Christian Church.* 14 vols. Grand Rapids, MI: Wm. B. Eerdmans, 1956.

Schaff, Philip, and Henry Wace, eds. *A Select Library of Nicene and Post-Nicene Fathers of the Christian Church: Second Series.* 14 vols. Grand Rapids, MI: Wm. B. Eerdmans, 1952.

Schroeder, H. J. ed. and trans. *Canons and Decrees of the Council of Trent: Original Text with English Translation.* St Louis: B. Herder, 1941.

Scott, Tom, and Bob Scribner, eds. *The German Peasants' War: A History in Documents.* New Jersey: Humanities Press, 1991.

Simmons, Thomas Frederick, ed. *The Lay Folks Mass Book or the Manner of Hearing Mass with Rubrics and Devotions for the People in Four Texts and Offices in English according to the Use of York from Manuscripts of the Xth to the XVth Century.* Early English Text Society, o.s., 71. London: N. Trübner, 1879.

Smith, Lucy Toulmin, ed. *A Common-Place Book of the Fifteenth Century, Containing a Religious Play and Poetry, Legal Forms, and Local Accounts.* London: Trübner, 1886.

State Papers, Published under the Authority of His Majesty's Commission. 11 vols. London, 1830–52.

The Statutes of the Realm. 1810–1828. 11 vols. Reprint, London: Dawsons of Pall Mall, 1963.

Swinburn, Lilian M., ed. *Laterne of Li3t.* Early English Text Society, o.s., 151. London: Kegan Paul, Trench, Trübner & Co., 1917.

Tanner, Norman P., ed. *Heresy Trials in the Diocese of Norwich, 1428–31,* Camden Society, series 4, 20. London: Royal Historical Society, 1977.

Toller, T. Northcote, ed. *Correspondence of Edward, Third Earl of Derby, during the Years 24 to 31 Henry VIII.* Chetham Society, n.s., 19. Manchester, 1890.

Tyndale, William. *The New Testament 1526.* Reprint, London: D. Paradine Developments, 1976.

Tyndale, William and John Frith. *The Works of the English Reformers: William Tyndale and John Frith.* Edited by Thomas Russell. 3 vols. London: Ebenezer Palmer, 1831.

Vitry, Jacques de. *The Exempla or Illustrative Stories from the Sermons Vulgares.* Edited and translated by Thomas Frederick Crane. Folklore Society, 26. London: David Nutt, 1890.

Vocht, Henry de, ed. *Acta Thomae Mori: History of the Reports of His Trial and Death with an Unedited Contemporary Narrative.* Humanistica Lovaniensia, 7. Leuven: Publications of the Institute for Economics of the University and Librairie Universitaire Ch. Uystpruyst, 1947.

Wenzel, Siegfried, ed. and trans. *Fasciculus Morum: A Fourteenth-Century Preacher's Handbook.* University Park, PN: Pennsylvania State University Press, 1989.

Whitford, Richard. *A Werke for Householders.* Vol. v of *Richard Whytford's The Pype or Tonne of the Lyfe of Perfection.* Edited by James Hogg. Salzburg: Inst. für Anglistik und Amerikanistik, Universität Salzburg, 1979.

Wood, A. C., ed. *Registrum Simonis de Langham Cantuariensis archiepiscopi.* Canterbury and York Society, 53. Oxford University Press, 1956.

Wright, Thomas, ed. *Three Chapters of Letters Relating to the Suppression of Monasteries.* London: John Bowyer Nichols and Son, 1843.

Wycliffe, John. *Johannis Wyclif tractatus de mandatis divinis: accedit tractatus de statu innocencie.* Edited by Johann Loserth and F. D. Matthew. 1922. Reprint, New York: Johnson Reprint, 1966.

   Select English Works of John Wyclif. 3 vols. Edited by Thomas Arnold. Oxford: Clarendon, 1871.

Zwingli, Huldrych. *Zwingli and Bullinger: Selected Translations with Introductions and Notes.* Edited by G. W. Bromiley. Philadelphia: Westminster Press, 1953.

SECONDARY SOURCES

Aston, Margaret. *Lollards and Reformers: Images and Literacy in Late Medieval Religion.* London: Hambledon Press, 1984.

Aungier, George James. *The History and Antiquities of Syon Monastery, the Parish of Isleworth, and the Chaperly of Hounslow.* London: J. B. Nichols and Son, 1840.

Baskerville, Geoffrey. *English Monks and the Suppression of the Monasteries.* London: Jonathan Cape, 1937.

Bernard, George W. *The King's Reformation: Henry VIII and the Remaking of the English Church.* New Haven, CT: Yale University Press, 2005.

   'The Making of Religious Policy, 1533–1546: Henry VIII and the Search for the Middle Way'. *Historical Journal* 41 (1998): 321–49.

   Power and Politics in Tudor England. Aldershot: Ashgate, 2000.

   'The Tyranny of Henry VIII'. In *Authority and Consent in Tudor England: Essays Presented to C. S. L. Davies*, edited by G. W. Bernard and S. J. Gunn, 113–29. Aldershot: Ashgate, 2002.

Bowker, Margaret. *The Henrician Reformation: The Diocese of Lincoln under John Longland, 1521–1547.* Cambridge University Press, 1981.

   'The Supremacy and the Episcopate: The Struggle for Control, 1534–1540'. *Historical Journal* 18 (1975): 227–43.

Brigden, Susan. *London and the Reformation.* Oxford: Clarendon, 1989.

   New Worlds, Lost Worlds: The Rule of the Tudors, 1485–1603. London: Penguin, 2000.

'Popular Disturbance and the Fall of Thomas Cromwell and the Reformers, 1539–1540', *Historical Journal* 24 (1981): 257–78.

Bruce, John. 'Observations on the Circumstances which Occasioned the Death of Fisher, Bishop of Rochester'. *Archaeologia* 25 (1834): 61–99.

Bush, Michael. *The Pilgrimage of Grace: A Study of the Rebel Armies of October 1536*. Manchester University Press, 1996.

Bush, Michael, and David Bownes. *The Defeat of the Pilgrimage of Grace: A Study of the Postpardon Revolts of December 1536 to March 1537 and Their Effect*. University of Hull Press, 1999.

Carrafiello, Michael. 'Robert Parsons and Equivocation'. *Catholic Historical Review* 79 (1993): 671–80.

Chester, Alan G. *Hugh Latimer: Apostle to the English*. Philadelphia: University of Pennsylvania Press, 1954.

Chibi, Andrew A. *Henry VIII's Bishops: Diplomats, Administrators, Scholars and Shepherds*. Cambridge: James Clarke, 2003.

Henry VIII's Conservative Scholar: Bishop John Stokesley and the Divorce, Royal Supremacy and Doctrinal Reform. Berne: Peter Lang, 1997.

Craun, Edwin. D., '"Inordinata Locutio": Blasphemy in Pastoral Literature, 1200–1500'. *Traditio* 39 (1983): 135–62.

Lies, Slander, and Obscenity in Medieval English Literature: Pastoral Rhetoric and the Deviant Speaker. Cambridge University Press, 1997.

Cressy, David. 'Binding the Nation: the Bonds of Association, 1584 and 1696'. In *Tudor Rule and Revolution: Essays for G. R. Elton from His American Friends*, edited by Delloyd J. Guth and John W. McKenna, 217–34. Cambridge University Press, 1982.

Cruickshank, C. G. *The English Occupation of Tournai, 1513–1519*. Oxford: Clarendon Press, 1971.

Cummings, Brian. 'The Conscience of Thomas More'. In *Representing Religious Pluralization in Early Modern Europe*, edited by Andreas Höfele et al., 1–14. Berlin: Lit Verlag, 2008.

'Swearing in Public: More and Shakespeare'. *English Literary Renaissance* 27 (1997): 197–232.

Darby, Harold S. *Hugh Latimer*. London: Epworth Press, 1953.

Davies, C. S. L. 'The Cromwellian Decade: Authority and Consent'. *Transactions of the Royal Historical Society*, 6th series, 7 (1997): 177–95.

Demaus, Robert. *Hugh Latimer: A Biography*. London: Religious Tract Society, 1869.

Dickens, Arthur G. *The English Reformation*. London: B. T. Batsford, 1964.

Diefendorf, Barbara. *Beneath the Cross: Catholics and Huguenots in Sixteenth-Century Paris*. New York: Oxford University Press, 1991.

Dodds, Madeleine Hope, and Ruth Dodds. *The Pilgrimage of Grace, 1536–1537, and The Exeter Conspiracy, 1538*. 2 vols. Cambridge University Press, 1915.

Duffy, Eamon. *Fires of Faith: Catholic England under Mary Tudor*. New Haven, CT: Yale University Press, 2009.

The Stripping of the Altars: Traditional Religion in England, c.1400–c.1580. 2nd edn. New Haven, CT: Yale University Press, 2005.

The Voices of Morebath: Reformation and Rebellion in an English Village. New Haven, CT: Yale University Press, 2001.

Elton, Geoffrey R. 'The Evolution of a Reformation Statute'. *English Historical Review* 64 (1949): 174–97.

Policy and Police: The Enforcement of the Reformation in the Age of Thomas Cromwell. Cambridge University Press, 1972.

The Tudor Revolution in Government: Administrative Changes in the Reign of Henry VIII. Cambridge University Press, 1953.

Eubel, Konrad et al., eds., *Hierarchia catholica medii aevi sive summorum pontificum, S. R. E. cardinalium, ecclesiarum antistitum series.* Vol. III, *Saeculum XVI ab anno 1502 complectens.* 1923.

Febvre, Lucien. 'The Origins of the French Reformation: A Badly-Put Question?' In *A New Kind of History: From the Writings of Febvre,* edited by Peter Burke, translated by K. Folca, 44–107. London: Routledge & Kegan Paul, 1973.

Fletcher, Anthony, and Diarmaid MacCulloch. *Tudor Rebellions.* 5th edn. Harlow: Pearson, 2004.

Forster, Ann M. C. 'The Oath Tendered'. *Recusant History* 14 (1977): 86–96.

Freeman, Thomas S. 'Over Their Dead Bodies: Concepts of Martyrdom in Late Medieval and Early Modern England'. In *Martyrs and Martyrdom in England, c. 1400–1700,* edited by Thomas Freeman and Thomas F. Mayer, 1–34. Woodbridge: Boydell, 2007.

Fuller, Thomas. *The History of the University of Cambridge, and of Waltham Abbey with the Appeal of Injured Innocence.* Edited by James Nichols. London: Thomas Tegg, 1840.

Gasquet, Francis Aidan. *Henry VIII and the English Monasteries.* London: John Hodges, 1888.

Gray, Jonathan Michael. 'Conscience and the Word of God: Religious Arguments against the Ex Officio Oath'. *Journal of Ecclesiastical History,* forthcoming.

'Vows, Oaths and the Propagation of a Subversive Discourse'. *Sixteenth Century Journal,* 41 (2010): 731–56.

Guy, John. 'The Elizabethan Establishment and the Ecclesiastical Polity'. In *The Reign of Elizabeth I: Court and Culture in the Last Decade,* edited by John Guy, 126–49. Cambridge University Press, 1995.

The Public Career of Sir Thomas More. New Haven, CT: Yale University Press, 1980.

'Thomas Cromwell and the Intellectual Origins of the Henrician Revolution'. In *Reassessing the Henrician Age: Humanism, Politics and Reform, 1500–1550,* edited by Alistair Fox and John Guy, 151–78. Oxford: Basil Blackwell, 1986.

Tudor England. Oxford University Press, 1988.

Haigh, Christopher. *English Reformations: Religion, Politics, and Society under the Tudors.* Oxford: Clarendon Press, 1993.

Hauser, Henri. 'Le Traité de Madrid et la cession de la Bourgogne à Charles-Quint: étude sur le sentiment national Bourguignon en 1525–1526'. *Revue Bourguignonne* 22 (1912): 1–180.

Helmholz, R. H. 'The Privilege and the *Ius Commune*: The Middle Ages to the Seventeenth Century'. In *The Privilege against Self-Incrimination: Its Origins and Development*, edited by Helmholz et al., 17–46. University of Chicago Press, 1997.

Hickerson, Megan L. 'Negotiating Heresy in Tudor England: Anne Askew and the Bishop of London'. *Journal of British Studies* 46 (2007): 774–95.

"'Ways of Lying": Anne Askew and the Examinations'. *Gender and History* 18 (2006): 50–65.

Hill, Christopher. *Society and Puritanism in Pre-Revolutionary England*. New York: Schocken Books, 1964.

Hindle, Steve. 'The Keeping of the Public Peace'. In *The Experience of Authority in Early Modern England*, edited by Paul Griffiths, Adam Fox, and Steve Hindle, 213–48. New York: St Martin's Press, 1996.

Hoyle, R. W. *The Pilgrimage of Grace and the Politics of the 1530s*. Oxford University Press, 2001.

Hoyle, R. W., and A. J. L. Winchester, 'A Lost Source for the Rising of 1536 in North-West England'. *English Historical Review*, 118 (2003): 120–9.

Hudson, Anne. *The Premature Reformation: Wycliffite Texts and Lollard History*. Oxford: Clarendon Press, 1988.

Hughes, Philip. *The Reformation in England*. 3 vols. London: Hollis and Carter, 1950–4.

Ives, Eric. 'Henry VIII: the Political Perspective'. In *The Reign of Henry VIII: Politics, Policy and Piety*, edited by Diarmaid MacCulloch, 13–34. New York: St Martin's Press, 1995.

'Stress, Faction and Ideology in Early-Tudor England'. *Historical Journal* 34 (1991): 193–202.

Jones, David Martin. *Conscience and Allegiance in Seventeenth Century England: The Political Significance of Oaths and Engagements*. University of Rochester Press, 1999.

Jones, Norman. *The English Reformation: Religion and Cultural Adaptation*. Oxford: Blackwell, 2002.

Kelly, Henry Ansgar. *The Matrimonial Trials of Henry VIII*. Stanford University Press, 1976.

Kelly, Michael. 'The Submission of the Clergy'. *Transactions of the Royal Historical Society*. 5th series, 15 (1965): 97–119.

Klinck, Dennis. *Conscience, Equity, and the Court of Chancery in Early Modern England*. Aldershot: Ashgate, 2010.

Knowles, David. *The Religious Orders in England*. Vol. III: *The Tudor Age*. Cambridge University Press, 1959.

Lake, Peter, and Steven Pincus. *The Politics of the Public Sphere in Early Modern England*. Manchester University Press, 2007.

Lehmberg, Stanford E. *The Reformation Parliament, 1529–1536*. Cambridge University Press, 1970.

Levy, Leonard W. *Origins of the Fifth Amendment: The Right Against Self-Incrimination*. New York: Oxford University Press, 1968.

Loades, David. *Henry VIII: Court, Church, and Conflict*. Kew: The National Archives, 2007.

    Mary Tudor: A Life. Oxford: Basil Blackwell, 1989.

    The Reign of Mary Tudor: Politics, Government, and Religion in England, 1553–1558. New York: St Martin's Press, 1979.

MacCulloch, Diarmaid. *The Boy King: Edward VI and the Protestant Reformation*. New York: Palgrave, 2001.

Maitland, Samuel Roffey. *The Reformation in England*. London: John Lane, 1906.

Marsh, Christopher. *Popular Religion in Sixteenth-Century England: Holding Their Peace*. New York: St Martin's Press, 1998.

Marshall, Peter. 'Papist as Heretic: The Burning of John Forest, 1538'. *Historical Journal* 41 (1998): 351–74.

    Reformation England, 1480–1642. London: Hodder Arnold, 2003.

    Religious Identities in Henry VIII's England. Aldershot: Ashgate, 2006.

Marshall, Peter, and Alec Ryrie, eds. *The Beginnings of English Protestantism*. Cambridge University Press, 2002.

Mayer, Thomas F. 'On the Road to 1534: the Occupation of Tournai and Henry VIII's Theory of Sovereignty'. In *Tudor Political Culture*, edited by Dale Hoak, 11–30. Cambridge University Press, 1995.

Moyes, J. 'Warham: An English Primate on the Eve of the Reformation'. *Dublin Review* 114 (1894): 390–420.

Mullinger, James Bass. *The University of Cambridge*. 3 vols. Cambridge University Press, 1873–1911.

Murray, James. *Enforcing the English Reformation in Ireland: Clerical Resistance and Political Conflict in the Diocese of Dublin, 1534–1590*. Cambridge University Press, 2009.

Nicholson, Graham. 'The Act of Appeals and the English Reformation'. In *Law and Government under the Tudors: Essays Presented to Sir Geoffrey Elton Regius Professor of Modern History in the University of Cambridge on the Occasion of His Retirement*, edited by Claire Cross, David Loades and J. J. Scarisbrick, 19–30. Cambridge University Press, 1988.

Noake, John. *The Monastery and Cathedral of Worcester*. London: Longman and Co., 1866.

Oxford English Dictionary Online. Oxford University Press, March 2012. www.oed.com/view/Entry/351?redirectedFrom=abjuration.

Porter, H. C. *Reformation and Reaction in Tudor Cambridge*. Cambridge University Press, 1958.

Reinhard, Wolfgang. 'Reformation, Counter-Reformation, and the Early Modern State: A Reassessment'. In *The Counter-Reformation: The Essential Readings*, edited by David Luebke, 107–28. Malden, MA: Blackwell, 1999.

Rex, Richard. 'The Crisis of Obedience: God's Word and Henry's Reformation'. *Historical Journal* 39 (1996): 863–94.

'The Execution of the Holy Maid of Kent', *Historical Research* 64 (1991): 216–20.

The Lollards. Houndmills: Palgrave, 2002.

'Which is Wyche? Lollardy and Sanctity in Lancastrian London'. In *Martyrs and Martyrdom in England, c. 1400–1700*, edited by Thomas Freeman and Thomas F. Mayer, 88–106. Woodbridge: Boydell, 2007.

Ridley, Jaspar. *The Tudor Age*. London: Constable, 1988.

Rouse, E. Clive. 'Wall Paintings in the Church of St. John the Evangelist, Corby, Lincolnshire'. *Archaeological Journal* 100 (1943): 150–76.

Russell, Henry G. 'Lollard Opposition to Oaths by Creatures'. *American Historical Review* 51 (1946): 668–84.

Ryrie, Alec. *The Age of Reformation: The Tudor and Stewart Realms, 1485–1603*. Harlow: Pearson Longman, 2009.

'Counting Sheep, Counting Shepherds: the Problem of Allegiance in the English Reformation'. In *The Beginnings of English Protestantism*, edited by Peter Marshall and Alec Ryrie, 84–110. Cambridge University Press, 2002.

The Gospel and Henry VIII: Evangelicals in the Early English Reformation. Cambridge University Press, 2003.

Scarisbrick, J. J. *Henry VIII*. Berkeley and Los Angeles: University of California Press, 1969.

'The Pardon of the Clergy'. *Cambridge Historical Journal* 12 (1956): 22–39.

The Reformation and the English People. Oxford: Basil Blackwell, 1984.

Schilling, Heinz. 'Confessional Europe'. In *Handbook of European History, 1400–1600: Late Middle Ages, Renaissance, and Reformation*, vol. II, *Visions, Programs, and Outcomes*, edited by Thomas A. Brady Jr., Heiko Oberman, and James D. Tracey, 641–81. Leiden, E. J. Brill, 1995.

Religion, Political Culture and the Emergence of Early Modern Society: Essays in German and Dutch History. Translated by Stephen G. Burnett. Leiden: E. J. Brill, 1992.

Shagan, Ethan. *Popular Politics and the English Reformation*. Cambridge University Press, 2003.

Sharpe, Kevin. *Selling the Tudor Monarchy: Authority and Image in Sixteenth-Century England*. New Haven, CT: Yale University Press, 2009.

The Sixth Report of the Deputy Keeper of the Public Records. London: Public Records Office of Great Britain, 1846.

Smith, Alan G. R. *The Emergence of a Nation State: The Commonwealth of England, 1529–1660*. 2nd edn. Harlow: Addison Wesley Longman Limited, 1997.

Sommerville, Charles J. *The Secularization of Early Modern England: From Religious Culture to Religious Faith*. New York: Oxford University Press, 1992.

Sommerville, Johann P. 'The "New Art of Lying": Equivocation, Mental Reservation, and Casuistry'. In *Conscience and Casuistry in Early Modern England*, edited by Edmund Leites, 159–84. Cambridge University Press, 1988.

Spurr, John. 'Perjury, Profanity and Politics'. *The Seventeenth Century* 8 (1993): 29–50.

'A Profane History of Early Modern Oaths'. *Transactions of the Royal Historical Society*, 6th series, 11 (2001): 37–63.

Strype, John. *Annals of the Reformation and Establishment of Religion, and Other Various Occurrences in the Church of England, During Queen Elizabeth's Happy Reign: Together with an Appendix of Original Papers of State, Records, and Letters*. 4 vols. Oxford: Clarendon Press, 1824.

Ecclesiastical Memorials: Relating Chiefly to Religion and the Reformation of It, and the Emergencies of the Church of England, under King Henry VIII, King Edward VI and Queen Mary the First. 3 vols. London: 1733.

Memorials of the Most Reverend Father in God Thomas Cranmer, Sometime Lord Archbishop of Canterbury. 2 vols. Oxford: Clarendon Press, 1812.

Thomas, Keith. *Religion and the Decline of Magic*. London: Penguin, 1971.

Thompson, E. Margaret. *The Carthusian Order in England*. London: Society for Promoting Christian Knowledge, 1930.

Tutino, Stefania. 'Between Nicodemism and "Honest" Dissimulation: The Society of Jesus in England'. *Historical Research* 79 (2006): 534–53.

Ullmann, Walter. 'This Realm of England is an Empire'. *Journal of Ecclesiastical History* 30 (1979): 175–203.

Vallance, Edward. 'Protestation, Vow, Covenant and Engagement: Swearing Allegiance in the English Civil War'. *Historical Research* 75 (2002): 408–24.

Revolutionary England and the National Covenant: State Oaths, Protestantism and the Political Nation, 1553–1682. Woodbridge: Boydell, 2005.

Wabuda, Susan. 'Equivocation and Recantation during the English Reformation: The "Subtle Shadows" of Dr Edward Crome'. *Journal of Ecclesiastical History* 44 (1993): 224–42.

Preaching during the English Reformation. Cambridge University Press, 2002.

Walker, Greg. 'Saint or Schemer? The 1527 Heresy Trial of Thomas Bilney Reconsidered'. *Journal of Ecclesiastical History* 40 (1989): 219–38.

Walsham, Alexandra. *Church Papists: Catholicism, Conformity and Confessional Polemic in Early Modern England*. Woodbridge: Boydell, 1993.

'Ordeals of Conscience: Casuistry, Conformity and Confessional Identity in Post-Reformation England'. In *Contexts of Conscience in Early Modern Europe, 1500–1700*, edited by Harald E. Braun and Edward Vallance, 32–48. Houndmills: Palgrave Macmillan, 2004.

Providence in Early Modern England. Oxford University Press, 1999.

Walter, John. 'Public Transcripts, Popular Agency and the Politics of Subsistence in Early Modern England'. In *Negotiating Power in Early Modern Society: Order, Hierarchy and Subordination in Britain and Ireland*, edited by Michael J. Braddick and John Walter, 123–48. Cambridge University Press, 2001.

Watt, Tessa. *Cheap Print and Popular Piety, 1550–1640*. Cambridge University Press, 1991.

Wood, Andy. '"A Lyttull Worde ys Tresson": Loyalty, Denunciation and Popular Politics in Tudor England.' *Journal of British Studies* 48 (2009): 837–47.

Wood, Anthony à. *The History and Antiquities of the University of Oxford, in Two Books*. Edited by John Gutch. 2 vols. Oxford, 1792–6.

Woodforde, Christopher. *The Norwich School of Glass-Painting in the Fifteenth Century*. London: Oxford University Press, 1950.

Wooding, Lucy. *Henry VIII*. London: Routledge, 2009.

Woodward, G. W. O. *The Dissolution of the Monasteries*. New York: Walker and Company, 1966.

Woolf, Rosemary. *The English Religious Lyric in the Middle Ages*. Oxford: Clarendon Press, 1968.

Zagorin, Perez. *Ways of Lying: Dissimulation, Persecution, and Conformity in Early Modern Europe*. Cambridge, MA: Harvard University Press, 1990.

Zaret, David. *Origins of Democratic Culture: Printing, Petitions, and the Public Sphere in Early-Modern England*. Princeton University Press, 2000.

UNPUBLISHED THESES

Beckett, Neil. 'Sheen Charterhouse: From Its Foundation to Its Dissolution'. Ph.D. diss., Oxford University, 1992.

Gray, Jonathan Michael. 'So Help Me God: Oaths and the English Reformation'. Ph.D. diss., Stanford University, 2008.

Mohr, Melissa. 'Strong Language: Oaths, Obscenities, and Performative Literature in Early Modern England'. Ph.D. diss., Stanford University, 2003.

Nicholson, Graham David. 'The Nature and Function of Historical Argument in the Henrician Reformation'. Ph.D. diss., Cambridge University, 1977.

Index

Printed in the United States
By Bookmasters